"BEYOND THIS NARROW NOW"

NAHUM DIMITRI CHANDLER

"

BEYOND

THIS

NARROW

NOW

"

....

Or, Delimitations, of W. E. B. Du Bois

DUKE UNIVERSITY PRESS *Durham & London* 2022

© 2022 DUKE UNIVERSITY PRESS

All rights reserved

Designed by Matthew Tauch

Typeset in Garamond Premier Pro by Westchester Publishing
Services

Library of Congress Cataloging-in-Publication Data

Names: Chandler, Nahum Dimitri, author.

Title: "Beyond this narrow now" or, Delimitations, of W. E. B.
Du Bois / Nahum Dimitri Chandler.

Other titles: "Beyond this narrow now"

Description: Durham : Duke University Press, 2021. | Includes
bibliographical references and index.

Identifiers: LCCN 2021001990 (print)

LCCN 2021001991 (ebook)

ISBN 9781478013877 (hardcover)

ISBN 9781478014805 (paperback)

ISBN 9781478022121 (ebook)

Subjects: LCSH: Du Bois, W. E. B. (William Edward Burghardt), 1868–
1963—Criticism and interpretation. | Du Bois, W. E. B.
(William Edward Burghardt), 1868–1963—Political and social views. |
Du Bois, W. E. B. (William Edward Burghardt), 1868–1963—Influence.
| African Americans—Intellectual life—20th century. | Politics and
literature—United States—History—20th century. | BISAC: SOCIAL
SCIENCE / Ethnic Studies / American / African American & Black
Studies | LITERARY CRITICISM / American / African American &
Black

Classification: LCC PS3507.U147 Z55 2021 (print) |
LCC PS3507.U147 (ebook) | DDC 973/.0496073—dc23

LC record available at https://lccn.loc.gov/2021001990

LC ebook record available at https://lccn.loc.gov/2021001991

Cover art: W. E. B. Du Bois, identification card for the *Exposition
Universelle*, 1900, Paris, France. Paul Nadar
(1856–1939), photographer. W. E. B. Du Bois Papers (MS 312).
Courtesy of the Special Collections and University Archives,
University of Massachusetts Amherst Libraries.

DUKE UNIVERSITY PRESS GRATEFULLY ACKNOWLEDGES THE
HUMANITIES COMMONS OF THE SCHOOL OF HUMANITIES AT
THE UNIVERSITY OF CALIFORNIA, IRVINE, WHICH PROVIDED
FUNDS TOWARD THE PUBLICATION OF THIS BOOK.

CONTENTS

ACKNOWLEDGMENTS

....

I give thanks to those many friends—who remain so close for me—who have supported my efforts as realized in this volume. This work is first of all—so too in the last instance—an expression of family, of the pyramid, of generations. For them, as gift, I give thanks.

1

In various formats, parts of "A Notation: The Practice of W. E. B. Du Bois as a Problem for Thought—Amidst the Turn of the Centuries" were presented on three occasions during my academic year as a Fulbright lecturer at Tohoku University in Sendai, Japan. Most especially, I presented it at An International Conference: W. E. B. Du Bois and the Question of Another World, which was held on June 15–17, 2006, in the Graduate School of Education at Tohoku University. An earlier version was presented on March 4, 2006, for the Tohoku Association for American Studies as part of its annual winter public lecture series held at Tohoku University, on the occasion of which Koji Takenaka, professor and chair of the Department of American Studies at Tohoku University, was kind enough to serve as translator. At Tohoku University, I also thank Professors Morimichi Kato, Kumiko Ikuta, and Yoshimichi Sato for their dialogue and engagement throughout the whole year. I wish to thank the Japan-U.S. Educational Commission and the U.S. Fulbright Program for the lectureship grant that made this experience possible. In addition, on June 20, 2006, this text served as the basis of a lecture for the seminar on American transcendentalism led by Professor Naoko Saito in the Graduate School of Education at Kyoto University. The support of Maria Phillips and Franc Nunoo-Quarcoo, perennially, has been of the essence. In addition, earlier versions of the principal ideas of this essay were presented over the course of a bit more than the past half dozen years as part of lectures on several occasions in the United States and Germany: on November 20, 2003, for the Lehigh Valley Consortium in African American Studies, Lehigh, Pennsylvania, as part of two days of lectures and seminars on the work of Du Bois by the kind invitation and hospitality of Professors David Luis-Brown and William R. Scott; on September 23, 2003, at Villanova University, Villanova, Pennsylvania, in the Program in Africana Studies by the kind invitation of Professors Kevin Thomas Miles and Meghan Keita; on February 18, 2003, in the Honors College at Sweetbriar College, Sweetbriar, Virginia, by invitation of Professor Deborah Durham; on February 4, 2003, at Paine College, Augusta, Georgia, by invitation of President Shirley A. R. Lewis; on December 4, 2002, in the Senatsaal at the Humboldt-Universität, Berlin, Germany, as part of a yearlong lecture series on secularization in the faculties of philosophy and theology by the kind invitation of Professor Christina von Braun of the Institut für Kulturwissenschaft; on November 14, 2002, as part of an especially gratifying two-day seminar conducted with Professor Fred Moten in the Department of English, Michigan State University, East Lansing, by the kind invitation of Professors Scott Juengel and Scott Michaelsen and the chair, Patrick O'Donnell; at two University of California campuses, on May 4, 2002, at Davis, as a public lecture presented on behalf of the Department of African and African American Studies as part of their series of events during the annual Black Family Week celebration organized by John Ortiz-Hutson, and on April 18, 2002, in the Department of English at Berkeley—its thesis was the guide of a lecture there—given by way of the invitation of Professors Saidiya Hartman and Steven Goldsmith; on March 10, 2002, at the University of Pittsburgh at a conference on Du Bois and Henry Adams organized by Professors Ronald A. T. Judy and Paul Bové; and on June 3, 1999, at the Humboldt-Universität as part of the inaugural W. E. B. Du Bois Week organized by the Institut für Amerikanistik by invitation of the chair, the late Professor Gunther Lenz, during which the generous collegiality of Professor Sieglinde Lemke, then of the John F. Kennedy Institute of the Freie Universität, was much appreciated. Perhaps the earliest presentation occurred on February 10, 1999, as the opening of a lecture in a series on work in progress presented by current members of the School of Social Science of the Institute for Advanced Study, Princeton, New Jersey. I was supported there by fellowships from the National Endowment for the Humanities and the Ford Foundation.

William Gaboury, labor historian, offered the first and only course that I followed as a student that was focused entirely on the work and itinerary of W. E. B. Du Bois, in a beautiful setting perched among the tall fulsome pines on the slopes of the low green hills of southern Oregon one rainy autumn more than a generation and a half ago. In this sense, he was my first *professor* of matters Du Boisian. I doubt that he could ever have imagined what he helped so graciously to set in motion—a kind of rein-auguration—in the rhythm of my step and the course that my path has so far taken. He was also a consummate host, of the essence, in his generosity of spirit. This notation is offered in his memory.

2

Certain motifs of part I were presented under the title "W. E. B. Du Bois and 'The Spirit of Modern Europe'" for The Future of Utopia: A Conference in Honor of Fredric Jameson, organized by Alberto Moreiras in the Literature Program at Duke University, April 23–24, 2003. I warmly thank Professor Moreiras, a friend and former colleague, for the invitation. A portion of the opening section of part I, in its present form, was presented at An International Conference: W. E. B. Du Bois and the Question of Another World, II, which was held on June 6–8, 2007, at the Renaissance Center, located in Shinagawa, Tokyo, under the auspices of the School of Global Studies, both of Tama University. (On the latter, please note "Toward a New Parallax: Or, Japan in Another Traversal of the Trans-Pacific," special issue of *CR: The New Centennial Review* 12, no. 1 [Spring 2012].)

For many years, first as a colleague and then as a friend, Fredric Jameson's affirmation of my work on Du Bois has been unstinting. Yet this is not to say that he would endorse all of its gestures. Nor would I wish it to be so. I thus dedicate part I of this study to him, with respect to his superb example in the practice of thought, recognizable in the catholicity of his reception of discourse, artistic practice, and cultural form, but above all with respect to his hospitality.

3

Under the title "'The Riddle of the Sphinx': *John Brown* and 'The Spirit of Modern Europe,'" some parts of part II were presented on February 11, 2005, to the Department of English, Michigan State University, East Lansing. And on March 4, 2006, a section of it was presented as part of a lecture given for the Tohoku Association for American Studies as part of their annual winter public lecture series held at Tohoku University, where

I held a Fulbright appointment. I also thank Keiko Toyama and Dr. David Satterwhite for supporting the latter lecture event, especially given that it was at Tohoku University and in Sendai.

For an entire academic year, from September 2005 to July 2006, Professor Koji Takenaka resolutely, and rather kindly, acknowledged, translating when absolutely necessary, my densely convoluted discourse given in the form of lectures for our seminar on Du Bois's sense of modernity—defined across the two terms respectively by our reading of the essay named in my title and of Du Bois's magnum opus of his maturity, *Black Reconstruction*. What may not have been evident at the time to the other members of the seminar, which I here wish to acknowledge, is the extent to which his careful formulation of questions assisted me greatly in proceeding a step further in my attempts to understand Du Bois's thought. In addition, it was an invitation, given at his initiative, to speak in that March 2006 lecture series that led me to elaborate the present form of the statement proposed in the *essay* at hand. And on the occasion, even with my late-arriving and rather long text, it was he who suffered through the difficulty of translating my prose for a Japanese general audience drawn from the community of Sendai, Japan. Although it came to the form of a general public presentation somewhat slowly—arriving for him only once he became emeritus—I thus dedicate part II of this study to him, in gratitude and respect.

4

Although it was published first, my book *Toward an African Future—Of the Limit of World* issued in 2013 unfolded in tandem with the preparation of the present study (see Chandler 2021). While they are diverse in elaboration, in my own conception, the books are of a common theoretical locution.

5

Portions of "A Notation: The Practice of W. E. B. Du Bois as a Problem for Thought—Amidst the Turn of the Centuries" were previously published in CR: *The New Centennial Review* 6 (3) (2006): 29–55. Portions of part I: "'Beyond This Narrow Now': Elaborations of the Example in the Thought of W. E. B. Du Bois—At the Limit of World," were previously published in *Journal of Transnational American Studies* 2 (1) (2010): np.

6

Three decades and three years ago, I was first gifted with the friendship of Ken Wissoker. If there is a tender touch in this book, it has come by way of his first gesture, as editor, from then, until now. Also, I thank Ryan Kendall, for the care that she has brought to this project throughout; so too for the exact attention brought to it by Ellen Goldlust and Jessica Ryan of Duke University Press. A member of the very first advanced seminar on W. E. B. Du Bois at Duke University, from the early years of the last decade of the last century, Lily Phillips has remained one of the most essential of my fellow scholars; here, she assisted me precisely in the preparation of the index for this study.

NOTE ON CITATIONS

....

1

While I have taken scholastic reference to the original publication or to the unpublished manuscript of texts by W. E. B. Du Bois, in every case of his writings engaged in this study, with citations noted within the text, where possible or appropriate, I have also without exception also consulted the versions of all published texts included in the thirty-seven volumes of the Complete Published Works of W. E. B. Du Bois, published from 1973 to 1986 by the Kraus-Thomson Organization and edited and introduced by the late Herbert Aptheker, as well as the six volumes of Du Bois's texts published from 1973 to 1985 by the University of Massachusetts Press, also edited and introduced by Aptheker, which include three volumes of selected correspondence and three of selections of other texts, including previously unpublished texts and documents. The bibliographical details of those texts edited by Aptheker, if cited herein, are listed in the reference list at the end of this study.

2

The Souls of Black Folk: Essays and Sketches is cited herein from the first edition of its original publication (Du Bois 1903l). A full-text version of the second edition (Du Bois 1903m), which has no major changes from the first, is available in electronic form through the University of North Carolina's Documenting the American South project, available as an open access online text at https://docsouth.unc.edu/church/duboissouls/dubois.html. I consider that presentation of the book (in its second edition, June 1903) an accurate and reliable work of scholarship. The pagination is the same in the first and second editions. In-text citations are given below in parentheses with the relevant page number(s), the chapter number, and the paragraph number(s) within the chapter. For example, (Du Bois 1903f, 213, chap. 11, para. 13) indicates page 213, chapter 11, paragraph 13, with pagination based on the first and second editons of the book, each issued in 1903.

3

When quoting or referencing *The Philadelphia Negro: A Social Study* (1899), published under the authorship of Du Bois, with an additional text by Isabel Eaton (the report of a study on African American women domestic workers), I cite it by the abbreviation PN and the relevant page number. My citation refers to the original edition of the text, that is the first published edition (Du Bois and Eaton 1899). It is the first edition that is the decisive basis of my references. Hence, if the reader consults the first edition of this text, a citation by page number given in this study, such as (PN 385), will *also* enable the reader to easily recognize the appropriate section of Du Bois's book to which I am making reference. As the most singular example here, in part two of this book such in-text citations should lead the reader to chapter eighteen, "A Final Word," specifically to a page number within "The Meaning of All This," the important brief opening section in that chapter of Du Bois study. In general, thus, an attentive reader will note the location of that specific citation in a chapter that addresses in larger frame the theme named by that specific citation. This matters; for other subsequent editions of *The Philadelphia Negro*, notably those issued posthumously, of which there are several, may be abridged and may thus not yield a reliable match with that first published edition; several of these also leave aside Du Bois's own original and important preface.

4

When quoting or referencing passages from *Dusk of Dawn: An Essay toward an Autobiography of a Race Concept*, originally published in 1940, I have cited the 1975 version published as part of the Complete Published Works of W. E. B. Du Bois series (Du Bois 1975d). While the 1975 edition is not a facsimile of the 1940 edition, the pagination follows exactly that of the first edition. Since the pagination varies somewhat among other editions of this text, in a manner similar to my references to the *The Philadelphia Negro: A Social Study*, as I indicated above, my citation to the 1975 edition of *The Dusk of Dawn* should enable the reader to easily locate within Du Bois's text the context of my discussion or references.

5

Four early essays by Du Bois—"The Afro-American" (1894a[?]), "The Conservation of Races" (1897b), "The Present Outlook for the Dark Races of Mankind" (1900a), and "The Development of a People" (1904)—are always cited by an abbreviated title and the page in the original or first publication of the text and paragraph number, with the paragraph enumeration determined according to the original publication or manuscript. For example, (CR 5, 1–3) refers to the original publication, issued in 1897, of "The Conservation of Races," page 5, paragraphs 1–3. Since these four essays are also included in *The Problem of the Color Line at the Turn of the Twentieth Century: The Essential Early Essays* (Du Bois 2015h) and the paragraph numbering is included there, readers with that collection at hand may find the relevant text simply by reference to essay title (noting the abbreviations that I use for in-text citations below) and paragraph number. That collection includes complete versions of the essays as originally published or as extant in Du Bois's unpublished papers, edited and annotated, according to contemporary scholarship.

6

Finally, I occasionally refer to material that may be found only among the W. E. B. Du Bois Papers (MS 312) (as part of series 3, subseries C) at the Special Collections and University Archives, University of Massachusetts Amherst Libraries, housed in the W. E. B. Du Bois Library, or in the microfilm version of those papers (Du Bois 1980f). These papers have been digitized under the University of Massachusetts Amherst Libraries online repository Credo and are now available as open access material at https://credo.library.umass.edu/view/collection/mums312. Additional bibliographic detail for some notable specific citations from among these papers may be found in the notes or in the reference list at the end of this study. The original papers were compiled and edited by Herbert Aptheker, whereas the microfilm edition was supervised by Robert C. McDonnell.

AN OPENING—
AT THE LIMIT OF THOUGHT,
A PREFACE

....

In the considerations that follow, I have been guided by two interrelated concerns.

The first is scholastic: to produce a more patient understanding of the early writings of W. E. B. Du Bois than has yet become common—even still—in engagements of his earliest initiatives in thought.

The second is theoretical: to pose a general problematization in contemporary discourse of the character and status of the problematic of matters Negro or African American for thought—the latter of which has heretofore, perhaps, been too easily engaged as congenitally specific, only partial, provincial—by way of a paleonymic engagement with the itinerary of thought in writing by Du Bois.

In turn, there are three primary questions according to which I have carried out this study.

The first is, Who or what is W. E. B. Du Bois as a problem for thought, for knowledge? My answer, in brief, as given in the introduction to this study, "A Notation: The Practice of W. E. B. Du Bois as a Problem for Thought—Amidst the Turn of the Centuries," is that he is above all a thinker-writer, the producer of formulations of problems for knowledge, notably with regard to matters African American—but not only. For his problematization concerns matters of the human in general. The approach that I have proposed herein is to mark out the analytical dimension for an approach to his thought in its itinerary: autobiographical and historiographical. The opening section of part I of this study—under the nominal generic term "Apologias"—in a manner is in continuity with my work on this theme in Du Bois's writing that I have offered elsewhere, proposing an elaboration of his distinct approach to his formulation of that problematic under the practical-theoretical heading of autobiography.

The second question that I have addressed herein is, Who or what are the matters African American for W. E. B. Du Bois? In a word, my judgment is that, for him, the ensemble of matters that may be configured under that heading are an originary example of the general problematization of modern historicity—for thought. In order to organize a somewhat more deep-seated resource for Du Bois's intellectual formation (other than the prescriptive and externalized basis for assessment that is common in such study), so as to enable a more patient understanding of the first stages of the itinerary of his thought as a matter for him of its achieved declarations, our own judgment notwithstanding at such a juncture, I have retrieved two exemplary early formulations of this thinking. The first is the essay "The Afro-American," most likely prepared sometime late in 1894 or early in 1895 and published for the first time in 2010. I consider this essay as the heart of part I of this study. The second exemplary formulation that I consider is given in the essay "The Development of a People," a text that was produced as the basis for an ongoing lecture by Du Bois during the winter of 1903–4. It was issued for publication in early 1904 (Du Bois 1904). In an essential sense, the elaboration of these two texts and the ensemble of discussions by Du Bois that I consider directly entailed may be most profoundly situated as in common with the problematization of which *The Souls of Black Folk: Essays and Sketches*, gathered and prepared for publication in the period from September 1902 to April 1903, is the quintessential production. Accordingly, I have sought to remark this internal textual and epistemological context throughout my considerations in part I of this study.

The third question that is addressed in this study formulates the domain of problem that provides the guiding subtext, if you will, for my work in this volume. How does Du Bois understand the relation of matters African American to modern historicity, most specifically, but not only, that configured under the heading "America"? One of two principal aspects of Du Bois's perspective is considered in my discussion of "The Development of a People" in part I of this study. There, I elaborate Du Bois's presumptive theorization of matters African American as fundamentally of and about historial possibility—the possibility of that historicity announced as forms and practices of social being with regard to such matters as the articulation of illimitable possibility in historial being. In part II of the study, I address the long-obscure essay "The Present Outlook for the Dark Races of Mankind," first presented as the presidential address at the third annual meeting of the American Negro Academy in late December 1899, in which Du Bois may be understood to have first presented his formulation "the problem of the twentieth century is the problem of the color line." As I consider this text, issued by Du Bois to address a specific occasion, to nonetheless mark the incipit of one of his principal theoretical offerings to contemporary thought, given extensive annotation across the whole of his long itinerary,

I have proposed and sought to exemplify in part II of my study the interest of an elaboration of this early enunciation by him.

Perhaps it is apposite to note here that despite and apart from any expectation or anticipation on the part of thinkers and scholars of our own moment, Du Bois does not so much nominalize, produce, or himself elaborate any narrative of the production of the idea and concept of race. This remains even though such a concern is at stake in his problematization of the idea and concept of race in the essay "The Conservation of Races" from early March 1897. Too, this is notwithstanding that in his thought the question of the self-understanding of the enslaving and the enslaved—of self and the other—in modern systems of enslavement in the United States of America (before, during, and after the formal inauguration of a political entity under that name, and throughout the Americas and the Caribbean) is throughout a standing problematization, already from 1894, as it were (in "The Afro-American," for example).

Du Bois gives us instead a thought of "the problem of the color line." For him, it is understood on a scale of reference that is at once epochal (all of modernity in whatever guise we might choose to construe it) and planetary (worldwide or global, as one may be wont to nominalize the references) in its implications. Likewise, its depth of determination is such that it is historically constitutive, implicating the initiatives of the Renaissance (and various subsequent instances of resurgence in knowledge and understanding across the planet and over the centuries of the modern period), the openings toward at once modern European imperialism (and its aftermath), modern colonialism (not only European), and the tendentious emergence of capitalism, in distinctive part by way of its inception in, through, and in relation to forms of sustained coerced labor, including the sexualization and engendering thereof, in which formal (ostensibly legalized) systems of modern enslavement, across the modern period, from 1441–42 to 1883, are perhaps the most poignant nodal articulation. It is essential that we understand Du Bois's thought of "the problem of the color line" as the conception of a constitutive production, tendentiously global in its bearing, and thus not in any manner the underside or alternative side of the entirety of modern historicity, in its material, as well as ideological, being.

The decisive implication for Du Bois's understanding of modern historicity, including the thought of "the problem of the color line," is that we can recognize thereby the way in which it is not only the case that matters African American may be historicized by recognizing them in the context of modern history and thought on the whole but that our understanding of modern historicity, under whatever dominant theoretical or ideological heading, is thereby in itself powerfully historicized (put in relative frame and thus rearticulated in its pertinence, in general).

If I may be allowed to extend in catachresis the deployment of a metaphor once given by the late writer Toni Morrison, when she remarked in conversation on the expression of an idea of a "melting pot," in which it was proposed that African Americans might be included, "We are the pot." We might then say with Du Bois, in our own extension of the turn that Morrison gives to the staid usage of that metaphor, matters African American, if thought on the track of the global-level "problem of the color line," allows one to recognize in just what way the whole of the world is "African" American; that is to say—if we may go by way of this lineage of the metaphor—we are at once the example and the thing itself by our historicity: *we* are the melting pot.

In a subsequent volume of study on the thought of Du Bois and the discourse of the Negro, a kind of companion to the present study, for it is of the same solicitation from which *"Beyond This Narrow Now"* issues, I address directly this question of the status of discourses of knowledge, notably on the concept of race (Chandler, forthcoming). There I consider Du Bois's critical reformulation of the concept of the human in terms of the concept of race as the inherited epistemic formulation of difference for him at the turn to the twentieth century. While each of these studies indicates something of the manner of my engagement with Du Bois's conceptualization of ipseity with regard to matters Negro or African American as always at least and never only double in its presumed references for social and historical being, that which we know famously under the heading of "double-consciousness," that problematization—the thought of "double-consciousness"—is of such massive reference in his discourses and implicates such a fundamental, excessive, and large domain of contemporary thought, from the Enlightenment era to now, and relates to a planet-wide topography, wherever modern enslavement and modern colonialism may be indexed, as to demand an engagement on its own terms, in a study devoted solely to its terms of question.

As already formulated as at stake here, in *"Beyond This Narrow Now,"* we can recognize that for Du Bois anything that might be understood under the heading African American is not given all in one go; rather, it is always more than one, notably always still in fact yet to come. And then too, in a related manner, *à partir de* the thought of Du Bois, that is to say by way of and in relation to, but not simply reducible to, his early thought, I propose in the companion study (Chandler, forthcoming) that one might develop a distinctive conceptualization of historicity as it is of or related to all matters African American. Therein Du Bois may be understood to propose a thought of the multiple and the heterogeneous (of both self and other, the self as always itself other—in which the conjunction *and* [which paradoxically still operates in a philosophical manner as copula] may be emphasized rather than the nonconjunctive conjunction *or*—as resolutely other than a supposed simple singular or singularity), always of the future that is plural, in which any past is thus likewise rendered plural.

This is at once a very simple thought and one that imposes considerable difficulty for contemporary forms of critical reflection and practical theoretical projection. With regard to *istoria*, of time, place, and the ways of making existence (otherwise than a simple habitation), the horizon of reference for any decision or judgment is a matter only and always of peoples, multiple, heterogeneous, with regard to both any future, and hence any futural claims to any understanding of the past, even for any reference than might be taken as an example. It is thus recognizable that the most abiding register of temporality, or all that we may think under the term *historicity*, for Du Bois is the question of the future. The study at hand, however, is simply on the threshold of such a formulation. Most properly, it is simply put at stake here as a theoretical question that must be explored in subsequent reflection.

Too, emphasis ought to be given to the political force of Du Bois's itinerary and expression in thought. His practice here ought not to be thought of as contemplative. It is activist. Du Bois seeks to intervene immediately and directly in matters that issue in the everyday social life of African Americans, indeed of all concerned with heightened conscience and hopefully enlightened persons. Yet he wishes to do so on the basis of the deepest and most far-reaching understanding and knowledge that his time, his historical time, might allow him to bring to bear. For Du Bois, at the turn to the twentieth century, this knowledge is science, including philosophy as science, of which a nascent sociology would be the most forward looking, the harbinger, of the possibilities of a new science of the human. However, here, too, it is instructive to understand that Du Bois, while committed to impartiality in judgment, or in the formal determination of truth, nonetheless could not abide a simple neutrality in assuming the instituting rationale for study or in assessing its practical value. On the latter, Du Bois's concern was to use knowledge to effect the best outcomes for the future, perhaps a distinctive sense within the nascent human sciences or forms of thought of human sociality and historicity. For Du Bois, a thought on the bias, as it were, in all truth posed the general question of humanity—the humanity of the future.

As this matter of futurity might well be considered the guiding thread of my effort herein, perhaps it is acceptable if I refer the matter to the spaces of metaphorization, elaboration, and reflection that may find their way to exposure or into relief within the work of this study at hand—unceasing—perhaps seeking to accede to the horizons of *atopia* or of possible passages of a cosmic imagination, something other than cosmopolitan (even if as apparition its outlines are remarked only in miniatures) that as such might articulate within the text of the following study itself.

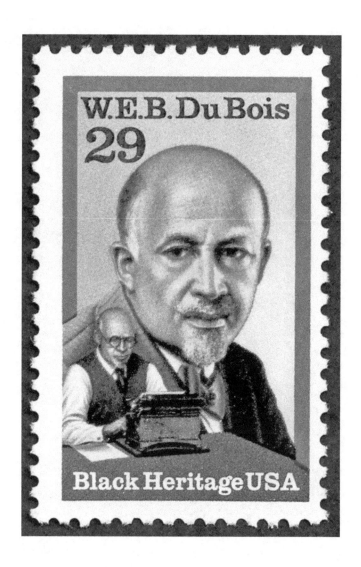

W. E. B. Du Bois postage stamp. U.S. Postal Service Black Heritage
Series, issued January 31, 1992, Atlanta. Source: Smithsonian Institution,
https://postalmuseum.si.edu/object/npm_1993.2015.229.

The Practice of W. E. B. Du Bois as a Problem for Thought—Amidst the Turn of the Centuries

PREAMBLE

In a ceremony at Clark Atlanta University two generations past, on January 31, 1992, just in time for the advent of Black History Month that year, the U.S. Postal Service unveiled a mellow gold-and-orange-toned stamp, with black, blue, green, and brown accents, commemorating the life and work of W. E. B. Du Bois. The stamp was part of the Black Heritage series, which the service had inaugurated in 1978.

The face of the stamp is dominated by a bust-like portrait of Du Bois in suit and bow tie, dressed in his usual dapper and inimitable fashion. This portrait was probably drawn from photographs of the late 1920s or early 1930s, when Du Bois entered his sixties. The handsomeness of Du Bois's high, full, and rounded forehead, which is matched by a distinguished gray mustache and goatee, is elegantly captured in the lines of this image by the illustrator Higgins Bond. Even the famous sternness or moral rectitude of the Good Doctor, as he is still widely known, especially among African Americans, is revealed in the sense of repose that seems to mark Du Bois's expression. Yet his face remains, for the most part, inscrutable. Perhaps one can imagine a hint of a sense of loss or regret, even a slight longing or desire, registered in the shaded lines that mark his countenance. However, the most sustained sense of Du Bois's expression here is the instance of an almost passive thoughtfulness. This is a memorial representation of Du Bois as a political figure—the one who was the advance architect of the Civil Rights Movement in the United States, the principal figure in the development of the global Pan-African movement, and a champion of a new global humanity, and known as such around the world. Here he is posed in a paternal guise, appearing perhaps even as a monumental persona or as an icon—a historic character—who has been affirmed in our time as one of the titans of the social, political, and intellectual life of the twentieth century, not only in the Americas and the Caribbean, but in Europe, Asia, and Africa and thus throughout the world.

Inset within this relatively large portrait, however, to its left and toward the bottom of the stamp face, is a second, much smaller one. It is so small, in fact, that its detail might be hard to fully detect at first glance. In contrast to the magisterial repose of the larger portrait image, which tends to deflect close comprehension, this smaller one, once one's attention is drawn to it, seems to invite further attention, giving rise to an almost visceral sense of the warmth, clutter, and clatter of daily life. In this second portrait, a portrait within a portrait, Du Bois is shown from the waist up, in a vest, straight tie, and shirt sleeves, without a suit coat. He is seated. His hands are at a typewriter, and his face is matter-of-fact in its composure, but his eyes are directed to a sheet of paper in the machine, as if in concentration, perhaps intensely so. Another sheet of paper lies beside the machine. Du Bois is writing.

The hierarchy of this double portrait produced in the late twentieth century remains representative of the mainstream understanding of Du Bois almost two generations later, at the end of the second decade of this still new twenty-first century. Such perspective—then and now—is one in which Du Bois as a memorialized political figure that is larger than life, whether as an aloof genius (or its opposite, a kind of political villain), or as a paternal figure (or its opposite, as a militant outcast and exile), is privileged in our recollections and projections of him over and above Du Bois as a committed intellectual, laboring at his task and practicing his craft, the task of thinking and the craft of writing.[1]

I. PROBLEMATIZATION I

Thus, amidst the generations in our time, whether in the United States or throughout the world, we still have yet to fully understand the extent to which Du Bois was first and last, preeminently I might say, a thinker.

More precisely, Du Bois was a thinker whose practice was writing.

It is the image of Du Bois as a thinker-writer, as a thinker who writes, that we should come to consider most compelling in our recollection and representation of him in our time. We should recall Du Bois as a thinker who thinks as writing, who thinks in writing, as a thinker who writes: in the sense that thinking is his way, his very path of existence and his vocation, and writing is his discipline, his definitive practice, his craft and artistry, or his métier.

It is this way and practice, as ground and reference for all of his other activity, for example, as a social and political activist and scholar, that can and must come to form the basis for our understanding of Du Bois within the history of modern thought in general; in the social, intellectual, and political life of both the nineteenth and the twentieth centuries and these still early moments of the twenty-first century; and in the life course of the contemporary centuries to come.

His first commitment, that to which he belonged in the primary instance, was to the practical doing of thinking, the practical doing of thought. It is an understanding of this way and this practice in all its complexity and specificity that is most necessary in order for us to come to understand, in turn, and in what way, W. E. B. Du Bois remains our contemporary.

Born on the February 23, 1868, in Great Barrington, Massachusetts, just after the end of the American Civil War, Du Bois died on August 22, 1963, in Accra, Ghana, on the eve of the first great civil rights march on Washington. He began publishing at the age of fifteen, serving as the local correspondent for an African American newspaper. His last published texts were prepared at the age of ninety-five, three days before he died. He published in every major genre of literature, including poetry, drama, fiction (including five novels and numerous short stories), biography, and, above all, the essay. Du Bois, it must be said, was one of the great essayists of the twentieth century; his most famous book, *The Souls of Black Folk: Essays and Sketches*, first published in 1903, is a collection of some of his earliest essays. He also practiced in other forms, such as full-scale historical narrative and journalism. And throughout his long professional life, he published within the social sciences, producing over a dozen full-length studies, editing more, publishing several dozen scholarly essays, and maintaining multiple well-followed newspaper columns for several decades. This remarkable output is as voluminous as it is varied. From the early 1960s through the mid-1980s, Herbert Aptheker curated and edited thirty-seven volumes as The Complete Published Works of W. E. B. Du Bois, as well as a volume of his previously unpublished papers and, too, several volumes of Du Bois's selected correspondence. The main literary papers, correspondence, and other documents of Du Bois are housed at the W. E. B. Du Bois Library (named in 1994) at the University of Massachusetts Amherst; they run to more than 100,000 items. And there is a significant body of documents at Fisk University, in addition to other smaller collections throughout the world. While the vast majority of these documents are correspondence, referring to both the published and unpublished works, complete and fragmentary, and following a calibration once proffered by Aptheker, we can estimate that Du Bois wrote an average of six pages of publishable text each day for well over half a century. If, essentially, one includes the massive correspondence, the sense of the daily volume of writing increases in a somewhat dramatic fashion.[2]

It is this archive of writing that stands at the root of the contemporary worldwide resurgence in engagement with the work of Du Bois. In 2003 the centenary of the publication of his most famous book, *The Souls of Black Folk: Essays and Sketches*, simply widened and extended, in its own rather dramatic fashion, the scope of this reconsideration. Thus, Du Bois's work—already a perennial concern since the first edition of that most famous of his writings in 1903, especially among the two intellectual generations of the end of the twentieth century—is in fact the object of a newfound attention in the twenty-first century and is now becoming a common object of new general scholarly labor that is being elaborated with considerable sophistication and acute theoretical learning.

Yet it remains that after all these years, for the most part, this work continues an approach to Du Bois's writing and other practices that is predominantly contextualist in orientation; that is, one begins with premises that are organized according to a *thetic* or *telic* structure that takes its definitive shape according to terms that are outside of Du Bois's own discourse, that is, outside of the declared organization of his own enunciations, statements, and texts.

Even if such a practice is an affirmative one—such as the ongoing and ubiquitous and perennial practice of quoting Du Bois in order to use his authority to throw perspective on a contemporary debate—not to speak of those same kinds of gestures that move from a primarily negative prejudgment, the critical disposition essentially starts from some contemporary author's own commitments, whether political or scholarly, and assertively places the discourse of Du Bois under that heading, and in this way it thus often has quite limited grounding in the movement of Du

Bois's thought. Nothing is more common today in the reengagement with Du Bois that is afoot around the globe. Thus, although this reengagement has been underway now for more than two generations, it remains that the overwhelmingly dominant, the primary or the heading, characterization of Du Bois in this work has been to adduce him as a political figure, one that can be used and abused for contemporary purposes.

The written texts of Du Bois, at the level of their most specific concept metaphors, statements, and elaborations of thought, have, for the most part, only in the past decade and a half or so become the object of our full and most patient attention. And this situation holds a fortiori with regard to his *discourse*, the course of thought and terms of art that gather around those forms of statement, linguistic gesture, and graphical presentation, issued within, as, or in relation to his own declarations of intent and value.

Yet the limit of our own inhabitation is not in and of itself the decisive form of our problematic.

Rather, the decisive matter is whether or not, and if so how, Du Bois's own commitments and practice, at the level of the locution and the metaphor (his operation of the *trope* in general), may be allowed within our practice to place in question, in turn, the forms and premises that organize the terms of our own judgments of his discourse.

His understanding of his own time and practice must be allowed in turn to question our understanding of our own time, most precisely to the extent that the latter indelibly informs our judgment of the former. We, too, are given in discourse, just as, and to the same extent that we may find access to the words, the texts, the discourse, that is to say, the writing of Du Bois.

Our own scholarly and interpretive practice must account for this necessity.

If nothing else, my suggestion in this study is that a new reading or rereading of the writing of Du Bois and another kind of attention to his discourse in general, by way of its solicitation of our own, should or must be undertaken and sustained in our contemporary moment. Not only should this be so for the generations of scholars, thinkers, and activists just emerging but also for those generations at the apogee of their wisdom and understanding, not only within the Americas and the Caribbean but globally, not only in Europe or Africa but also in Asia. For Du Bois was truly, in a metaphorical sense, a citizen of the worldwide horizon in general. And he was an intellectual, a thinker and writer, whose concern was the whole of what we can call *our* world. His ultimate concern was the possibility of another world, not one that existed in the past and not the present in the future, but another world, one that has not yet been and remains yet to come.

I propose that in order to understand this Du Bois, we must *think* with him, allowing his questions to become our own.

This includes both its limits and its possibilities. This is to say that we must first acknowledge *his problematic*, the problematizations that set his itinerary adrift or the questions that set his practice afoot. And, in so doing, we should not accept Du Bois's manner of inhabitation of those terms in any simple sense. However, it is only in thinking by way of the form that his questions took for him, that is, by moving with them and thus *through* them, that one can mark or remark their limit. It is paradoxically only on the cusp of this fold, at such a juncture in thought, that we might find or recognize the form, perhaps, of those paths or passages that lead beyond such exposed limits in a thought such as his and into the domains that can sustain our inhabitation in thought in the future, or even the future of the future, one that is yet to come.

This approach requires that we understand something of Du Bois's thought on its own terms, that we think first in terms of the problematic and movement of thought that is specific to it, that we contextualize it internally, so to speak. Such an understanding would radicalize and extend our capacity to understand in what senses Du Bois's practice as thought was political in its very being and in its most mundane implication, this large and fundamental sense of all that we might think under the heading of the political as indeed, perhaps, rendering a critical (that is self-questioning) the passage of sense and understanding for his formal labor and activity of organization. This critical sense, the self-reflexive and self-questioning dimension of his thought, was a fundament for his activity in general.

Such an approach requires that we must accept his thought first as the responsibility of our present. This means, above all, that we approach his thought as the contemporary of our time and, perhaps, as the contemporary of our future. We have only just begun such an approach.

This is *our problematic*.

II. PROBLEMATIZATION II

We can think of a problematic, or problematizaton, in the sense that I propose it here, as the ensemble of questions that are given to a thinker as a task by the conditions of time and situation, by the historicity of his or her emergence as an intellectual. We might specify this idea a bit more by suggesting that what compels our attention here is not simply history as an organization of external condition that constitutes a demand or obligation for a thinker. Rather, what we want to understand is a movement of thought and social existence in which a certain order of life becomes the object of sustained attention and preoccupation, of reflection and reelaboration, as thought and discourse, as practice, in the terms and circumstance of a practical theoretical engagement.

Thus, what should interest us is formed as a certain relationship between what is announced at the level of history and social condition in general and the movement of critical engagement that takes shape as a form of inhabitation: as the work and thought of a thinker (an intellectual, a scholar, an artist, a teacher, an activist).

A problematic, or, better, problematization, is thus the organization of social or historical condition as a relation that is announced in or as thought. In the terms of traditional formulations of the matter: a problematic or problematization is thus a *relationship* of thought and context.

Yet, to specify a bit more our own theoretical sense: context is thus also always plural, configured in the movement of thought and not simply and purely given, beforehand.

Our own practice, then, can be announced only as itself *of* (both from and about) this movement.

Historicity, here, that which situates both Du Bois and us (whoever we are), would thus have the shape of a possible future of a future and a future past as much as it would have the character of a given past.[3]

The character or mode of appearance of a problematic or problematization at the level of the constituted, or the mark in general, is always a figure of relation, perhaps even an agonistic relation. As a mark in the form of a sign or symbol, specifically in a linguistic form (although this is not its only or even always its most important form), it appears in the rhetorical organization of the interrogative: What (or when)? Or why? Or, even, how? The organization of a question for thought or a difficulty for a practice, and even of existence in general, is the very movement of problematization. This movement can be understood as the very character or texture of thought. This movement can be understood by a historian of thought as both an elaboration and an inhabitation. And yet what is also at stake is the potential practice of a kind of *desedimentation* of both the given (to stake the metaphor we might say, perhaps, as *ground*) and the possible. It is thus the dynamic, and perhaps agonistic, dimension of the process of the production of the very historicity of a practice as thought.

A. If we turn to the question of Du Bois as an intellectual, as a thinker, as one who tries to understand and come to terms with the social conditions of his time and place in the most fundamental manner possible, then in a general sense a certain order and organization of questions may be understood to announce themselves.

(1) Du Bois's problematic, in the sense that I have just proposed, acquires its incipit within a historical situation: the devolution of the modern institution of slavery in the Atlantic basin, involving Europe, Africa, and the Americas (North and South) and the Caribbean. In terms that are relevant for Du Bois's thoughtful relation to the historicity of his present, the events of this process produce, as effects, as the very condition of the historicity most specific to him, a radical displacement of his inhabitation, in every sense, from any supposed simple or pure ground of habitual reference in a supposed origin.

This condition would be the threshold of a historicity that might most specifically be attributed to a group called African American.

(2) At the level of an inhabitation of thought, how might one go about understanding this situation? (a) Certainly, one must try to understand the whole of the various so-called contexts, at their most general level, that might situate this specific historicity: this would include not only a certain history and possibility of "America" but that of the modern West in general and then also the history and present of the modern world in a global sense. (b) Yet one must also undertake a certain critical reflection upon the conditions and means of such an understanding. This reflection would be about possibility and impossibility: a certain consideration of the ground of chance and necessity (or law), in the context of knowledge, of truth or science, especially as logic; and a certain consideration of the ground of freedom and responsibility (or duty), in the context of ethics and morals, of human "will." All that is named under the heading of religion (or theology) would be at stake here as well. How can one know, for example, the truth, or the right? And if one might know truth or right, what is the chance, as possibility or opportunity, for realizing it in its proper fashion?

(3) For Du Bois, the relation between this historical situation and his own possibilities in thought took on a fundamental character and distinct organization.

(a) This was first and foremost an abiding concern with the question of the general conditions of possibility for the construction or reconstruction of *ideals* for social life. Thus, we can underscore that the most general and singular concern of the work of Du Bois across the entire itinerary of his thought was the construction or reconstruction of what he called "ideals of life," those headings of value and distinction that would orient a collective social life, the terms that would assist in the organization and sustenance of a collectivity. While such terms would give the social and historical space for individuals to realize themselves, they would, above all, be operative at the level of the group (humans in general, civilizations, "races" or cultures, nations, and states, or a political entity as such). This general concern yielded a certain practice of principle in Du Bois's thought: an affirmation indeed of the possibility and authority of truth and law as a guide in the organization of life but, equally, a resolute and unfungible affirmation of *freedom or chance* in human doing. In fact, the latter might be understood as the root possibility of the former in Du Bois's terms. There is a principle of freedom that operates as the organizing premise of the most fundamental dimension of Du Bois's thought. And this principle is rendered and maintained as a theme—that is, reflexively and critically—in a manner that is distinctive to his discourse. At the level of his critical reflection, it is something other than simply one theme among others. It is the most fundamental path of organization in his thought. In a practical sense, this organization of principle might be understood to stand at the root of Du Bois's *affirmation of democracy* in all aspects of collective social life and an *affirmation of universal opportunity* for the production and realization of ideals, especially in the form of education, as an illimitable horizon for human existence in general. In this sense, education might be understood as a formalized practice of the transformation of the self, at the level of either the individual or the social group, in relation to an ideal.

(**b**) Second, Du Bois's affirmative concern with *possibility* sustained an abiding critique of all practices and institutions, historically or in the present, that would foreclose such chance or freedom in the realization of human faculty, capacity, or ability. This certainly took shape as a critique of all peremptory modern proscriptive distinctions among humans, whether of birth or race, sex or gender, social class, learning or education, occupation or employment, general wealth, religion, political belief, nationality, or forms of enculturation in general.

Above all, however, Du Bois was concerned with a certain idiom and practice of such proscription. It is the form of distinction that he came to place in a critical sense under the analytical heading of the concept-metaphor "the problem of the color line."

With regard to the U.S. context, especially in *The Souls of Black Folk: Essays and Sketches*, Du Bois elaborated the metaphor of *the veil* to account for the operations of this practice.

We might describe "the problem of the color line" in Du Bois's sense in a summary fashion as an agonistically derived and hierarchically ordered mobile articulation of the differences and relations among groups of humans situated on a dimension of generality that we would today, in the early twenty-first century, tend to colloquialize as *global*. Its operative premise is that distinction can be rendered *effective*. This is the threshold of its operative mode whether or not its promulgation is immediately understood or inhabited at the level of the subject as a sense of an oppositional or categorical difference. And yet the logic of opposition remains the form of its philosophical emergence and destiny. In a worldwide sense, "the problem of the color line" is produced in *modern* history as a basic and fundamental aspect of new historical relations among groups of people. In this history the institution of Atlantic slavery and its relation to modern forms of imperialism, including its devolution in and as the practices of colonialism, would be a central reference. This is to say, forms of labor subordination and exploitation are fundamental to the history in which "the problem of the color line" in Du Bois's sense is produced.

Yet this is an idiom and practice of proscription that is not *simply* one historical form of hierarchy among others. The paradoxical character of the specificity at issue here—a paradox because this specificity is given in the peculiar relation of this idiom of proscription to ideas of the general and the universal—can be named on two levels. In one instance, it is uniquely connected to the history of modern systems of knowledge, as science and philosophy, and of authority, as law and political right, as they were elaborated in Europe and the Americas. While Du Bois does not elaborate an account of the production of "the problem of the color line" in thought, in the formal discourses of thought—especially by way of what can be summarized under the heading of the relation of philosophy to the idea of sovereignty, as such—and we may surmise that perhaps he was circumscribed by his own ambivalent inhabitation of the legacies of eighteenth-century critical thought, which could pertain especially to his epistemic inhabitation in a general sense of the promise or hope of the human sciences or to his preeminent focus on the practical task of producing an intervention in the general field of political and social subordination and exploitation, it remains that an elaboration along these lines can be proposed on the basis of fundamental premises in his work.

This is a task that I have undertaken both here and elsewhere.[4] In another instance, this form of proscription is constitutively concomitant with the threshold production and articulation of a common worldwide, or global, horizon of value and meaning in the understanding of the ground of the relations among groups of humans. It announces the form in which the question of the human as a kind of whole becomes at issue for thought as science, that is, in the terms of the devolution of human knowledge and understanding. It is produced in the warp and woof of the historicity that makes the practical questions of such relations general or situated as an issue of the whole as an absolute; and here the whole is not just that of groups, of nations, cultures, or states, for example, in their individuality or differences, but of their status in terms of any sense of an ultimate whole *as a practical issue*. On both levels, while formed by way of genealogies that brook no absolute break with its pasts and configured in a diversity of elaborations, it has a unique standing as *a specifically modern* ensemble of practices and institutions of proscription. While Du Bois referenced this problematic by the colloquial name of "the color line," common at the turn of the twentieth century, he elaborated an understanding of his historical present, an interpretation of modern global history as a whole, under the critical heading of this term in a manner that was distinctive to his thought and according to a protocol of attention that made possible an immediate and acute analytical productivity at the time of its first enunciation. And some of his most poignant and consummate historiographical and political contributions that were given relatively late in his itinerary took their root in this epistemological soil. It can be shown that the theoretical possibility exposed in that productivity retains considerable bearing for any effort to understand our own historical present and future.

B. Two clarifications are in order at this juncture of our sketch of Du Bois's problematic.

The first is epistemological with implications for scholarship of his work; the second is scholastic with an epistemological bearing for our contemporary interpretation of his thought.

This is to emphasize as a threshold notation that it is of fundamental epistemological importance for the contemporary interpretation of the work of Du Bois that his complicated negotiation with the concept of race as the nominalization of the fundamental ground, often supposed as ontological, for a historical positivity that he would seek to affirm, for example, a group that might be called Negro or African American, should not be simply subordinated to or amalgamated with his epistemological nominalization of the term "problem of the color line" that he proposed in order to bring into analytical relief a dimension of modern historicity that he wished to make the object of a fundamental critique.[5]

What he ambivalently names under the heading of race in the inaugural moments of his itinerary he would affirm and never disavow, even as he questioned any premise that would ground its determination in physical, natural, or biological character: the possibility of an original announcement of a Negro or African American inhabitation of world (even if woven of heterogeneous strands, a form of intermixture) and, beyond such an example, the originary capacity of any group that might contribute to a sense of the full inhabitation of the chance or freedom of human existence. Certainly, this movement of his thought carries within it all that is at stake as the core concern of later, more formalized disciplines of the humanistic and social sciences, and their putative aftermath, during the past century, which have been conceptually and theoretically placed under the heading of a concept of culture or a concept of historicity.

What he named under the heading of the problem of the color line he sought to radically challenge, disrupt, and transform such that it would eventually be worn away or rendered meaningless by a revolution of values and social organization or fade away in the midst of historical change as surely as "the morning mists fade before the rising sun."[6] In this sense the critical thought of the problem of the color line proposes the terms of an epistemic desedimentation of historicity, not only of the past, but also of the present, in such a manner that one can remark the limits of such historicity as yet also outlining the thresholds by which one could reimagine possibility. It is in this sense that a continual desedimentation of the past is of fundamental necessity in practical thought. In this sense, a certain thinking of "the problem of the color line" might allow a different sense of world, a different sense of horizon, to arise. It would be one that is different from what has been given in the present. This is the scene of a fundamental epistemological contribution by Du Bois that has yet to be fully elaborated as a theoretical intervention in modern thought as critical discourse.

In such a world, another one, different from those that have yet existed, and specifically one in which "the problem of the color line" has been rendered obsolete, groups such as the African American, *whose originarity necessarily remains at stake in every instance of its promulgation* and thus always in a sense yet to come, might be exemplary for human existence: not exemplary as the final or absolute example but, rather, as exemplary of the historicity of our time and of the possibility of the making and remaking of ideals in, or as, the matter of existence in general.

Second, however, it must be remarked that one of the astonishing facts about the current resurgence in the reading and study of Du Bois's works is the absence of any true scholastic account of his formulation and deployment of the thought of a global "problem of the color line."[7] While it remains that his most famous words are "the problem of the twentieth century is the problem of the color line," this oft-quoted statement has been understood or used primarily for its apparently prosaic truth or as if it were merely apocryphal (see Du Bois 1900a, 2015g). Thus, the phrase has primarily been used over the decades, if taken up at all, as a slogan or idiom. It has not been taken up so much as the name of a fundamental motif in Du Bois's thought or as a problem for contemporary thought in general: one that would fundamentally be epistemic even as it is irreducibly political. (Part II of this book examines at length the place of this phrase in Du Bois's thought and itinerary.)

In terms of the discussion of Du Bois's discourse itself, due, perhaps, to this same limited effort to think with him on this line, it has often been deduced or implied that a global perspective arose more or less suddenly for him as an effect of his participation in the Exposition Universelle, held at Paris, and the first international conference called by the name "Pan-African," held in London during the months of June and July in 1900.[8] And then others have operated this logic with reference to many other dates in his later career, with some mentioning the 1920s as a time when such a perspective developed, with others proposing that such an event occurred as late as 1945, when Du Bois was in his late seventies. This kind of premise and such logic have governed much of the interpretation of Du Bois's thought with regard to modernity as a whole or concerning the global in general, no matter what period of his itinerary has been under discussion. Yet such a premise does not bear up under scholastic scrutiny, and the theorization and interpretations deduced by way of it are profoundly misleading for any attempt to judge the implication of the itinerary of Du Bois's practice for contemporary thought. Thus, it should be understood as both a scholastic paradox and a political conundrum, certainly definitive in the American and Anglo-European academic discourse, but perhaps decisive in other geo-epistemic domains by way of the dissemination of such discussion, that most people—including many Du Bois scholars—know the famous line "the problem of the twentieth century . . ." from the reprinting of his 1901 essay "The Freedmen's Bureau" as the second chapter of *The Souls of Black Folk: Essays and Sketches* (Du Bois 1901b, 1903g), with virtually no idea of the fundamental level of sedimentation that it has within his thought: (a) that the global perspective adumbrated in that chapter was developed initially from Du Bois's attempt to understand the specific African American situation; (b) that it bespeaks a whole conception situated at a global level that Du Bois had begun to formulate during the half dozen years before the publication of his most famous book; and (c) that it remained an epistemological formulation that he would elaborate on many registers across his entire career, serving to formulate the theoretical horizon for the most ambitious works of the later stages of his career, from *Black Reconstruction*, in 1935, including both *Color and Democracy* and *The World and Africa* from the signal era at the end of World War II, to the time of the *Black Flame* trilogy, the latter of which was written and published from 1955 to 1961 (Du Bois 1935, 1976 [1935], 1945, 1975b, 1947, 1976d, 1957, 1976c, 1959, 1976b, 1961b, 1976e).

For this reason, an ongoing annotation of the paradoxes engendered by this approach remarks the persisting pertinence of a clarification of the issue at hand (see also Chandler 2021, 12–16). So, on the one hand, those who know of the line just quoted from the second chapter of *The Souls of Black Folk: Essays and Sketches* usually have a quite limited sense of its global framing in Du Bois's thought; or, if they do gesture toward such a frame, they have little or no grip on the depth of the conception involved. But, on the other hand, those who rhetorically grasp this line as a way to link Du Bois's thought to a global context in a general sense tend to do so by using it as a kind of weapon, under the authority of his name, against what they mistakenly think of or opportunistically characterize as a kind of parochialism in the discourse of African Americans in the United States, or the apparition of the supposed dominance of such a topic in discussions of the question of the African Diaspora or the problem of race in a global context.[9] Yet the pertinence of such announced interventions might at best be found in their rendering legible matters of position and authority in our contemporary discursive and institutional scene. For beyond any matter of polemics, it remains that the most troublesome aspect of readings of Du Bois that would conscript his discourse primarily for affirming our own ideas about the truth of modern global history is that it makes it very difficult, if not impossible, to access and to judge, first on the terms of Du Bois's own declarations, what he thought he was saying.

If one undertakes such an examination, it renders a quite legible track that shows that Du Bois was first led to this global frame precisely by trying to think the African American situation in the United States in the most fundamental and general manner possible. That he was, in this sense, first solicited by the specific ground of his own emergence articulates a general protocol of a commitment to thinking immanence that one disavows at one's own epistemic peril. That he sought to situate such immanence in relation to a passage of thought to the most general itself solicits and radicalizes this thought of the specific and the immanent. In an empirical sense, this meant that he was led to a global frame precisely *by way of* this preoccupation with the situation of African Americans in the United States and *not despite* it. Yet, in a theoretical sense, Du Bois was *simultaneously* insisting that the African American situation could only be understood as part of a global horizon and that global modernity could only be understood if one recognized the constitutive status for the making of modern world history as a whole of the historical process by which this group was announced in history.[10] The African American situation was a global one for Du Bois. And, *in this way*, at a ground level of historicity, shall we say, it was an exemplary example of a global problematic.[11]

Let me also annotate the scholastic question that indicates profoundly what is at issue. What if the apparently most local and parochial chapters of *The Souls of Black Folk: Essays and Sketches*, if situated, for example, in relation to the labor of thought presented in the essay "The Present Outlook for the Dark Races of Mankind" (which first appeared in print in October 1900), can be rendered as profoundly marked by a global perspective (Du Bois 1900a, 2015g; Chandler 2021)? Yet what if it is also the case that it therefore becomes clear that the means to the development of such a perspective for Du Bois, that of a certain sense of global modernity, was through and through by way of his concern with the only apparently parochial or relatively local situation of the African American in the United States? I suggest that this double remarking can come into profound relief by such a juxtaposition. Yet it remains that up to now there is no contemporary approach to Du Bois's work that has accomplished such an interpretive positioning. The project at hand is a part of such an undertaking.

It can therefore come as a jolt to a scholar approaching Du Bois's work from this perspective to discover that "The Present Outlook for the Dark Races of Mankind," which was first presented in public in December 1899 as the presidential address at the third annual meeting of the American

Negro Academy, has received at most extremely limited citation in the contemporary literature and in an essential sense remains unread in our time. Yet it is one of Du Bois's most important essays: for it is in fact the first place where he actually enunciates his most famous statement—"the problem of the twentieth century is the problem of the color line"—according to an achieved principle of formulation and clarified epistemological frame. This essay is easily as important as "The Conservation of Races," an essay that has become perennial on both sides of the Atlantic over the course of the past three or so intellectual generations. "The Present Outlook for the Dark Races of Mankind" is now available in an annotated scholarly edition of his early essays (Du Bois 2015g). Thus, it is only an apparent paradox that Du Bois's essays on the African American situation in the United States from the time just after the completion of his doctoral study in 1895 to the years immediately following the publication of *The Souls of Black Folk: Essays and Sketches* in 1903, and especially the chapters of the latter text that in a superficial reading would appear most particularistic, for example, those on the Freedmen's Bureau or on the relations of "Black" and "White" Americans (as one might call them) in the South, acquire their most powerful legibility and theoretical importance, then or now, only when seen as the very path for Du Bois's development of an interpretation of modernity in general, certainly of America as a distinctive scene of its devolution, but also of a global or worldwide historical conjuncture understood from the trajectory of human history as a whole. For, taken as a whole, singular enunciation, even as it is threaded with multiple motivations, claims, and levels of utterance, Du Bois's discourse at the turn of the twentieth century bespeaks a powerful sense of the way that the question of the African American is a question about the possibilities of a global modernity in general. Such an understanding should play a large role in getting rid of an often unstated but widely held sense that the study of African Americans in the United States is a parochial or naively nationalistic discussion and so forth. It can also go far in showing that in fact the problem of the Negro in America was long understood within the African American intellectual community in the United States as a fundamental part of the question of colonialism and its aftermath, that the differentiation of the two discourses, one concerned with "African American" matters and another concerned with "the colonial" in general, in contemporary academic discussions in the Americas and in Europe, but especially in the United States, is an instituted one of recent and superficial lineage. We can underscore that Du Bois, for example, from the very inception of his itinerary had announced a conception of a thought of the African American in which the premise and implication of this common historicity were the very terms of enunciation.

In the context of contemporary discussions about the aftermath of colonialism, or postcolonial discourse of one kind or another, or debates about globalization, Du Bois's early negotiation of the epistemological paradoxes involved in conceptualizing the modern history of imperialism, slavery, and colonialism in a way that accounts for the worldwide provenance of the problematic and does not simply reproduce a self-congratulatory narrative of the making of the West, along with his prophetic thematization of *the way in which* the question of historical difference within a global horizon of reference at whatever level of generality (for which we have no good names, including those common today—such as ethnicity, race, nationality, culture, or even social class) among groups of people would come to dominate future discussions of politics and authority in general on a planetary scale in the twentieth century and beyond, bears renewed and somewhat paradoxical force. Thus, the current discussion of Du Bois must be rearticulated such that it may become possible to thoroughly think through the implications for contemporary thought of his understanding of the African American situation as part of a worldwide problematic, whether we call it modernity or postmodernity, the persistence of colonialism or postcolonialism, a conflict of civilizations, or simply globalization or *mondialisation*, or something else altogether. Du Bois's thought of the future may indeed remain profound for our time.

FORMULATION

With this sketch in mind, a summary statement of just what an imperative to read Du Bois anew might mean can be formulated as two conjoined subsidiary demands.

On the one hand, it means that *a new sense of the whole* of Du Bois's itinerary itself must be adduced. At the scholastic level alone, this prerequisite is a daunting task for most scholars: its scale leads most to give up, to pull their research up short, or to turn elsewhere. Yet this recalibration of the positions of Du Bois in the history of thought—of intellectual and political practice—by way of a new sense of the whole of his work is a necessary task for critical thought in our time. There is no existing horizon of theoretical context that can become commensurate with the problematization that is at stake within this itinerary. All of the concepts by which we would comprehend an entire historicity remain necessarily and fundamentally in question in our time. All of the concepts of contextualization by which we once thought that we could appropriate, annex, or append the thought of Du Bois to a given or already accepted theoretical sense of horizon (especially those governed by the epistemic determinations of a formal discipline of knowledge) are at issue in the attempt to think through the problematization of Du Bois. Why? If it can be gathered in a word, it is because there is no absolutely sovereign figure of authority or example of historicity and historical becoming in the thought and practice of Du Bois. This remains despite or beyond his persistent gesture—across his entire itinerary—of affirming a resolute form of leadership, even in the face of the chance or risk of the greatest form of cost. Within this very torsion, precisely with regard to our historical present, his path shows in a fashion that is both paradoxical and yet exemplary what is at stake for the contemporary practitioner of thought who does not presume the absolute singularity or paramount status of what can be called in the self-referential terms of philosophy the transcendental historicity of the figure of modern Europe and the concomitant presumption of the simplicity of a putatively European-derived America. And such reserve also pertains to any other claim to such exemplarity. In a generalization of this negative formulation: there is no singular example of the passage beyond limit. Or, put in other terms, affirmatively, according to his discourse, the possible example of the passage beyond a given historical form was illimitable. All this can be proposed only by way of a critical practice in which the whole of Du Bois's thought and the whole of context are not assumed; rather, it must be developed by a theoretical sense in which both, in relation, appear only as the terms of a question. If produced with a desedimentative practice in which the sense of whole is taken as always itself immanently at stake, Du Bois's itinerary exhibits a profound thinking inhabitation of the historicity in which the situation of a figure such as himself—American, African American, Negro, Caribbean, European, European American, African—was possible. Across the distended organization of temporality in which it is announced and along the multiple paths, passages, and fault lines therein, it gives a legible form to the possibilities of thought in our time. As such, it marks, or makes possible the remarking of, two sides (at least and never only) of the limits of our historicity. It remains a solicitation to think the yet impossible future. If a critical or desedimentative practice would sustain the possibilities for the practice of a certain freedom on the order of existence that has been yielded by way of its dispositional practice, this work of Du Bois cannot be apprehended simply as a finished or finally accomplished whole. It must be inhabited as a practice—as a practical theoretical projection or elaboration—in which the whole or the general is always at stake in the instance. Never simply given, this whole or possible limit (or delimitation) takes shape only as the form of another problematization. The sense of limit, as resolution or impasse, is only the form of another organization of problem. The whole of Du Bois's itinerary, if there will have ever been such, is its dynamic, never simply given, ensemblic organization of practical theoretical problem for thought. This difficulty that we have just remarked—in the form of the solicitation that it sets afoot, that is to say, this questionable status of the relation of thought and historicity— remains exemplary of a fundamental problem of our time, of our historicities. That problem is that all concepts by which a whole process might be comprehended remains, for us in our time, as it were, at issue.

On the other hand, this imperative also means that such a sense of the whole must be sustainable by way of a consideration of his discourse, of his texts and the practice of this thought, of the infrastructural figure, step, or gesture, that is, according to the organization of the microscopic, so to speak. A *radical sense of the partial* must be developed. In one register of this imperative, the relation of Du Bois's thought to all forms of contextualization must remain in question. This is to say that only in this manner can critical discourse keep open the question of Du Bois's thought. It is in this way that the critical discourse can sustain the relation to his thought as a form of question. In such an engagement, limit is only one face of a more general structure. The other is possibility. The appearance of this relation (or, Du Bois's thought according to this general structure) is as an opacity: that which remains withdrawn within its promulgation. This is certainly the idiomatic code of its historicity. Yet it is more. For in another register of this difficulty of thinking with the partial, it poses the question of the methods and the techniques, or technologies, by which we might engage Du Bois's practice. One could remain open to the question in his discourse by addressing it at the microlevel modes of its organization and the infrastructures operating in his practice. In the discursive sense, these would be the orders of the concept-metaphor and the rhetorical gesture. In the social and political sense, Du Bois's practice always takes the form of position(s), forms of political relation. Du Bois's discourse must be engaged on the level of the *seme*, the *mark*, "*l'énonciation*."[12] The critical discourse as a form of political practice (and it cannot fail to be one, for an apolitical posture is also a politics) must itself inhabit the *movement* of thought, the *gesture*, the *vocative*. In all cases, a desedimentative practice must maintain an openness to the forms of the here and now of Du Bois's practice as relation. This latter is to say that such critical or desedimentative practice, the work of our own efforts, must distantiate the *instance* of a practice such as that sustained across the itinerary of Du Bois by recognizing the way in which it is not yet or is still at stake in that within it which is still yet to come, as a form of interlocution, as provocation, as elaboration. The forms of its beyond might yet be available thereby—as the form of a kind of reinscription.

The pertinence of the contributions from his itinerary have a distinctive bearing for how we inhabit our future: such bearing for our own historicity is something other than that of serving simply as one example among many others. The paradoxes attendant to the relation of any such partiality to a putative whole (which is most spectacularly proposed in the grand projections of transcendental philosophy) are what grant this distinction. Any gesture that would propose to disrupt a thought that posits a claim of the absolute or the absolutely singular could only sustain such by way of the apparition of its own claim to essence. Du Bois's practice puts such paradoxes at stake at every step, turn, and conjuncture of its itinerary. In this sense, it solicits the whole of modern thought on a global level from the middle of the eighteenth century through the nineteenth, twentieth, and twenty-first centuries, and perhaps beyond. It is thus the case that a certain tarrying with his announced partiality can bring into relief how it always also places at stake any thought of a putative whole. Partiality here is simultaneously formal and historical. There, at the site or seam of such apparent parochiality, what is at stake in the *here and now* of a historical present—Du Bois's, in this instance—gives itself to a practice that would propose to sustain the illimitable chance of becoming in the future that is yet to come.

Further, it is thus the case that a certain labor of scholastic and theoretical inhabitation of Du Bois's writings—at the level of the *instance*, the *seme*, the *step*, the *reflex*, the *mark* on the bias—would yield a kind of paleonymic production. And there partiality would grant the future as much by way of its opacity as its lucidity or apparent clairvoyance. The labor of critical thought in this sense (our own practice) would always carry the imperative of judgment. (And here a certain ambivalence can hold a conceptual edge—still on the bias, such as that of a *deba bocho*—the leading cut of which, with a certain attunement in the sharpening, could match that of the finest scalpel. It would be fundamentally distinct from impartiality.) In such practice, we would be required to respect the way in which that which becomes legible for us in Du Bois's thought is given by way of this partiality: it is the very path for the announcement of the universal or the cosmic, whatever is such; it is otherwise than the oppositive of such. Partiality must be understood as capable of proposing another passage beyond limit.

However, in the engagement with Du Bois, it has been all too common that a certain order of critical judgment (which amounts to a form of prejudgment) happens most often, analytically speaking, prior to any sustained resting with the dimension of limit in his practice. Certainly, no matter its depth or its superficiality, a judgment must be rendered operable in the critical work. Yet, if it would be otherwise than dogmatic, the attributes of Du Bois's practice—theme, topic, element, position, method—must be adduced according to their infrastructural organization and microlevel concatenation. But it is in such rendering that the limit of the seemingly perennial preemptive forms of engagement with Du Bois's work show itself, in turn: an apparent nominalization (parts and pieces of Du Bois's discourse, usually presented as a heterogeneous agglomeration of changing positions and declarations) in fact always proceeds from the basis of a fundamental theoretical declaration that was reached prior to any critical inhabitation of Du Bois's discourse. Whether to affirm or to denounce, Du Bois's discourse, especially at the level of its most specific mark, is usually submitted to a kind of blinding lucidity.

Yet what matters most in our own engagement with Du Bois's thought as given is the capacity of our interpretation, or thoughtful inhabitation, of his itinerary to sustain the sense of the opacity and limit of that itinerary even as our practice attempt to recognize the fecundity of his discourse within the terms of its own practical and theoretical vocation and projection. For this apparitional limit is also the encoded forms of a thought of possibility. It is only in the traversal of Du Bois's discourse in its nodal specificity that such an order of recognition can be announced and sustained in a critical and desedimentative work.

The order of attention that can carry both imperatives—that of an immanent sense of whole and that of judgment with regard to any sense of the partial—in thinking with Du Bois is the enigmatic order of the example. Du Bois is everywhere concerned with the character, status, and implication of the example. By way of a cut or break on the bias, a certain declension produced in the form of a judgment as an act, the figure of an example can be adduced. It is partial and ineluctably limited. Yet in it *also* is a certain deposition, disposed perhaps as those concatenations that might have once been called system or the general forms of order. Yet, too, it is radically otherwise than such. The latter can be organized only by way of a passage (never only one) beyond or in the remains of the always distantiated dispersal that is another name for possibility in general. Form, which is a kind of dispersal as much as apparent deposition, if there is such, may be usefully described as dendritic. On this order of attention, the example within such critical practice, then, is always a certain immanent thought of whole, of becoming, and of possibility. In this sense, then, the example exposes at once both the circumstance and the possible. Thus, it is the guiding problematization of part I of this study.

* * *

Working under the heading of what he formulated as an autobiographical example of a concept, Du Bois himself remarked this order of problematic in 1940, in *Dusk of Dawn: An Essay toward an Autobiography of a Race Concept* (Du Bois 1940, 53; 1975d, 53). A septuagenarian who would remain strong and present on the scene of thought and activity for nearly a quarter century more, he wrote at that time:

> Little indeed did I do, or could I conceivably have done, to make this problem or loose it. Crucified on the vast wheel of time, I flew round and round with the Zeitgeist, waving my pen and lifting faint voices to explain, expound and exhort; to see, foresee and prophesy, to the few who could or would listen. Thus very evidently to me and to others I did little to create my day or greatly change it; but I did exemplify it and thus for all time my life is significant for all lives of men. (Du Bois 1975d, 3–4)

What might such exemplarity mean today? Certainly, it remains in part because of the precocity, depth, and persistence with which Du Bois wrote about the monumental historical events of the past five hundred years that constitute and shape our epoch in a general social and historical sense, events that have given shape to the modern world, especially the conjoined history of colonial slavery in the modern era *and* its aftermath.

But not only this.

It is also because our futural capacity to think the historicity of our existence, in the form of its present and its future, in a theoretical and philosophical sense, our capacity to discover paths where there is no way in the world of the future ("to make a way out of no way," in that African American phrase from those who have gone before), to gather ourselves in coming upon the question of a horizon of possibility that remains in the present enigmatically yet to come, is at stake that we we must search out those examples in our intellectual heritage of figures who were willing *to place themselves at stake* at the limit of given forms of historical possibility *in the name of the future here and now*. Failure in this sense is of the order of necessity. It is only an apparent paradox that it is also of the order of freedom. As such, there will always only have been examples. I would propose that the figure of Du Bois, his thought, gives us such an example.

It is thus at the juncture, those crossroads of the past and the future, the known and the unknown, that one will most often find the figure of Du Bois. We can nominalize it somewhat: the thinker who questions (reflects on our ethics, morals, and ideals), the scholar who inquires (seeks understanding of our historical and social conditions), and the writer (who, in exercising his craft, resolutely affirms the freedom of being in the practice of the imagination, always given in the form of a writing, in general, the practice of which is his very habitation in thought). This is also the Du Bois whose entire mode of being is thus a political activity. We might recognize thus, across the flow of time and effort, not only the young, hopeful, and effervescent Du Bois of the fin de siècle, or the imperious and indefatigable intellect of the *renaissance years* between the world wars, but, beyond all, the Grand Old Man, gray, mustached, and gaunt with age, yet still beckoning energetically to us to hasten our steps and get on with the responsibility of grappling in thought and critical reflection with the implacable matters of existence in our time. It is this commitment to the work of thinking, to that within thought that opens onto the infinite and bequeaths to us an infinite task, an infinite practice, that renders legible within Du Bois's practice an exemplary inhabitation of our common horizons, even if the problematic that he still shares with us, one which we still share with him, exceeds horizon, as such.

Yet the example means still more.

For the broad order of problem that announces matters African American in general within or as historicity, in general, as given within his own thought, situates Du Bois's own itinerary as simply an example of a more general order of our epoch—of the centuries, not only of the past, but also those centuries yet to come. Therein, too, the exemplary status is not simply of limit—for example, "the problem of the color line"—but also exemplary for us of how we might put at stake existence as possibility, of the terms of a generous future that may remain such, as futures, even within or as supposed necessity. Herein I have followed it under the heading of the historiographical dimension of practice as it shows forth in some of Du

Bois's earliest formulations. The example of Du Bois himself, even when annotated in autobiographical mode, is an articulation of the historiographical example, of all that may for a time be thought under the heading of the African American example in general. Whereas what may appear as the autobiographical takes the apparition of the unfungible, the singular, and perhaps the irreversible terms of the historial, that which is rendered legible within the order of attention that operates as the practice of the historiographical may be shown also as a name for possibility. The example on this order of attention brings into relief possible terms of address to the futures of historicity. This sense of radical hope, perhaps an "unhopeful hope," is also given within this practice of the example in the thought of Du Bois. Given across the threshold of one turn of the century, it remains that it is still becoming such for those centuries—both future and future past, thereby—yet to come. It is under this heading, of possible delimitations, on the track of two paths of the example, that I have sought herein to offer the question of the delimitations, which may yet be configured for us, of the practice of W. E. B. Du Bois, as a problem for thought, within our time.

PART I

For Fredric Jameson

"Beyond This Narrow Now"

Elaborations of the Example in the Thought of W. E. B. Du Bois—At the Limit of World

The silently growing assumption of this age is that the probation of races is past, and that the backward races of today are of proven inefficiency and not worth the saving. Such an assumption is the arrogance of peoples irreverent toward Time and ignorant of the deeds of men. A thousand years ago such an assumption, easily possible, would have made it difficult for the Teuton to prove his right to life. Two thousand years ago such dogmatism, readily welcome, would have scouted the idea of blond races ever leading civilization. So woefully unorganized is sociological knowledge that the meaning of progress, the meaning of "swift" and "slow" in human doing and the limits of human perfectibility, are veiled unanswered sphinxes on the shores of science. Why should Aeschylus have sung two thousand years before Shakespeare was born? Why has civilization flourished in Europe, and flickered, flamed, and died in Africa? So long as the world stands meekly dumb before such questions, shall this nation proclaim its ignorance and unhallowed prejudices by denying freedom of opportunity to those who brought the Sorrow Songs to the seats of the mighty?
—W. E. B. DU BOIS, "The Sorrow Songs" (1903k)

What is good and better and best in the measure of human advance? and how shall we compare the present with the past, nation with nation, and group with group, so as to gain real intelligent insight into conditions and needs, and enlightened guidance? Now this is extremely difficult in matters of human development, because we are so ignorant of the ordinary facts relating to conditions of life, and because, above all, criteria of life and the objects of living are so diverse.

—W. E. B. DU BOIS, "The Development of a People" (1904)

INCIPIT

If one accepts the epistemic imperatives of the example, its status as an always ensemblic apparition of the supposed proper and also, thus, its status as a certain order of name for both the limit and the possibility of thought, it might well be engaged as the announcement of an *atopic* order of existence that nonetheless *is*, if you will, only in its immanent appearance: as a site or a seam, an irruption yielded by way of the concatenation that is a fault line; or as something like the fractual force of waves on the high ocean; or as the terrible heat of a sudden and massive efflorescence, of flame, moving across the desert of the mind's-eye memory, arising from the sharp and textured frisson of rock against rock; or according to a distribution of force that takes form, if at all, in the general figure of the cantilever, whether as mountain or bridge. The *atopic* in this sense is simply an otherwise-than-proper name of the passage beyond—at the limit of world.[1]

A critical practice—understood otherwise than in simply a modern and now classical sense of that phrase—that would move according to such an order of imperative calls for the development, or operation, of certain techniques that would comprise an inhabitation that sustains itself, if at all, at the limit of habitus—techniques of sounding, of gesture, of reception or hospitality—in the practice of thought. Such modes of attention may remark, in the infra-organization of the instance, or the circumstance, some possible movements, gestures, or steps, perhaps, or some forms of maintenance, of the passive in constitution, in a practice that would accept the responsibility given in a general desedimentation, one that would remain, open, and generous, to its own possible becoming, by which one could traverse the limit of world.[2]

Approached on the path of the bias of this situation of the example, W. E. B. Du Bois's thought may yet be understood as a certain order of organized epistemic ensemble. As a kind of objectivity, here nameable as a formation of life, it can thus be engaged according to the guidance given by the demands of the topographical in a general sense as the dispensation of metaphor—of air, of water, of soil or earth, for example. Yet it would remain the case that the example in the Du Boisian modes of thoughtful practice, like habitation or architectural production in general, can be announced only according to the forms of its ensemblic temporalities. There could be no radical disjunction of the topographical and the topological: or, rather, the latter is always already at stake in the former. In this sense, the distinction of the topographical might also be understood to extend itself as a dispensation of metaphor for temporality—of space and spacing as temporization and of the plane and the parallel as duration, for example.

The problematization that we can notice, track, and critically announce as the forms—of historicity, of the itinerary of one W. E. B. Du Bois— then can be understood as the general topographical figuration of a force that is, so to speak, always and already *atopos*. It is always otherwise than the simple or punctual present. Yet such an atopic movement is also the dispensation of paths of traversal for the utopic: it is the announcement— within the forms of existence—of an illegible legibility that appears only in the remark or an impossible possible future that is yet at stake in the present. It is the form of the here and now that is yet "beyond this narrow Now," as we receive such a thought in the penultimate paragraph of Du Bois's elegy to his lost son (Du Bois 1903i, 213, chap. 11, para. 13).

Proposed here by way of a tarrying with the thought of Du Bois: the temporal would extend beyond time as duration and configured plane; the *atopic*, as movement or rhythm, would announce the passage to form of the *utopic* and remark its impossible passage beyond possible limit, yielding that which remains as a measure of possibility. Such practice can be rendered available by paleonymy and placed at stake for a contemporary thought—whatever its time—if we think of Du Bois's thought as a name for both sides of a limit: this is to say that at the limit of limit, there will also always have been the name of possibility.

At the threshold of our own basic practical decision, so to speak, accepting the rhetorical dispositions just given as our guide in traversing a domain beyond that which is accessible simply by way of an analytics, the principal features of Du Bois's practice in turn may be understood at an epistemic level to exhibit or expose two forms of concatenation, among perhaps other examples: one we might call the autobiographical, and the other we can mark as the historiographical. The interpretive premise that is operative here, in such a formulation, which I began to propose from the outset of this study, is that before one analytically organizes Du Bois's practice as thought and itinerary into the shape of various given traditions of discourse, disciplines, or political stratagems, one should attempt to accede or attend first to the forms of problematization as they are announced as something that is at stake *for* him as thought—as simultaneously adducing the contours of his profile in thought as such and acquiring a distinct practical organization by way of this production. The concern in the first instance of critical engagement—even if understood as an analytics or a methodology—must be the way in which the major questions took shape as his intellectual formation and inhabitation at the level of his existence and the manner in which the broad historical situations announced their epistemic shape as the sustained solicitation of his critical attention. This is the first order of seam or concatenation. It marks the measure of thought articulated according to possibility in general, we might say. And then, in both instances, the autobiographical and the historiographical, the order of historicity that Du Bois came to call by the name "the problem of the color line" can be understood to inscribe itself in the articulation of every aspect of the problematizations that are announced in his itinerary. It is an instituted form of limitation that would announce itself in both axes of orientation—the spatial and the temporal. And, too, analytically, then, it is a constitutive dimension of both forms of concatenation that I am proposing as the shape of the itinerary of Du Bois—the autobiographical and the historiographical. Yet it takes form if at all not as a thing-in-itself but as a form of relation, its ostensible being at stake as eventuality in each and every instance of its possibility: hence, its announcement on the order of knowledge and understanding is as a problem for thought. It does not preexist objectivity, nor does it issue from a preexistent organization of materiality. It takes its configuration from the force of relation. Thus, it remains that this latter dimension, "the problem of the color line," a heterogeneous ensemble of productive forms of practiced proscription, can still be usefully rendered distinct—by interpretive elaboration and analysis—from the question of possibility in general, even as the two remain inseparably interwoven. It solicits its own form of elaboration: thus, I consider it directly elsewhere (see part II of this study).

Yet the general question of *istoria*—the historical and the historiographical, of the *historial*—is the very organization of world for Du Bois as a practitioner of critical thought.[3]

Specifically, one is thus led to ask the following question: What, then, is the organization of the "narrow Now" of Du Bois's contemporaneity as a historical topography? This question tracks, then, a second order of concatenation in an approach to the practice of Du Bois. I propose that what must gain our attention is that in both forms of the itinerary of Du Bois's practice, the autobiographical and the historiographical, there is no precomprehended limit that can sustain itself as of ultimate pertinence. This may be a practical way to receive or accept a thought as participation in that which opens toward *atopos*. The fundamental question, then, is not only about given circumstance—what shows in the critical discourse as a stubborn commitment to think the African American situation (to reference an on-hand example of the issue at stake) or that of the historically subordinate (for example, the so-called poor) in realms of social power in a general sense (to notate another ready-to-mind exemplar of the question) only under the heading of abjection or pathology—for it is also, and more radically, about historical possibility. It is at such a juncture of epistemological problem that the question of the status of the mark that would announce thought to itself in the form of its own distantiation takes shape in the critical discourse—a discourse that would portend to approach the figure of Du Bois. The turn, the reflex, the *trope*—as metaphor or catachresis—becomes within this difficulty of practice not the finality of thought but the mark of its passage. It is the form of a guide that can only appear as such after the fact. It demands from us—those who might try to think with Du Bois, for example—a certain kind of engagement with the impossible task of remaining open to the impossible possibility within thought. For only within such openness might one gain ground on that which is beyond, or, better, discover configurations of force that may remain susceptible to epistemic desedimentation, a disarticulation of conceptual and theoretical presumption, enabling thereby the capacity to think otherwise than the given. Herein, thus, what follows is an elaboration of *the question of historial possibility* in Du Bois's thought, along the lines of the autobiographical and the historiographical, as this can be adduced according to the rhetorical, methodological, and theoretical protocols required for an engagement with the order of the example. Our order of attention—however limited our access to such—must be toward the very terms of possibility of the practice of thought.

It is in this irruptive sense that the following takes the form of a sustained excursion on the question of example—by way of the example here—of the thinking of one W. E. B. Du Bois, on two orders of example.

It is Du Bois himself who, in the prefatory "Apology" of *Dusk of Dawn*, places three of his texts in a genealogical relation as "autobiographical" reflections of a distinct kind (Du Bois 1975d, 1–2). They are not simply narratives of his life, or even at a larger level the story simply of the Negro American, but a discourse of exemplification, of a situation, a historical problematization, perhaps as a certain object of thought, and of the struggle to understand or engage this situation as a problematic, perhaps as a subject of thought. These three texts are (and such listing here certainly does not preclude the addition of other texts, especially later ones; indeed, it calls for such interpretive extension) first, *The Souls of Black Folk: Essays and Sketches* of 1903, which Du Bois calls in this "Apology" "a cry at midnight thick within the veil, when none rightly knew the coming of day" and whose titular opening and path of elaboration was the question, "how does it feel to be a problem," or, in other words, the movement of "double-consciousness"; then, *Darkwater: Voices from within the Veil*, which Du Bois presented in 1920 just after World War I as a sequel to *The Souls of Black Folk: Essays and Sketches* and which, in the opening paragraph of the prefatory "Postscript," was proposed as offering to the devastated world a distinct "point of view" "from a veiled corner, where all the outer tragedy and comedy have reproduced themselves in microcosm within" (Du Bois 1920, vii; 1975c, vii); and, finally, for our annotation here, the text at hand in a most signal manner, *Dusk of Dawn*, the subtitle of which, *An Essay toward an Autobiography of a Race Concept*, announces a thought of the autobiographical example as the titular heading for an investigation of what he calls in 1940, at the incipit of World War II, "the central problem of the greatest of the world's democracies and so the Problem of the future world." He continues, immediately:

> The problem of the future world is the charting, by means of intelligent reason, of a path not simply through the resistances of physical force, but through the vaster and far more intricate jungle of ideas conditioned on unconscious and subconscious reflexes of living things; on blind unreason and often irresistible urges of sensitive matter; of which the concept of race is today one of the most unyielding and threatening. I seem to see a way of elucidating the inner meaning and significance of that race problem by explaining it in terms of the one human life that I know best. (Du Bois 1975d, 2)[4]

In each case, Du Bois sought to understand the limits of the present world from the situation of this example, certainly not in isolation or alone, but as indeed a guiding example. It is the case, however, in a fundamental way that is not often enough remarked or understood, that Du Bois also proposed a horizon of possibility by way of the question of this example: it yielded a thought of an illimitable movement of possible being that would be at stake here and now even as it was as yet, in the present, impossible. It is thus that just a few passages after the lines quoted in extenso above, in the opening section of *Dusk of Dawn* that he calls "The Plot," Du Bois presents two layers, in an ontological sense, according to which one might approach the question of possibility *in the world as something yet to come*. For the Negro subject, he writes that they "must live and eat and strive, and still hold unfaltering commerce with the stars" (Du Bois 1975d, 7); and for the world in general, as it engages the problem of its future by way of the problem of the color line, while the negative or limit dimension demands that "the scientific task of the twentieth century would be to explore and measure the scope of chance and unreason in human action" (7), the affirmative or imaginal dimension would open toward "conceiving the world not as a permanent structure but as changing growth" and "the study of man as changing and developing physical and social entity" (4).

Let me now take up only one sheaf from among the many pages of this triptych of the autobiographical example in Du Bois's thought, as it announces itself in the opening paragraphs of the opening chapter of *The Souls of Black Folk: Essays and Sketches*:

> To the real question, How does it feel to be a problem? I answer seldom a word. And yet, being a problem is a strange experience,—peculiar even for one who has never been anything else, save perhaps in babyhood and in Europe. It is in the early days of rollicking boyhood that the revelation first bursts upon one, all in a day as it were. I remember well when the shadow swept across me. (Du Bois 1903d, 2, chap. 1, paras. 1–2)

We have entered the text en medias res, across the conjuncture of the first and second paragraphs. (And as these famous lines, and this text in general, are now more and more widely read as well as well as relatively easily accessible, in this part of the present study, I will more often cite this text, rather than offer full quotations or any extensive reference [Du Bois 1903l; see also 1903m]).

A. BEING AS A PROBLEM. He has never been anything else, always a "problem." His, the narrator's, sense of experience, sense of being, is of always existing as a problem, a social and historical problem, certainly, but also an existential problem. The matter of existence takes shape as an always previous organization of problem. In "The Conservation of Races," it is announced on the order of what is often thought as an ontological question (Du Bois 1897b, 2015c). But even though it is the most common and perduring of experiences (that is, consciousness, and above all self-consciousness, of being), the most familiar, this sense, this "feeling," is "strange," "peculiar." This becomes the opening and, thus, the framing formulation of the opening essay. Thereby it is such for the entire text. The inhabitation in question produces a sense of double identification, an American, a Negro, which form, for Du Bois as the narrator, the headings of two ideals: the famous line from the third paragraph reads, "two warring ideals in one dark body." This in turn yields a moral and ethical question (as this problematic is through and through political) as a matter of position, power, alliance, strategy, and tactic, that is, a matter of policy and program. The question as I would state it is either, "What is the relation between these two identifications (or two figures of a double identification)?" or, "Is it a matter of choosing allegiance to one or the other of these senses of identification?" The question is: Is it possible to be "both a Negro and an American" without proscription?

The response of Du Bois, as author, in the form of the narrator's declaration, is to affirm both identifications, in a double fashion.

He affirms them together, in reciprocal relation. He affirms each beyond its orientation or referral to this given other. Just how either reference might be *nameable* beyond this other is not so much the issue here, at this passage in the first chapter of *The Souls of Black Folk: Essays and Sketches*, but both within this text and elsewhere (as we can see in his discussion of Europe's formation, or of the formation of Africa), Du Bois speaks of any civilization or culture (I would say mode of inhabitation in general) as produced out of multiple, that is, heterogeneous, sources and references. This is his conception in such texts as "The Spirit of Modern Europe" (which our best supposition dates to 1900) (Du Bois 1985f, 2015j) and *The Negro* (Du Bois 1915b, 1975e), but this conception is already put forth in the speculative narrative that provides the principal thetic transition of "The Conservation of Races," notably in its tenth paragraph (Du Bois 2015c, 1897b, 1986a). That is to say, there is in Du Bois's thought, along with a powerful commitment to the sense of the whole and to unity, a certain maintenance of an affirmation of the heterogeneous. Here it can still be maintained in our own time under the metaphorical heading of the double.

This sense of double identification then opens up a space of critique. At the level of the social order, of the subject's inhabitation of a social and historical situation, Du Bois calls it "second sight," in this context, what he calls "this American world." At the level of the social entity or being, of the subject's consciousness of his own way of inhabiting this situation, that is to say the self-consciousness of the subject, Du Bois calls it "double-consciousness."

What must be underscored is that this double sense is set in motion by the violence of a symbolic proscription that is given its force and bearing by acute real social practices of violation, exploitation, and oppression that are distributed beyond the punctual present of the occasion of its promulgation. It is thus that the movement of critique that arises within the formation of this sense, if it acquires legibility, is indeed a turning back, a fold, if you will, operating within the movement of symbolization that is the formation of sense, upon the very conditions that set it in motion. And then, further, it can be shown that at that threshold level of existence, the inhabitation of sense, it both disorients and deters the simple fulfillment of that violence. Let us then follow this more precisely, restricting ourselves principally to these few lines highlighted from the opening paragraphs of this first chapter of *The Souls of Black Folk: Essays and Sketches*.

For Du Bois, in the phrase that we have already recalled, there are two autobiographical exceptions to that experience, "babyhood" and "Europe."

B. OF BABYHOOD. The appearance of the term *babyhood* implies a conception, more or less formal, of stages of a life course, such as infancy (or babyhood), childhood (or boyhood), adolescence, and adulthood (entailing stages of maturation, fullness, and decline). Here, in the passage at hand, Du Bois mentions two stages.

First, babyhood has for its pivotal example in the book *The Souls of Black Folk: Essays and Sketches* the figure of Du Bois's son Burghardt, who died at eighteen months of age in May 1899. This is most poignantly articulated as the eleventh chapter of the text. And it is to Burghardt, along with his sister Yolande, that the book is dedicated. Here it can be said that the figure of the child always clusters around *matters* utopian; this is certainly true for Du Bois. The father writes, "A perfect life was his, all joy and love, with tears to make it brighter,—sweet as a summer's day beside the Housatonic" (Du Bois 1903i, 211, chap. 11, para. 10). And then he remarks this vision a bit later: "Blame me not if I see a world thus darkly through the Veil,—and my soul whispers ever to me, saying, 'Not dead, not dead, but escaped; not bond, but free.'" Du Bois goes on to follow this vision by way of his reception of his son's passing and marks its nonsimple horizon (if it can still be called such) as "beyond this narrow Now":

> All that day and all that night there sat an awful gladness in my heart,—nay, blame me not if I see the world thus darkly through the Veil,—and my soul whispers ever to me, saying, "Not dead, not dead, but escaped; not bond, but free." No bitter meanness now shall sicken his baby heart till it die a living death, no taunt shall madden his happy boyhood. Fool that I was to think or wish that this little soul should grow choked and deformed within the Veil! I might have known that yonder deep unworldly look that ever and anon floated past his eyes was peering far beyond this narrow Now. In the poise of his little curl-crowned head did there not sit all that wild pride of being which his father had hardly crushed in his own heart? For what, forsooth, shall a Negro want with pride amid the studied humiliations of fifty million fellows? Well sped, my boy, before the world had dubbed your ambition insolence, had held your ideals unattainable, and taught you to cringe and bow. Better far this nameless void that stops my life than a sea of sorrow for you. (Du Bois 1903i, 213, chap. 11, para. 13)

There is a complex movement of affirmation at work here. By a deft affirmation of the negative, it simultaneously produces a desedimentation, or destabilization, of the status of negativity and forestalls any simple recuperation to the given. The sense of loss that is recorded in the text encodes more than the sign of negativity. The narrator father's declaration in these lines of a temporality beyond presence can be understood as calling into question the status of the historicity named therein. While the father cannot be certain of some putative other horizon, for he most especially cannot find and does not propose a proper name for it, there is no absolute here, neither in the sense of canonical religion, nor in the terms of philosophy as metaphysics. However, it is certain that, for this father, the passing of the son cannot and will not be apprehended simply as loss. What the text encodes here in the form of rendering a record, a kind of elegy, under the heading of temporality, is a radical disjuncture, a rending, in the heart of being as existence. And, then, in the most decisive move of this essay, it affirms that lability. It affirms it for the passing of the son. And it affirms it for the survivance of this father. The implication is certainly that the father's sense of self—in the temporality of his life course—was in fact reinaugurated, already, we might say, by way of the force of a delimitation of a putative horizon, which had previously appeared as unlimited, by the coming to legibility of the mark or "problem" of the color line. Thus, it has taken shape within the horizon of this "Now." Yet paradoxically, it is this *break*, this *décalage*, this sense of "*time out of joint*" ("The time is out of joint; O cursed spite! / That ever I was born to set it right!"—as Shakespeare's Hamlet bequeathed the unholy thought to us [Shakespeare 2006, 1.5211–12] that will announce *in existence* the very form of the passage to another horizon (Spillers 2003d, 262; 2006; Derrida 1994, 18–31). It is certainly one in which passage is form, and, perhaps, form is passage. In this movement that is yet a break, the sense of both the instituted break and an unlimited horizon becomes susceptible to remark—that is to say, in another register, acquires nameability—only in retrospect. And yet the process of rendering such legibility is the very means of a passage to and beyond the given limit. It is the disorientation of time as or according to "Now." As such, its affirmation names without naming the possibility of an illimitable becoming, not in terms of a received idea or canonical horizon. And yet it has bearing and is at stake *here and now*. And here, as we shall be able to confirm again later, in that other register, it is the very passage to narration. The text that *we* are reading is rendered possible by way of the itinerary that we are tracking within its folds.

The figure of childhood, or boyhood, is given as Du Bois himself in the first chapter. "I was a little thing, away up in the hills of New England where the dark Housatonic winds between Hoosac and Taghkanic to the sea" (Du Bois 1903d, 2, chap. 1, para. 2). And as this figure is the very subject of the narration that we are following, we will address it momentarily.

Elsewhere in the text, Du Bois describes another stage, a figure of adolescence, we might say a textually doubled figure, for it has two interwoven examples: that of Josie, the dark young woman of the harsh hills of eastern Tennessee, who dies of a loss of hope, in the early chapter of *The Souls of Black Folk: Essays and Sketches* called "Of the Meaning of Progress," and that of John Jones, in the later chapter "Of the Coming of John," the Negro John in the story (for there is also a White John), from southeastern Georgia, at the mouth of the mighty Altamaha, on the restless shore of the Atlantic, who is lynched for defending his sister against rape (and she does survive unscathed in a physical sense), not yet a prophet perhaps, but one who fulfilled the duty that was bequeathed to him—the form of historical possibility—and whose voice or the voice of those like him, but for this twice-told tale, would be lost in the wind and the sea of history (Du Bois 1903h, 1903f; see also 1903i).

Du Bois, or the narrator, at any rate the boy of the first chapter, as it is given in the second paragraph, encounters a glance, a line of force, we might say, that sends him back on himself:

In a wee wooden schoolhouse, something put it into the boys' and girls' heads to buy gorgeous visiting-cards—ten cents a package—and exchange. The exchange was merry, till one girl, a tall newcomer, refused my card,—refused it peremptorily, with a glance. Then it dawned upon me with a certain suddenness that I was different from the others; or like, mayhap, in heart and life and longing, but shut out from their world by a vast veil. I had thereafter no desire to tear down that veil, to creep through; I held all beyond it in common contempt, and lived above it in a region of blue sky and great wandering shadows. That sky was bluest when I could beat my mates at examination-time, or beat them at a foot-race, or even beat their stringy heads. Alas, with the years all this fine contempt began to fade; for the worlds I longed for, and all their dazzling opportunities, were theirs, not mine. But they should not keep these prizes, I said; some, all, I would wrest from them. Just how I would do it I could never decide: by reading law, by healing the sick, by telling the wonderful tales that swam in my head,—some way. With other black boys the strife was not so fiercely sunny: their youth shrunk into tasteless sycophancy, or into silent hatred of the pale world about them and mocking distrust of everything white; or wasted itself in a bitter cry, Why did God make me an outcast and a stranger in mine own house? The shades of the prison-house closed round about us all: walls strait and stubborn to the whitest, but relentlessly narrow, tall and unscalable to sons of night who must plod darkly on in resignation, or beat unavailing palms against the stone, or steadily, half hopelessly watch the streak of blue above. (Du Bois 1903d, 2–3, chap. 1, para. 2)

While elsewhere I have sought to establish the way in which there is an asymmetrical reciprocity in this movement, one that brings into configuration the limit as given in the social mark, here I will propose the way in which it is productive of possibility, according to which the mark can be remarked such as to exceed that which is already simply given within it (Chandler 2014c, 129–70, 233–46). Thus, we can note that there is a temporality to this figuration; it is one in which the "glance" as a socially productive force (while not simply conclusive) would mark him as different, as "a black boy." And, indeed, he then sees himself in terms of this difference, this position. However, within this movement, the text records a paradoxical fold or movement otherwise, a properly semiotic configuration, within the formation of the mark. First, he seeks or declares a strict or putatively pure opposition to the mark. However, with this move, he discovers that he cannot succeed, that it gives him no hold within the system in play. So, second, he undertakes a double move of simultaneous opposition and declaration of commonness across the distinction that the glance would institute. In understanding Du Bois's autobiographical texts, this track or trace that I have outlined is crucial. I consider it the motif of *internal dissociation*, certainly within the self, or supposed ipseity, and in a corollary fashion from, or within, a given context. It opens the space or time of a critical apprehension and reflection, which although announced under this determined heading has no necessary limit. Thus, simultaneously so to speak, by way of an act that might be called a metalepsis, in seeing himself in this way, as the narrator describes the time of experience, he begins to render relative this way of seeing. He names himself as part of a putative group, "black boys." He typologizes the lines or types of negotiation of the position by skin color, some fiercely resistant (him), some resigned (others). Thus, a nascent critique of the distinction and its real concomitant material effects announces itself. To the extent that the narrator by way of a certain movement within the experience of violence has been enabled to see and describe its effects, it is not a simple, or the only, horizon of his sense of the social field or of himself within it. That is to say, the frisson of the movement of violence is rendered only by way of its tracking of a possible movement of distantiation in the field of historicity in play. It thereby leaves the disfigured marks of the path of its own becoming such that there remains a tractable rift in its own apparent repleteness as outcome. This tractability is open to multiple and quite contradictory forms of reinscription. Yet, to the extent that such a gesture is indeed a claim that would, at the symbolic level, as both fact and fiction, portend its own absolute ground or possibility, an act that in its distended temporality takes notice of this process, that of the production of distinction, which thus also takes notice of its own tendential position as well as a distribution of positions within a social field, even among the subordinated, notices such a gesture as an act of force and deployment of power, as a gesture that generates effects on the basis of other already established or operative hierarchies. As the narrator writes, "The worlds I longed for, and all their dazzling opportunities were theirs, not mine" (Du Bois 1903d, 2–3, chap. 1, para. 2). Following this rift reflexively, then, in the form of this double gesture, at the level of the character, the young boy "Du Bois," and a redoubled one at the level of the narrator, the young intellectual Du Bois (the one who has been solicited in the form of his writing), make possible the opening of a track for a general desedimentation of the historicity of the present. As the mature Du Bois, as the world-famous intellectual, will write of the younger Du Bois after some seven decades of living—the young boy, the young man, the young intellectual on the threshold of writing *The Souls of Black Folk: Essays and Sketches*, perhaps:

> Had it not been for the race problem early thrust upon me and enveloping me, I should have probably been an unquestioning worshiper at the shrine of the social order and economic development into which I was born. But just that part of that order which seemed to most of my fellows nearest perfection, seemed to me most inequitable and wrong; starting from that critique, I gradually as the years went by found other things to question in my environment. At first, however, my criticism was confined to the relation of my people to the world movement. I was not questioning the world movement itself. What the white world was doing, its goals and ideals, I had not doubted were quite right. What was wrong was that I and people like me and thousands of others who might have my ability and aspiration, were refused permission to be part of this world. (Du Bois 1968, 155–56; see also 1975d, 26–27, 13–15, 51–52, 54; 1940, 26–27, 13–15, 51–52, 54)

As I have remarked elsewhere in an elaboration of this text, situated between Friedrich Nietzsche and Michel Foucault, it is certainly "genealogy" avant la lettre in either or both senses of the term given in the discourses carried out under those names, and something more (a tracking on the fold of difference that neither of those figures would avow in their practice). And, then, the practice of a critical reinscription of the world within and by way of this peculiar point of view will not only be maintained and affirmed by Du Bois across his entire itinerary but devolve as one of his most powerful epistemological interventions, and it remains as a still excessive resource for critical thought in our time (Chandler 2014c, 129–70, 233–46).

c. EUROPE. The other exception offered in the second paragraph of the first chapter of *The Souls of Black Folk: Essays and Sketches* is Europe. This place is, at least and first of all, a habitation apart from the normal, apart from "this American world." But the experience of *not* being a problem is, at this juncture, otherwise than normal, the normal of his habitual residence. Even with just this bare reference we see the reflexive existential configuration of Du Bois's residential experience of Europe as marking for him a limit, a certain kind of inside and a certain kind of outside.

This text of Du Bois's, penned in the late spring or early summer of 1897, is perhaps his earliest *published* retrospective reference to his experience as a student in Europe.[5] And he experienced more than just Germany, where he studied at Berlin. The reference is also to his travels and exploration of historical and sociological examples and entails allusions to architecture and to art. Thus, doubtless, in one reading, Europe, especially Germany, can be shown to be a signal reference for Du Bois in this text. Across this book, completed as a whole in 1903, he cites, among many others, William Shakespeare; Johann Wolfgang von Goethe; Johann Christoph Friedrich von Schiller; Honoré de Balzac; Lord Byron; William Wordsworth; Alfred, Lord Tennyson; Thomas Carlyle; Richard Wagner; and then, too, Alexander Dumas. He describes the African American situation at the historical time of his writing at the end of the nineteenth century as one of "*Sturm und Drang*," with reference to the phrase that came to name the earliest movement within the work of Goethe and Schiller and some others in Europe of their generation during the last third of the eighteenth century. So, too, in three turnkey chapters of *The Souls of Black Folk: Essays and Sketches*—the seventh, eighth, and ninth, which together provide entry to the most interior depth explored in the books closing chapters, thereafter—Du Bois makes the interpretive analogy of the historical conditions of African Americans of the southern region of the United States, notably of the region across the American south that he metaphorized as "the Black Belt," as akin to the conditions of the peasantries of France and Italy (England too) during the era of the ancien régime, which led to the cataclysm of the French Revolution (Du Bois 1903l, 110–88, esp. 150–53 and 158–59, chap. 8, paras. 26–28, 36).[6] So Europe as a figure of comparison, remark, and reference can be seen to run throughout the entirety of the essays gathered under the heading of *The Souls of Black Folk: Essays and Sketches*—to take the main title for the book as a figurative heading, as it were. Yet Du Bois's main preoccupations here are otherwise than with Europe as such. Thus, in another sense, Europe is on the periphery of his principal thetic concerns and situated in the background of the primary declared work of the text. Thus it is also the case that it is in later autobiographical references and texts strewn across his long career that Du Bois elaborates upon the time and experience of this first trip to Europe and to Germany: for example, in *Darkwater*, *Dusk of Dawn*, and the posthumous text published as the *Autobiography*. In this sense, we can append them to this singular notation of Europe from the opening of *The Souls of Black Folk: Essays and Sketches*.

Du Bois studied in Germany at Berlin from September 1892 to March 1894, taking courses and writing a thesis for the doctorate (apparently since lost but perhaps still retrievable). Although nominated for the degree by his professors Gustav Schmoller and Adolph Wagner, it was not affirmed, for the brevity of his residency in situ, the duration of his stay, did not meet the university's declared rule. (And the university at Berlin did not formally recognize his study at Harvard.) He traveled widely throughout Germany and other parts of continental Europe, specifically Switzerland, Austria, Hungary, Italy, Slovenia, Poland, France, and the Netherlands. Approaching age fifty, Du Bois recalled:

> I crossed the ocean in a trance. Always I seemed to be saying "It is not real; I must be dreaming!" I can live it again—the little, Dutch ship—the blue waters—the smell of new-mown hay—Holland and the Rhine. I saw the Wartburg and Berlin; I made the Harzreise and climbed the Brocken; I saw the Hansa towns and the cities and dorfs of South Germany; I saw the Alps at Berne, the Cathedral at Milan, Florence, Rome, Venice, Vienna, and Pesth; I looked on the boundaries of Russia; and I sat in Paris and London. On mountain and valley, in home and school, I met men and women as I had never met them before. Slowly they became, not white folks, but folks. The unity beneath all life clutched me. I was not less fanatically a Negro, but "Negro" meant a greater, broader sense of humanity and world-fellowship. I felt myself standing, not against the world, but simply against American narrowness and color prejudice, with the greater, finer world at my back urging me on. I builded great castles in Spain and lived therein. I dreamed and loved and wandered and sang. (Du Bois 1975c, 16; see also 1920, 16)

At age seventy, he reflected further on this moment:

> Europe modified profoundly my outlook on life and my thought and feeling toward it, even though I was there but two short years with my contacts limited and my friends few. But something of the possible beauty and elegance of life permeated my soul; I gained a respect for manners. I had been before, above all in a hurry. I wanted a world, hard, smooth and swift, and had not time for rounded corners and ornament, for unhurried thought and slow contemplation. Now at times I sat still. I came to know Beethoven's symphony and Wagner's *Ring*. I looked on the colors of Rembrandt and Titian. I saw in arch and stone and steeple the history and striving of men and also their taste and expression. Form, color and words took on new combinations and meanings. (Du Bois 1975d, 45; see also 1968, 156)

And in his last years, his nineties, he wrote across this memory again:

> In Germany in 1892 I found myself on the outside of the American world look-
> ing in. With me were white folk—students, acquaintances, teachers—who
> viewed the scene with me. They did not always pause to regard me [with a cu-
> riosity or as something subhuman]; I was just a man of a somewhat privileged
> student rank, with whom they were glad to meet and talk over the world; par-
> ticularly, the part of the world whence I came. I found to my gratification that
> they with me, did not regard America as the last word in civilization. Indeed,
> I derived a certain satisfaction in learning that the University of Berlin did not
> recognize a degree even from Harvard University no more than Harvard did
> from Fisk. (Du Bois 1968, 157)

Europe, then, opened another horizon. As Du Bois describes it in these
autobiographical recollections, he treasured his solitude, the stillness of a
rather new inhabitation of thought. Equally, he discovered and held fast
to a kind of companionship that knew no simple boundary. In a corollary
fashion, he found that he could delimit any given context by way of such
reflection. Thus, the American context became a limited and particular
one. Moreover, elsewhere, he speaks not only of other "Whites" in Europe but specifically of his reception in eastern Europe, as he was "several
times mistaken for a Jew." "*Unter den Juden?*," he is asked by "the driver
of a rickety cab" in "a town north of Slovenia," and, accepting the terms
of the "mistake," he "stayed in a little Jewish inn" (Du Bois 1968, 174–75).
This solitude and new sense of possible companionship delimited his
imagination in such a fashion that he could envision a New Negro vanguard and a renewed (New) Negro "race" participating in a peaceful world
revolution of ideals.

An imaginary or fantastic sense of an illimitable collectivity, even if
not a simple unity, took shape within this experience. I would propose
that we can formalize a sense of this motif under the theoretical heading
of *external association*.[7]

It might appear an obvious conclusion to understand Du Bois's time
in Europe, especially in Germany, during this moment as the culmination
of a certain humanism and the birth of a certain internationalism thereby
in the understanding of himself and of the world in general, as the passage beyond a sedimented parochiality, as the discovery of a path to a true
universalism. And while this is certainly so in one sense, and indeed one
would wish such in general for anyone, not only for Du Bois, in the discovery of what it means to inhabit a whole other way of existence, perhaps

another world, and to discover a radical sense of the manner that the given can be rendered otherwise, perhaps it remains that there is another sense, even more radical, in which the question must also be understood: simultaneously. What if Du Bois's whole inhabitation of Europe during the early 1890s should be understood as a scene (and not the only one when viewed as part of an early stage of the life course of thought) of the dynamic unfolding of his nascent self-critical understanding of himself as a Negro and a Negro American? What if, for him, a dream of an illimitable concatenation of association among humans took its existential predication and form in a possibility that announced itself by way of his experience of existence as a form of dissociation? Reserved from our first access, it is nonetheless the form of this organization of subjectivation, that might allow for the reflexive naming of two sides of a limit and in so doing thus announce an inhabitation of an originary complication in the constitution of a sense of being, given to us (within our own inquiry) under the heading of the autobiographical, by way of the example of Du Bois. It is this form, or the apparition of such, that must occupy our attention.

It is here, then, that we can properly situate the ambivalence of a fundamental passage in Du Bois's intellectual development. As we retrieve it through an account that he prepared of his somewhat privative celebration of his twenty-fifth birthday in Berlin, the question that arose might be put thus: To what do I belong in my historical present and future?[8] The question is the status of the sense of historial limit within subjectivation.

For a reader of this memorial notation, the answer that Du Bois gives is perhaps first distinguished by its tone: a combination of arch bravado and a somewhat defiant and inaccessible melancholy. This tone in turn directs one thus to the most abiding sense, perhaps, that one gathers upon reading this text: that the narrator is alone. Alone. And that this is not simply in fact but in principle. It is from this unfolding self-reflexive sense of his lived experience, if you will, that the narrator's answer will be given.

The writing of this text precedes the inscription of Europe in the second paragraph of *The Souls of Black Folk: Essays and Sketches* that we have been following above and are in the midst of following throughout our discussion of the autobiographical here. It was written in February 1893, seven months into the time of his experience as a student living in Berlin. The first inscription of the textual passage speaking of Europe amidst the discourse of *The Souls of Black Folk: Essays and Sketches* dates from the late spring or early summer of 1897. I quote freely here of the passage from the late winter of 1893:

I am striving to make my life all that life may be—and I am limiting that strife only in so far as that strife is incompatible with others of my brothers and sisters making their lives similar. The crucial question now is where that limit comes. I am too often puzzled to know. . . . God knows I am sorely puzzled. I am firmly convinced that my own best development is [not][9] one and the same with the best development of the world and here I am willing to sacrifice . . . and now comes the question of how. The general proposition of working for the world's good becomes too soon sickly sentimentality. I therefore take the work that the Unknown lay in my hands and work for the rise of the Negro people, taking for granted that their best development means the best development of the world. This night before my life's altar, I reiterate, what my life . . . (Du Bois 1985c)

A note from the editor, Herbert Aptheker, indicates that "pages 8–10 of the original manuscript are missing" (Du Bois 1985c). In the extant pages, when the text resumes, near its end, the narrator is in the midst of an apparently wistful memory. Mentioning his experiences at Fisk and Harvard, and his past loves, he writes, "Then Europe where the heart of my childhood loosed from the hard iron hands of America has beat again in the great inspiring air of world culture" (Du Bois 1985c).

Let us briefly work back across several layers of the rhetorical and semantic strata of this passage. The narrator has already made a decision. He will dedicate his life to "work for the rise of the Negro people." According to to his stated logic, beyond the first blush of a declaration, this is not a simple chauvinism. For it is based on a judgment that is presented as prior: "that their [the Negro people's] best development means the best development of the world." What is the status of this generalization? It should certainly not be understood as a simple or naive reduction of the whole of *the* world to that of the Negro. Perhaps it could mean that in order to understand the Negro, one must understand *the* whole world. Perhaps it could also mean that in order to understand the world, it might be essential to understand the *whole problem of the Negro as world*. The Negro as example then cuts through and beyond the "narrow American world" and yet gives the question of *the* whole of the world its tractable historicity. It is thus, perhaps, that we might apprehend the even more previous judgment, given in the form of a refusal of the misleading apparitional neutrality of the universal, when he writes, "The general proposition of working for the world's good becomes too soon sickly sentimentality."[10]

Now, proceeding according to the text, perhaps we can remark the traces of some rather disparate imprints or impressions that remain of a complex movement. In terms of the status, then, of the experience of Europe in the unfolding sense of world for our narrator, the text tells us that the horizon has already been broken. The simplicity of an inherited idea of America, given as if a form of his natality, has already been complicated. Yet there is a maintenance here, so the narrator declares, of something that appears as almost primordial and indestructible, "the heart" of his "childhood." But is that which is recorded here only (if at all) a primordial root or stem that has survived into the present of his writing? Perhaps. But even if so, what is also registered here are the remains of a cut, division, or restriction, an instituted limitation, whose bearing or effects can only announce themselves within the subject in formation as figures of ambivalence.[11] But they can yet assist in making possible a delimitation. (One says something like, "So, if that is your idea of the game, then I am really not sure that I wish to be a part of it at all"; the child declares threateningly, "I'll take my marbles and go home!") Such figurative moments of hesitation are susceptible to a metaleptic retrieval, and such retrieval would not always be benign or containable within a sanguine disposition. Perhaps it is this operation that we see moving through the semantic instability of the declarations of this text. Du Bois's discourse of full-throated youthful bravado then would yield not only a putative continuity from the "heart" but from this metaleptic inhabitation of his present. Such inhabitation here proceeds by way of a kind of breaking up of the compressed sedimentation or fault lines of an instituted limitation. As a response to a solicitation, it retraces or tracks the disfigured remains of the line of force by which that mark was instituted. Such a response is a folding that displaces the apparitional punctuality of the mark, concatenating its supposed primordial originarity with other lines of force. This concatenation might be understood to produce an *atopic* dispersal or dissemination of such a line—even if configured as a scene of emergence. On occasion, at the level of the formation of sense for the subject, the effects of such relations of force might be available for metaphorization on the order of the rumblings of a small volcano or the tremors of a barely tenable earthquake. Yet while we cannot ourselves declare some pure or primordial ground for what is yielded by way of such desedimentation, we can affirm that this declaration by our narrator is effective for him at the level of its enunciation: it relativizes the American scene—one that would have relativized and restricted him, rendered him parochial in every sense—and delimits another horizon, even a beyond of any given horizon, as the orientation of hope, desire, and becoming.

For us, at the level of a retrospective analysis, if not for Du Bois the subject or narrator, this whole movement has the form of a nonsynchronous simultaneity. In this sense, then, as descriptor and cautionary protocol for our own approach to this moment in Du Bois's thought, it might be reasonable to say that before his arrival in Europe, Du Bois had certainly already begun to insist that no matter the presumptive limits of the mark of the color line, *for him*, his future was *not yet decided*. For it can be understood that it was such a perspective, that of possibility in his own life, that led him to pursue study in Europe.[12] It was a sense of possibility that remained, during those years of the early 1890s, open in his thinking—receptive for whatever it could *come to mean for him*. Thus, the European experience should certainly not be misunderstood as determinate of his entire sense of the African American situation or as the only basis for his thought of an illimitable sense of human existence. As I noted above, Du Bois himself described the experience in Europe, saying that it "modified profoundly my outlook on life and my thought and feeling toward it." Neither the profundity of this modification of his sense of the parochialism of the American division along the color line nor that it come to that function by working over an ongoing inhabitation of his sense of the African American as a name for a possibility yet to come should be left aside.

What we must countenance, in the terms of the formulations that I have proposed here, is the thought that Du Bois's dream of an illimitable concatenation of *external association* took its *historical* predication and form from the possibility opened by way of his supple inhabitation, simultaneously negative and affirmative, thereby radical in a critical sense, of an ongoing reflexive practice of judgment and decision, of a movement of *internal dissociation*. Thus, we might say in the biographical or autobiographical register that Du Bois inhabits European historicity, including European discourses of critique, say a certain philosophy or a nascent science of the human, by way of a historicity that we can properly name as African American without any presumption of pure essence. In this specific sense, it is his own, his peculiar, historicity. This is certainly to say the obvious: that he inhabits Europe on the basis of his previous history and social experience. Yet it means something more fundamental. The autobiographical reflection and account of the experience of Europe is formulated by way of a certain inhabitation of his specific or peculiar historicity. An affirmation of the spacing of this dissociation, its formation as the articulation of the heterogeneous is then, paradoxically, an announcement of a peculiar and originary inhabitation of the historical.

This is thus to say that the passage of a movement of dissociation is the name of the structure of a retrospective metaleptic inhabitation of the sense of Europe that we can without any presumption of simple essence or primordial obligation name in the historical sense as Negro or African American. The status of Europe in the unfolding of Du Bois's sense of self is given in an autobiographical account whose epistemological possibility and form are themselves, in part, but in a fundamental way, the manifestation of a certain inhabitation of his most specific and peculiar historical possibility. Thus, it can be seen that the Europe that Du Bois announces here, at the opening of *The Souls of Black Folk: Essays and Sketches*, as the opening to the imagined sense of an illimitable possible association, in the first instance has its configured implication as example, for him and for us, by way of its taking epistemic shape in the movement of a kind of double inhabitation or inhabitation of the double—a certain form of internal dissociation that is otherwise than simply passive—that is the narrator's critical inhabitation of his peculiar historicity.

Yet we would restitute in our own discourse the apparition of the oppositional logic of this form of proscription if that were all we could adduce in Du Bois's practice. The critical inhabitation of the economy of thought and practice that we are tracing here in Du Bois's discourse can only become commensurate with the question at stake for it in his thought if it practices *along with his discourse* a certain exorbitance in relation to the logic of opposition. It is here that we can affirm that it is *also* the case that the figure of Europe, this example, in this opening passage of *The Souls of Black Folk: Essays and Sketches*, marks a possibility beyond the limits given by this problem of the color line. It is here that we can see that at the end of the nineteenth century, for Du Bois, the experience of "Europe"—perhaps allegorically tractable in the form of the travels of the young twenty-something Du Bois—made possible the tracing of a legible frame or horizon that could nonetheless relativize all previous experience. As such, the experience of Europe would affirm, in this young figure, the powerfully political aspect of his ambivalence in the engagement with the oppositional or categorical premise of the color line. As such, it should be understood as an example that could refract the logic operative at the root of this historicity in such a fashion that it could disrupt the ultimate pertinence of the line. And, for him, this devolution took such fractual patterns of dispersal (perhaps always otherwise than fractal), most precisely even as there was no absolute necessity in the realization of this possibility. And then, further, if such a refraction were attached to the kinetic force of the violence that would install this line, by way of the double movement of identification named in this autobiographical account, the form of this line could paradoxically begin to twist, to defract and to refract, such that the possibility of passage to an illimitable inhabitation of being, the atopic passage that maintains both sides of a limit, perhaps metaphorizable here according to the apparition of a virtual geometric figure that articulates as a kind of *élleipsis* or the apparition of an open circle, or a broken line, or, better, a movement by which such could be announced at all, the possibility of inhabitation of existence beyond even that which can be given in outline, beyond the simple plane or parallel, such is rendered—perhaps, in the form of question. At best, it is a movement that yields doubled parallaxes. As such, the dynamic operative here is a movement of the imagination— as freedom or chance—such that an inhabitation beyond any boundary given as a form of proscriptive limitation is proposed as of existence. In this manner, the discursive recollection of the sense of the double, the inscription of a sense of internal dissociation in the temporality of thought, is rendered in a fashion that is inextricably interwoven with the recollection of the hypothetical sense of external association, the existential space of which is named for thought in a narrative of the coming of age of a Negro American—one William Edward Burghardt Du Bois—as such an experience opened as a scene of the habitation of critical thought in the horizons of Europe at the end of the nineteenth century. It is for this reason that it must also be affirmed as autobiographically unfungible that the sense of dissociation announced therein, with all of the productivity that we have sought to notice above, acquires a certain legibility for thought in this passage beyond the existing or given limits of the American scene that is the retrospective experience of Europe for the young Du Bois.

In this way, then, the sense of dissociation and the sense of association, each and each in relation, are announced and elaborated in thought according to the discourse of Du Bois's autobiographical accounts in a fundamentally elliptical reciprocity. That is to say, understood together, their form as constitutive movements in the historical production of a subject is that of a dynamic dissymmetric relation or difference. Each is announced in its own irruption. And, thus, they are not subsumable within the other in any sense. Yet neither could be announced except by way of a metaleptic retrieval carried out in the atopic inhabitation of the scene or horizon that is opened by way of the other. The recollection of the experience of dissociation is named in a retrospective account of the experience of association that acquires its nodal organization across the layers of the sedimented epistemic subsoil of the historicity that would render a critical sense of such dissociation as the form of a possible lived experience. The temporality operative here is such that it distends any presumption of the priority of time as a given present. The geographic distension of this movement is the name of a duration that is thus the very form of existential possibility. The event of experience, if there is such, occurs in both the before and in the after of its incipit and then, too, remains in that which is yet to come, both here and there. It is a complicated *atopic* movement of temporalities.

It can now be said that in this discussion of the sense of the autobiographical example in the practice of Du Bois we have outlined a movement of reflexivity or sense that marks out the path by which the subject of critical thought—a thinker, a practitioner of thought, an intellectual, a writer—came into relief, or into itself, rendered as a form of problem. But, equally, we have remarked the process of bringing into relief the terms of a critical inhabitation of world, of history, of a historical present, for such a putative subject. The subjectity in question is rendered according to the terms of another horizon whose sense is announced as illimitable by way of an experience of dissociation that takes the form of a nonsynchronous simultaneity as the becoming of the self in the practice of thought. At each step or level of the elucidation, what has been remarked is the extent to which such practice in the itinerary of Du Bois acquired its form through, or as, a maintenance of an affirmation of a chance or freedom in the organization of experience. We might say, then, that the figure of the double is simply a concept metaphor for this possibility and this complex process.

Such would be the announcement of historicity, as existential, as such might be specifiable or tractable in terms of a putative individuation of person or subject announced in the order of the autobiographical.

II. HISTORIOGRAPHIES

What is now at issue is the status of the historiographical as an order of example of possibility and not so much as a supposed simple and direct thought of the whole in general, whatever is such. The dimension of problem to which we now turn cannot be named by way of the analogy of a simple linearity or discrete contiguity.

In its eventuality, it might yield the problem of a difficult thought of horizon as otherwise than the given or that which could be—even in the staid sense of the term—as thought or concept. Orchestration of thought and practice in this dimension would always be of at least more than one continent (for the matter is *of* relation); this would mean a sense of space and spacing that would always be in its very immanence beyond or otherwise than the simple form of a here and now.

This matter of the-way-in-which, or the question of possibility in its actuality, this is the matter that should remain our guide. Thus, at this juncture in my own discourse, a kind of fold, another fold, if you will, I propose an affirmation of this thought-metaphor of spacing, the movement that forms space, which I began to annotate at the outset of part I as a way to track Du Bois's concern with the figurations of historicity.

Thus, if I present my discourse henceforth as if an unfolding of sheaves upon which we might discern inscription, the matter of the binding of such sheaves would be that they must remain loose and undrawn, if not undrawable. For indeed the matter of the form of discourse must accord, even if as an agonism, with the status of the topographical as itself *of* the topological, in general—even if ultimately, in a new sense, the matter remains *atopos*, otherwise than simply given according to topos.

This is also to say that at this juncture of contemporaneity, in our time, along with Du Bois and his time, we must take reference to the dominant orders of thought, even as we might question them. Hence, I propose that we recognize that the general question of historicity in the thinking and political practice of W. E. B. Du Bois was situated at the level of existence that might have once been understood as ontological in the terms of the inheritance of Greek thought as conceptuality as it has issued forth in the modern epoch. This is not at all to declare that Du Bois's thought should be understood or construed as itself an ontology. Thus, it can be said that it concerned for him the sense of being or the way in which something is announced in or as a form of existence. Thus, the question of historicity for him was not only, or first of all, a problem for thought, one concerned with the gathering and establishment of references that would confirm a claim about the material aspects of a form, or forms, of existence—even though it was also such a project. In the epistemic sense of practice as thought, it was simultaneously a question of the possibility of rendering an account of the status, the ground, as genesis or revelation, of a form, or forms, of existence. As an inquiry the question might be summarized by three interlaced interrogatives and a coda: (1) What kind or form of entity is or can be understood as a bearer of historical devolution? (2) Whence comes such a form of existence; that is, from what, or how, does it emerge or arise? (3) What is its end or telos, or is such a formulation even the proper one to ask about the character of its becoming, its past, its present, its future? And then the coda, the motif of which actually runs through each previous question: What are the means by which such questions can be considered, engaged, perhaps answered—if the given, supposed being in its possibility, is itself (if there is such) only as a question? What if the sense of being is always only as a form of question?

Within our own discourse and yet beyond the horizon of our own historicity, the matter of status and sense as question ought not be understood here according to the premise of a putative presumption of the anterior or ultimate determination of the present.

Beyond such reference to the epoch of that which has been understood as ancient Greek conceptuality, the question is about a certain impossible possibility, the opening toward a domain that cannot be thought, as such, but can be announced, if at all, in a movement that cannot be given to a proper name. As I have begun to annotate within Du Bois's discourse, such immanence is about the status we may give to the thought of relation in all senses, in its radical sense, the very possibility of relation, relation as possibility, even as the differences of force that may organize the formation of form, that is to say, also, power.

If I characterize his thought in general on this question, that of historicity, or, better, the historial, I have sought to cultivate a sense of Du Bois's own approach or practice as best understood as from or of a history of the problems of existence. An account of such, his or our own, for example, is neither the chronicle of the greatness of the sovereign (whether as person or people) as conqueror, nor simply the narrative of the realization of a given truth in the form of the idea or the supposed absolute. Historicity, or the apparition of existence as problem, as I understand Du Bois to proffer it across his discourse, is announced in the promulgation of an engagement with problems, with the dynamic constitution of a difficulty as existence itself, its coming into being, in the forms of existence. To place this as a pragmatic matter, historicity emerges in the forms by which an engagement with the difficulties posed as existence configures a group for a time, perhaps, including *both* its possibility, its survival, *or* its becoming something else altogether. This maintains within it the movement of that which will always have been—in a certain sense—inhuman. Historicity, or the historial, is then beyond the question of the status of any particular group; rather, it is about possibility in general: the relation of chance and necessity, that is to say, the configured character of possibility as relation.

In such a light, I can now propose that the question of the subject, or example, of historicity—the historial example—takes on a profound status in the work of Du Bois. By way of the relation of the question of on-tological ground to the question of who can be a subject of history, what exemplifies historicity, this supposed ontological level of the question of historicity (no matter that it may or must be given to desedimentation) is for Du Bois profoundly political—concerned with the organization and bearing of the force of power. The determination of the question of ground is decisive in the practical theoretical judgment of who or what is the bearer of historicity, whether or not such is understood as a proper, the proprietary, or a property. It is thus the crux on which all of Du Bois's major judgments about the political are situated, and, too, it is the question of who is responsible and for what in the making of the future world(s).

In this sense, Du Bois's ideas about the historial might be construed along two dimensions: one, a concern with the possibility of the origi-nary emergence (not only as past but also, and especially, as future) and profile of social groups of one kind or another; the other, a concern to characterize the structure of limit in a historical domain. The necessity of an engagement with both of these questions was given to Du Bois by his situation, by the terms that solicited his reflexive and critical inhabitation.

The first of these two dimensions, the question of originary possibility—that is, the question of the possibility, in all senses, of the realization of forms of existence according to judgment, perhaps as value, perhaps as ideals—is the guiding order of this problematization.

The second dimension of Du Bois's critical engagement of the historial, the form of historical limit, is a constitutive form of the organization of the first dimension within his thought. This latter dimension as part of a project of science in the broad philosophical sense would pose the ques-tion of elucidating the general process of historicity, certainly of a domain of history in general, such as the modern epoch, if not of the absolute of history as a system. Yet the paradox of Du Bois's approach to the general or the whole is that it is only and always by way of the nodal irruption of historicity as example or problematization. That is to say, it accedes to the general form of limit by way of the tractable example.

As I indicated at the opening of part I, I will reserve this second di-mension for an initial consideration and elaboration on its own terms; see part II of this study. Here, as the first dimension will appear as the titu-lar motive in the discussion at hand, it might be salutary to at least state, in a word as it were, that the production and operation of the concept-metaphor of "the problem of the color line" in Du Bois's thought across more than sixty years offers an account in this domain—of historical forms of limit—that cannot be set aside without epistemological consequences for even the most contemporary of theoretical discussions of modern forms of historicity.

For his thought here, in its elaboration, is one that attends to systems of material forms of hierarchy and subordination as domination, exploitation, and oppression, just as much as it names so-called ideational systems. It is most certainly about the operations of power. And, for Du Bois, the mode of historical appearance of the "*problem* of the color line" (my emphasis) would always be material even if the forces in play cannot always be represented.

In the epistemic sense, these two dimensions—possibility and limit—are aspects of one general problematic. They are simply respective ways of conceptualizing the same objectivity: the character and implication of collective forms of historical existence. They are conjoined and tractable only in the irruptive emergence and devolution of the example.

The example, at once autobiographical and historiographical in general within discourse, becomes the site of epistemological conjuncture in Du Bois's thought. It articulates the given as a situation to existence as a committed practice. On the one side, it is the situation of an individual, as singular or collective, as group, as revelatory of historical circumstance. On the other side, it is the activity of an order of individual, notably as a form of group, as an exemplification of both limit and possibility. Du Bois was committed, it must be emphasized, we might even say ultimately, to the question of historical possibility: to the movement of that which is illimitable within the possible as existing limit.

It may be confirmed beyond even the present context of our discussion (which is a certain form of an overture to some essential dimensions of Du Bois's thought by way of some of his earliest writings) that—as I have proposed elsewhere—all of the forms of historial example that one may find decisive across the whole of Du Bois's later itinerary were already adduced as signal examples on both an epistemological and a theoretical level in the earliest moments of his intellectual maturation (Chandler 2021).

A. OF HORIZON I: "THE AFRO-AMERICAN" (CIRCA 1894)

Now I propose to render a turn in the organization of our passage through the discourse announced under the heading of Du Bois. Further, I will proceed by folding over or under, across, and through the plane of the previous autobiographical exploration another level of passage, the historiographical.

Yet, in this study, the value of this turn from the autobiographical to the historiographical is acquired according to the virtual and rigorous responsibility of a contemporary sense of an *origami*, a fold on the bias, for these so-called parts of our discourse here are not at all equivalent: that is to say that this fold is the configuration of a radical asymmetry in which it is the case that while the autobiographical is here the form that allows us passage in thought and discourse to the historiographical, the latter domain is yet in all propriety the general terms of possibility of the former. For therefrom, or in the form of a kind of swiveling movement, I propose to unfold, as a sheaf, a different possible articulation of sensible forms of topography, of historial specificity or example, now thought in terms of another order of generality, the historiographical, not only of limit or necessity but also of imagination and possibility. In this consideration, I propose that Du Bois operates in terms of a concept of the collective as the level of individuation or discursive nominalization. Yet, layered within the imprint of each sheaf of writing, if you will, is the ineluctably intermingled passage of the autobiographical—that is, as both individual and collective and, too, of the given and the as yet impossible possibility.

Thus, while a rendering of this thought of the example by way of a passage through the texts of Du Bois is indeed and in all truth the concern of the whole of this study, at stake in the instance of each one, here I wish to remark, is the incipit of its enunciation in his discourse. And this remarking may have the additional value of allowing us to notice the form of the turning within Du Bois's practical-theoretical reflection, one that in all truth never stops but remains as a recurrent and renewed oscillating gesture and movement, from an existential preoccupation on the order of the autobiographical to one that extends itself to the limits of the historial understood on a planetary scale and on an epochal horizon of temporality.

The first locution of the statement in question is given in the form of an essay that is provocatively titled "The Afro-American," the composition of which most likely dates from sometime over the course of the late autumn of 1894 to the late spring of 1895—during the half a dozen months or so after his return to the United States by steerage from Germany (where he had studied from midsummer of 1892 to the early spring of 1894), via France and England.

While the original twenty-page typescript can be found among the papers of Du Bois housed in the special collections of the library named after him at the University of Massachusetts Amherst, it was recently published for the first time.[13] We can reasonably adduce the approximate time—within a given eight-month period—of the composition of this text by Du Bois on the basis of the hand-script signature and title that are given on the last page of the original typescript. It is signed "W. E. Burghardt Du Bois (A. M., Professor of Ancient Classics in Wilberforce University)." We know several facts—that Du Bois was in possession of a master's degree that had been awarded by Harvard in 1891, that he assumed his duties as a faculty member of Wilberforce at the very end of August 1894, and that he submitted his doctoral thesis to Professor Albert Bushnell Hart at Harvard University in midspring in 1895, which the latter signed in official approval on June 1 of that year (Du Bois 1973e; Aptheker 1989b, 9–10; 1989b, 2; Lewis 1993, 155). Thus, it is reasonable to suppose that the text of "The Afro-American" may have been written (or at least completed) sometime after the assumption of his professorial duties and before his official designation as holder of a doctor of philosophy degree. More specifically, two different time frames seem most plausible for the text's composition: early to late autumn in 1894 and late spring in 1895. On the one hand, the reference by Du Bois to his train travel on the "continent" in the opening line of the essay suggests an ongoing reflection, implying that Du Bois may have written this text with the memory of a last sojourn (alone) across Germany during the last weeks of March 1894 very much present to mind (Du Bois 1968, 175–76; 1894b). On the other hand, given that we know that Du Bois had been hard at work redrafting the text of the thesis throughout the early months of 1895 (the initial research for which dated back to 1889–91) and that he delivered an address on the occasion of the death of Frederick Douglass for a memorial service held on March 9, 1895, at Wilberforce (some themes of which overlap with "The Afro-American"), it also seems quite plausible that Du Bois could have been led to engage the question of the direction and leadership of African Americans as a group and prepared the essay "The Afro-American" sometime after posting the final pages of his doctoral thesis to Professor Hart at Harvard (Du Bois 1985d, 23–25, 1973f; Aptheker 1989a, 1–3; 1982e).

We can notate here, as well, that if the latter time frame is adduced, we can retrospectively remark the temporality of its construal in the development of Du Bois's thought about leadership as reciprocally punctuated by the appearance of Alexander Crummell as a commencement speaker at Wilberforce University in the spring of 1895 (a man, as Du Bois would later write in *The Souls of Black Folk: Essays and Sketches*, to whom he "instinctively bowed" upon their meeting) (Du Bois 1903l, 216, chap. 12, para. 2;

and see whole essay 1903b), on the one hand, and Booker T. Washington's famous Atlanta Exposition speech in the early autumn of that year (to which Du Bois responded on the occasion as "a word fitly spoken"), on the other (Du Bois 1973a, 39).

For our concerns at this juncture in our inquiry about Du Bois, this essay, "The Afro-American," renders traces of the form, the legible relief, of a certain historical passage in thought of an African American intelligentsia.

This essay can rightly be taken as a decisive step in Du Bois's attempt to formulate for himself the theoretical and political terms and project of a putative vocation that could become his own. The title of the essay, then, should in all propriety be taken as Du Bois's first attempt at announcing his own reflexively chosen nominalization of a sense of self in terms of a supposed group or horizon of historical situation. It stands at the inception of a crucial phase in Du Bois's development, at the beginning of a period of three years in which he struggled to clarify for himself his sense of intellectual problematization and a way of engaging it—the sense of a vocation. In the chapter titled "Science and Empire" in the remarkable text *Dusk of Dawn: An Essay toward an Autobiography of a Race Concept* of 1940, which might be understood in relation to "The Afro-American" as simply a late extended reprise of the fundamental thought of the original composition with the addition of an elaborated up-to-date coda, Du Bois gives us the pivotal formulation in the form of a recollection: "I tried to isolate myself in the ivory tower of race. I wanted to explain the difficulties of race and the ways in which these difficulties caused political and economic troubles. It was this concentration of thought and action and effort that really, in the end, saved my scientific accuracy and search for truth. But first came a period of three years when I was casting about to find a way of applying science to the race problem" (Du Bois 1975d, 54–55; see also 1968, 208). We can reasonably understand the denouement of this period of vocational and theoretical searching as given a nodal articulation in the pivotal programmatic statement calling for a "scientific" study of the situation of the Negro in the United States that Du Bois presented to the American Academy of Political and Social Science in November 1897, which was subsequently published in early 1898 in the *Annals* of the academy (as the opening text for the January issue of their periodical) and then (a month later) also as a freestanding pamphlet in its special publication series, both under the title "The Study of the Negro Problems" (Du Bois 1898c, 2015b, 1898b, 2015l). I consider this the founding programmatic

statement calling for the systematic practice of an African American studies. If this is so, following Du Bois's own periodization as a thumbnail
guide, we can propose, then, that the essay at hand, "The Afro-American,"
stands at the inception of Du Bois's effort to announce to himself the
terms of his possible intellectual projection. It thus offers a legible passage
of reflexive discourse that can be remarked as outlining the conjunctive
terms by which the so-called Negro problem acquired its incipient organization within his practice as thought. And in this organization, the autobiographical and the historiographical are explicitly conjoined, and the
local and the global appear as figures always announced in relation to each
other. This so-called Negro problem—in America—is anything but parochial in the terms of Du Bois's discourse, as we may be able to recognize
already in this very early essay of his first maturation as a thinker. Yet it
must be noted for the scholastic record that the epistemic and theoretical
sense that we are adducing here for Du Bois's late autobiographical recollection of the passage of time that we hereby demarcate, from late 1894 to
late 1897, has remained essentially unremarked in the critical discussion of
his thought, biographical or otherwise.

First, it may be useful to briefly extend here a critical sense that I formulated and began to outline above concerning the autobiographical with regard to how we may understand Du Bois's relation to Europe in general and
Germany in particular. Here I note that the scholarship concerned with Du
Bois's itinerary during the 1890s on the whole has been primarily oriented
toward adducing what we today might wish to claim Du Bois received from
Germany and Europe (Barkin 2005, 2000; Schäfer 2001). On the whole,
not much scholarship has been situated theoretically to think of his relation to the historial figure of a supposed Europe as a whole as a kind of
engagement, critical and variegated, a realized perspective, assiduously and
distinctly cultivated. This latter approach would recognize in this engagement an affirmative critical inhabitation of disposition and thought as the
leading edge of Du Bois's relation to Europe, and it could account for such
a practice by Du Bois as one in which the history, the political situation
(in specific but also in terms of a global horizon), and its intellectual discourses of science and philosophy are all at stake and not simply assumed;
moreover, it would recognize the dynamic, yet principled, unfolding of his
relation to Europe in general across the first six decades of the tumultuous
twentieth century. Despite the apparent consolidation over the past two
decades of the postwar discussion of Du Bois's relation to Europe, within

that relatively recent discourse, some efforts have gestured in the direction of remarking his relation as a whole engagement (Rothberg 2001; Sollors 1999; Beck 1998). The text at hand by Du Bois, especially its opening dialogue (among others across his discourse), might well be taken as a legible indication of the possibility of a more balanced and supple understanding of this relation. Two other texts by Du Bois from the 1890s, both of which remained unpublished during his lifetime and were brought to publication at the turn of the twenty-first century by Kenneth Barkin—"The Present Condition of German Politics" (1998a) and "The Socialism of German Socialists" (1998b)—give further indication of the depth of Du Bois's critical inhabitation of Europe at that time. They provide a poignant engagement with the whole crisis of liberalism and the social question (especially the problem of a certain "socialism" in the general sense) afoot in Germany and Europe at the time.[14] These two texts stand then—along with the essay "The Afro-American" (circa 1894–95), the memorial speech "Douglass as Statesman" (circa 1895, published for the first time in 1964 by Herbert Aptheker), and the public lecture "The Art and Art Galleries of Modern Europe" (circa 1896, also published for the first time by Aptheker in 1985)—as a quite rich set of intertextually related documents marking the young Du Bois's far-ranging and yet deeply probing critical thought on the historical (both political and economic) and supposed historial situation (that is, on the terms of the whole question of historical possibility) of African Americans, the project of America, and modern Europe (Du Bois 2015a, 1964, 1985a; note also 2010 and 1982e). On one fundamental level, they form an intertextual discourse in which the problem of leadership (its moral and intellectual projection of duty to uplift society) is the foremost theoretical guide. Europe, then, is both part of this problematic as an example and a source of thought and ideas for its address. Yet, as I suggest later in this commentary, so is "the Afro-American" and a certain "America," of which (with regard to both) Douglass is—for Du Bois in the 1890s—the stellar example. Thus, here too, one must index the gathering of this understanding specifically with regard to Du Bois's solicitation of a new African American leadership under the heading of the "talented tenth" in mid-1903 (Du Bois 1903n, 2015m).

Now, second, with regard to "The Afro-American," we can annotate our reception at the outset to the effect that this essay is the theoretical form of Du Bois's return from Europe to the United States of America.

Organized as an ambulatory discourse of four paragraphs and a main discourse of four sections, the essay is oriented toward one concern: to articulate a sense of the situation of the "Afro-American" from the point of view of this putative historical and social subject itself.

The turning that we have begun to remark is made across the crucible of the problem of representation. That is to say that the stage-setting problem of the essay as a whole is that of the question of understanding or knowledge and the concomitant question of the representation of the situation of the Negro in the United States at the end of the nineteenth century. The question can be further unfolded as the problem of the representation of the so-called Negro problem both by others and by the putative "Negro himself." And, in an apparently small but ultimately decisive formulation, Du Bois will come to proclaim that in America, "Americans" in general (other than the Negro) "veil" the situation of the American Negro from themselves. In the thought of the young Du Bois of the middle of the 1890s, the problem at its root is one of "understanding." The project, then, is to engage the prevailing discourse on "the Negro question" and to intervene in its terms by way of announcing the Negro's own representation of their own sense of themselves as a form of problem—and this sense will mean in part, in its eventuality, a form of solution.

The essay opens and closes with an autobiographical reference, the first situated on the level of the individual and the latter on the level of a collective. In its middle stages, it formulates a sense of problem, the so-called Negro problem, and outlines a series of approaches to it, three different ones proposed by others and a nascent perspective that would be proffered by a putatively new "Afro-American" intelligentsia at the end of the nineteenth century. Across the discourse of this incipient essay, all of the most poignant and famous themes and concept-metaphors of Du Bois's thought of the turn of the century are already announced—in thoughtful gesture and reflexive distinction, if not in the fullness of their lexical and theoretical nominalization. In a sense that could be sustained at all levels of its discourse—lexical, rhetorical (conceptual and metaphorical), and theoretical—it could be demonstrated that the pivotal essay "Strivings of the Negro People" from mid-1897, which was subsequently positioned as the opening chapter of *The Souls of Black Folk: Essays and Sketches*, is in every sense a performative and transformative reinscription of the essay "The Afro-American." The fullness of Du Bois's attempt to think the whole of the historically given present situation of the Negro in the United States at the time of this inscription gives the latter essay its most distinctive character. It is thus the political-theoretical form in which Du

Bois first attempts to announce himself as an independent intellectual persona within the American scene.

1. A PASSAGE. The discourse of the essay opens with the flush of a searching gesture of self-reflexivity, which, paradoxically perhaps, is formulated by reference to his sense of the apperception of his persona by others. Across the cusp of this perambulatory statement and fictional dialogue in its conjunction with the opening of the first section of the essay proper, the first formulation of a certain structure of critical self-reflexivity begins to take shape. It is a movement of self-reflexivity that would justly become the definitive epistemic passage in opening the most radical order of Du Bois's own gestures in thought. In these opening paragraphs of "The Afro-American," we see the first discursive appearance of a practical theoretical problematization on the order of *thought*, a certain critical reflexivity, of the sense of inhabitation of the historically rendered forms of identification that would define one W. E. B. Du Bois or the putative forms of collectivity to which he might be understood and understand himself to belong. In this specific sense, we can say only retrospectively that it is the first rhetorical form within Du Bois's discourse of the problem that he will in its eventuality construe under the heading of "double-consciousness." As this essay has remained essentially unremarked or unknown in the critical literature, I will quote its ambulatory paragraphs and embedded dialogue in full here:

> In a third class continental railway carriage, my neighbors at first stare at me—sometimes a bit impudently, sometimes with an inquisitive smile. I have grown so used to this that I can sit quietly for an hour or so with from three to six pairs of eyes focused on my brown face, my closely curled hair, my hat, my clothes, my hands and the visible part of my soul, without betraying any considerable impatience. After satisfying their eyes and becoming more or less assured that I am neither wild nor a member of a passing circus, one of the bolder ones usually seeks to open a conversation, through the weather, the speed of the train, the window, or some such railway topic. It depends of course on my mood as to whether the conversation is particularly successful. Sometimes when there are [not many] with us, and my neighbor is pleasant and gentlemanly, I let the talk run on, well knowing whither it will eventually drift. I agree that the weather is pleasant, that the open window is to my taste, *et cetera*.
>
> My friend then generally sees fit to compliment my accent and says:
> "Your native tongue is—?"

"English."

Here comes always the first look of surprise. Oh! he thought I spoke French, or Spanish, or Arabian.

"You are then from English India?"

"No, I am an American."

"Ah, yes—South American of course; I've a cousin—"

"No, I'm from the United States, North America."

"Indeed, but I thought—were you born there, may I ask?"

"Yes, and my father, my grand father and my great grand father."

"Is that so! Excuse me, I had thought from your color that—"

"I am of Negro descent."

In this manner it gradually dawns upon my inquisitive friend that he is face to face with a modern "problem." He recollects the emancipation of several millions of slaves in the United States some years ago, and he has since heard more or less of the trouble which naturally followed with this horde of partially civilized freedmen. In common, however, with the rest of the European world he had always thought of these people in the third person, and had no more imagined himself discussing this race problem with one of them, than he had planned talking Egyptology with a pyramid. The curiosity of my neighbor, therefore increases. He hesitates at openly prying into my private affairs or into such public ones as may be painful to me. Yet he is interested, for here, says he is a young man whose very existence is a kind of social paradox: removed but a couple of generations from barbarism, he is yet no barbarian; and again though to all appearances the civilized member of a civilized state, he represents the 19th century problem of barbarism.

I am not always unwilling to satisfy my friend's curiosity. Yes, I tell him, I am one of those nine million human beings in the United States, who constitute the so-called "Negro Problem." The majority of us are not of pure Negro blood, and therefore, as a people, cannot be described as Negroes; neither we nor our ancestors for generations were born in Africa and thus we are not African. We describe ourselves by the perhaps awkward, but certainly more accurate term of Afro-American. If, now, the interest of my neighbor still continues, I proceed to enlarge on a subject which naturally lies near my heart. (AA paras. 1–4)

In these opening paragraphs of "The Afro-American," Du Bois begins by hypothesizing a description of himself through "the eyes of others." And this formulation of a narratological or epistemological point of view will certainly come to stand as exemplary across his entire itinerary of discourse.

It is related to all of his subsequent major statements of the problematization that defined his thought. Its richness is such that it can and must sustain multiple approaches to its discourse. Here we will mark out only a certain track of reflection in the context of our discussion at hand—the question of example.

The scene, as it opens, is of the Negro abroad, beyond the borders of his natal habitation in a local, regional, or national sense. Perhaps it should occasion no surprise that the very incipit of the discourse of the young Du Bois in maturation is a discourse of transnational "travel."[15] The autobiographical narrator is on a completely different "continent" from his natal one, and the world is named, if at all, from a different shore or heading than one that might presumptively be considered his own. And it is precisely the question of heading, under the question of nominalization, that is at issue. He is in Europe in the general sense and on the continent itself. Yet he is in transit. The question remains, From where to where? In all senses, this is a conversation "of between," that is, both from and about a movement that is otherwise than a coordination of a punctual present of a determinate space and a given time (Chandler 2014a).

The theme is his sense of the perception of him by others around him. This is self-reflexivity of the second degree, at least and never only. On the implicit level, the entire background of the discourse is that they perceive him as "different from the others," from themselves and the others, those other than him. He formulates their implicit questions as to whether in some sense he is monstrous—whether he renders the space unsafe for them, as in "wild," or whether he is abnormal in some definitive manner, as in a member of a "passing circus." Here, before the incipit of a stated dialogue proper according to Du Bois's text, he represents their perception of him as a certain order of phenomenal problem. His appearance for them is outside of the norm: thus the question "What is . . . ?" But their eventual judgment is that he is within the compass of their anticipation of the possible forms of human. He is comprehendible by way of their notions of civility. In a moment, this form of precomprehension will be shattered, at least for one hypothetical member of this circumstantial and fictional group.

Du Bois, the "Afro-American" narrator, then outlines a typical course of conversation. It proceeds by way of indirection. It is in all senses a discourse of "between." Expressions of curiosity mount, about the weather, the speed of the train, the aperture of the window, and so forth. His response is to meet such indirection with the same: "I agree that the weather is pleasant, that the open window is to my taste, *et cetera*." And, so far, he describes his supposed interlocutor as "gentlemanly" or, with a gesture of politesse, as "my friend." In its eventuality, the course of the conversation picks up an orientation toward a question of his origins or his identification. It unfolds as a series of questions and responses that are punctuated by statements of repeated surprise, which acquire their rhetorical implication by their appearance against the foil of an indirectly spoken but nonetheless relentlessly declared statement of always already achieved knowledge on the part of the autobiographical narrator. This narrator is a worldly one.

The explicit register of the first question is the narrator's language. Perhaps the language of the conversation is German, for it takes place in "continental" Europe, and French, Spanish, and English, along with Arabic (Du Bois writes "Arabian"), are queried in the dialogue. Here we simply note the biographical facts as we have them at present, that after some initial study of German as well as Latin some years earlier at Fisk, Du Bois really began to speak the language during his first months in Germany during the summer of 1892 (Du Bois 1985d, 6; 1975d, 45–46; 1968, 160–61). He makes no mention anywhere in his autobiographical recollections of learning Italian, perhaps the only other language that would likely function in a synonymic manner in this example. Yet the specific and presumptively literal truth of reference is not decisive. At issue is the narrator's relation to the language of the interlocution. Is it natal or not? Or, better, does its availability *belong to him*? His accent in that language, although perhaps worthy of compliment, is perceived as otherwise than native: "'Your native *tongue* is—?'" (emphasis mine). And what goes unasked is the real question, perhaps given as two implicit interrogatives: initially, "Where are you from?" which in all truth means "Who or *what* are you?" When the narrator answers "English," it only causes greater confusion. It occasions the first "*look*" of surprise (emphasis mine). But this is really the second (or even a third) form of surprise after a hidden or implicit one that stands before and behind the entire opening of spoken interlocution. The first one noted in this recollection was the surprise of his appearance in general. But another unspoken surprise has perhaps also already occurred, the one that yielded a perhaps overly polite judgment that he has already been better spoken than they would have anticipated: "My friend then generally sees fit to compliment my accent." They both bespeak the character of a hidden—unspoken, perhaps unspeakable— order of presumption in this context.

Yet another turn of question can be noted here in that this open register of the stated form of interlocution, as just noted, carries an implicit one. It is a query about his natal place, the place of his natal origination. Here the stress is on the first term of this nominalization: "Your *native* tongue is—?" (emphasis mine). And here, it can be recognized, the whole implicit order of presumption moves ever so obliquely onto the threshold of the realm of the speakable. The question here is "To what do you belong?" In a general sense, place, as in place of origination, is here presumed by the interlocutor almost as a form of given ontological determination. Language then would be its sign. Thus, "English India," in the interlocutor's aggressively inquisitive reply, carries the paradoxical mark of civility at this juncture of the discourse, of which the implication here—without any paradox according to the horizons of colonial discourse and its offshoots—is that it issues from a form of colonial philanthropy. The term "English," the one shared term of these two respective locutions, in all of the instability and polysemic capacity of its putative reference, is the modifier that bespeaks the presumption. Otherwise, the figure and term of "India" might be enough. Yet even the statement of this latter figure would leave intact the idea that language and place, as in origination, bear a fixed relation. The narrator's answer disturbs all of the layers of such presumption within the terms of this interlocution: "No, I am an American." The force of this statement comes from its deepest paradox. While it appears in the form of a statement of essence, an answer to the question "What is . . . ?" or "Who are . . . ?" in all truth it resolutely announces a heterogeneous genealogy all the way down, so to speak, and in all of the orders of reference at issue in the interlocution. The sense of possible reference of the term "English" is simultaneously distended from any fixed origin—the term is "American" and not "English American"—and multiplied in the implication of the horizons of world that it might assist in naming.

Yet the figure of whatever it is that is "American," as that has been named, is also not simple. This is the third turn of question. It appears, however, not in the explicit form of the interrogative but as a reassertion in even stronger terms of the implicit presumption. It is almost a declarative statement. The interlocutor raises the profile of a certain "South America" in which he would recognize "a cousin." It is given as the "of course" of a statement of precomprehension in which this "other America" would be apprehended as an extension of the "gentlemanly" interlocutor's supposed world, not to say family, that is to say, *of* a certain "Europe." The "South American" would be the derivative cousin of the European in the latter's imaginal horizon. We note, however, that at least the question of another "America" (whatever is such) appears on the edge of this dialogic scene. The strongest disruption of any thought of a simple essence attached to an appearance—that of the practice of language, here as speech—comes in the flat insistence by the narrator that his natal origin is "the United States, North America." In so doing, he proposes against his interlocutor's repeated presumption of a predetermined recognizability a different truth: that this America, of the north, has anything but a simple form of identity or identifiable sense of essence. Just what is "American" is being problematized for his interlocutor, or at least any precomprehension of what might be such.

It is at this juncture that the interlocution reaches a decisive turning point, in the sense of the dynamic play of perlocutionary force that would determine for this interlocution the order of name attached by both parties to the narrator. It is the most complicated moment of the discourse. The interlocutor's presumption appears in an implicitly self-reflexive statement as an explicit admission: "Indeed, but *I* thought—" (emphasis mine). And then, finally, interrupting the ever so briefly exposed hint of self-reflection, the question about natality appears explicitly and is posed in starkly direct terms: "Were you born there, may I ask?" This is the presumptive and precomprehended query of the whole dialogue for the interlocutor. It arises from a complication at the root: phenomenal appearance has not yielded the base for a determinate judgment of essence, supposed here as a certain necessary conjunction of natality and language. Likewise, we can remark then that the narrator has continually exacerbated that indetermination rather than relieved it.

Let us turn, then, and follow this exacerbation to its conclusion. The narrator proposes that this complication of the American scene goes, so to speak, all the way down. "Yes," he was born in "the United States, North America." But, more important, much more important in the terms of this interlocution, he continues in a manner that has the status of an emphatic gesture, almost an aggressive one, "And my father, my grand father and my great grand father." With this statement, the questions cease. The next locution, which could well have been expected to take the form of an interrogative, is not such at all. And Du Bois's punctuation here guides us. It takes the form of a mark of exclamation and not of interrogation: "Is that so!" This locution is simply the beginning of a two-part statement from the interlocutor. In all truth, it is a statement of agreement. Yet, in the rhetorical sense, it is one that is given under the aegis of a certain perlocutionary force that might be said to arise by way of the narrator's complicated ironic operation, as we have followed it, of the very premises by which the interlocutor had instituted the conversation. It yields also an apology and the admission, again in the ever-so-brief flash of an explicit register of self-reflexivity, of a mistake and a form of prejudgment on the part of the interlocutor: "Excuse me, *I* had thought *from your color* that—" (emphasis mine). Having already fundamentally questioned the premise and the whole logic of this presumptive admission, the narrator can then give a final statement in a manner that is peremptory and appears in the context of this interlocution almost as a triumph: "I *am* of Negro descent" (again, emphasis mine). And yet all of the ambiguities of this statement of apparent being (given in the unavoidable use of the copula) and descent that has been set afoot over the course of this interlocution remain.

We can say, then, that a certain presumption is adduced both rhetorically and thematically as subtending the whole conversation of the narrator and his interlocutor. A certain engagement with that presumption is the concern of this opening stage of the essay "The Afro-American."

We have so far been able to track the rhetorical level of this problematic within the dialogic rhythm of this interlocution. The matter pertains to the syntax of the respective locutions: a contrapuntal movement in which, respectively, a presumption, unstated or not, is given in the discourse of the interlocutor, which is then met by a certain counter, in the form of a confounding contradiction of that presumption and the eventual revelation of a different truth, so to speak, on the part of the narrator.

2. THE CONCEPTION—OF WORLD. The thematic level of this problematic is given in the two closing paragraphs of this ambulatory discourse. We can sketch it as the relation of two forms of question or two forms of representation of question. The first is that of the Negro American in the United States as perceived in "the European world" as a "modern 'problem,'" that is, a form of being "whose very existence is a kind of social paradox." As the narrator describes it, he is perceived in the eyes of his interlocutor in this railway carriage as of apparently "barbaric" origins but is yet "to all appearances the civilized member of a civilized state." Du Bois here calls it "the 19th century problem of barbarism," which might well be understood as a nascent formulation of the problem that he would later call "the problem of the color line." If, in the opening scene of the interlocution, just before its incipit in the form of an actual statement, the problem was understood by the narrator's putative interlocutors as one of a certain comprehendible monstrosity,

a borderline "wild" man or a "member of a passing circus," now we can recognize that for the "gentlemanly" interlocutor proper, a far more profound sense of problem is also operating within his discourse, on its lower registers or among the resonances of its cavernous subterrain. The figure of the narrator, under the heading of the Negro, appears as the name of a great modern social problem. And it takes the reverse form of the one we noticed at the outset. It can now be said that, according to the view of his interlocutor, the Negro has seemed on the terms of his initial appearance— decisively marked here by his linguistic capacity, perhaps his ability to speak in German, a so-called European tongue—within the norm of civility, but, according to the eventuality of the conversation, it has been revealed that he *is*, in actuality, according to this view, descended from "barbaric" and uncivilized origins. Yet interlaced within the whole of this apparently given form of social problem in general is a specifically discursive one. In this view of the question, the so-called Negro is an object of discourse but not at all a possible, let alone probable, subject of such discourse or of a critical reflection. As the narrator poignantly puts it, "In common, however, with the rest of the European world he had always thought of these people in the third person, and had no more imagined himself discussing this race problem with one of them, than he had planned talking Egyptology with a pyramid." In a sense, the whole discourse of this essay is an intervention and interruption of this form of objectification and its underlying premise of the absence of a critical and reflexive form—in this form—for the announcement of a putative subject. Not only has the table begun to walk, but the walls have also begun to talk. Thus, the second form of question is the one given by the putative object/subject of the conversation—the "Afro-American" himself. And the key is given in that he proposes to self-reflexively name himself in a certain manner: "I am one of those" whom you think "constitute the so-called 'Negro Problem.'" That is to say, in the initial breath, he names himself to his interlocutor in the terms that would be given by others. However, almost immediately, in the decisive gesture of the interlocution, he proceeds to re-name, to reinscribe the name, of the so-called Negro in America according to premises that would define such a figure otherwise than those already given. In logically negative terms, he specifies in two terms or two forms of reference what the Negro in America is not: not of "pure . . . blood," not of "pure Negro blood, and therefore, of the Negro in America as a people , one ought not describe them as "Negroes" (thus, in part, the complication posed for his interlocutor by the narrator's "color" or appearance); and not of a simple or single natal origin in a genealogical sense; that is, "neither we nor our ancestors for generations were born in Africa and thus we are not African" (even as the question of "What is American?" is opened and held in abeyance, as any closure that would exclude the figure in question is forestalled or put at issue). Thus, the narrator concludes, "We describe ourselves by the perhaps awkward, but certainly more accurate term of Afro-American." This figure, in the voice of the narrator, proposes to intervene here directly and in its own name on the terms by which it would be represented—to the whole of the possible world, we might say.

And then we must recall that this ambulatory discourse is just an overture to a discourse that would attempt to name and rename the terms by which this figure of the "Afro-American" might be announced within the lineaments of Du Bois's historical present of the end of the nineteenth century. Over the course of the next decade, he will definitively elaborate this thought problem at the level of a self-reflexive discourse as the historical terms of a specific organization of subjectity—of subjectivation and the pronouncement of a putative subjecthood—here called "Afro-American." Yet the gradual or eventual character of the processes of this emergent theorization must be adduced. All does not appear in one moment or gesture. Nor does it eventuate in a fully accomplished statement on the level of a generalized theoretical proposition. We will maintain here in our own reinscription this sense of a thought in movement, in process, yet to be finished, or, better, yet to come. The implication of its epistemic irruption remains, even in the form of this emergent enunciation, nonetheless.[16]

In the first step into the main discourse of the essay, across the conjunction of the ambulatory discourse and a first statement of problem, a formulation of an understanding the problematization at stake, Du Bois maintains the self-reflexive register of his discourse even if the specific autobiographical motif has moved somewhat into the recesses or interstices of the explicit statement:[17]

> The European child is born into one of several superimposed worlds; he sees in the various social grades and walks of life, so many different and more or less completely separated spheres to only one of which he belongs, and from which he views the others as so many strange and unknown planets. With the white American child, the case is not so different as many democrats would have men believe. With the Afro-American the case is quite different; he is born into a universe which in addition to all horizontal boundaries is separated by a straight perpendicular fissure into a white and black hemisphere. These two halves both have their horizontal differences of educated and ignorant, rich

and poor, law abiding and criminal. On the black side these grades are not, to be sure, so highly differentiated, and the average of culture is far below that of the white side, still they are adjacent and not superimposed spheres.

This fissure between white and black is not everywhere of the same width. Naturally it is the widest in the former slave states and narrowest in the older and more cultivated East. It seldom, however, wholly closes up in New England, while its threatening width in the south is the "Negro Problem." (AA paras. 5–6)

The question that Du Bois adduces here—following the figure of the child—is that of a peculiar sense of world. Du Bois, it may be understood, is on the track of outlining a complicated sense of world. The world in question is always one of worlds. It is a world that is itself, as such, an infrastructural organization of discontinuities. In this sense, the world has, perhaps always, already been "broken." It will always have been a "wounded world."[18] At its limit, it may be that, paradoxically, it will always have been this break or "wound" that will also always have already made possible a complicated epistemic passage of standpoint from which the sense of world in question might be remarked.

Du Bois outlines two contrasting experiences of the sense of world. The "European child" and the "white American child" exist within a world of separate worlds marked by a series of horizontal distinctions, layers, or gradations, configured as distinct "social grades and walks of life." It is a stratified social order. But, in the telling as given here, however, "world" is yet more or less experienced as if a whole, indeed as a "sphere" (even as we can note that at its root, in its genealogy, the distinction of supposed social class could purport from a certain position of hegemony to function as a categorical mark). The existence of the "Afro-American" child also takes place within separate horizontal worlds but, according to the text at hand, with a radical difference. A vertical or "perpendicular" line of distinction, which Du Bois describes as "a fissure," divides the horizontal layers into two different "hemispheres," one "white" and the other "black." Thus, "world" here, while experienced in a certain way as if a whole, is yet also always already re-marked within that form of experience, that is to say, explicitly marked, as a categorically or oppositionally divided whole. The sense of whole here is always already that of the originarily nonsimple. And even if only in the form of the remark as an infrastructural organization of its possibility, the nonsimple would always remain precisely *as the sense* of "world"—in the apparent here and now of this situation. The sense of world will always have been already phenomenological.

In describing the situation of the Negro in America from a putative third-person point of view, which would yet simultaneously be a partial one, that is, one announced on the bias of a concern to adduce the terms of an "Afro-American" situation, Du Bois accedes to an account of the general structure organizing the social and historical field in question. Just how such an accession unfolds at the epistemological level we will not try to completely address or determine here. The eventuality of its announcement must retain its theoretical opacity for us. Yet the moment of this essay "The Afro-American" is a pivotal stage of theoretical projection, and it is one from which Du Bois in all propriety will never retreat. According to this statement, the problematization that sets afoot the conditions in which something like a Negro or "Afro-American" is announced takes shape as a peculiar organization of relation, one that is yet distributed across the entire social field in general. This is a specific historically produced organization of social field and horizon.

Across four subsequent paragraphs that form the remainder of this opening section of the main body of the essay, Du Bois produces the perhaps apocryphal, yet truthful, figure of a young "black boy" as a coded mark to guide his representation of this heterogeneous sense of historicity (AA paras. 6–9). Making reference to John Greenleaf Whittier's figuration of the same in the sixth stanza of his poem "Howard at Atlanta," which was composed in the aftermath of the Civil War and in the advent of Reconstruction, in a gesture that he would reprise in one of the two epigraphs that stand at the head of the fifth chapter of *The Souls of Black Folk: Essays and Sketches*, titled "Of the Wings of Atalanta," Du Bois proposes to describe the "peculiar world in which he [the young black boy of the poem] had to 'rise.'"

This reference is a nodal mark of a deep ore line within Du Bois's discourse, marking the connections of the reflexivity of his practice to a certain distribution of the historical sedimentation within his thought. On the one hand, it gives legible passage to the historical nexus that gathered upon the formal ending of the Civil War (the deep and vexed historicity encoded therein) and to an epistemological index of the inception of the project of Reconstruction (and its complicated relation to the future of the project of America as a whole, both at the turn of the twentieth century and beyond). On the other hand, this line also indexes Du Bois's own life course. Born in 1868, Du Bois is fully writing *of*—both from and about— the historicity of which he is an issue. And near the end of this opening section of "The Afro-American," he will make this explicit, declaring in the ninth paragraph that the conditions of which he writes pertain to "even the boy born, as I was, in Puritan New England."

We can recognize the depth of the reference here by two forms of annotation. In the instance, John Greenleaf Whittier's poem "Howard at Atlanta," referring in its titular frame to General Oliver Otis Howard, a Union military commander during the Civil War, who was with General William Tecumseh Sherman at Atlanta in September 1864, was first published in the *Atlantic Monthly* in March 1869 (Whittier 1869). It may thus be understood to index on supposed literary terms directly and broadly one form of potential audience for Du Bois's essay, even as the latter remained unpublished. Du Bois refers to the fifth and sixth stanzas:

> *And he said: "Who hears can never*
> *Fear for or doubt you:*
> *What shall I tell the children*
> *Up North about you?"*
> *Then ran round a whisper, a murmur,*
> *Some answer devising;*
> *And a little boy stood up: "Massa,*
> *Tell 'em, we're rising!"*
>
> *O black boy of Atlanta!*
> *But half was spoken:*
> *The slave's chain and the master's*
> *Alike are broken.*
> *The once curse of the races*
> *Held both in tether:*
> *They are rising,—all are rising,*
> *The black and white together!*

Also, however, the specific reference to this poem, in addition to this essay in general, is more than a literary citation; for it is also in all truth a kind of trace or residual mark of the emergent *historial* articulation of what would later become a signal reference in Du Bois's early thought—the status in the aftermath of war and reconstruction of the immediate generations of those talented among African Americans who somehow found the opportunity to realize some substantial aspect of their capacities.

The "black boy of Atlanta" of the sixth stanza thus refers to an event in 1868, during which a young Richard Robert Wright, a student in a "new" school for Negro children at Atlanta, in response to a query from a commissioner of the Freedmen's Bureau on behalf of General Howard, replied, "We are rising." The event and the poem are each something other than apocryphal.

For Wright eventually graduated from Atlanta University in 1876 as the valedictorian of his class, going on to become a pioneer in education, a prominent political activist, a major in the U.S. Army, and a banker in Philadelphia (after study at the Wharton School of the University of Pennsylvania), as well as a founding member of the American Negro Academy in 1897, along with Du Bois, among others. At the time that Du Bois wrote this essay—perhaps sometime from late 1894 to early 1895—Wright was head of the State College of Industry for Colored Youth in Savannah, Georgia. William Sanders Scarborough, a native of Georgia and the first graduate of Atlanta University, also a founding member of the American Negro Academy, wrote in his autobiography of being a participant in the events on the occasion and noted that Wright's phrase had been written in "good King's English" but that "the newspapers insisted on putting it into a dialect form" (Scarborough 2005, 43–45). As well, during this same time frame, having just returned from doctoral study in Germany and upon being offered a position at Wilberforce University, Du Bois had thought covetously that he would become an assistant professor to Scarborough, a brilliant scholar of classical languages, but the latter had been unceremoniously displaced from his position of fourteen years at Wilberforce and shuttled into its new offshoot, the Payne Seminary, with no regular salary provided. Yet the older scholar would later return and serve for twenty-three years as a distinguished president of that university.

This reference thus indexes the historicity configuring the course of three of the most distinguished men (for one notes the masculine implication of the literary and historical archive's reference and the essay's citation to the "black *boy*," even if not simply expressing a declared self-reflexive intent by this author, that is indexed therein) of the African American intelligentsia of this pivotal moment. Du Bois, it ought to be noted, has thus already remarked (inscribing himself therein)—in 1894—a possible historical intellectual and political formation that he would come to conceptualize nearly a decade later as a "talented tenth" among African Americans in the United States (Du Bois 1903n, 2015m). Within this same purview, we might well recognize the difficult and real ambivalence—of unsentimental sorrow and ambiguous, yet still resolute hope—encoded as a remark across the representation of this same historicity within the narrative arc of *The Souls of Black Folk: Essays and Sketches* during the same time as the essay on the "talented tenth." For the historical figure of Josie (the young woman of thirty who dies of loss and exhaustion in the back-woods and hills of eastern Tennessee) who appears in the fourth chapter of the classic text as the signal example of the generations left aside from the grand hopes and dreams of the Reconstruction era and now caught and ground within the gears of the resurgent old in the form of sharecrop-ping and peonage and the insurgent new of an industrial reorganization of the proclaimed New South (Du Bois 1903h), along with the fictional Jen-nie of the penultimate chapter of that same text (the young woman who is protected by her brother—the willful protagonist and ostensible hero of the story—from an ensuing rape), who survives, so it seems, within the apparent truth of the fiction to *potentially* find a way forward into a new horizon (Du Bois 1903f), neither of these figures can appear in a fulsome mannner and on their own historial terms within that archive and that the idiomatic resources of the forms of telling such stories at that time—the last decades of the nineteenth century—within Du Bois's path of thinking.[19]

Yet, in a thetic sense, the leitmotif carried within the reference to the "black boy" of Atlanta, so to speak, in Du Bois's telling, in which the matter of "education" is the most decisive passage of the life course, is that of "Afro-American" capacity—to "secure a common school educa-tion," to struggle to rise above "the old menial positions" that he had been perennially encouraged to accept, and to move beyond the segregation and prejudgment that had both historically and in the present of the fin de siècle "strictly hedged in" his mature social and political life (in homeown-ership and in participation in civic life, such as the use of "public libraries, theatres . . . , lecture courses, white churches, etc., and . . . hotels, cafés, res-taurants, and the like," but also in the negotiation of the relative absence or limitation of protection by public law for the freedom of movement, e.g., railway transport, freedom from insult or injury, and the right of the franchise) (AA paras. 7–9).

In terms of the whole sweep of the early discourse of Du Bois, he will adduce two orders of concept-metaphor to name the operations of social and historical distinction or forms of relation that concern him here.

On the one hand, he adduces a metaphor to name the distinction as a structure of social relation in general that appears almost as a given form of objectivity. Here Du Bois is trying to represent what he thinks of as a certain reality—a real situation rendered by an account that would be concerned to present the truth of and about that situation. In the text at hand, such distinction is named by way of a geologic term, *fissure*. Elsewhere, and most often, he renders it by various syntactic deployments and semantic shadings of a geometric or geographic term, *line*. This was a term that had become a constituent lexical and semantic element in the general colloquial formulation of the matter of the turn of the twentieth century, as in the phrase "the color line." However, it is given a distinctive theoretical weighting in Du Bois's reinscription of it in the phrase and thought of "the *problem of the* color *line*" (emphasis mine). Du Bois will adduce this name to characterize the general form of the problem that he wishes to remark, which he will construe as pertaining to all of modern history on a global scale. And he will attempt to exhaustively report and characterize its functioning in the American scene, even its distinctiveness within a comparative horizon, across these early years of his projection of scientific study from the middle of the 1890s through to the World War I. The characterization of this "fissure" as a social condition, then, is the concern of the entire first section of the main body of the essay "The Afro-American," the first paragraph or so of which I have noted above.

Here I must index Du Bois's essay of the turn of the century, "The Present Outlook for the Dark Races of Mankind," even though in part II of this study, by way of a close attention to this essay, I attempt to track some aspects of the first declarative statements of Du Bois proposing the theoretical question of "the problem of the color line."

Likewise, we may note here that fifteen years after preparing "The Afro-American," in a closing chapter titled "The Legacy of John Brown" within his biographical study of that figure, Du Bois will thematize this relation of hierarchical "horizontal" distinction by "class" with a kind of "vertical" form of hierarchical distinction by socially ascribed "race"—on a global scale of comparison. He writes in paragraphs 38 and 39 of that closing chapter of the original edition of the book *John Brown*:

> We are, in fact, to-day repeating in our intercourse between races all the former evils of class distinction within the nation: personal hatred and abuse, mutual injustice, unequal taxation and rigid caste. Individual nations outgrew these fatal things by breaking down the horizontal barriers between classes. We are bringing them back by seeking to erect vertical barriers between races. Men were told that abolition of compulsory class distinction meant the leveling down, degradation, disappearance of culture and genius and the triumph of the mob. As a matter of fact it has been the salvation of European civilization. . . .

The same is true in racial contact. Vertical race distinctions are even more emphatic hindrances to human evolution than horizontal class distinctions, and their tearing away involves fewer chances of degradation and greater opportunities of human betterment than in the case of class lines. On the other hand, persistence in racial distinction spells disaster sooner or later. The earth is growing smaller and more accessible. Race contact will become in the future increasingly inevitable, not only in America, Asia and Africa, but even in Europe. The color line will mean not simply a return to the absurdities of class as exhibited in the sixteenth and seventeenth centuries, but even to the caste of ancient days. This, however, the Japanese, the Chinese, the East Indians and the Negroes are going to resent in just such proportion as they gain power: and they are gaining the power, and they cannot be kept from gaining more power. The price of repression will then be hypocrisy and slavery and blood.

This is the situation to-day. Has John Brown no message—no legacy, then, to the twentieth century? He has and it is this great word: the cost of liberty is less than the price of repression. (Du Bois 1973d, 286–87; but see also 274–301)

Hence, we may reasonably recognize the profundity of the question—at least for Du Bois and within the cadence of his thought—announced in its nascent articulation within the "The Afro-American" of 1894. This world-historical reference was already at issue in his first efforts at the enunciation on this order of problematic, say in 1894; it is thus no surprise to recognize its stakes in the a most emergent moment of his intellectual maturation, say in 1909, approximately a decade and a half later, from the end of the first decade of the twentieth century. Du Bois's distinctive critical conception of modern historicity as a whole came into resolute focus, across the turn from this latter decade to the beginning of the next one, which then was punctuated by the advent of the first war on a planet wide scale of reference.

Yet, on the other hand, as he turns to address at least a putative part of the audience for his representation of the situation of the African American in the United States, the matter of representation itself begins to acquire the character of an explicit part of the problematization. In order to address it, Du Bois will eventually be led to coin one of his most poignant concept-metaphors, "the veil," as the name for the *problem of representation*—both to the self and to the other, constituting thus an entire social field of articulation, of values and norms—of the dynamic social infrastructures in question, of the elusive play of social distinction according to a *practical* idea or concept of race. The term *veil* appears as a descriptive verb, rather than as a theoretical nominalization, three-quarters of the way through the essay at hand, "The Afro-American." In what is apparently the first lexical appearance of the term *veil*—here as the description of an action, *to veil* and not *the veil*—in Du Bois's discourse in a manner that is yet epistemologically proximate to the implication that we have come to recognize in it in our time, it appears as the name for the act of avoidance that defines the "American people['s]" engagement with "the kernel of the Negro problem." That "kernel" is the question of the status (supposed ontology, understood and enacted as moral, political, and legal judgment, almost always with economic consequence, although Du Bois does not make the latter a privileged theme in this essay) according to which the Negro will be recognized in America. The question is whether this figure will be proscribed within the horizon of the American republic "solely because he has Negro blood?" This, we might suggest, following the manner of his statement, could well be simply called the *American* problem with the Negro (my emphasis). At this juncture, Du Bois deploys the word *veil* in its verbal form as the name for the specifically American way of grappling with "the problem of the color line," a certain denegation, which is the act of "*veiling*," hiding or disguising, the basic question. And that question is about the presumptive practice that is carried out in the blind of a peremptory judgment (in all truth, a prejudgment) about the status of, the Negro as a form of being. He writes, "This is the kernel of the Negro problem, and the question which the American people have never boldly faced, but have persisted in *veiling* behind other and dependent problems" (AA para. 23; emphasis mine). The order of problem here is, precisely, that of the *representation* of the so-called Negro problems.

We can begin to confirm this sense of the emergence of the term *veil*—*to veil* and *a veil* or *the veil*—as a lexical mark and its eventual acquisition of the status of a theoretical nomination within Du Bois's interpretive disposition toward the so-called Negro problem by noticing its announcement within what appears to be its next deployment, which in all truth is the epistemologically decisive one, within his discourse. It appears in the famous second paragraph of the essay "Strivings of the Negro People," which Du Bois completed sometime between the middle and the end of June 1897, while he was still in Philadelphia and just before he left to undertake summer fieldwork in the small southern town of Farmville, Virginia. It was then published in August of that year in the *Atlantic Monthly*. It opens an autobiographical reflection that recalls the young "black boy" of the essay "The Afro-American" of some two and a half years earlier. He describes its appearance as a reflexive figure in the relation of a failed exchange of "greeting cards": "The exchange was merry, till one girl, a tall newcomer, refused my card,—refused it peremptorily, with a glance. Then it dawned upon me with a certain suddenness that I was different from the others; or like, mayhap, in heart and life and longing, but shut out from their world by a vast veil" (Du Bois 1897c, 194; 2015k, 68, para. 2).[20]

In the account of June 1897, the term *veil* undergoes a decisive metaphorization. Under the impress of a theoretical projection, its semantic and grammatical character begins to shift from a description of a discrete action, which could almost appear as voluntary, to the performative nominalization of a constitutive dimension of the organization of a social field. If the 1894 deployment purported to account for an incipient action, then the 1897 operation names a repetitive and sustained outcome of an ongoing social process. If its first appearance was in the form of a verb, then its grammatical accretion in the latter presentation is now that of a noun. The "veil," then, is adduced here as the fictional name of an *infrastructure* of passively inhabited yet *actively* operated representation, a form of denial or denegation in every sense, that becomes effective as the rendering of social ordination, the implication of which can be understood to function on every level of social existence from the relation of supposed collectivities to the subindividual mark of apparent self-reflexivity.

And then, in a fragment of writing titled "Beyond the Veil in a Virginia Town" that most likely dates from the late summer or early autumn of 1897, perhaps composed during the time of his fieldwork in and around Farmville, Virginia, or shortly thereafter, Du Bois describes this order of presumptive, yet effective, distinction, this representation that is a concatenated form of a certain social "fissure," in some detail, and he does so under the heading of the concept-metaphor of "the veil." Its yield on an epistemic level is a theoretical generalization of the problematic named therein to the whole of the social field in question:[21]

> Midway between the memory of Nat Turner and John Randolph of Roanoke, beside the yellow waters of the Appomattox, lies a little town whose history winds about the falling stars in '32 and about "The Surrender." One would not call——ville a pretty town, nor yet has it the unrelieved ugliness of the west. There is a certain southern softness and restfulness not to say laziness about it that gives a charm to its sand and clay, its crazy pavements and "notion" stores. But the most curious thing about——ville is not its look—old brick mansions

and tiny new cottages, its lazily rolling landscape and sparsely wooded knolls that beck and nod to the three-peaked ridge of the blue Alleghenies—the most curious thing about——ville is the Veil. The great Veil—now dark, sinister and wall-like, [now?] light, filmy and silky, but every[where] a dividing veil and running throughout the town and dividing it: 1200 white this side and 1200 Black beyond the Veil.[22]

You who live in single towns will hardly comprehend the double life of this Virginia hamlet. The doctrine of class does not explain it—the caste misses the kernel of the truth. It is two worlds separate yet bound together like those double stars that, bound for all time, whirl around each other separate yet one.

Two little boys are walking along the street. "Big execution in town today," says one; "white or colored?" asks the other. Two men are standing in the post office. "I'm running fifty hands in the foundry now," says one. "White or colored?" asks the other. Two countrymen urge their jaded mares across the Appomattox and up main street. "Big meeting at the country," says one; "white folks or niggers?" asks the other. And thus it runs through life: the Veil is ever there separating the two peoples. At times you may not see it—it may be too thin to notice, but it is ever there. And we have added an eleventh commandment to the decalogue down here: you may have other Gods before Me, you may break the kill commandment and waver around adultery but the eleventh must not be broken; and it reads: Thou shalt not cross the Veil.

Of the life this side of the Veil you all know much; it is the twice told tale of country town life flavored with war memories, and a strange economic experiment, curiously influenced by the other world, but withal quite like [to] Illinois or Connecticut in its business and gossip, its Church [fairs] and [_____], its courting, marrying, and dying.

But beyond the Veil lies an undiscovered country, a land of new things, of change, of experiment, of wild hope and sombre realization, of superlatives and italics—of wondrously blended poetry and prose (Du Bois 1897a[?][circa], 1980b, 1985b).

The epistemological significance of this fragment for us is that here the desedimentative force of the thought of the "veil" is brought to term and directly proposed. And this force moves on two registers or along two lines of concatenation. In one register, Du Bois seeks to describe what we might call both sides of the veil, in their irreducible relation, in a "Southern" town. The general epistemological implication of the thought of "the veil," that is, its capacity to name the production of a putative "white" social horizon as well as that of a supposed "black" or "Negro" one within a general

"American" scene, is brought into explicit relief. This general implication, that is, its capacity to bring into relief something fundamental about the subjectivation of a putatively "white" social and historical subject as well as that of an ostensibly "black" one, is one of the most original dimensions of Du Bois's discourse.[23] Yet, of equal import, in another register of his discourse, indeed, appearing as its frame, he proposes a movement beyond the mark of limit, outlining it without a discrete nominal term as its proper name yet remarking it as "beyond the veil." The task of a re-representation of this "beyond" then might well be understood as the first naming of the project that he would undertake five years later, more or less, in September 1902, when he began to work in earnest on the production of the text *The Souls of Black Folk: Essays and Sketches.* This remarkable book then would appear as the elaborative realization in narrative form of the proposal of this fragment that such a "beyond" might remain as a yet-to-come horizon of "new things, of change, of experiment, of wild hope and sombre realization," the imagination of which could well be rendered in another form of representation than that given by way of "the veil" in its proscriptive sense—a representation that would be one "of superlatives and italics—of wondrously blended poetry and prose." It hardly need be said, then, that this has been perhaps the most widely recognized contribution of Du Bois's work at this stage of its itinerary. In this latter form, then, that given by the rhetorical dynamis of the concept-metaphor of "the veil," the problem of the representation of a vertically "fissured" social horizon would come to provide the rhetorical frame and theoretical impetus for the narrative that issues as *The Souls of Black Folk: Essays and Sketches.* And the thought of going "beyond" the limits of such a horizon would remain its most radical contribution, that of proposing the necessity of a certain practice of interpretation, which indeed stands at the far edge of the human sciences and the humanities in general, certainly then and perhaps even *now,* whatever the latter is as such.

Returning, then, to the letter of the text of the essay "The Afro-American," the whole thought of this social "fissure" and the related "veiling" of apperception by which it is engaged by "Americans" in general as it is given herein may rightly be taken by our critical and retrospective discourse as the first enunciation, within Du Bois's own thought according to the terms of concatenation that would eventually be specific to his discourse, of the theoretical proposition of "the problem of the color line" and the theoretical metaphorization that takes shape under the heading of the term "*veil,*" within Du Bois's discourse.

What is the status and implication of this social "fissure," according to Du Bois's thought in this essay? The most obvious impact is its negative effect upon the group that he calls "Afro-American." It imposes or effects a proscriptive limitation of opportunity, on the level of the group, individually and collectively, to fully realize the potential of the gifts or capacities that they may be able to announce within historicity. Assuming that some would claim that "these discriminations may, in some cases, be merely protective measures of society against its proletariat," Du Bois nonetheless declares, "They change this character however, when they force back rising talent and desert among blacks, and leave uncurbed ignorance and lawlessness among whites" (AA para. 9). The marks that produce such a fissure are then primarily a means of maintaining a practical status quo of privilege and presumption that is without any fundamental justification. Yet also the impact of this "fissure" on America as a whole, in his view, has been to foreshorten its historial projection and to confound its actions on the level of the nation-state, producing both unwise and contradictory gestures.

3. THE PECULIAR SENSES OF DISCOURSE. If such a condition is a historical limit on this project, how has it been addressed by reflective thought? According to what organization of thought and understanding has it been engaged? Have the dominant critical discourses, political, legal, and economic, proposed a viable understanding of this situation such that a real transformation could be produced?

Du Bois makes a basic distinction in this essay among the discourses concerned with the so-called Negro problem, between that of others, collectively configured under the heading of "the American State" (AA para. 10), and that of the so-called Negro American himself, understood as a self-reflexive collectivity.

A. OF THE STATE. The discourse of "the American State," for Du Bois, is formed by way of three diverse but interwoven perspectives. These are the "Ricardean" (the laissez-faire approach of the government proper), the "Philanthropic" (inheritors of an abolitionist disposition), and the "Radical" (a certain maintenance of the projection of the Old South) (AA para. 11). In Du Bois's view, the Negro American's own idea of the so-called Negro problem remained distinct from such positions but was still only nascent at the midpoint of the 1890s. What, then, is the relation between these three schools of thought pertaining to the Negro problem that have been given by others and the nascent viewpoint of the "Afro-American" intelligentsia, especially the ideas of one of the latter's young, up-and-coming members, one W. E. B. Du Bois? In essence, none of the three positions given from outside of the discourse of African Americans themselves provides a perspective commensurate with the problematic named as the so-called Negro question, according to him. At the root, however, is a failure of policy and leadership on the part of the national-level state.

The hitherto dominant position has been that of the "Ricardean" (or "Smith-Ricardo") school, taking nominal reference to the figures of Adam Smith and David Ricardo. The position named by this reference had proposed to "emancipate" the slave, in which such action meant only the legal decree of the abolition of the practice of enslavement. It would then, and in fact did, leave the freed slave to so-called free competition (as Du Bois describes it). According to him, the policy proposed and enacted by this school of thought was the "most extreme" case of the application of the "Smith-Ricardo" doctrine of laissez-faire that had issued from the eighteenth century:

> The situation violated every condition which the English school of social philosophy presupposed as necessary for the application of their laws. Instead of a stable state of society, an absence of great class differences and prejudices, and an approximate equality of opportunity for the competitors, there was a state of society only to be described as revolutionary, a maximum of class hatred and unreasoning prejudice, and the competing "equality" of master and slave. Scarce a single step was taken by the State to remedy this." (AA para. 11)

In a crucial comparative reference, Du Bois scores this policy as outside the norms of recent historical experience as given on the continent of Europe:

> Russia, to whom America has often thought it fit to read lectures on national morality, gave the emancipated serfs a part of the land on which they and their fathers had toiled: not an inch was given America's freedmen; the builders of the monarchic Prussian state took care that the ignorant German bauer was in a condition to compete before he was left to "free competition:" the democratic American state did not give its freedmen so much as a spade." (AA para. 11)[24]

This school of thought, according to Du Bois, was inapplicable in theory, and the policy that issued from it was historically abnormal, if not moribund, from its inception. And this censure of the American scene would hold regardless of our own judgment with regard to the Russian and Prussian examples.[25] Obviously, so to speak, the "Smith-Ricardo" approach had simply continued and often even exacerbated the difficult problems faced by the Negro American in the United States, yielding the present of Du Bois's earlier description of the limits on opportunity experienced by this group.

Fortunately, in Du Bois's reading of the mid-1890s, "the private efforts of philanthropists in some measure, hindered its radical application, the patient stubborn striving of the freedmen accomplished unawaited results, and the white showed itself more friendly to the blacks than the freedmen had expected" (AA para. 12). Otherwise, the outcome of the state-level "Smith-Ricardo" policy might have been far more grave than its actual dire effects. But this "Philanthropic" school, also a product of eighteenth-century thought, was "a development of those one-sided moral and social ideals which made man purely the result of his individual environment" (AA para. 12). While striving for "the highest ideals of humanity," they have yet been fundamentally limited in their approach:

> They have seldom escaped narrow fanaticism or great-hearted blindness to facts. Seizing upon the Rousseau-Jefferson half-truth: "All men are created free and equal," they sought to secure the rise of the Negro by a course at College, and the recognition of his rights by legal enactment, or executive dicta. Here naturally, they largely failed. Their laws remained dead-letters, their mandates were hooted down by the mob, while the vast system of private charity which they set on foot to aid the helpless and forsaken freedmen was without general plan, expensively distributed and, shortsighted in its object. The whole philanthropic movement in regard to the Afro-American forgot the real weakness of his situation, i.e., his economic helplessness and dependence; that whatever "equality" he could be said to hold in the American state, was an equality in "poase" and not in "ease."[26] It gave him churches before he had homes, theories of equality instead of personal property, theological bickerings instead of land and tools, and mushroom "colleges" instead of a good common school and industrial training system. (AA para. 13)

And even as this perspective gradually broadened and became more systematized, it remained, although "a huge work of highest importance," that it was "built on the narrow vacillating and humiliating basis of personal charity" (AA para. 13). Thus, finally, as Du Bois so deftly put it at this moment, "The better self of the American people has not yet realized that this situation is something more complicated than a case of pariah almsgiving" (AA para. 13). This "spasmodic charity" of a generation by the time of Du Bois's writing had ultimately shown its inability to conceive of the whole of the so-called problem of the Negro as one pertaining to the whole of the possibility of the United States as a historial projection.

Even so, in the face of the indifference of the national state and the incoherence of the philanthropic gesture, a reaction had set in that would renounce the Negro's status as an equal political and historical figure within the project of America as a whole and at all levels of the socius. This was the thought of the "Radical" school, in Du Bois's nominalization:

> The grand thought of this radical school of opinion lies on the oft-repeated phrase: "This is a white man's country," i.e., in all questions affecting the weal or woe of America, the only people whose interests are to be considered are the members of the Caucasian race. This 15th century phrase is stated baldly and bluntly by some classes; by others it is dressed in 19th century clothes; it is said: We are dealing with facts, not theories of morality; there is among us a vast horde of people, alien to us in looks, in blood, in morals and in culture; our people will not associate with them, and cannot live in peace beside them; they stand on a lower plane of humanity than we, and never have in the past evolved a civilization of their own, nor under a favorable trial today do they show any ability to assimilate or forward modern culture; therefore as a lazy, shiftless, and bestial folk, they must in accordance with the universal law of the survival of the fittest yield before the all-conquering Anglo-Saxon, and must be either transported, isolated or left to slow and certain extermination. (AA para. 14)

Du Bois describes this view as belonging to "many Americans and Europeans" (AA para. 15). Indeed, it must be noted that throughout this essay he is at pains to differentiate a certain reactionary radical disposition within the southern states from the whole of the American South and especially a relatively progressive wing of its leadership. Beyond the South, this disposition could be found throughout America and even abroad in Europe. Du Bois sharply and directly questions two core premises of this "school" of thought. Contrary to their presumption, he holds that their view is not the attitude of the American people as a whole and that the Negro has shown much in their development since Emancipation (as it is commonly understood in African Americanist discourses of the time of Du Bois's writing, as he indexes it this text). While he does not respond here in the form of a declarative statement to the most general and peremptory claim of this school, that is, that the Negro as a group "never has, and never will, do anything to aid and advance the culture and civilization of the day" (AA para. 15), the whole of the remainder of the essay "The Afro-American" should yet be understood as an effort to formulate a decisive answer.

It is an answer that moves on multiple registers. And it is here that the problem of the discourse of the Negro American himself is announced.

B. OF "THE THING ITSELF." In order to engage the terms of this latter school in their most deep-seated dimensions, a whole line of intervention is proposed by Du Bois. It is a formulation that is of signal epistemological importance for our understanding of Du Bois's thought, for it will come to retrospectively name the initial course of his specific vocation. The terms of this "school" of thought, as Du Bois's characterizes it, encode the most fundamental metaphysical order of question that subtends the entire discourse of the Negro at this time, distributed across all three of these positions as described so far by Du Bois, despite its variegation within their respective locutions. A kind of knowledge that would be new in terms of the discourse of the Negro in the United States at this time would be necessary in order to propose a way to go beyond the dispute of opinion and the poor empirical measure of the present and to decisively displace the root presumption of this "Radical" school. Du Bois describes this problem of knowledge as "the kernel of the whole problem." The "real truth and the real problems may be laid bare" only by way of a new practice of knowledge with regard to the question of the Negro (AA para. 17). As we have already noted above, Du Bois would be led to formulate and elaborate this necessity in a systematic fashion during late 1897 while engaged in the research that would eventually yield *The Philadelphia Negro: A Social Study* (Du Bois and Eaton 1899, 1973). However, already in "The Afro-American," the most decisive epistemological dimension of that later statement, and indeed of all of Du Bois's subsequent work, is already given its definitive theoretical place. It is the formulation of the Negro American as otherwise than a putatively simple object of knowledge. He conceptualizes the Negro as also a possible subject of such a project. The Negro, if there is such, is a fundamentally composite entity in terms of the question of human reflection, understanding, and forms of knowledge: "Meantime one of the most important elements of the problem is without doubt, the attitude of the Afro-American himself, his opinion of his situation, his aspirations, and ideals. For it is the peculiarity of problems in social science, as distinguished from physical science, that the thing studied as well as the student, is a living breathing soul, all of whose numberless thoughts and actions must be ascertained and allowed for in the final answer" (AA para. 18). As I notice elsewhere, this dimension of "the study of the Negro problems," as Du Bois will come to name them in general, that which pertains to the Negro's subjectivity, is eventually understood by him as the epitome of the problematic of such study. He will later call it in epistemological terms "a distinct social mind."[27] And this order of a "distinct" social life might be understood itself to yet manifest two interwoven subsidiary dimensions within it: that of the social life of the group as a whole and that of its self-reflexive discourse, in this last sense that of its own self-criticism or self-reflexive leadership (especially that form which might be called the work of an intelligentsia, although not necessarily or predominantly an academic one).

And so for Du Bois at the end of 1894, the problem a generation after the legal abolition of slavery and the failure of the project of Reconstruction is that no perspective had arisen within this group itself that could be commensurate with its situation. It is this form of problem that takes shape as the most proper concern of the essay "The Afro-American" in a theoretical sense. Its task is thus to announce a new—"Afro-American"— understanding of the situation of the Negro in America from within the subjectivity of this group itself. As we have already noticed from the outset of our consideration of this essay, Du Bois presents the so-called Negro question in America according to a frame of reference that is fundamentally comparative on a global scale. This group, he proposes, faces a historically abnormal situation with regard to the production of a leadership:

> The peculiarity of the rise of the Afro-American is that he has been compelled to advance by means of democracy toward ideals which American democracy has set before him. The invariable rule of advance among peoples is the gradual evolving of leading, ruling classes among them, who guide the masses, and incorporate strata after strata with themselves until a sufficient number of the whole race become raised to that average of culture which we call civilization. So to place a nation that [for whom] this usual method of advance was hindered, did not mean the substitution of some new method—it did not result as 18th century social philosophers taught, in the lifting of the race bodily from the bottom into one dead level of equality; it mearly [merely] meant that the natural development should be slower, and the natural aristocracy longer deprived of their rightful places as leaders of their own people. Thus it has happened that the majority worship and deification of mob-rule, which has too often in America displaced the high ideals of true democracy, has within the ranks of the freedmen themselves, acted as a disintegrating force at a time when unity and subordination was most needed. (AA para. 19)[28]

In the comparative sense, Du Bois formulates two ways of understanding the development of leadership and ideals. One, given in his own theoretical voice, declares that such development follows an "invariable rule," in which there is "the gradual evolving of leading, ruling classes," a "natural aristocracy," who "should assume that legitimate leadership and beneficent guardianship which the cultured classes of all nations owe their proletariat" (AA para. 19).[29] The other, the conception of which he attributes to "18th century social philosophers," imagined "the lifting of the race bodily from the bottom into one dead level of equality."

At variance with both of these ideas—the historial norm and the revolutionary ideal—is the Negro situation in the United States, which from the end of the Civil War to the fin de siècle had taken a peculiar path: a slower development of a leadership and no simple uplifting of the whole. Without the availability of any true established comparative norm for such, a situation that Du Bois will shortly describe as one in which the Negro can be understood to have "suddenly broken with his past" but yet remained "out of touch with his environment," the Negro "ex-slave was compelled, out of the dead-level of his degradation to evolve his leaders and his ideals" (AA para. 20, 19). Thus, while the ideals of the "American State" had inevitably influenced those of the Negro, their effect had actually but yielded confusion for the Negro. That is to say, while the Negro "instinctively" withdrew from "that soul-blunting competition, that Sturm und Drang of the gigantic business life, as the great cause of all the disabilities and indignities he suffered," this withdrawal only "increased the prejudice against him," for his disposition was not "profitable" (AA para. 19). Yet, within the group itself, this absence of any "natural aristocracy" meant that "it has happened that the majority worship and deification of mob-rule, which has too often in America displaced the high ideals of true democracy, has within the ranks of the freedmen themselves, acted as a disintegrating force at a time when unity and subordination was most needed" (AA para. 19). Approaching the midpoint of the 1890s, the matter can be seen in this light as a distinctive moment in African American intellectual-political history: Frederick Douglass would shortly pass from the scene, as would Alexander Crummell shortly thereafter; Booker T. Washington would be collaboratively anointed (in late 1895, by a kind of joint disposition on the part of both northern and southern white economic and political leaders); and a new leadership from among the ranks of African American women would begin to announce themselves, namely, Anna Julia Cooper and Ida B. Wells-Barnett, among others.[30]

The young Du Bois then would try to announce himself and his vision within this volatile and difficult moment of transition in leadership and the production of a new sense of ideals among African Americans.

Positioning himself autobiographically, he writes in the form of the first person plural. In all of its apparent simplicity, it is the rhetorical level of the most decisive theoretical course of thought moving within and across the essay as a whole:

> We Afro-Americans claim that the United States has made the dangerous mistake of calling a mass of complicated social problems which lay before the nation, by the common name of "Negro Problem," and of then attempting to find some one radical remedy for all such distresses.
>
> We claim to see under what is commonly called the Negro problem at least four different problems; We regard the Negro problem proper as nothing more nor less than a question of humanity and national morality. Is the American nation willing to judge, use, and protect its citizens with reference alone to their character and ability, and irrespective of their race and color? Is the conscience of the American Republic so far behind the social ideals of the 19th century, as to deny to a human being the right of "life, liberty, and the pursuit of happiness" solely because he has Negro blood? This is the kernel of the Negro problem, and the question which the American people have never boldly faced, but have persisted in *veiling* behind other and dependent problems. (AA paras. 22–23; emphasis mine)

The vocative position adduced here will in all truth announce another order of perspective within this American discourse of the Negro. In brief, it announces a metalevel perspective. In so doing, it shows how the discourses of the Negro are themselves a constitutive part of the so-called Negro problems. In essence, all three of the schools of thought as Du Bois has described them, even the most benevolent (the "Philanthropic" project), along with the apparently, or supposedly, most benign (the "Smith-Ricardo" doctrine), presume in effect, if not as their declared first premise (as in the "Radical" position), that the Negro group itself is the root of the problem. If one does not presume an ontological root as in the last of these three, it remains that for the other two the fundamental issue is ultimately still understood to take the shape of the historical forms of limitation manifested within this group itself. The position announced by Du Bois under the heading of the "Afro-American" begins from an equally fundamental but very different presumption: that the form of problem named as the so-called Negro problem is produced by the organization of

American society in general and on the level of the nation-state as a whole. It is in this sense, then, that one can simultaneously name its "kernel," "the Negro problem proper," and yet insist that in its fullness it is not one but several "other and dependent," interwoven problems.

On the one hand, in a gesture that should perhaps be understood as a counter to the premise of the Negro himself as the root of the problem, Du Bois proposes that if any conceptual breadth should be given to the nominalization "Negro problem," then it should most properly be understood as a quite general one that is situated "as nothing more nor less than a question of humanity and national morality" (AA para. 23). The Negro question, if there is such, is not first of all or only a question about the Negro. In a philosophical and practical-theoretical sense, it is first a fundamental and general question about the dominant conceptions of humanity, morality, and nation afoot within the domain of the socius called America.

On the other hand, the social difficulty encoded here takes shape as a whole ensemble of social problems. Subsequently, over the remainder of the fourth section of this essay, Du Bois enumerates three domains of reference: the *educational* condition of the Negro, the *political* capacity of the group, and the *moral* forms of habitation and socialization. It must be annotated at this juncture that while Du Bois thematizes the economic condition of the Negro throughout this essay, even emphasizing the role of Negro labor in the nascent and partial economic recovery of the so-called New South, he does not theorize it here as a distinct sphere or order of social problem as such. In all propriety, however, it should be understood according to his stated discourse in this essay as not only interwoven within but subtending, *in a specific theoretical sense*, all that he remarks under the heading of the Negro problems in the plural: the persistence of the Negro's economic debility renders intractable each solution in every other sphere. The most essential theoretical statement here, however, is that the so-called Negro problems are something other than a form of the simple. They are not in any sense given all at once. Described by him in the context of the Negro, they actually name the forms of a general social problem within the American field in general. This fundamental postulation of the essential heterogeneity of the problematic at issue here will be elaborated across his entire career. For example, it is maintained by Du Bois some three years later, in the late autumn of 1897, at the end of his period of theoretical and vocational "casting about" (as we have notated it above), when he returns to this epistemic threshold again as the opening of the programmatic essay in which he outlines a certain conception and approach to "the study of the Negro problems":

> Thus a social problem is ever a relation between conditions and action, and as condition and actions vary and change from group to group from time to time and from place to place, so social problems change, develop and grow. Consequently, though we ordinarily speak of the Negro problem as though it were one unchanged question, students must recognize the obvious facts that this problem, like others, has had a long historical development, has changed with the growth and evolution of the nation; moreover, that it is not *one* problem, but rather a plexus of social problems, some new, some old, some simple, some complex; and these problems have their one bond of unity in the fact that they group themselves about those Africans who two centuries of slave-trading brought into the land. (Du Bois 1898c, 3, para. 6; 2015l, 78–79, para. 6)

Whereas proximate to the end of 1894, Du Bois emphasized the nonsimplicity of the so-called Negro problems (even as he remarked their historical development), in late 1897 he will insist on their temporality (thus intensifying the sense of their nonsimple root or their heterogeneity). In the later moment, he is able to render the question of the historicity of such forms of problem into distinct theoretical relief. And in the later moment, this insight is conjoined with a rapidly maturing sense of his conception of a general "sociology," or science of the social, and of his specific vocation within its project. Already engaged in his work on the study of the Negro in Philadelphia, over the course of late 1896 through late 1897, Du Bois would begin to clarify for himself just what task was set for him if he would recognize an engagement with the so-called Negro problems as the most specific and concrete form of problematization that would define his own work. We see the first precocious steps along that path in this closing section of the essay "The Afro-American."

For the young, effervescent Du Bois, the Negro at the mid-1890s does not measure up to the standard that he would set: "We Afro-Americans acknowledge freely that we form a larger part of those many social problems that confront the American nation; we must educate ourselves, we must learn our duties as voters, we must raise our moral standards" (AA para. 26).[31] However, just as equally, he maintained that every categorical claim about the condition of the Negro, whether presented as empirical or not, was untenable. Across the closing section of the essay, he systematically defends the efforts of the Negro to uplift themselves, as a group. Announcing himself on the register of the orator and the preacher, he declares in the closing paragraph, "Few peoples have ever striven more earnestly to gain the respect of civilization than we in the last quarter-century" (AA para. 26). As this project will unfold in Du Bois's discourse over the next decade, it will eventually acquire, in the closing chapter of *The Souls of Black Folk: Essays and Sketches*, for example, the implication not only of producing the Negro within a given horizon of respectful "civilization," whether understood as America or the modern world in general, but eventually of deepening and improving it. The impossible possible world of the Negro "beyond the veil" becomes there, as it was already becoming in the mid-1890s, the name of the project of immanent striving that will yield another world in the time to come. In this sense, we can say, too, that the figure of the "Afro-American," announced within the confines of all manner of historical limit, is yet for Du Bois a name for the futural form of possibility within this American "world."

It remains, however, to remark perhaps the most powerful theoretical aspect of this text as a discursive intervention. As part of the project of announcing an "Afro-American" sense of the Negro problems, Du Bois has been led to challenge the forms of understanding and knowledge by which the Negro question has been understood. And, more radically still, he has questioned the very terms by which the hegemonic discourses would name the problem in question. That is to say, he has questioned the terms of their *representation* of the Negro problem. And, by way of this critical riposte, the way in which the discourses themselves are part of the problem in question appears in distinct relief. This is to say that Du Bois practices a recognition that the discourses of the Negro are themselves part of the problem, even if he does not himself thematize it on a metalevel of his own discourse or in the manner that we have done here. The "*veiling*" of the "question of humanity and national morality" that is at issue is not just a failure of understanding or knowledge with implications for an abstract construal of the question but rather a practical-theoretical failure that leaves aside from the debate the very premises that predetermine and precomprehend the whole of the supposed question. If it would be critical and not only reflexive, the approach to this question according to the terms of a subjectity that would understand itself in the first-person plural to be named by such a heading turns the whole question over and indeed puts at issue not only the terms of its self-representation but the terms of the representation of the supposed Negro question in general. The "Negro problem" then is simply the name given within discourse to an entire dimension of historicity that has constituted the domain called America, or more specifically in this instance the United States of America.

4. THE THOUGHT OF THE EXAMPLE. It can now be said that it is on this horizon of historicity and within the interstices of problem announced therein that the discourse and practice of Du Bois took its initial orientation and acquired its most specific sense. As we have just recognized in our recollection of the essay "The Afro-American," it had been the very threshold condition for the announcement of his ownmost trajectory. In the autobiographical engagement, we have been able to recognize the initial steps of a self-reflexive intellectual and the first political maturation for the young thinker, one W. E. B. Du Bois, in terms of such an order of reference. However, we have also already begun to recognize that the dynamic movement of question that opened this autobiographical passage to the historicity in question acquired its enunciative form only retrospectively, by way of the metaleptic and reciprocal passage from one form of historicity to another: of the individual as supposed ipseity, of nation (or nation-state), or of something else altogether on a more general level than that of the national state. It acquired its legibility in the passage that opened for him joining a certain Europe and a certain America. Certainly, the question of the Negro in the United States is discursively projected into a comparative horizon that should be understood as global in its extension. It is an order of horizon that is global in space and epochal in temporality. Now we can remark that it was this dynamic reflection announced in the idiomatic form of the autobiographical that has yet opened a distinctive epistemic view that could lead to the conceptualization of an entire dimension of historicity as a problem for practical-theoretical engagement. That is to say, we have also been able to suggest the practical-theoretical fecundity in thought that began to announce itself within Du Bois's inhabitation of that formation. In essence, the forms of such inhabitation as reflexively produced within his discourse—here remarked especially as the internal discourse of the essay "The Afro-American"—are understood to be anything but simple, always other than the one, somewhat and somehow always other than the simplicity of a given here and now. In this sense, we have now been able to fold across and through each other these two main registers of Du Bois's discourse that we have been following, the autobiographical and the historiographical. While we note that it enabled the critical remark of limit—in the practice of both policy and discourse—it yet should be emphasized that for Du Bois it also opened an affirmative sense of the heterogeneous—of the more-than-one, of the double, of the peculiar and problematic sense of world (that of, say, the little "black boy of Atlanta")—as a name of possibility, beyond the here and the now. For Du Bois in the 1890s—in America (whatever is such)—the "Afro-American" announced itself as a practical-theoretical name for such a thought of the beyond.

A decade later, Du Bois will outline this thought with direct reference to the world-historical horizon of modern historicity, on a planetwide scale of implication.

B. OF HORIZON II: "THE DEVELOPMENT OF A PEOPLE" (1904)

In the opening paragraph of the essay "The Development of a People," Du Bois gives the incipit, antecedent to the text proper, according to which his discourse is presumptive with regard to its own possible value:

> In the realm of physical health the teachings of Nature, with its stern mercy and merciful punishment, are showing men gradually to avoid the mistake of unhealthful homes, and to clear fever and malaria away from parts of earth otherwise so beautiful. . . . But if we have escaped Medievalism to some extent in the care of physical health, we certainly have not in the higher realm of the economic and spiritual development of people. Here the world rests, and is largely contented to rest, in a strange fatalism. (Development 292, para. 1)

On the basis of a disposition that operates in a theoretical sense as a matter of principle, Du Bois will propose in his essay a first order of reference to knowledge, both science and the learning of those who would seek to know, for the adjudication of the terms of "a people's advance," or, more properly put, for humanity in the most general sense of the imagination.

The essay is organized as some forty-seven paragraphs over twenty pages, divided into three discursive components: a conceptualization (paras. 1–16), a narration (paras. 17–29), and a statement, this last given in the form of judgments and propositions (paras. 30–47).

With regard to the conceptualization according to which Du Bois will organize the epistemological domain of his essay, the topical heading of concern is a form of human collective that Du Bois names as "a people." It is notable that this reference is not a "race group," as in the 1897 essay "The Conservation of Races" (Du Bois 1897b, 2015c). Too, the reference in this essay is more formal than the sense of "folk" in the 1902–3 gathering of writing that yields the book *The Souls of Black Folk: Essays and Sketches*, published in April of the latter year. But the term of reference here is not yet that of a "culture" group, as that would come to be somewhat formally nominalized in the work of Franz Boas and his students across the second and third decades of the twentieth century; for the concept of culture was not yet a stable lexical term of art, let alone a formal epistemic premise, in discourses in the Americas or Europe, for example, in the years 1903–4 (Boas 1911, 1989; Stocking 1982).

Yet the idea of "a people" is for Du Bois a general heading (perhaps presumptively universal in pertinence). It might be thought of as an idea or concept from the sciences—the human sciences, we might say today—but then, if so, we might specify it as of a nascent sociology, or a science of "man," which would be a general "anthropology," including an ethnology, and perhaps even some index of the discourse under the heading of *Geisteswissenschaft* of Germany in the decades on either side of the turn to the twentieth century (Gooding-Williams 2009, 19–66, esp. 37, 47–49; Clarke 2015). In any case, in his conception, it would concern the social problems of any society, in a comparative horizon on a worldwide basis, and encode a commitment to bring forth reform for the benefit or uplift of all (Du Bois 1897d, 1897e, 1898c, 2015i, 2015b, 2015i). It recalls Du Bois's statement, in his principal early essay "The Conservation of Races," that any judgment of the status and value of an African American *historial* articulation must accord with the "constitution of the world" (CR 5, 8, paras. 3, 9). Likewise, it projects a conceptualization of human social being as historical (perhaps as part of an evolutionary process but not a predetermined one, in any sense), and this would specifically take its concern from an orientation to think matters African American in the frame of human sociality as a kind of whole. Du Bois's analytical understanding of his problematic can be remarked in its distinction with regard to the subsequent itinerary of the concept of culture within the human sciences as it was contested and promulgated across the twentieth century. Whereas the dominant sense of this conceptualization, of "culture," if taken as a viable premise, approached it as if a thing, accomplished, that ought be understood as such and then analyzed (understood by practices of interpretation), in this essay Du Bois's thought of "a people" would include the past in its concern; however, in order to account for the African American situation, his order of attention and criteria of assessment turn on the basis of an approach that seeks an understanding of that which is yet to come. Hence, his concern is not so much a critique of the past as it is a commitment to the future. He wishes to wrest from knowledge some theoretical anticipation in thought as to the futural demands of existence for such a group. We may further specify this matter. Nor would it be that for him the limits of the past could serve as criteria for ascertaining the terms of the future. Finally, his sense of futurity would not maintain the future as something immemorial that might be retrieved or projected into a future. Rather, his attention in this essay is toward that which is not yet (and could in all truth remain unrealized and, on the terms of any given present, unrealizable). All just might be at stake in the future of "a people."

With regard to the determination and judgment as to how "a people" ought to function, at least as idea, that is to say, the putatively general terms according to which one may understand the "development" of "a people" (general, even if not so explicitly declared by Du Bois as universal), that of seeking to know what is necessary to enable a kind of liberty, freedom from necessity—for this one can outline an evolutionary process (in the mundane sense). The process can be thought of as "steps": from a concern with physical reproduction, "subsistence," through maintenance, to "accumulation," and to the priority of learning in conjunction with a decisive commitment to "train the young into the tradition," to an eventual and possible preeminent and privileged freedom to engage in the imaginary and symbolic production of values. The dimension that constitutes the epitome of such traditionalization for Du Bois is the "spiritual," that is to say, "the transference and sifting and accumulation of the elements of human culture which makes for wider civilization and higher development" (Development 295–96, paras. 10–11).

A narrative is at the theoretical center of the text. He describes the constitution of the Negro American, or even the African American, as historical, a development, a duration marked by events, that can be specified, named, and remarked, which he will do in this essay. It entails a broad historicity. It is an account of the production of modern international systems of enslavement, from the trade in Africans across the Atlantic basin from 1441–42 to 1883 and the organized practice or emplacement of systems of coerced labor throughout the region of the planet soon called as the "Americas" and the "Caribbean." The historiographical core of this narrative is a conceptualization of the modern historical epoch as a whole. As such, modern systems of enslavement produced in and as the Atlantic basin— from Luanda (organized in the sixteenth century) on the southwestern coast of the continent of Africa; to the islands off the southernmost coast of the continent now thought of as "South America"; to the bays of the area that has come to be known, within this geographic system, as Nova Scotia; to the Scandinavian region; on, through the British isles, and the continental regions of the peninsula now known as western Europe; to the domains of the Mediterranean—were entailed as the threshold and determinant level in modern commercialism, in all of its diversity and depth, as the inception of modern imperialism, modern colonialism, and the world-historical efflorescence of capitalism as an integrated system of economic organization (Development 298–304, paras. 17–29). For Du Bois, for some quarter of a millennium, the most distinctive form of exploitation and economic accumulation within the domains that we came to think of as world-historical in the modern period derived from modern systems of enslavement across this basin, what he describes in this essay as rivers of "Black Gold" (Development 299, para. 17).[32]

The commercial imperative remarked in this narrative may be given theoretical amplification. We now know that at this early modern juncture, a considerable amount of the gold in circulation in what is now western Europe derived from the goldfields of Africa—already from Kush-Nubia in the ancient period and then, in the early modern period of the thirteenth through fifteenth centuries, including both the empires of Ghana and Mali in the west, on the edge of the Sahara, and as well the gold trade centered in the early modern kingdom of Zimbabwe, within the southeastern region of the continent. Hence, although many Europeans already had gold as a guiding fantasy within their diverse forms of imagination of the African continent, the Portuguese upon the purchase on the northern west coast of Africa and resale at Lisbon of a group of some thirty-five persons, whom we now describe as "African," such as Du Bois describes it in this essay, when a bit of gold dust entered the exchange of the explorers along the coast of Africa out of Portugal, the general historical extension and elaboration of such an idea was rendered practically commercial and thus became something more than what had been as primarily a mercantile or imperial venture (Robinson 2000a [1983]). Thus, in terms of Du Bois's thought, it may not be wont to take the date 1441–42 as a theoretical metaphor, given in narrative, for Du Bois's thought of early modern historicity, in which modern enslavement stands neither inside nor outside of modern imperial colonialism, of a supposed European world economy, of what in contemporary understanding is often taken as the inception of capitalism as a system, of all that we have come to think of as modernity as a global or planetwide horizon (Development 299, 17).[33]

Although not declared by Du Bois, the first order of thetic statement that one might take from his narration—with Du Bois's conceptualization of the developmental processes entailed in the making of "a people"—is that the eventuality that he describes produced in simultaneous and reciprocal manner a kind of "freedom" for those promulgating the enslavement and a kind of forced "subsistence" of un-freedom or inextricable determination by necessity, by way of coercion, for those who were inscribed into such systems as enslaved (Development 298–304, paras. 17–29).

It was this eventuality that yielded the world-historical order of the time of Du Bois's writing, most precisely as one would see it in the southern Virginia town of Du Bois's example in "The Development of a People"—perhaps it is the example of Farmville, studied by him in 1897 to which I made reference earlier in the discussion of Du Bois's 1894 essay "The Afro-American" (Du Bois 1897a[?], 1898a, 1894a[?], 2015a).

As a secondary-order thesis but a thetic corollary to the first, Du Bois proposed that this inscription induced a double "revolution" that led to the outcome in the southern town of his example. The first was the destruction of a context that he describes as African, of supposed primordial and immemorial *historial* linkages, bonds, and ideals, for those persons who would come to be known as African American. An outcome and eventuality of this revolution was then the system of extreme mundane violence enforced as servitude. (Although he does so here without naming the matter of its direct role in the historical constitution of "Europe," he will do so elsewhere.) Likewise, Du Bois would throughout his itinerary annotate the matter of the impact of this "revolution" for the continent of Africa itself. Such notations may be found, for example, as principal terms of the essay "The African Roots of War" and the book *The Negro*, each of 1915, and *The World and Africa: An Inquiry into the Part Which Africa Has Played in World History*, of 1947 (Du Bois 1915b, 1915a, 1947). The second "revolution" was a result of emancipation, which yielded another destruction of bond and premise, in the sense that the historical world in terms of which the now formerly legally enslaved had constructed symbolic horizons of some integrity, of values and ideals of living, even otherwise, or despite, the existential basis of the determinations of this variegated symbolic order, was no longer extant; it was no longer emplaced. Another displacement was the order of this new historicity. The yield in Du Bois's historical present was the production of "degradation and uncleanliness"—according to centuries-long systems of social and political terror and domination and economic exploitation (Development 304–10, paras. 30–47).

As a theoretical premise, we are justified to suggest that, given this persistence of a sense of world for African Americans (as we might ourselves name them in our own moment) despite or even within the historical experience of degradation, Du Bois would insist on an "infinite gradation" of patterns of habitation among the people so configured by history, from low to high. The high perhaps might best be thought of not so much as a simple exception to this historicity but as an expression thereof, from this historicity. There is nowhere in Du Bois's thought the suggestion that such a group might have some preternatural dispensation. The matter might best be thought of in terms of the nineteenth-century discourses of duty—of obligation that is given, decided always already, within tradition. (It might be understood as something otherwise than a choice, for the latter, choice, would be given as a matter of individual decision and responsibility.) In this sense, in such a situation, "leaders" must supply "ideals." For Du Bois, in this essay, they must simultaneously make up for the twofold destruction of the past, as well as for that from the past that ought to be adjudged as not worthy of passage to coming generations. In his schema, they ought to be the primary source: for setting "the tone to that all-powerful spiritual world that surrounds and envelopes the souls of men; their standards of living, their interpretation of sunshine and rain and human hearts, their thoughts of love and labor, their aspirations of dim imaginings—all that makes life *life*" (Development 306–7, para. 35).

The essay's explicit theme, apparently dominant, yields in the main a narrative of the imposition of limit. It yet remains that the primary and motivating concern of the essay (its *incipit*), its guiding orientation, the object of its thought, is to adduce the distinct possibility (in both conception and action) of the reconstruction of the potential and actual experience of the lives of the progeny of the Africans enslaved in the New World since the fifteenth century. The concern is to ascertain the potential for the construction by them and by way of them of a more generous and truly new sense of world—a future—that is still yet to come. Such would be a world that in its arrival could become a generative sense of further possible worlds, perhaps all that could yet be imagined, in its gift.

It may now be understood that for Du Bois, in this essay, all is *istoria*— there is history; or all is historical; or all knowledge is or must be historiographical. Which is to say with philosophy as science, of an understanding which modern philosophy (perhaps since the critical project of the European Enlightenment, especially during the twentieth century) has sought to claim as its own, all is *historial*—of duration, indefinite, perhaps illimitable. Herein, put in apparently simple terms, there are three primary temporalities of *istoria* for Du Bois: past, present, future. Of those three, the most decisive is the futural aspect, that is, with regard to the temporality that attends to "a people." This is also, then, to say that "a people" is a temporal reference; that is to say, the key matter is the group's relation to the future. Said another way, still, their relation to that which is not yet, has not yet been, remains yet to come, becoming; this is the decisive matter for thought and action. This aspect of temporality, precisely as the terms of *istoria* for Du Bois, can be affirmed as—in principle—illimitable. It cannot be limited by prejudgment or predetermination. If telos, it remains open. This we can think of in contemporary thought as a delimitation within and of the thought of Du Bois with regard to his sense of an African American collectivity.[34]

Setting the thetic mark of the essay, its thought, by resounding the lower registers of *The Souls of Black Folk: Essays and Sketches*, a perennial disposition on his part, as its central tonal register, Du Bois proposes the theoretical reception of a twofold initiative for a figure that might too easily be taken in thought as *ahistorial*. One is the historiographical recognition of the decisive or originary constitutive status of the "Negro"—even as enslaved—in the making of the modern world. The other is a theoretical imagination of the illimitable possibility that may be understood as encoded as the enslaved. For Du Bois, in this essay, in turn, this latter possibility goes under two subheadings, leadership and learning. In this dimension of the text, a submerged generic order of the text, as also a form of appeal or petition to the conscience of the enlightened, might be adduced.[35] What can be rendered which has not yet been but could in being rendered become available for existence? "Development" would be something that can be cultivated, that is to say, made; something that is an expression, if you will, of a process or a practice, in the plural. The project of the essay is to conceptualize or outline a way. While this essay itself does not provide so much of an elaborated specification of the character of the sense of possibility that could become legible, this theoretical reticence or forbearing may perhaps be understood as felicitous. For it is the insistence on possibility itself in this essay, on the futurity of possibility, that remains decisive for thought in our own time, in our contemporary time, astride the second generation, if you will, of the twenty-first century. This whole way of thinking, Du Bois's, is then somewhat different from what has now become a traditionalized conception of culture, via the human sciences, and now a generalized cultural studies (wherein culture is too easily understood as if a thing already fulsome in its emergence and duration, which may be codified, more or less, and analyzed). The matter at stake in Du Bois's thought, although his approach certainly includes such a project, ought still be available for thought in our own century as radically otherwise than such an itinerary. For all remains at stake.

1. FIRST NOTATION. According to the trajectory of this affirmation—already nascent in 1894—across the opening years of the new century Du Bois would propose the figure of the African American (in fact under diverse names) as the principal metaphor for this opening, that is to say a new *sense of world* in general that emerges as modern historicity. This epistemological temporality, if you will, of the coming of the new century in thought for Du Bois, should assume our attention even if we recall that the autobiographical sense of this metaphor was already legible in Du Bois's reflections in Berlin in the winter of 1893, on the occasion of his twenty-fifth birthday (Du Bois 1893). More simply, yet emphatically, it may be said that while remarked everywhere in Du Bois's discourse of the turn of the century, the conception was realized in its quintessential articulation in the thought and writing gathered in the text of *The Souls of Black Folk: Essays and Sketches* of early 1903 and then also articulated in the handful of texts that followed almost immediately in its wake, as it were, within the next eighteen to twenty-four months. Certainly these texts include the famous essay under the title "The Talented Tenth" (Du Bois 1903n, 2015m). Likewise, we ought to include here the incisive and prescient theoretical text under the heading "Sociology Hesitant," likely prepared in late 1904 or early 1905, even though it was published posthumously, approximate to a century after its composition (Du Bois 1980i, 1905?, 2015i, 2000b). So, too, ought we place here the writing (done in English in its original) gathered by Du Bois in early 1905 and published in 1906 in a German translation (with the translator not attributed) by Max Weber, and translated back into English as a kind of whole, in the manner that Du Bois apparently conceived it for a European intellectual audience, with suitable annotation, only a century after its original publication (Du Bois 1906b, 2006, 2015f; Chandler 2006b, 2007). However, this conceptual eventuality in Du Bois's thought is especially marked by our essay "The Development of a People," issued in early 1904 (Du Bois 1904, 1982d, 2015d).[36]

2. SECOND NOTATION. Yet, after the epistemic maturation across the second half of the nineteenth century of a general discourse and thought

of human societal development in Europe and America, Du Bois's early twentieth-century concern with the "development of a people" under the heading of the Afro- or African-American could appear to some as anachronistic, not to gainsay perspectives or standpoints contemporaneous to the time of our present discussion, astride the opening quarter of this so-called twenty-first century.

Yet, in this still new century, our own, the pertinence of the question that is proposed in Du Bois's 1904 essay under that title is somewhat more radical now than at the time of its first enunciation. For the question—of the relation of the so-called darker world of peoples, supposed as underdeveloped, to the so-called lighter peoples of the world, supposed as more civilized in some expansive sense of this latter term—has become existential on a planetwide scale of reference.

The question of that larger frame is "the problem of the color line," as Du Bois formulated it (a matter that is elaborated as part II of this study).

That is to say, with regard to its enunciation in his discourse, the relation of the "darker" to the "lighter" peoples, of the world, known in the thought of the eighteenth and nineteenth centuries in Europe and America as "nations" and then as "races." Now, since the early twentieth century, in genteel company, with regard to such geographic contexts, one might reference "cultures." It has now become polite, in the twenty-first century, to no longer admit this question, at least not in an open manner, or in explicit terms. Yet it remains afoot.

For this old, worn-out question, which was previously understood by many who have at the times in question been emboldened by their own access to hegemonic forms of power (both within and among localized domains, that is to say, so-called nations and states, yet also on a worldwide scale of a common scene) as *their* problem, a problem for those folks over there, has returned. One might have once put it as a problem of the so-called darker peoples, or, less astutely, as a problem for colonized folks, or as an issue for those who have in the past been colonized. Yet, the question has returned, alas, astride the twenty-first century, in a newly existential manner, at once concrete and specific *and* apparently universal, planetary, in scale and implication.

If in the moment of Du Bois's writing one could imagine that what was at stake pertained to those "darker" peoples by way of the initiative and the actions of those "lighter" peoples, now, in our own time, the very future of the whole of the world, so to speak, is at stake by way of the very forms of the new ways (even if proclaimed as of ancient, or even archaic, lineage) of becoming as such, the coming-to-be of peoples, that is of the so-called darker peoples of the world.

If it was once thought, in part by way of certain aspects of Du Bois's discourse as well, that the African American must accede to the hospitality of the world (and thereby become properly civilized), now, under the heading for thought that we develop from the *assay* of Du Bois (to stake the metaphor), the whole of the world is becoming, or rather has become, African American. It is no longer, if it has ever been, a question of the becoming of *a* people; it is, rather, a matter of understanding the way in which a supposed "people" have become such, which is to say, most precisely, the being at stake as such.

At this juncture in our inhabitation of his thinking, we can note that the center weight of the essay "The Development of a People," apart from any expectation, is not in its declaration of premise (although the merits of his formulation, as noted above, are more general than some might suppose), nor is it in its statement of judgments and propositions, however telling they were at the time of the essay's original publication and, indeed, notwithstanding its striking continued relevance after almost a century and a quarter, in the passage of time. For, indeed, contemporary thought in general commonly finds a suitable conceit that can allow it to either step aside from the question of "what was slavery and the slave trade" (Development 304, para. 29) or thoroughly assimilate the answer to that question to an assumed or affirmed already given, accepted account of modern historicity, in which the history of modern systems of enslavement is treated as a derivative expression of a more general and fundamental order of social process.

The decisive presumption, that is the theoretical bearing, of the essay is indeed in its brief narrative.

The pivotal terms of this narrative and the essay may now be understood as expressed in one sentence: "The African slave trade was the child of the Renaissance" (Development 299, para. 17).

In this analysis, Du Bois may be understood to adumbrate, but declare with lucidity, a turnkey historiographical perspective.

For there were, we might propose, in fact two "renaissances" in early modern Europe (if in fact we are to assume there were any). One of them was humanistic and is justly closely and widely regarded. The other was scientific; its bearing was practical, most distinctively given in its technology. For Du Bois, it is the latter that ought to be understood by contemporary thought. And of this latter sense of renaissance, while it is most certain that he is noting and affirming, profoundly, the principled commitment to inquiry, the idea and practice of science, of philosophy in, of, and as science, in all of such ancient initiatives of the Mediterranean, and including its conduit into the modern period by way of the Arabic and African (notably Islamic, as well as Christian) learned world, indeed including its recollection in the early periods of the modern epoch, it is notably its technical eventualities that Du Bois may be understood to index with this insight.

Likewise, from this same perspective, we may note two pivotal technologies that operated within this historicity as arising in the context of the Sinophone sphere of world. This is to remark both the compass, a measure of divination for centuries before its full deployment for navigation in the eleventh century CE, during the Song dynasty, and gunpowder, developed during the Tang dynasty of the ninth century CE. Along with certain technologies for shipbuilding and maritime habitation, they were turning points in the Portuguese project, more than a quarter of a millennium in duration by the 1440s, to find their way by ocean, down the west coast of the African continent, and eventually to India, and to the eastern coastal regions of the Indian Ocean, to China, Korea, and Japan in the "East" (Lach 1965b).[37] If, then, the modern systems of enslavement are decisively rendered in part by way of the ascription of ancient learning in a modernizing Europe and the conscription to a military sense of purpose of foreign-born technologies (of the so-called East), and if in turn the history of such incipient enslavement produced in part the historical problematization, in its turn, of the terms of the *historial* emergence of a possible collective of persons under the heading "African American," then it is indeed a history and our understanding of it that is most at stake for thought and action, both then (at the turn to the twentieth century) and now (at our own moment amid the early decades of the twenty-first century).

There are, then, four senses of revolution at stake herein: three senses of the past and one of the present-future. With all the presumptions of modern histories of what is known as Europe, the western peninsula of a greater Asia was radically revolutionized in its being and possibility in the early modern period, by way of incipient processes that were not so much defined or determined by the horizons of its indigeneity or natality. It was neither primordial nor preternatural in its emergence or maintenance. Likewise, a certain incursion of such revolutionizing was rendered afoot on the African continent, initially through its corridors of exchange that took shape along the western coastal regions but most precisely as what in a paradoxical sense might be understood as ostensible modernization, throughout the continent, including its southern and eastern shores and the hinterlands thereof. Yet, too, the very modalities of trade, the general exchange of knowledge, and the senses of historical time, place, and imagination may also be considered to mark out a sense of revolution (even if tertiary, according to an analysis of some kind, a certain form of judgment). That is to say that in this third sense of revolution, modernity is marked, if you will, by the distinctive doubled inhabitation of all that is Africa and Europe. To tell of this history, as does Du Bois in the course of his narrative of modern enslavement, is to speak of the mutually agonistic constitution of all that is Europe and all that is Africa, in the modern world.

Taking its mark from this latter sense of revolution, the violence that Du Bois remarks in this essay as the destruction of "African" ideals (not tout court, even if he does not specify the matter here) is a fourth sense of the manner in which he speaks of revolution in his brief narrative. Emancipation was a "second" break, a "partial breaking with the past," as Du Bois conceptualized it. The double destruction, from an originary African domain and then from the contexts (at once geographic and temporal in specification) of centuries of formal systems of enslavement, gave shape to a distinctive problematization: leadership for a group whose conditions of emergence are such that they cannot simply accept present or extant "standards" for living. Rather, they must "make up" for the destructions and losses of the past. Rather than anything reducible to compensatory work, it is a solicitation to the possible terms of a genesis, or geneses, that is, originary production of the highest values, ideals, perhaps at least novel in their dispensation, if not entirely new. A demand for a revolutionary production of values, of ideals, issues in terms that are at once *historial* (in its reference to the collective) and *existential*: the world of what might be African American, of "a people" known as such, arises from the capacity of such a group (with a mark set by "leaders," of which he gives a nominalization of the moment) to respond to the present and whatever might be yet to come, by whatever resources may be at hand or can be cultivated. Without any declaration, the implication of his statement in the latter stages of his essay of 1904 is that African Americans ought to be led to revolutionize this second break, or second sense of a historic revolution, that is upon them. As such, the African American situation is given in and as history.

For Du Bois, the telling of their story is positioned as a demand for the ethical enlightened. Yet, too, in its deeper registers, I am wont to suggest, it may pose or propose an exemplary example of possibility, in the future (of the turn to the twentieth century). At the penultimate moment of the closing chapter of *The Souls of Black Folk: Essays and Sketches*, Du Bois notes three gifts brought to the horizon of America by Africans and their descendants in this new context of world: the gift of "sweat," the brawn of labor, mental (of care) as much as physical, for centuries; the gift of "song," the cultivation of arts, of making a way out of no way (in the proverbial African American phrase), of which all that is art may be named; and then the gift of "spirit," that is to say, of hope and capacity to believe in the future (Du Bois 1903k). There, as I noted earlier in our discussion of "The Afro-American," that is at the end of *The Souls of Black Folk: Essays and Sketches*, Du Bois offers a metaphor, or, better, a concept metaphor, for nominalizing this process. African Americans are the "warp and woof of all that is or has been the making of America" (Du Bois 1903k). (Du Bois's text has a common or colloquial form of the word, that is woof, where the word "weft" is perhaps more in use in our own time.) Amid the ongoing systems that would produce only ignorance and degradation, for Du Bois, the Negro or African American is already afoot in the production of the terms of a new, perhaps ongoing, revolution of values, of habitation, and of imagination of the future.

This lesson, if understood according to the imperatives of the example, as theoretical resource or provocation, is worldwide. It is "global." And yet its full implication is still yet to come. For the sense of "development" at stake in Du Bois's text is a conception of African American historicity, or, better, historicity in general, that is not so much turned to attend what has gone by, or what is given, but toward the very possibility of the remaking of the very sense of the world, the very origin, or, better, genesis, of world, of the sense of *the* world, perhaps the generation of another world, as it were, of a new world.

With this understanding, the question concerns the making of all that is, or may be, all that we may articulate by way of time, which is also to say, already and first as it were, as space. It is not, nor can it be, simply, given. By way of this reference in thought, to Du Bois's specific essay, the concept metaphor of the existential horror that has been understood under the heading of the "middle passage" (or perhaps one may recall the euphemism "the hold of the slave ship"), as one might index it, of persons that will have been enslaved, is perhaps or potentially radical for *only* a time. For what remains at stake and beyond such a "narrow Now" is the possibility of a commitment to become—that is to say, to give, to enable, to allow hospitality, or to receive, to accept or affirm the passive in generation. In a *historial* sense, it is to affirm passage, the ways of passage, not only within but "beyond this narrow Now." This is the thought that I propose to continue to track and elaborate in the path of thinking of Du Bois at the time of the turn to the twentieth century, notably in the discourse of 1904 as given in our essay, "The Development of a People."

3. **THIRD NOTATION.** It may be understood then, that in this essay, Du Bois provides a historical account, marked by its distinct and specific character, of the present situation of the African American in 1904. In so doing, he would not abide the hegemonic representation, which might present the Negro simply, as abject, a sense that is even now, still, too often given and taken as a normal account of matters. In order to do otherwise Du Bois proposes an intervention among the conceptions at the root of the common narratives of modern history as a whole.

Whereas, in his accounts of the mid-1890s, 1894 or 1895, he may have posed his discourse as a narrative of moral failure, on the part of Europe and the colonists in the Americas, with an indictment thereof, his account abreast the middle of the first decade of the new century is one that accents and annotates the eventualities that are produced by willful, motivated, and antagonistic judgments and actions, which are in turn susceptible to assessment by a certain disposition and judgment (which of necessity is reflexive, or self-critical). Such antagonistic production in turn produces concomitant effects, social and historical (even if also theological), that will eventually issue as an entire historicity, or a fundamental and general dimension thereof, that is, of a historical epoch. Yet from this self-reflexive thought and critical perspective comes a reconceptualization of modern historicity in a general sense.

For even if in 1904 Du Bois attunes this historiographical sense to the frequency of eventualities, with this thought he enters a dimension that is not circumscribed by the event of enslavement nor the operations of emancipation, but one that sustains a frequency that encodes the *futural* sense of such eventualities, including a sense that might be beyond, or otherwise than, even the legible mark of such futurity. It is a thought of the centuries, we might say, the *futural* sense of the twentieth century, or of the twenty-first century (even if it is the so-called Asian century), that may be understood here, that is to say, a thought of the possibilities of a sense that has not yet been, and thus remains (Adelson 2017). Du Bois's purpose, as it were, is then both to propose the possibility of human action and to do so by way of a critical philosophical, as well as historiographical, operation of judgment, that is, the use of reason, the practice of supposed rational inquiry, a form of critical self-reflection upon the conditions of existence and knowing, expressed as the practice of science. He proposes this basis for action among the Negro American and among the supposed "friends" (who are in the main referenced in an unspoken, undefined manner and thus are not enumerated).

In providing this account, even though he does not declare it as a scientific contribution in itself, we may not be on the wrong foot to suggest that nonetheless Du Bois presents the perspective that he adduces as a contribution to understanding, in a political sense. It may be understood as an effort toward good social relations, a beneficence of knowledge that is rooted in the practice of scholarship and research—motivated by an effort to make critical sense of the world of the late nineteenth century and the century to come, that is the twentieth. Quite specific to Du Bois's enunciation is his own previous work in scholarship: the research for his doctoral dissertation project, from 1892 or so, and its final textual encoding, as presented for the degree in 1895 and then published in 1896 as *The Suppression of the African Slave-Trade to the United States of America, 1638–1870* (Du Bois 1896, 1973h). By the time of the preparation of the discourse of "The Development of a People," Du Bois has been at work, thinking through the historicity that he offers as the concern of its core narrative for something on the order of a decade or more. In his essay, we are receiving knowledge by way of Du Bois's emplacement, at the time of his writing, at the leading edge of scholarship on this dimension of modern historicity.

4. **FOURTH NOTATION.** This order of question was adduced by Du Bois in the opening stages of his essay "The Conservation of Races," already, as it were, from early on in 1897. That is to say, everyday political and social and economic matters—such as "questions of separate schools and cars, wage-discrimination and lynch law" while always potentially decisive in the existential instance, remain overdetermined and may not in and of themselves, simply and discretely on their own terms, be of general implication or determination for thought and, eventually, for action. In Du Bois's formulation, the matter must be approached on a higher (or more fundamental) order of understanding. As he writes in paragraph 3 of the essay, one must "survey the whole question of race in human philosophy." He then specified it according to two reciprocal formulations: "the hard limits of natural law" and the "constitution of the world" (CR 5, para. 3). Du Bois then proceeded, from the very next paragraph in "The

Conservation of Races," to pose a philosophical questioning of the concept of race that one might suppose could be inscribed into any project of a science of race, the object of which would be understood as simply and directly given in nature (or, its reciprocal opposite, the categorical disavowal of the ostensible social and historical implication of forms of natural difference as such). There, in an incipient moment for his intellectual practice, Du Bois offers a critical epistemological judgment with regard to any form of knowledge as science that would presume the possibility of a natural science of race: "that the grosser physical differences of color, hair and bone go but a short way toward explaining the different roles which groups of men have played in Human Progress" (CR 6–7, para. 5). The disposition of Du Bois's questioning in early 1897 was notably one that would seek a guide for judgment in "philosophy." From, or within, "philosophy," as he names it there, such an inclination would seek to understand and follow the "natural law" that could be known by way of its practices and the accumulation of knowledge that might be configured thereby. This disposition to philosophy may be understood even more precisely as the practice of philosophy-as-science, that is to say, the operations of a subject that would seek to understand, or come to know, an object, in some fundamental sense of its character or existence. In this case, it is a sort of being that would seek to know (as a kind of subject) something of itself (as object). That reciprocal subject and object is most precisely the human, understood as a whole in common, as a form of being. One should address the matter in terms of "human philosophy," or, as I would specify it with other words: a philosophical understanding of the human. While the referential index to values remains (the disposition that is dominant in the 1894 essay "The Afro-American," or in the writing of 1895–96 in his doctoral dissertation), above all to values as ideals, the highest form of values, as Du Bois understood such, most especially all that one might consider as morals, forms of morality, in the 1897 text another order of reference for judgment has become articulate within Du Bois's thought. That additional manner of reckoning, now ascendant in Du Bois's articulations, is the bequest of philosophy, understood and practiced as science, in the general sense of knowledge, here interpretive and historiographical.

Seven years later, early on in 1904, in the wake of the gathering, under the heading of *The Souls of Black Folk: Essays and Sketches,* a sheaf of the essays that he had cultivated from early 1897, just past a decade following his return to the United States from study in Europe, taking the statement of problem and the terms of elucidation in that book as a fundamental reference (for which the essay "The Afro-American" of 1894, which we have retrieved and marked in this study, may now be understood as an emergent, preliminary, as yet compressed *essay*), Du Bois staged anew the question of the historial status of the African American, the Negro in America, the distinct place of the so-called Negro in the context of modern world history as a whole.

5. A PENUMBRA. It may now be indicated in what sense that restaging took place in the concise form of the text "The Development of a People" (Du Bois 1904, 2015d).

For to the extent that it unfolded in the wake of the completion and reception of *The Souls of Black Folk: Essays and Sketches* in 1903, "The Development of a People" may stand not only as an extension of the guiding problem of the very early forms of thought encoded in the unpublished text "The Afro-American," which as we have seen had already posed the problem of leadership and the construction of ideals for a social group, but also and most poignantly as an elaboration *of*—in both senses, from and about—the book *The Souls of Black Folk: Essays and Sketches*. For the conception of the 1904 essay deployed the book's problematic on the scale of a multiply constructed presentation of an entire social field, African American, American, and otherwise; this latter notation is to say that such a domain, the social field in question, may be understood as also hemispheric and worldwide in reference. Likewise, if the "Afro-American" essay marked out Du Bois's initiating concern to place matters African American within the maelstrom of any conceptualization of the American project, then "The Development of a People" as a statement of theoretical concern produces another horizon of reference, the epoch as a whole on a planetwide scale of reference as the genetic possibility of that supposed incipit of world. The referential question of the latter essay concerns the arena of comparison of all times and all places of the world, or the "world of worlds" since the fifteenth century of what we may consider today the common era.

It therefore may be understood as apposite that the essay had a more-than-decade-long penumbral gathering and opening within Du Bois's writing, that is, the scriptural record of his intellectual maturation. Of this itinerary, as already remarked, we may summarize the question posed in the essay of our concern here as already open within the text of the effort that is "The Afro-American" of 1894; as decisively inflected into the philosophical organization of matters of historicity, by way of the concept of race, in "The Conservation of Races" of 1897; emplaced within a willful historiographical articulation and a nascent sociological horizon of indices in the closing of *The Philadelphia Negro: A Social Study* of 1899, and the essay "The Present Outlook for the Dark Races of Mankind" of 1900; and then, too, as brought to a visionary, even prophetic, political-theological clarity, yet as a legible inscription, in the essays gathered as *The Souls of Black Folk: Essays and Sketches*, this latter a text completed in its textual suturing from September 1902 to April 1903 (even as the writing therein dates from across the whole of the previous seven years). Our essay of focus, "The Development of a People," of early 1904, is thus the culmination of a tendentious global-level vision of the making of a supposed "New World," pertaining to the entire modern epoch, modern in a sense that might be inclusive of almost all the diverse notions of such contemporaneity.

6. FURTHER PROBLEMATIZATION. In our essay of focus, Du Bois may be understood to assume the kind of radical bearing for thought, a pertinence that I propose is at once epistemological in general and theoretical in its specific implication, of the questioning and understanding that he had formulated in "The Conservation of Races" of 1897 as also the domain of concern in his inquiry here, in 1904. (As I noted earlier in this study and have elaborated elsewhere, in the 1897 text Du Bois formulated the thought that the general possibility of "intermingling" of form or attribute rendered incoherent any conception of difference among humans in bodily form or natural attribute as an unfailing expression of the essential capacity and limit of a form of being as human [CR 5, para. 4; Chandler forthcoming]). In 1904, however, the matter is staged as *historial*—here understood more in the sense of the actual, the historiographical, than the possible, the virtual—rather than as a matter of morals. It is now not so much a speculative commitment that leads Du Bois's thetic practice. Rather, it is now an attention to the given, the supposed empirical organization of matters, then or now, that is to say, the eventual (the sense of which may be noted as that which has happened or may still be happening, forms of the *futural* pertinence of which may still be yet to come). The idiomatic register given at this juncture is still philosophical (or in a sense postphilosophical, proceeding always in light of that tradition of thinking but otherwise and putatively beyond it). Yet, now, it is no longer speculative in its attention but attuned to eventuality, the legibility or even *leitmotif* of events, and of their telling, in their utterly irreversible, yet exemplary, singularity. Indeed, to describe it in more general terms, I propose that it is *historial*, of or about

the very possibility of the making of sense, as historicity. In this sense, its tonal center, so to speak, its rhetorical register, is historiographic (more representational than expressive): at once nascent and schematic, yet distinctly authoritative in the concatenation of its locution, the syntax of its delivery, in what it yields for practices of inquiry and knowledge. That is also to say that the author of the essay—even though the text has the register of an appeal or petition—may be understood to insist, by presuming its value, on a commitment to the exemplary practice of a science, herein in terms of the accumulation of knowledge, less in terms of fact (for such is not contested or allowed to become the terms of contest, for example, between writer and reader, perhaps) than in terms of an inhabitation and setting forth of a certain learning; and only as such, by way of this presumptive reference of understanding, may one understand matters as then of or related to an articulation of facts, or a factum, of knowledge.

Two annotations may be useful here, one national-local in reference, the other global-level in indication.

Within the story of all that may be thought as national-local, as "America" in project, the essay carries out its work by elaborating the *historial* question that may be analytically emplaced at the heart of *The Souls of Black Folk: Essays and Sketches*, traversing hard-won access paths to terrain that might belie its marks of historical possibility and limit that are layered within its apparently recessed but heavily impacted deeper sedimentations, even finding ways in the discourse of this specific essay, just as he had done in that book of essays, to theoretically limn—in metaphor and apostrophe—perhaps of fragments, broken inscriptions, the cryptic apparent resonance of rasps of *asonic* whispers and wails, as well as the telling forms of silence, that may be gathered, or scattered, thereby, according to these otherwise than dormant (even if not so present) modes of habitation, past and *futural*, perhaps, at once (Du Bois 1903n, 2015m).

Too, while in the planetwide horizon of our story, the place of Asia and Africa, so too a certain Europe, are geographically of nodal moment and location for reckoning the emergence of the epoch, it is the inception of a historial entity—which Du Bois places herein under the heading of "a people"—through and beyond systems of enslavement contemporaneous to the eventuality that concerns us and their aftermath that is at stake for our understanding. Further, while the Americas—the erstwhile misnamed New World—are the geo-locus of his directed attention, or tendentious theoretical intention, the matter at stake in all truth concerns the possibility and implication of the emergence of an originary historical configuration, in principle and in general. The problematization, the problem for thought, that sets loose the formulation of question that articulates in the form of our essay is the contemporary status of the so-called Negro American in the context of the American world and the turn to the twentieth-century world, this latter on both a hemispheric and planetwide scale of reference.

Du Bois proposes a context—which I note, simply, as epistemic and theoretical, in the general senses of these terms—for adjudicating this status. In this essay, it is not so much a determination of just what is the situation, as it were (a matter that is a central overall concern of his study, a sociology of African Americans, and America, during the decades framing the turn of the century); rather, the question is how to explain and alter, to improve, radically if possible, the conditions of those understood as African American and the whole question of the Negro in and for America in general.

This question arises within the general historicity of the centuries-long, nay, half-millennium-long, eventuality that, in its effects, rendered a configuration of social being, a kind of sociological entity, if you will, even into the present of the writing of the text, of early 1904, just after the turn to the new century, at the beginning of the twentieth century. That is to say, Du Bois adduces a privileged historical or eventual horizon that he proposes must be gathered and rendered available for thought in order to assess the standing of his guiding example, this new historial being—presumptively and tendentiously understood as Negro-or-Afro-or-African-or-Colored-American (Development 298–304, paras. 17–28). That horizon is the institution and promulgation of systems of enslavement that articulated forms of relation—in virtually all senses of this notion, from theological, to political, to economic, to aesthetic, to technological, to philosophical—that were new in the denouement and the aftermath of the ancient Roman Empire. The key, then, is the abiding clarification offered in the essay of the status of enslavement in the historicity of the epoch. Notably, for Du Bois, the horizon acquired originary articulation only in the wake of the so-called Renaissance in the region of the world that will come to be known as Europe (Development 299, para. 17). Marked in terms that reference the Christian calendar, no matter its intention to articulate a common era, the temporal indication for the time in question is the duration astride the time of 1441–42, when the first persons, whom Du Bois will describe as African, from the Senegambia region of what we now consider as West Africa (captured or purchased), were sold into slavery in Lisbon, Portugal, that may be understood to articulate within modern historicity through to the time of the early 1890s, within the half dozen years following the last legal abolition of modern enslavement in the Americas (in Brazil) in 1883. While the geographic breadth of remark and interpretive comparison is worldwide, if you will, the touchstone of theoretical reference is to recognize anew the general emplacement and import of all matters considered that may be or will come to be understood as African, including its diaspora of persons (multiple and plural in almost all senses) within a planetwide ensemble of references astride the opening years of the twentieth century.

What may herein now be proposed is that in the narrative as given to us by Du Bois, the protagonists articulate less as replete, or self-possessed, or abiding, subjects, in any sense, as if sovereign, the countenance of which would provide the standard for our understanding of any historial form of being; rather, the historial reference for our story may be gathered only as the double-sided configuration of a form of problem: the relation of a certain Europe, that is, if you will, only in and by way of all that is considered as of Africa, or a certain Africa that is reannounced to the contemporary centuries in its futural or intentional apparition by way of a certain figuration *of* Europe. On the one hand, *in fact*, what is entailed is the coming to historical articulation, as such, of all of the major "trading nations" of what will come to be understood as western Europe—the Portuguese, the Spanish, the Dutch, the English. On the other hand, the *productions* that will constitute *the factum* of all that will yield the epoch that we often call modern (its articulation including not only the Americas and the Caribbean but also, notably, all that we take as Asia, from India, to Korea, Japan, and China, to Southeast Asia, and to the regions too easily remarked as Micronesia and Indonesia) take their nodal incipit in and by the productions *of* Africa (both from and about such), first of all West Africa but, in fact, the whole of the continent and more, of matters African.

The most decisive dimension of this problematization for Du Bois is that aspect of it that is our understanding—in all senses and in general. In this text, Du Bois is not so much concerned to privilege formal practices of knowledge, even as his mode of critical reflection places the status of learning as of paramount value. That is also to say that his insistence on learning and the cultivation of knowledge, in combination with his exemplification of his own learning, and then too his solicitation of his audience to claim or accede to a learning complementary with that of the writer, produces a profound historical understanding. It is an understanding that may be construed as an insistence on the fundamental pertinence of historiographical practice for leadership of all kinds, from pedagogy to politics, to practices of art (notably all that might be called aesthetic), to religious belief, for example. The essay seeks to intervene on that dimension of problematic—that is to say, how we understand the terms of the question of the Negro. Du Bois produces a distinct conception, one that may be regarded as original, of the terms of this problematization.

7. PREMISES. I suggest, in light of this problematization, that at the outset of the essay, in a theoretical sense, there is a distinct ensemble of premises (an organization of concept and analytical commitment) that Du Bois proposes. It composes a kind of epistemological reference, a certain kind of analytical presumption, or a topographical metaphor, with bearing for the mapping of the terrain that is taken as an object for analysis (Development 292–98, paras. 1–16; Du Bois 2015d).

The guiding premise is that there is for any historial being a measure of indetermination in its devolution. Considered as an object of analysis, its being may be translated as illimitable, such that it may be understood to yield possibility. Human action might thus operate such indetermination as the terms of possibility, through self-reflexive, critical, even rational thought, toward a chosen form, a practice of reformation. Such action would seek perfectibility in the human and in the organization of society in general. It may be understood as a kind of directed evolution of the being social of the human, of working together for a common good.

Then, there is a corollary premise: that the problem in question has been produced. In this sense, it is indeed historical—historial—of and by way of eventuality on the part of humans, above all in some collective sense.

Hence, as a further relative premise: the situation, as given, in a historical instance or circumstance, can be altered. A thoughtful, critical, even self-critical understanding, one that is historiographical in its references, can be realized so as to enable judgment as to what might be done to address the situation. Action can then be undertaken to change the present conditions, indeed, to seek to change society, as it were, in general. At the beginning of the twentieth century, in the schema of Du Bois's thought at this time, in terms of this essay, such action would first be that of the Negro, the Negro American. In the sense of priority only, others—the putative learned addressees of the essay—would need to admit the problematic character of past collective action and then abide by the principle of do-no-harm, or commit to a policy to remove obstacles, or the potential for such, such as themselves or the institutions of which they are the determining force, as any form of unnecessary or unjustifiable limit.

To enable the establishment of such a possibility without stepping back from any of the claim of moral value that is the abiding register of his formulations in "The Afro-American" of 1894, "The Conservation of Races" of 1897, "The Present Outlook for the Dark Races of Mankind" of 1899–1900, and the essays as gathered under the heading of *The Souls of Black Folk* of 1902–3, in "The Development of a People" of 1904, Du Bois turns to single out the authority of knowledge for the adjudication of what should be done. The actual can be understood—historiographical practice can enable self-critical understanding to bring to light, if you will, the root character, or even cause, in a theoretical sense, of the problem. If not exactly as science in the prevailing sense of the turn of the century in America, then as a practice on the order of a science, the bringing forth of analysis of a supposed actuality, taken as an empirical referent, might allow a nonsentimental, nondogmatic, and ostensibly objective use of human understanding to determine whence the problem has emerged and taken a given form. The analogy here is the nineteenth-century arrival of a biology, which determined the cause of the disease of the human body, the physical, as from a biochemical pathogenesis—not from the willfulness of a malevolent God or gods. So, too, then is the implication—undeclared though it is, at the lexical level of the text—that a sociology (suitably historiographical, perhaps) of the turn to the twentieth century might be able to determine that the dis-ease of human society (in all senses but not metaphysical) is by way of a *historial* semiosis. This latter would be the analysis of a different sort of pathogenesis, perhaps a metaphysical one, if you will, the devolution of certain kinds of morals, that is to say, immorality, incoherent ideals, or the absence or vacuity of ideals, perhaps indifferently pursued or practiced. The premise is that an understanding of the character that Du Bois's is proposing is both of and about the very "constitution" of the world, as Du Bois had put it in "The Conservation of Races" (CR 5, para. 3). In like manner, as simply the other side of the same coin, if human understanding and action thereby are not in accord with such an order, that of the general and fundamental constitution of existence and its articulation within or as historicity, human social existence will not prosper. It will wither away and die.

This disposition is practical, perhaps pragmatic; yet it amounts to the proposition of a kind of political epistemology. He seeks to stake the tenability of human social being on a combination of knowledge and leadership.

His premise entails a commitment to a philosophical ground for such inquiry. The example of biology offers an odd allegory, or allegorical presumption (for a learned intellectual class), that although unremarked as such is then construed by Du Bois as an exemplar, by a nascent catachresis, or kind of unconventional metaphor, for a sociology—theoretical in his enunciation but practical in its intention.

Perhaps the matter can stand for emphasis: that for Du Bois, the premise here is not theological. It was taken as a domain of the divine by Thomas Jefferson, in a related line of query, both in his *Notes on the State of Virginia* (astride 1785) and in his epistolary ruminations toward the end of his life (in the 1820s)—remarking the wrath of a just "creator"—on the future of the American republic configured by the conjoining of a distinctive projection of democracy to a historical system of enslavement (Jefferson 1984, 269–70; Chandler 2014c, 27).

Notable, too, is that Du Bois's perspective here ought to be understood as distinct from the kind of mistaken biological metaphor of Herbert Spencer (as Spencer put forth a supposed sociology during the latter part of the nineteenth century), even as this reference remains without declaration in the lexemes of his text. Even though the essay "The Development of a People" was produced by Du Bois almost a year before he would write what ought be a touchstone text for any consideration of his early thought, "Sociology Hesitant"—the composition of which dates to late 1904 or early 1905, responding to the massive Congress of Arts and Sciences held in St. Louis, Missouri (which was itself presented as an international scene of putative practitioners of the human sciences, which he will criticize in this response) in September and October 1904—Du Bois's perspective in the *early* 1904 essay on "the development of a people" may notably be understood as distinct from the kind of mistaken biological metaphor that Spencer had supposed.[38]

Likewise, in addition to the two distinctions that I have just annotated, in the midst of the early passages of the essay articulating his opening premises, Du Bois distinguishes his sensibility from any idea that might seek to construct an analogy of human social organization to mechanical process, a process that would be theorized as already given in its adherence to a set of rules and procedures (Development 296, para. 11).

It is human action, learned or enlightened, that would set the mark toward which Du Bois turned, that he eventually proposes should serve as both the basis and the means of the adjudication of the terms of the possible futures for "the development of a people," such as those that may be understood as African American, at the turn to the twentieth century.

8. ANNOTATIONS AND A BRIEF ELABORATION. The conceit of the narrative that Du Bois constructs in "The Development of a People" is that along with the presumptive terms of a lead narrative of the making of a putatively common modern worldwide historicity often told in Europe and the Americas that projects the rise and consolidation of practices that promulgated the ideal of the dignity of the human, I suggest that his account in this essay enables us to recognize the lineaments of the terms of another dimension of the historicity entailed. The narration gives us the thought that the modern epoch also saw the promulgation of an interwoven set of marks and practices that produced and consolidated a tendentiously novel sense of the denigration of the human. The devolution of this practical sense ought to be understood as simultaneous, perhaps coterminous in the early stages of its emergent articulation, with the development of the ideal of human dignity, within modern historicity.

A. FIRST ANNOTATION. I offer here an *epistemological* annotation.

At 1441–42, as given its historical remark in the opening third of Du Bois's essay, with regard to the terms of the historicity of thought and knowledge, the epistemic orders of general historicity (as analytically distinguished from the events or eventuality of the general social, economic, and political orders, for example), we would be wont to assume a coherent common concept of the human—a theological, philosophical, or political thought or idea—taken as a universal premise or predication, for a form of social and historical being (Development 300–301, paras. 19–21).

Taking our own mark from a thoughtful inhabitation of Du Bois's discourse (notably his writings of 1894 to 1904, for example, already in "The Afro-American," even if such reference is not given literally or in the text of our specific essay, "The Development of a People," of 1904), we are not remiss to indicate that at the historical moment of 1776–90, taken as a distinct historial reference (even if not utterly singular), an idea of such dignity of person, with all of the crooked manifestations of its birthing, had taken shape within philosophical and political discourse within the Americas, namely, the discourse of the British colonies of North America, attendant to its concomitant devolution within the diverse arenas of a nascent configuration that would begin to suppose itself under the heading of

Europe; I have annotated the discourse encoded under the name Thomas Jefferson as an example of such (Chandler 2014: 20–30; Jefferson 1999).

In terms of understanding and knowledge, matters of the episteme in a general sense, leaving it without discrete nominalization in our consideration so far, the novelty at issue here might be clarified in a twofold manner. It is attached to the emergence of the concept of the human—afoot and at stake in the domains of Europe a still nascent Americas and the Caribbean by the midpoint of the seventeenth century. It is produced and at stake in a manner coextensive with the rising discourse of science (which is the lead mode of formulation or gesture toward a formalization within discourse here), including philosophy as science—notably in the centuries-long emergence given in the nodal eruption of the supposed sciences of the human across the second half of the eighteenth century (not so much the religious discourses, nor so much those of politics and legality, even as each is articulated therein and thereby) (Foucault 1990, 314–53, chap. 9; 1973, 303–43, chap. 9; Mudimbe 1988, ix–xiii, 1–43, 187–203; Wynter 2003; D. F. D. Silva 2007, 95–151, 287–92).

Rather than beginning with the presumption that the idea of the human ought to be taken as a domain marked out by the terminal establishment of pylons, as some might suppose, we can begin with a different premise. We might proceed by way of recognition of the pertinence of a different kind of analogy, not of the architectural but rather of the textile: that of the *warp* and *weft* in the construction of fabric for a cloth or a tapestry. This is to stake and extend to matters of supposed knowledge the metaphor that Du Bois proffered in a related locution, concerning the symbolic and the historial in general, as a notation on the idea of "America," in the penultimate paragraph of the closing essay of *The Souls of Black Folk: Essays and Sketches*, as noted above (Du Bois 1903k).

For the question that arises in the modern epoch, as the very concept of the human, is the supposed relative status of sameness and difference within the emergence, maintenance or duration, and denouement of any form of social and historical being that may be understood as utterly originary in its genesis. Such being ought to be understood, thus, as indefinite in its historial articulation. Hence, it is also, thereby, illimitable in its realization. While one dimension, supposed sameness, is usually proclaimed as the basis for a sense of the common, the other dimension, the necessity of difference is usually presumed, without proclamation or radical problematization (or, presumption is usual with regard to the implacable imperatives that arise thereby and according to such). Or, that is to say, this latter is put into practical operation without critical consideration, despite all manner of disavowals, except in the most benign forms of politesse. What remains for philosophy in the general sense, for critical reflection and discourse, is the question of how one might conceptualize the maintenance of both sides of the limit—of the distinction of sameness and difference, ostensibly one marked off from the other—in weighted asymmetry, in an otherwise-than-classical sense of balance in its ostensibly reciprocal devolution. The thought is that there may not be any preternaturally given devolution in the unfolding of *historial* being. Rather, all is at stake: here, now, then, there. If so, the emergence and articulation of "a people" as such encodes the question of the very historial order of being as human.

For indicative purposes here, to offer a few discrete nominalizations, as a matter of situating the conceptualization that I have just proposed, one can recognize in Du Bois's locution in this essay several diverse orders of historicity of the sixteenth century through the eighteenth: from the ideological dynamics of the political and economic revolutions of the demos in the British Isles (notably the so-called Glorious Revolution); to the discourses of some of the leaders of the indigenous groups of the Caribbean and the Americas in relation to the imperial invasions of Spain and Portugal (for example, that led indigenous leader of the Taino nominalized by the Spanish friars as Enrique); to the historically late, supposedly enlightened, yet dappled discourses under the heading of philosopohy of Jean-Jacques Rousseau or Immanuel Kant; to the precocious ruminations in the form of *poësie* of those enslaved in the supposed New World, as such could find articulation in the writings of Phillis Wheatley; or the poignant world-historical initiatives of Polydor, Möise, or Toussaint L'Ouverture, on the island known during the eighteenth century as Saint-Domingue.

A horizon of historial reference at once nodal and perennial in temporization may be given.

Although not yet coherent in explanatory claim, nor stable in semantic reference, nor simply available in lexical entity for thought and discourse astride the middle decades of the seventeenth century, by the midpoint of the following century, a full century later, this novel sense began to acquire articulation as a kind of classification that was adumbrated as a potential scientific and philosophical heading for thought and research: the concept of race.

A century thereafter, over the second half of the nineteenth century, the concept of human culture acquired a certain status in the rising sciences of the human (taking strong lexical reference from the German, *Kultur* and *Bildung*, yet nonetheless encoding therein references to the Romance legacies, namely, *sensus communis*) as the dominant heading for address of the difficult matter of difference among the supposed humans. Such a heading, the latter, the concept of culture—for how we think about difference among humans—remains dominant in our own time.[39]

In this essay Du Bois does not remark this tendentious novelty as a theme, as I have nonetheless adduced it here. Indeed, while named virtually everywhere in his writings of the two decades straddling the turn of the century, his analytical judgment as to the effects of the practices that denigrate groups of humans is acute, precise, even resolute—for he would brook no compromise on the tenability of the moral status of all those understood as human; all for him are *person*. There is nonetheless an abiding theoretical ambivalence in his discourse—legible according to the protocol of critical fidelity to the integrity of his thought—as to the epistemic determination of the sense of difference among humans that is at stake. That is to say that even as he ought to be understood to bring into critical elucidation the contradictions of logic and the concomitant incoherent conceptual formulation of the philosophical and supposed scientific discourses of the human that proposed such denigration, there abides within Du Bois's thought an apparent irresolution on the order of the *strategy* in thought (not at all with regard to his clarity about the practical-theoretical character of the problematization) in the address to matter of the determination of the tendentiously novel gathering of the senses of denigration of the human. Yet, as I have proposed elsewhere, this difficulty is constitutive.[40] Further, the practical theoretical terms of what is at stake for thought can be elaborated by way of Du Bois's early engagement with this problematization (Chandler, forthcoming).

B. SECOND ANNOTATION. I now offer an annotation, with emphasis on the historiographical event, of *historical eventuality*, in thought as practice. With regard to the moment of 1441–42, within the historical domain that will come to consider itself common in some sense, despite all manner of differences, as Christian and of a putative Europa, there begins to emerge within the social field (certainly for the literate and ruling economic and political classes) a certain order of sense that a possible determination of the status and pertinence that one might adjudge for any being encountered as a foreign "human," that is to say, even if taken as perhaps "human," that such being might be construed as categorically different from oneself, different from one's sense of one's self—different in kind, in essence. This would be a self that is conceived as the subject of, or under the aegis of, a religious authority, or theological sovereign, namely, God (or, in Catholic Lisbon, or even within the domain of the Crown of Aragon, under the pope), thus Christian. So, too, in an understanding that could run in a parallel or subterranean manner to the theological, in the reference to a sense of self, one would be the subject of a political sovereign, a ruler (usually as monarch, of one kind or another, a king, usually, or queen, or even kaiser), a figure that might declare its own sense of self as the exception to all, within any social or historical dispensation (Lach 1965–93; Pagden 1987).

In the aftermath of the political declarations of 1776, or in elaborations thereof, while retaining in sedimented form the principle of opposition, the legible surface of this historically novel practice (the tendentious judgment according to the terms of a putative conception of distinction gathered under the heading "race"), as precisely the articulate promulgation of the new epistemic sense of a historial being under the heading human, the titular claim may be understood to shift in apparition to a distribution of mark according to the logic issuing from that first and founding premise. The other (as foreign, alien, radically new in both being and bearing) might be adjudged as not yet *fully* human, or perhaps *not yet* perfected, as human. Such judgment in the epistemic and historical instance proffered itself (perhaps as its only means) by way of the tutelary image of the relatively recently consolidated idea of the European.[41]

This historicity in its devolution might be given in and by way of the example of the emergence of that perennial exemplar of the world-historical known in historiographical discourse and knowledge as Virginia. Already afoot as historical figures as part of the arrival of the Spanish in Mexico and Florida in the sixteenth century, Africans were also among the first in the incipiting decades of what is now know in the historiography as "Jamestown" in the early seventeenth century. With practitioners of labor subjected by contractual financial overdetermination, as well as by the military violence of the English against the indigenous peoples of the region (after the Spanish in the previous century and ongoing), from the first decade of the century through to the beginning of its sixth decade, determinations of status (in all senses—from theological to legal) were perhaps decisively inflected by one's relation to coerced labor. Conditions of indenture and then, too, of enslavement, and likewise the terms of sexualization by gender and forms of marriage, would articulate profound and perhaps existentially ultimate forms of hierarchy and subjection, of one's person to that of another. Yet our understanding would be remiss if we propose to claim a presumptive status during those decades in this historical domain for something that we might today place under the terms of a concept of race.

In the critical epistemic sense (in which what concerns me here would include any stable formation of general understanding as well as tendentiously formal practices of thought and knowledge), in this historiographical sense, such terms did not yet exist. The nascent legibility of any lexical index of what we might nominalize with the term race, or its derivatives, as an idea, is in the processes of its emergent articulation. The formal efforts to place a concept of race as a heading for knowledge or philosophy is not yet apparent in any definitive manner at the midpoint of the seventeenth century, in the historical domain that we know as either "Jamestown" or "Virginia."

Across the century, the devolution to the articulation of differences unfolded: by way of the eventful refusals to release Africans or their descendants from coerced labor across the 1630s, clustered at the turn to the decade of the 1640s, as distinguished from the indentured English and others of the British Isles, for example; to the 1643 law (of the colonials of a supposed English provenance in situ) supporting the assignment of African women to field labor, notably taxing them as laborers (as opposed to the more common domestic labor for women from the British Isles, understood as English); to the quietly cataclysmic 1662 law of the Virginia colonial legislature that made the status as enslaved of the African woman heritable (that "all children borne in this country shall be bond or free only according to the condition of the mother"), its articulation simply the historically specific expression in symmetrical converse form of the sedimentation of the logic encoded in an old Roman patriarchal principle (*patria potestas*); to the 1667 law of the colony that excluded enslaved persons from the beneficence of the legal covenants extended to Christians in the colony; to the 1691 legislative action that emplaced a declaration that any person understood as "white" who married a "negroe, mulatto, or Indian" would be permanently banished from the colony within three months of the act of marriage. By the end of the century, these actions had produced in situ, if accorded a retrospective thought, as if of principle, to the effect that it could be tendentiously claimed over the century that followed these eventualities to announce a new sense of the idea of *chattel*, portable and inheritable property, as pertaining to a form a being, ambivalently understood as "human," a certain legal fiction. An enslaving class, led by male property owners, of British provenance, proclaiming themselves as subject of the English crown, would promulgate this idea as if pertaining to those Africans and those descended thereof; this new idea, to remark the matter, would be declared to attend to those in the colony who earlier, that is, at an earlier time, within a century, were understood to stand within the colony of Virginia as *persons*, indeed as persons of the "commonwealth" (Hening 1810, 1:146, 552, 2:170, 260, 267, 270, 280–81; Holt 2010; Saller 1994).

At the turn to the eighteenth century, at least according to the dominant legality on the terrain, as it were, this latter supposition was no longer the case within the English colony of Virginia.

C. **THIRD ANNOTATION.** Marking this reference, from the unfolding of the dispositions of the law in colonial guise, in the apparition of what has been proclaimed as Virginia, there is promulgated within the colonial theater that we have come to know as America (something more and other than simply the world of the colonists), a distinct thought of the human, at once a discourse of a putative horizon of the common of the human as a form of being that is yet constitutively riven in both its emergence and maintenance, or apparition.

On the one hand, according to the discourses and the history that may become legible by way of the index that I have given above, there is a claim to the common, a putative worldwide sense, sensus communis, on a planetwide scale, declared universal in its becoming and in its implication. Such a claim makes it possible for the commoner, again in situ, precisely as "a people," to insist on status in common with the supposed aristocracy (within the frame of whatever whole is declared, of the supposed sovereign reference, of the home country or the colony, of home and colony, or the colonies of the crown), and likewise, eventually, also in relation to the sovereign. As such, this order of commonness is understood to issue as if a distinct and radical difference. It was the supposed emergence of another "people" on the world-historical horizon. In this instance, sameness is understood to affirm a claim to difference. This is the thought of the Declaration of Independence of the British colonies in North America of 1776, as proposed in writing by Thomas Jefferson (see Jefferson 1999).

This is a potentially radical understanding of either sameness or difference. It would announce the radical form of the very existence of any and all that might be construed as "a people," that is to say, the historial. It may be thought of as a name for the very making or production, or construction, of any ideal or morality thereof, of the human, perhaps as such that might subtend or guide a claim to the shared as a practice of idealization.

On the other hand, any refusal of the common, such a sense of the common, a certain sense of the same, always, ineluctably, yields another, a new, yet always derivative, sense of difference. Arising in a traditional sense of historial being, this other sense of difference is always understood or declared as categorical, as issuing from an oppositional logic (as either-or, all or nothing). In a philosophical sense, likewise within traditional legality, the categorical insistence on, rather than a pragmatic judgment of, the distinction as fungible is its definitive operation. It must or will always proliferate apparitional codifications as if to justify its principle. (The exemplar par excellence here is the legal system of the codes of apartheid in southern Africa in the nineteenth and twentieth centuries. Others would be various aspects of European colonialism in general, from the eighteenth to the twentieth centuries; so, too, it would include the legality attendant to the codes of law of the systems of enslavement throughout the Atlantic Basin in general, the Americas, and the Caribbean, from the fifteenth through the nineteenth century.) This other sense of difference is always understood as secondary, dependent, subordinate, and inferior to the supposed originary or radical emergence of difference. (The supposed inferiority of the difference understood as secondary or derivative could easily be inverted in its kinesis, from an ostensibly negative quality to an affirmative judgment. In colloquial terms, it is akin to the practice of a kind of "slumming.") It is always heavily marked by sexualization and engendering (gender in general).

The declaration of difference, "independence," of the sort marked out in Jefferson's discourse, debated and affirmed in situ in the early summer of 1776, has been supposed as of the former kind, a supposedly originary proclamation of difference.

The radical disposition within the discourse of African Americans that have been enslaved in the Americas and the Caribbean and of those who claim descent thereof has been taken in general as the latter sort of claim.

Perhaps it is apposite for critical thought to take as our exemplum a node of the problem of thinking what is often considered matters of kinship within ethnological discourses, anthropological and otherwise. For behind most of our general ideas of forms of human collective, almost as an immemorial reference, stands the image of a supposed traditional kin group. The idea is that of a group the relations of which are in some decisive manner *of* (both from and about) heredity. Such relations are a form of bond, thought of as the most unfungible sort of social relation. The metaphor of such a group circulates through our most common terms of self-reference—those of nation, of state, of religious belonging, of "culture." It is often taken as a sine qua non with common and dominant ideas of family. (In the twenty-first century, it is often used to speak of or describe shared interest groups—we are "family.")

In traditional guise, kinship or kin relations are the metaphorical extension of birth relations. Even now, in the twenty-first century, half a century after the consolidation in American ethnological discourses of the 1960s of a formal critique of such an idea and practice, such a disposition toward matters of kinship is common; such is typically expressed in genealogies, often represented in graphic form (Schneider 1972, 1984). One must either assume or change such inherited conceptualization in the form of knowledge.

In order to account for the principle that we limn from Du Bois's order of historiographical attention in "The Development of a People," another idea of kinship, if not entirely new, may be adduced: birth relations are a metaphorical expression of kinship relations (Sahlins 2012, ix, 65, 74). Alternatively given, we might say our understanding of birth relations is produced by way of the system of values and meanings by which we understand kinship relations.

Notably, in this second principle (a not yet traditionalized idea) for understanding kin relations, mutuality (mutual care) is but one possible aspect of such a system and not at all general, or radical. Whereas one might attend to the thought of mutuality with a markedly affirmative sense of existential connection, without any analytical presumption of the given stability of a distinction of self and other, in this second way of thinking of the matter (yet to become a traditionalized thought), kin relations are better understood under a generalized understanding of the idea of the *agon*. (The notation is by way of an initial reference to the ancient Greek linguistic topos—agonistic, perhaps the semantic sedimentations, in all senses, of the derivative lexemes, such as *antagonistic*, even possibly *protagonistic*; for such nominal references might remain generative for critical thought here. In principle, as well as practice, any list of the possible terms of art or reference must remain open. The agon is one among others.) A general conception of kin relations may be best thought under the heading of the agon. If we may think of mutual care, there is yet no principle of theoretical determination that would exclude its organization as agonistic. The general form can, and thus must, always be of at least two different registers. Indeed, to continue to stake our historical example, such differences are indeed the very kinetic organization of systems of kinship produced as "America," both then and now. This agon is at the root (both genesis and telos) of what has devolved as the historical projection most precisely understood in all of our discourses in general as "America" or "American"—in the horizons of the modern epoch.

In the context of the discussion that we have proposed as an annotation to Du Bois's thought in "The Development of a People," such a new disposition in thinking matters of kinship may appear as necessary for a coherent account of the double reference of the promulgations of the idea of the human across the early modern centuries, from the fifteenth to the nineteenth. Permit me to recall here my indication above that such double reference is my reference to the interwoven production of discourses and practices that give us the simultaneous and coextensive dignification *and* denigration of the emergent figure of the supposed human as definitive of modern historicity.

If for the stake of historiographical fidelity we remain with our world-historical exemplar of colonial Virginia, we have at hand the example of the relation of Sally Hemings and Thomas Jefferson (Gordon-Reed 1997, 2008; Spillers 2003c; Chandler 2014c, 109–11).

Sally Hemings (1773–1835), the birth daughter of Elizabeth Hemings and John Wayles, was inherited in the month of May of the year of her birth by her birth sister, Martha Wayles Skelton (also a birth daughter of John Wayles), who became the first wife, and the only one recognized in formal legality, of Thomas Jefferson. Hemings may then be described in museum curatorial provenance attendant to the first exhibition at historic Monticello on her life and relations as a "daughter, mother, sister, aunt . . . seamstress, world-traveler, enslaved woman, concubine, liberator, mystery."[42] After nearly a quarter century of genetic and historiographical query, at the inception of the second decade of the twenty-first century, we can now affirm with knowledge that beginning in Paris, when she was just past about fourteen or fifteen years of age, while she was serving there as an enslaved maidservant for Mary Jefferson (Thomas Jefferson's youngest daughter with his legally recognized wife, Martha, who had died in childbirth some four years earlier), Hemings was subsequently, eventually, inscribed within an approximately thirty-seven-year relationship of some intimacy (that is to say fulfilling many of the duties of a wife in care for a husband, leaving aside for another inquiry a critical understanding of the terms of such practice of intimacy, for either, both, or all, parties entailed) with Thomas Jefferson. It resulted in six birth children (four of whom lived to adulthood—Beverly, Harriet, Madison, and Eston).

Elizabeth's mother, Sally Hemings's grandmother, was Susannah, who is sometimes described in the scholarship as a "full-blooded African" woman; she was held enslaved by the Eppes family (nearby the plantation of John Wayles of Charles City County), by whom she was made sexually available to a visiting English sea captain of the name of John Hemings. In historical turn, Susannah's daughter, Elizabeth, delivered over her life course an extended progeny, of several generations, such that at Monticello they constituted approximately a third of that plantation's enslaved population, which included as many as 115 persons (Gordon-Reed 2008). Elizabeth Hemings may thus—according to a discreet dimension of historicity—be understood to have been one of the most powerful persons afoot on the plantation that was Monticello, in Virginia. At Monticello, too, the life of Elizabeth Hemings, Sally's mother, was closely entwined with that of Martha Wayles Skelton Jefferson. Historical notation reports that Elizabeth was even present, along with other Hemings women, at Martha's death. (Indeed, Martha might have been considered Elizabeth's "niece," by some reckonings of kinship.) There is no official record of John Wayles's birth children with Elizabeth Hemings. Nor is there such for Thomas Jefferson's birth children with Sally Hemings. Enslaved persons, notably those who were women, had no right by positive and nascent statutory law in the Virginia colony of the late eighteenth century to refuse sexual, or gendered, advances, or other such insistence, by their formally recognized legal owner, or his designee, as it were.

Yet, as we give thought to the mark of Africa, shall we name it—in this instance given by way of woman, enslaved, and her progeny—the matter of things African in modern historicity on a world-historical scale may not be understood as somehow apart from the modern epoch but rather as actively constitutive of its very possibility and manner of unfolding. Such an understanding is precisely at stake for any and all traditional historiography—or so Du Bois's thought in this essay leads us to acknowledge.

It is given above all in the example of the care for the other—as other.

We may attest to this thought by way of example—here as theoretical metaphor.[43]

On the order of our earlier notations with regard to "The Development of a People," a reading of the kinship relations supposed as afoot in the late eighteenth-century domain of colonial Virginia, if annotated according to the traditional analytical priority of an ensemble of births, by which then kinship relations may be ascertained, the interpretive yield is a more or less refined genealogy. Some of those births are understood and conceived as legitimate; others are understood as illegitimate. Such a supposition is easy to think, even intuitive in the context of contemporary discourse, then and now, of colonial Virginia. The matter is in all truth more simple, still. Hence, it is thereby much more difficult for thought to accede to a commensurate understanding.

For in late eighteenth-century Virginia, Sally Hemings and Martha Wayles were not understood as having legal kin relations. Or better, this supposed nonkin relation was the term of their kin relation, within the context of the Virginia of their time. Rather, their kin relation was determined by the eventuality of the condition of a system of legal enslavement (and its inverse, legal freedom, of a nonetheless gendered kind), on the one hand, and the valuation of a conception of a *historial* difference among humans, on the other. This latter was tendentiously an ostensible categorical difference (no matter if the difference is adjudged by only one drop, or alternatively formulated by only 99.9 percent of a supposedly possible 100) among humans. The difference is codified in symbolic form in the idea and concept of distinction by supposed "race," at once semiotic in its being or existence, yet quite actual (in whatever sense such actuality is reckoned). Yet by way of such emergence, it was also at stake for philosophy and science by the coming of the later decades of that century, the eighteenth.

As described earlier in this study, this distinction, which I continue to describe here as yet without name, as it were (within the terms of my analysis), was not yet stable in the "Jamestown" of Virginia of the opening three decades of the initiative of colonization by the English, say, perhaps, in 1632, for example. However, in the course of the devolutions of that century, the seventeenth, as I outlined earlier, its symbolic ground was decisively imprinted by the decree of *partus sequitur ventrem* of legislative action in situ led by a propertied minority of the colony in 1662. Thereby it was codified in the 1691 stricture against supposed intermarriage (which was not so much against the potential production of intermixture—an adroit misnomer, perhaps—in the form of progeny, as it was an effort at a prophylactic against its legal sanction or the production of any new status for such progeny).

Yet something more than a century later, abreast the last quarter of the eighteenth century, the terms of kin valuation in terms of the idea and concept of race were not only established and coherent in formal legality but presumptive in all general matters of the life of the colony, of Virginia.

Its bearing for our attention to Du Bois's problematization is multiple. By way of such presumption (of the late eighteenth century), the system in operation does not yield the further presumption of a categorical difference for a reading of the kin relation of Sally Hemings and Martha Wayles, nor does it yield only a distinction of enslaved and free person, for example (or man and woman, owner and "concubine," of Sally Hemings in relation to Thomas Jefferson, and vice versa, and so forth), but it articulates most precisely and most radically the terms of the kinship relation that matter (as determination, in all senses of this idea of force) for each progenitor as a birth parent, their relation to their sense of self in such relations, each in relation to the other, by others to each of them, and to both in relation, and most fundamentally by those who are or may be understood as progeny—of the relation or union of the supposed parent-progenitors.

At the most radical level of existence, on the order of the very possibility of the social, that is to say, the collective level of historiality, the matter—the terms of kinship—thus articulates the relation of such progeny to their "people": those that may appear socially and historically around and in relation to Sally Hemings, then and now, as it were; those clustered around and in relation to Thomas Jefferson; and then the relation of such progeny to the American "people," and thereby, too, to the African American "people," or, better, peoples. The matter may be that they always have "people," always and only in the plural. They are not only part of *a* people, as it were. They always have peoples, all of them, and then more to come. This is the real secret of the problematic for thought that Du Bois opened for address in his essay of 1904. Perhaps this is the true inheritance of "the souls of Black folk."

In the schema that may arise as a guide for knowledge and understanding that issues from that traditionalized conception of matters of kinship, the yield in the first instance is only a genealogy. It complicates rather than affirms a critical account of the motivation and production of values, in their social or historical effect. Further, that genealogy can yield only a bifurcated mapping, giving parallel lines of descent, doubled in appearance, but it cannot sustain a critical theoretical articulation of those lines (in relation, within a social domain or historical reference). The valuations that organize the kinship relations, beyond the supposed genealogical, produce a variegation in status accorded each line, of which a traditional understanding nonetheless cannot of itself give account for knowledge and understanding, historiographical or otherwise. That is to say, in traditional genealogical reference, one line is ostensibly legal (sanctioned). In the same such reference, the other line is supposed as para-legal (not exactly illegal but without legal sanction). This may offer a description as the premise of a native historiography; yet, it cannot account for the condition of possibility of what it describes nor the terms of its own access to or account of that history. It is a restricted, rather than general, sense of kinship, as a form of the social or relation, among humans.

Another approach, one that not only affirms the inversion of the metaphor (birth relations ought to be understood as the metaphorical extension of the organization of kinship relations, rather than vice versa) but also recognizes the *agon* as a form of *historial* relation of possible kinship system or domain of reference, not only accounts for the possibility of the late eighteenth-century Virginia outcome with regard to the progeny of Sally Hemings and Thomas Jefferson, but brings us to the task of rendering legible the motive forces that articulate their possible *historial* relation to the productions of their peoples—always at least and never only double.

So too, according to forms of reference enabled by this other approach to kinship, arise the terms of our own access in thought, to such historical eventuality (from "Jamestown" to eighteenth century colonial Virginia in general, as given in Monticello) as an articulation at once of possibility and limit or of dignification and denigration. That is to say that it arose of a historicity that is always at stake, then and now, now by way of then; and, we must note that it is a then that remains always at stake in its historical bearing in the now); the then in this sense is one that has not yet ascribed to itself the possible terms of its futural right of historial articulation, or rearticulation.

D. A BRIEF ELABORATION. The historicity gathered into view by Du Bois pertaining to matters African American, which forms the capsule narrative of the central third part of this essay, announces a distinct understanding of the problematization attendant thereby (Development 298–304, paras. 17–28). It is the question of the relation among generations as the instituting condition of tradition, rather than that relation appearing as the historically given outcome of tradition (an understanding in which the relation of generations is not in question but appears historically as the outcome of a presupposed tradition). The relation to the future is the decisive, perhaps even the only, pertinence of tradition. The matter of their being—all those understood as *of* all that may be placed under the heading African American—is at stake in the very apparition of existence.

On the order of reflection at which the problematic is announced for thought that would be radical, the question becomes: How does one receive and grapple with the hitherto unimaginable, such as in the situation of the historical Phillis Wheatley (ca. 1756–82), or those such as her (for example, those of her generational cohort, such as a Sally Hemings); or the circumstances of the practitioners of the making of the tradition of songs and music that we now know as the "spirituals" across the fifteenth to the nineteenth centuries; or the conditions for thought of one W. E. B. Du Bois (1868–1963), or those such as him; existential, always, in thinking, of the possible remaking of history?

Across the duration of distended belief, from one century, through a third, and into a fourth, and now a fifth, from ostensible acceptance without resignation to an "unhopeful hope," one discovers that the nodal concern, if not given so much as telos or a harmonic outcome, is a supple and resilient commitment to being at stake in the future (Du Bois 1903k). For here there is no purgatory or beneficent salvation, as ultimate claim (such as one might have found in the professions of Saint Francis of Assisi or the writings of Dante Alighieri). Rather, there is an insistence on the illimitable realization of that which is not yet, as an expression of responsibility in the here and now for that which is not yet available within the given. Unmarked though it is in the kinesis of the "striving," even as maintenance, it is nonetheless weighted heavily on the bias toward giving, generosity in general, as the opening for all that will come to have been considered of highest value or valuation. Thus, rather than pose the query: What if Phillis Wheatley, or the practitioners of the spirituals in their creation, knew the history of the modern world as did one W. E. B. Du Bois, or us (whoever we may be), for example, how might they have judged and taken action? Rather, the question is, How might W. E. B. Du Bois (for example)—not just receive the bequest of a Wheatley or the symbolic inheritance left by the givers of the spirituals, but rather in such reception—recognize how the being at stake for those past generations might be, or become, at stake for those generations yet to come? Perhaps it is a matter of being at stake as a determination of a decision, the outcome of a judgment (rather than simply a response to a demand), for the as yet impossible possible future?

So it may be, for those who might claim the status of the progeny of Sally Hemings.

In the course of Du Bois's essay, this question may be understood to unfold according to two interwoven senses of historicity. These two senses both appear in Du Bois's essay under the nominal heading of revolution. The initial sense is that of destruction, the destruction of ideals called or named retrospectively as African (given here only a brief lexical notice, totalized, monumental or mundane, undifferentiated in time or place—as if memorial—in nominalization). In such reference, they are always presumptively of patriarchy. The other sense of revolution is of production. It is the production of ideals and ways of existence in the face of ongoing destruction (destruction normalized and routine, or even specifically violence, violence not only of built space, or the body of a person, but of all that one may consider of "soul" or psyche, of imagination, of the order of so-called dreamworlds). Likewise, it is the circumstance of production amid new senses of relation—of new or novel contexts for their emergence, both toward diverse senses of the past and potential allegories of the future, for which no terrain, let alone any map, can be imagined, let alone proposed. There is in such revolutionary production no futural referent that one might assume. As an example, one cannot even hope to imagine, let alone know, the face of the ancestors yet to come (both future and past—there are those surely yet to be invoked as such), given only in the historicity that is not yet and has not yet been, in any yet possible sense. As Du Bois names it, a leader, as it were, in such historial problematization, faces not just the destruction of an archaic or immemorial past (of Africa; yet also in general), but so, too, the destructions within the the existential past, that is to say within the life-course of the generations afoot in the Americas, of productions announced in the midst of ongoing destruction (of such archaic referent and its concomitant aftermaths), of all those who might be configured, affirmatively or negatively, in relation to matters African American (Development 304–8, paras. 29–36).

This work of revolutionary production, in the face of originary and ongoing destruction, has always and already been afoot—as the very course of African American practices. Understood to be set on its course in the wake of the production of the book *The Souls of Black Folk: Essays and Sketches*, gathered in 1902–3, the essay "The Development of a People" may be understood—*à partir de*, we might say, the provenance and claim of the monumental essay "The Talented Tenth" (written in the months immediately following the publication of that book of essays)—to insist on the moral horizon of a responsibility on the part of all enlightened persons to the possibilities of the highest "culture" of "modern life" (Development 311, para. 47).

The question of new senses of ideal or idealization for a new leadership is staged as a problem as the tonal center of the soundings of the poetic voice in *The Souls of Black Folk: Essays and Sketches*, in whose wake our essay, "The Development of a People," has found its sonic registers. In that book of essays, the voicing of that locution is always biographical and autobiographical. It carries particular cadences and colors, yet marked by the particular timbre of our indefatigable narrator (and his avatars in character and problem).

In the memoir-essay on "Josie," "Of the Meaning of Progress," in which someone married another (we think it the narrator of our story), our heroine stands as the monogram of her community in general (or those such as her throughout the "New South" of the 1880s) but most especially she articulates as the paradoxical exemplar of her generation—at least one of several generations lost in the failures of leadership and social dispensation in the aftermath of the American Civil War. The loss in question, however, is most sonorously sounded when also heard in its resonances in the others of her generation and among those generations contiguous to hers, some that preceded it and some that succeed it (or those who arrive on the scene in the latter moments of the passing of the one that properly belongs to her). It is with the double elegy of those generations, the essays on the death of Du Bois's firstborn, his son Burghardt, and on the journey of Alexander Crummell, that we can attune to the somber tone of the last third of that book (the part that Du Bois, in the book's "Forethought," placed as addressed both from and to those "within the Veil").

Still, a certain resolute hope finds its distinctive legibility in the short story "Of the Coming of John," which sounds the book's penultimate sonic notation, just before any resolution of theme and consequence. So it is that in our story, upon returning to his hometown from a sojourn of higher education, John is politely and adroitly shouted down, so to speak, by an older "African American" generation, in the locutions of a deacon, when the young sojourner who has returned home speaks from the pulpit of the African American church of new worlds to come; and then, later, he is hanged in judgment, on penalty of death, in the woods by members of what is most likely an older "white" generation, subtending the perjorative disposition previously voiced or enacted by a member of a younger "white" generation, so as to in effect render silent the "voicing" of his action in defense of the hope and possibility of a younger African American generation. This is to say that beyond the limits of a subterranean narrative of a divinely given "white" knight in shining armor (which is the reference to *Lohengrin* in the story), one might hear the narrative resonance of the kind of rustle that comes as one's fingers brush unseen and forgotten pages of fine papers, once carefully set aside into the quiet corner of a drawer or small closet, with precious notations, of some night thoughts and morning dreams, perhaps hastily written down, with impatient fear of forgetfulness. Therein, we might find a few encodings that could recall a voice such as that of Jennie, John's little sister, for whose protection he would commit the mortal sin.

We note that it is Jennie who, as the story unfolds, follows him from the scene of his failed oratory at the church and asks of him the question of the ages:

> Long they stood together, peering over the gray unresting water.
> "John," she said, "does it make every one—unhappy when they study and learn a lot of things?"
> He paused and smiled. "I am afraid it does," he said.
> "And John, are you glad you studied?"
> "Yes," came the answer, slowly and positively.
> She watched the flickering lights upon the sea, and said thoughtfully, "I wish I was unhappy,—and—and," putting both arms about his neck, "I think I am, a little, John." (Du Bois 1903f, 242, paras. 19–24)

We recall that it was the memory of the eyes of his sister Jennie, along with the face of their mother, in his mind's-eye memory that led John to turn and commit himself to what he thought of as his "duty" in his hometown and thus to return from the North to the South and pursue his life's work there (Du Bois 1903f, 238, para. 16). While John's nascent vision was perhaps unimaginable, almost unspeakable, in his own time, it remains that in the conceit of the story, Jenny survives (unblemished we might venture)—perhaps to live, and to fight, in another time, for another day.

That is to say, it was some eight years after the book of *The Souls of Black Folk: Essays and Sketches* before Du Bois's writerly locution could realize in print the full-throated form of the fictional voice that we think might be considered akin to Jennie's. That is the voice of Zora, the heroine of Du Bois's first novel, *The Quest of the Silver Fleece* (Du Bois 1911, 1974b). Zora, born in a swamp, in a brothel, finds her way out, gains her schooling, and then saves from failure and refounds the school in which she was educated. She then, by way of a mighty vision, by way of a kind of "double-consciousness," one might say, leads a revolutionary coalition of local African American tenant farmers and sharecroppers, along with local Italian immigrant laborers and artisan-workers, to acquire, drain, and reclaim the swamp as arable farmland, which is then successfully farmed and cultivated by a cooperative of members of the local community. She accomplishes what John Jones was unable to realize in his fictional lifetime. Zora may be understood as Jennie-John, reborn in a full-scale fictional narrative. As a historical factotum, she was perhaps the first "dark-skin" heroine in African American fictional literature.

Across the doubled generation of its telling in Du Bois's book of essays, one the generation of Crummell, the other the generation of one Burghardt, as well as that of the fictional eventualities of its *récit*, this order of historiography encodes a vision that is perhaps potentially still radical, of an impossible possible new world.

That which was not given to Du Bois according to a traditional historiography, coming into its own professionalization at the time, he could come to produce in literature, a vision of a possible future. By all measures this text ought to be taken as an elaboration not only of the shadowed pathways that remain hidden in the rich undergrowth of the book of *The Souls of Black Folk: Essays and Sketches* but, too, as an elaboration, by the labor of a fiction, of those essays that follow immediately upon the setting forth of that big little book of thoughts, of which "The Development of a People" can be understood to give us a historical conception of suitable breadth and depth. That essay refers us back, perhaps through the historicity that was colonial Virginia, to the very inception of the epoch, with remarkable theoretical perspicacity.[44] For it may be considered the theoretical telling of the possibility of another historiality, one yet to come, perhaps of the sort that would be such as our fictional Jennie and her generations, and the potential for another kind of historiography, of both that eventuality and its retelling, or telling anew.

This staging in story and fiction can be our guide to a highlighted annotation of the singular status of the question of the relation of generations in Du Bois's thought. It is not so much that Du Bois's essays call to our attention the obvious or presumptive arbiters of mundane or intramural value (such as preachers or teachers, and clergy, or businesspersons, for example) that should hold us in reflection. Rather, it is the obscure or even submerged, almost hidden dimension of leadership that we might seek to bring within a resolute focus. Almost everywhere, Du Bois calls for an unconditional reception of "the gifted children" that find their way in the historicities attendant to matters African American. To our mind's-eye memory might come such figures: from historiography, Sally Hemings of Virginia and Paris, Phillis Wheatley of Boston and London, Josie of the hill country of eastern Tennessee, and the young Du Bois of Great Barrington, son or father, gone "south"; from fiction, Jennie Jones of eastern Georgia or Zora of southern Alabama. So it is with the voices of the children that "cheer the weary traveller" at the close of the last chapter of *The Souls of Black Folk: Essays and Sketches* (Du Bois 1903k, 263–64, para. 26). For the whole of the "duty"—a major word and thought for Du Bois at the turn to the twentieth century—of the supposed "talented tenth" is quite something other than a practice of elitism (Du Bois 1903n, 1982j, 2015m). In Du Bois's disposition, it is by way of an affirmation of each generation (namely—but not only—such children as gifted), *as the carriers of that which has not yet been and is, perhaps still, yet to come*, that there can be, or is, an affirmation of those already gone, of those who made a way out of no way, precisely when there was no way. For they will become what they were only by way of this affirmation of the future, even of a fictive future (Waligora-Davis 2006). Perhaps, indeed, in this thought of an affirmation of the future, as we have proposed to recognize it in the thought of Du Bois, there is available a new way to think of leadership, that is to say, by way of the affirmation of a certain followership. It may well be a radical and other way to think of tradition and the relation of generations.

CODA I

The nineteenth century was the first century of human sympathy,—the age when half wonderingly we began to descry in others that transfigured spark of divinity which we call Myself; when clodhoppers and peasants, and tramps and thieves and millionaires and—sometimes—Negroes, became throbbing souls whose warm pulsing life touched us so nearly that we half gasped with surprise, crying, "Thou too! Hast Thou seen Sorrow and the dull waters of Hopelessness? Hast Thou known Life?" And then all helplessly we peered into those Otherworlds, and wailed, "O World of Worlds, how shall man make you one?"
—W. E. B. DU BOIS, "Of Alexander Crummell" (1903b)

According to his thought in this passage, the matter of the relation of the example and the movement of "ideals" for Du Bois must be understood in a manner that is as fundamental and simple in premise as it is complex and ultimate in implication. In apparition here as a cipher, perhaps, the matter is toward the problem of thinking that which remains yet to come, beyond the line of today, of "this narrow Now," proposing another world, another sense of world, another possible world that is yet impossible; we can call it the general principle of "democracy": recognition of sameness is by way of the asymmetrical affirmation of difference. Or, rather, the affirmation of possibility should not be understood as rooted in the inhabited sense of loss as the passage to sympathy but rather in the irruption of possibility as the passage to the affirmation of empathy. Empathy would be otherwise than an accession to any form of a supposed sovereign, or the universal, or the absolute; rather, it would announce the kinetic possibility of the irruption of freedom. The sense of being in this way is always an affirmation of the possibility of the future that is at stake in the present: here and now. Du Bois's thought may be understood as an affirmation of a general principle of freedom in historicity. It is thus a parallax.

Toward an affirmative attention to such a thought, we have considered two orders of example in this first part of our study. One is existential in an autobiographical idiom of thought. The other is historiographical (nascently sociological) in a theoretical discourse.

The autobiographical register of Du Bois's writing, addressed most generally in the opening section of part I, may be thought of as a practice in which a subject of thought is rendered as an object. For this reference, one might take Du Bois's text *Dusk of Dawn: An Essay toward an Autobiography of a Race Concept*, of 1940, as the guiding or exemplary consideration.

This register marks a scenography in Du Bois's intellectual habitation that is the scene of massive metaphor and the play of the most thoughtful practice—of almost mundane, thoughtful, existential imagination—which yet in its implications could perhaps, at times, yield an irruption of catachresis. What has been leavened in this study of his discourse of the turn of the century is that his autobiography produces an affirmation of a sense of self as *ipse* that is always at least and never only double in both its possibility and that which it may become. That frightful apparition, while remaining otherwise than a domesticated doppelgänger, attuned the would-be protean thinker-writer to the ineluctable necessity that the journey given of the existence to which he belongs (without possession), also for those like him, remains without any accession or passageway to home, for such may never have been given. What is both required and given is a passage beyond any parochial formation, in its sedimentation. Here we might remark the thought of an illimitable concatenation of association, of like and unlike all at once, as it were, such that an asymmetrical rhythm might arise within the relation, of person—of peoples—by way of an indissoluble movement of kinetic dissociation. (Perhaps it might be akin to the fractual movement of the waves and sedimentation across the ocean bottom.) An existential journey, whether of the one or the many (as life story or as historiography)—even if as sojourn—is marked by such punctuation, may no longer be rendered as an experience only of faith. Rather, it would bring to relief the interminable markings of one's own limits, of the instance of ambivalence as legible trace of impossible possibility. A way forward, so to speak, might be found only by going forward. Here perhaps I may be allowed to remark in summary that we have an autobiographical writing of the most profound sense of hope, even in the face of the absence of almost all resources for a commitment to the future. Perhaps this writing was subtended by the historiographical availability of the sense that others had gone before, that they, too, found ways to make a way out of no way, or so the proverbial understanding comes to us.

In the historiographical practice of his writing, in thought and discourse, as considered here, we were able to follow the order of example by indexing two of Du Bois's earliest essays, the posthumously published essay "The Afro-American," circa 1894, and "The Development of a People," of February 1904, a threshold essay for his early thinking (issued by Du Bois less than a year after he completed and released the book, *The Souls of Black Folk: Essays and Sketches*, in March and April 1903). With these two references, marking the inception and the denouement of the decisive early decade in Du Bois's intellectual itinerary, we can ascertain the way in which a sense of general modern historicity was at once (simultaneously, reciprocally) productive of the specific apparition of African American historicity, thus general in pertinence and implication, and yet also constitutive in that according to a critical path of thought matters African American may be understood to announce a distinctive, perhaps originary, problematization general to modern history (for social and historical collectives in general) whether of nation or state, and perhaps also in terms of a heading that would soon be afoot, that is to say all that is now commonly understood under the heading of an idea or concept of culture. Without declaration, thematic claim, or remark in first-person guise, the latter essay may be understood to operate the rhetoric of an appeal or petition (to conscience) that insists on a doubled identification of both the writer and reader, the reader by way of the writer, with the object of concern, the object of the discourse, African Americans. Hence, even as the writer of the 1904 essay does not declare in his own voice, as the subject of the locution (as does the 1894 essay, even if at times only by implication rather than direct claim), he should also be understood as of the object, the demand that is put to the supposed reader—in part by way of a putative acceptance or affirmation of an implicit appeal from the writer—to recognize and affirm the object of concern, African Americans, as indeed "a people," of historicity as it were, of the same historical bearing as both the writer and reader—as we ought to understand all human groups—this appeal insists on an acknowledgment that would be hard-pressed not to include admission to a recognition of a certain perlocutionary force that would attend the status the first-person articulation of such a group, in whatever tongue or ensemble of such, in whatever idiom or diverse forms of such, that is as a subject of historicity.

It should be noted that although it is neither mentioned as text nor declared by thesis, for the decisive historial matter that is in question with regard to the ruminations in these two essays that I have marked as historiographical, "The Afro-American," of circa 1894, and "The Development of a People," from 1904—each indexed at an ostensible national level, of America as project, and then too in terms of a worldwide horizon, of African Americans as a world-historical reference—the thought of the later essay may be formulated in this context thus: if one takes in mind the Declaration of Independence of the United States of America, as both text and proclamation, as the touchstone example of comparison, ought "leaders" of or among the supposed "people" of which Du Bois is writing declare in turn an "independence" (understood here in light of that modern practice of "declarations of independence," perhaps of colony from supposed metropole or in the announcement of a new supposed nation as a political and legal state that would claim the right to be recognized on the contemporary world historical horizon, across the past two and a half centuries) with regard to the specific eventuality of their emergence, that is to say, as an originary historial genesis as a self-proclaimed singular domain of symbolization and sense of world and thus an irruption of "a people" (as Du Bois uses this term in 1904) onto the world-historical scene?

Although proposed in only a nascent fashion in the 1894 text (called forth in this study from its obscurity, for, as I have noted, it remained unpublished until 2010), as well as at best only indirectly stated in the published 1904 essay, across the decade in question, Du Bois's answer, even as it must be specified, is always an affirmation of recognizing an originary historial articulation from and among African Americans.

Yet, as I believe can be recognized, he does so in a manner quite distinct from that most famous "declaration of independence" of our time (see, for example, Jefferson 1999).

Yet, already in 1894, Du Bois came to consider knowledge, discourse, and practices of representation as a dimension of the problematization of matters African American. Indeed, a formulation of forms of representation, including practices of learning and knowledge, is perhaps the most powerful theoretical aspect of the essay "The Afro-American." In like manner, knowledge as science—perhaps especially its theoretical aspect, as a proposed nascent sociological perspective on human collective practices—is at the core of the project of the 1904 essay. Too, by producing a text that simultaneously proposes a general theorization of social practices as they pertain to "the development of a people," which takes the history of African Americans as both its declared object and a guiding epistemic problematization that would solicit fundamental thought, Du Bois's own accomplishment insisted that recognition of the originary genesis in the production of a historial being, at once social and historical, a historical sense, a certain sense of world, was at stake.

Indeed, by way of a practice of elaboration in the first part of this study, I have sought to render legible in what manner at the turn to the twentieth century Du Bois proposed that African American history carries the lineaments of a sense of world that has been "beyond the veil"—for his contemporary forms of knowledge and understanding—that might yet be dressed out in suitable apostrophes and periods, the quintessential example of the latter subsequently given during our period in the form of *The Souls of Black Folk: Essays and Sketches*, of 1903. More precisely, further, I have endeavored to begin to raise into hearing the still resonant tones of the lower registers of a discourse that proposed for theorization a conceptualization of a commitment to historial genesis that despite or beyond all manner of vicissitudes and disavowals in knowledge and forms of representation and overdetermination in the instance according to systems of exploitation and direct oppression, has carried forth by way of those most at stake in the subject position of this world-historical figure, which we too easily know under the heading African American or Afro-American, who have persisted in holding forth a solicitation of a world that has not yet been and remains yet to come. The historicity attached to this figure may thus mark the scene in which the harbinger of a new world may yet take shape.

However, a more lineal formulation of Du Bois's theoretical disposition can be offered, as enabled by the elaborations that we have been able to adduce so far in this study. There is not, nor can there be, any declaration of "independence." For their historial production is already a constitutive genesis—of the "warp and woof" of the fabric (to once again quote Du Bois from the closing of his 1903 book of essays)—of all that has come to be America. So, too, the historicity of their historical articulation is of the very constitution of all that has come to be understood as the modern world in general. Yet their emergence has also set loose something distinctly generative: a certain form of historial being the reference to which—as past or future, past and future—is *atopic*. That latter thought is to say that the very kinetic organization of historial being is such as to place at stake as the terms of emergence (as historical and as historial in the most profound sense of human existence), for any ipseity, that its very condition of emergence may be understood as otherwise than any presumption of the historial priority of its own natality—even in its ostensible constitutive address to itself. It can only see itself, as it were, and to suggest the metaphor, always at least and never only double in both becoming and apparition. This holds in both its possible geneses and the problematization that is always engendered in any supposed passage or accession to what may have been given as historicity. Thus, the problem bequeathed to contemporary thought by this example, as Du Bois positioned it at the onset of the twentieth century—"how shall man make you one"—is no longer available on those terms. Instead, the question has become, How did the world become only and always of one and the other, that is to say, always other than one?

CODA II

As we have sought to adduce, by reference to the opening stages of his itinerary, certain aspects of Du Bois's work had early begun to yield an ensemble of techniques, modes of practice, we might say, that were elaborated according to the imperatives of a thinking through of the status of the example.

They are a legible pattern of marks that remain from an indefatigable practice carried out across some nine decades. In part I of this study, I have attended to the opening stages of his itinerary. Yet the yield of this part of our study proposes that even the writings of the last decade of his itinerary, those of the late 1950s and early 1960s, should stand in contrapuntal relation to the imagination of an illimitable form of association of the young Negro Du Bois in Berlin, the capital of imperial Germany, more than half a century earlier. According to the perspective that I have been able to adduce in part I of this study, in the time of the inscription of even the last writings, one might anticipate that one might find maintained therein, within their near-octogenarian sense of knowledge of the world, both the still effervescent "unhopeful hopefulness" of resolute youth and the depth of insight delivered from a critical intelligence in the fullness of its power (Chandler 2021). Forms of historical example that one may find decisive across the whole of his later itinerary may be adduced as already signal examples on both an epistemological and a theoretical level within in the earliest moments of his intellectual maturation.

Still more, Du Bois's writings in general survive as a kind of epitaph of a thoughtful and receptive passion sustained until the end of nearly a century of living. While this work as a whole cannot and should not be taken to form a system—even if one were to track them across the whole life course attendant to his itinerary—they might yet be inhabited or rethought in a certain critical manner as an exemplary practical-theoretical organization of question and problem. They can be retrospectively gathered as the object of a critical discourse; they might be inhabited as a practical-theoretical organization of question and problem, even as such would always remain partial and their very form at stake in the eventuality of their elaboration. That is also to say that the exemplary example here would remain, if at all, only in the possibility of its dissipation and disseminal dispersal. Such practices, techniques, modes, dispositions remain as a form of problem for thought that might be desedimented and reinscribed, elaborated, in contemporary discourse by way of a certain practice of paleonymy. This, has defined my efforts so far in part one of this study.

And, in this latter fold of my text, along with, or within the bias of, the autobiographical and historiographical practices of inhabiting the difficulty of the example as we have followed it here, I have tried only to outline some of the terrain of Du Bois's discourse, or to gesture toward the openness of the horizon of his imagination, within which such practices might be reengaged as a problem for theoretical labor in our time.

The historial example then becomes the site of epistemological conjuncture in Du Bois's thought. It articulates the given as situation to existence as a committed practice. On the one side, it is the situation of a group as revelatory of historical circumstance. On the other side, it is the activity of a group as an exemplification of both limit and possibility. Du Bois, it must be emphasized, was committed ultimately, we might say, to the question of historical possibility: to the movement of that which is illimitable within the possible as existing limit. That is to say, once again, I have posed this order of problem for us: how to think with Du Bois a certain maintenance of both sides of limit.

It can now be said that if it is understood that thought is not only a derivative continuity of context in general but rather is also engaged as the operation of a freedom, as principle or surreptitious play, then Du Bois's itinerary in its possible forms of passage—autobiographical, historiographical—remains at stake for us as a radical possibility of practical theoretical organization of project in the contemporary moment. And, perhaps, it would be likewise in the future. It is, of course, a form of the example.

At such a conjunctural concatenation, the paradox is that it is the apparently "dead" order of the letter of his text, that which is in all its appearance opaque, that remains a legible carrier of a certain atopic movement of freedom or chance, showing at the level of thought. Thought may be understood here as a form of practice issuing from a constitutive opacity, that is to say, by way of such. Opacity as a name of possibility is thus its force of solicitation. It is thus by way of the movement of freedom or chance, showing forth in his discourse as a practice of thought, that I have proposed herein an example of the possible reelaboration of Du Bois's thought as a task for a critical labor in our time. It has taken the form of the proposition of our responsibility for conceptual, rhetorical, and theoretical labor in and across the topography—in the general sense—of his discourse. To attend to that in it that might remain atopic. Its time is always in this latter sense yet to come. It follows that the approach that I have offered with all of its limits and complications should be understood otherwise than simply as a statement. It is, rather simply, a certain formulation or reformulation of the problem of the thought of Du Bois for our time.

And then, further, on the other side, finally, I have proposed that one might most powerfully accept and engage the limits of Du Bois's thought by way of a hyperbolic practice—taking Du Bois himself at this letter. I have proposed, by my practice or my efforts toward such, to describe a historical sense of such practice as paleonymic—a certain reinhabitation of old terms of thought, old words, distinctions of value, in a radically new way of habitation, necessarily, of course, always more than only one.

In such a practice, the apparently given letter in both its perdurance and its dissipation remains open to its futural form. In this sense, as the limit, the given can yet be understood to mark "both sides," at least and never only, and as such registers the possible passage of form: of an auto-historiographical desedimentation that may yet turn up new soil on old ground; or of a discourse that accepts its formation as if the fractual formation of waves, for example, along the ocean bottom; or of the passage in thought as the irruptive dissipation and rending of remains without remainder, of both the shifting of earth and of flame. It is the practice of thought at the limit of possible world. It is thus under the heading of a response to the solicitation to such a practice—a material thought of the illimitable—that we might find and maintain in our own discourse the generosity of the writings of a certain W. E. Burghardt Du Bois on the question of the example.

Third Annual Meeting

of the

American Negro Academy

will be held in the

Lincoln Memorial Church, 11th and R Streets, N. W., Washington, D. C.,
Wednesday and Thursday, December 27th and 28th, 1899.

...PROGRAM...

Wednesday, 10 A. M.—Session called to order. Minutes of last meeting and of Executive Committee read. Reports of Secretary and Treasurer. Routine and New business.

2 P. M.—PAPER: Higher Education; Its Relation to the Future of the Negro. Mr. W. S. Scarborough, Wilberforce University, Ohio.
PAPER: Epidemic Manias with Reference to the Southern Situation. Mr. Peter H. Clark, Sumner High School, St. Louis, Mo.

7:30 P. M.—ANNUAL ADDRESS: The Present Outlook for the Dark Races of Mankind. President W. E. B. DuBois, Atlanta University, Ga.

Thursday, 10 A. M.—PAPER: The Ministry in Civil Affairs; Its Duty and Opportunities. Rev. Levi J. Coppin, Philadelphia, Pa.

7:30 P. M.—PAPER: America; The Modern Type of Democracy. Mr. W. T. S. Jackson, Washington, D. C.
PAPER: Right on the Scaffold; or the Martyrs of 1822. Mr. Archibald H. Grimké, Boston, Mass.

☞The public invited to all but the business meetings.

J. W. CROMWELL, *Secretary.*

Program for the Third Annual Meeting of the American Negro Academy, December 27–28, 1899, Washington, D.C. Reprinted by permission of the David Graham Du Bois Memorial Trust. Source: Papers of W. E. B. Du Bois, Special Collections and University Archives, series 3, subseries C, MS 312, W. E. B. Du Bois Library, University of Massachusetts Amherst.

PART II

For Koji Takenaka

The Problem of the Centuries

A Contemporary Elaboration of "The Present Outlook for the Dark Races of Mankind"—circa the 27th of December, 1899—Or, At the Turn to the Twentieth Century

The African Slave trade was the child of the Renaissance.
—W. E. B. DU BOIS, "The Development of a People" (1904)

And above all consider one thing: the day of the colored races dawns. It is insanity to delay this development; it is wisdom to promote what it promises us in light and hope for the future.
—W. E. B. DU BOIS, "Die Negerfrage in den Vereinigten Staaten" (1906b)

PREAMBLE

It must be said that for W. E. B. Du Bois the modern world proposed for the first time in history the possibility of the realization of the full meaning of freedom for man—humankind—understood as a certain ultimate whole. Yet it must also be remarked that for him, at the turn to the twentieth century, the modern history of the world had so far been defined as the sustained imposition of limit on the human practice of such freedom. And, most fundamentally, such imposition was proceeding according to forms of distinction that recalled previous epochs of human social organization. In this sense, it is the conceptualization of a tension between freedom and instituted limit that characterizes the most fundamental dimension of Du Bois's thought of modern historicity.

On the eve of the twentieth century, the question for a still quite young Du Bois was what—in the future—would be the relation of historical limit and the possibility given for humans as a certain *freedom*. Let us just say for now—if you will—being at liberty. What could be the form of freedom in a future that might be otherwise than the past in the future, a future that would thus remain a historical time, or historicity, that would be yet to come?

While Du Bois recognized many forms of limitation and proscription in human institution and practice, one mode of such proscription, despite diverse possible apparitions, is not just one among others. For it enfolds many others within its grasp and bespeaks a radical order of problem. That is the emergence of all that may be understood as *the* human as a problem for existence. Although, for Du Bois, questions of the human also entail the inhuman (this latter perhaps best be understood as illimitable within the orders of genesis and telos-in-general), in the modern epoch forms and practices of proscription would nonetheless tendentiously emplace questions of the human according to the projection of categorical limits. The matter articulated in his thought under the heading of the signal practice of such problematization in and as the modern era. He called it "the problem of the color line."

This problematization was not just one among others in the thought and itinerary of Du Bois. For the ultimate projection of its root premise concerned the very concept of "man" or humankind as a whole. And, specifically, it marked a recoil that has taken shape across modern history in the devolution of a sense of the commonness of the human as destination or end.

Of course, and indeed, the problematic for the Afro-American, or the African American, and so forth, might well be exemplary for the matter of the human—in general—as a problem of existence, and thus as a problem for thought.

As such, this concept metaphor, "the problem of the color line," was rendered as a distinct epistemological proposition in Du Bois's thought in the course of an effort to name the situation of the African American, or, that is also to say, an African Diaspora, on a global and world-historical scale. Yet the theoretical attention that was announced therein, maintaining within its orientation a certain capacity for a full axial rotation of view, a possibility rooted in the distantiation that was its own incipit, adduced an order of historicity that could also name the processes that produced the worldwide and variegated system of modern colonialism—a system that had reached an unprecedented height at the beginning of the twentieth century.

What matters in the context of the torsions and confusion of contemporary theoretical and scholastic discourse, here and now, in the opening decades of this so-called twenty-first century, is that this global perspective originated by way of Du Bois's attempt to think the question of the Negro in the United States: to think the question of the African American therein in terms of its most fundamental historical frame.

It was while he was conducting the fieldwork for his study of the social conditions of the Negro American in one city, that is, in Philadelphia, Pennsylvania, including the study of an associated rural area, Farmville, Virginia, and while he was trying to formulate a general and comprehensive plan for the study of the Negro in the United States as a whole, that Du Bois first began to attempt to name in a critical theoretical sense a thought of "the problem of the color line" as a fundamental issue in understanding the general situation, historical and otherwise, of this group (Du Bois 1899c, 1973g, 1898c, 1980c; see also Du Bois and Eaton 1899, 1973). He would arrive at a certain accomplished statement of such a thought over the course of the first years of his "study of the Negro problems," from 1897 to 1901—and these were his most intense moments of such study—while undertaking his first major independent research work (Du Bois 1897d, 1897e, 1898c, 1898b, 2015l, 2015b).

The first stage of this work took place in Philadelphia, Pennsylvania. The second moved from his base at Atlanta University in Atlanta, Georgia, but was national in purview, while granting a certain privilege to the South, above all to the state of Georgia.

Once he arrived in Atlanta, Du Bois began teaching and conducting academic-year surveys and summer-season fieldwork with his students on the rural conditions of Negro American communities throughout the state, especially in one of its southwestern counties, Dougherty (situated along the border of Alabama in the hinterland that rises up slowly from the Florida Panhandle) (Du Bois 1980j). It was on this very particular terrain that Du Bois began to arrive at a certain theoretical understanding of the problematic bequeathed to him—by all of the overlapping ensembles of his historical situation.

In the thought that he formulated, the problem was recognized as one produced on a global scale as a general form of the organization of modern historicity. In the second half of part I of this study, we recognized the 1904 essay "The Development of a People" as a certain achieved and succinct formulation and statement of that understanding (Du Bois 1904, 2015d).

Yet the course of his theoretical formulation must be understood with a certain regard for its immanence. By way of thinking through a quite specific situation, Du Bois was led to formulate an understanding of it in such a way that it in turn enabled him to propose a distinctive understanding of the general historical situation of which the so-called group in question was a part. The general historicity in question comprised the economic and political processes shaping a certain commonness of world on a global scale from the fifteenth century through to the turn to the twentieth century. And, for Du Bois's understanding of it, ontological claims in discourse (philosophical, legal, theological, political, economic, literary, "scientific," and so forth) made on the basis of the organization of this historicity were a constitutive dimension of its very unfolding. It was in order to come to terms with, render relative, and perhaps overturn such claims and to produce an understanding that might allow one to intervene by way of judgment and decision and organized action in the central processes of this history, that Du Bois produced a critically reflexive thought of "the problem of the color line."

This study proposes that we recognize Du Bois's formulation of "the problem of the color line" as an epistemological intervention, on the order of a conceptualization and a nascent theorization, naming an entire domain of study: a certain dimension of all that might be rendered legible for thought under the heading of modern historicity.

If so taken in contemporary discourse, in a certain way, what comes into relief is a sense of limit and possibility that might go beyond the impasse of a contemporary discussion that still presumes the possible projection of a singular horizon for thought, usually in the form of an imperial Europe or European America, as definitive of the terms of theoretical problematization, yet not reflexively acknowledged as playing such a theoretical role. It may be that an apparently parochial formulation of problem by way of the necessary and self-critical exposure of the limits of both its possibility and its becoming is more resolute *and* supple in its guide for critical thought in our time than one that would propose to accede directly to the limit and announce its discourse as the ultimate form of passage beyond such. A certain form of tarrying with the partial might well name in a felicitous manner the most intractable difficulties posed for thought in our time. If so, it proposes a certain patient restlessness in the promulgation of thought as theoretical practice. It maintains within its elaboration a responsibility that would not disavow its emergence according to the limit that it would seek to engage. Yet it also, by way of that very maintenance, inhabits a protocol that recognizes and insists upon the always previous responsibility of its impossible responsibility in the present to a possibility that remains yet to come. In this complicated practice, it would remain open to its own limit as the very form of its becoming. In this sense, the passage beyond for thought as practice is only according to the always immanent announcement of its own heterogeneity in its possible becoming otherwise than the given. Passage, if there is such, remains never only absolute. Possibility otherwise is never simply given. Affirmation of such, as a practice, maintains thereby its own critical form of responsibility to both sides of the limit as the terms by which historicity gives possibility.

Still, if a summary word can serve to orient here without proposing a final determination of meaning, then we might describe "the problem of the color line" for Du Bois as an agonistically derived and hierarchically ordered—mobile—articulation of the differences and relations among groups of humans situated on a dimension of generality that we would tend to call global in our contemporary sense of horizon.

In the U.S. context, especially in *The Souls of Black Folk: Essays and Sketches*, Du Bois has famously elaborated the metaphor of *the veil* to account for this mode of problematization as a certain order of social phenomenon (Du Bois 1903l). (We have remarked the first appearances of this metaphor in the previously unpublished essay "The Afro-American" which we annotated in the first half of Part I of the present study 2015a.) Such metaphor, if also taken as a concept, does not name an ontological structure even if it can be understood to announce the way in which being as existence is always other than the simple. It remains otherwise than the ontologically given as historial form. It names, if at all, the announcement of the historial as a form of problematization. It is, then, a historical structure whose specificity renders it tractable by knowledge.

The "line" and the "veil," respectively, are the concept metaphors of historicity by which Du Bois would name the limit as having, shall we say, always and everywhere at least two sides.

As an aspect of Du Bois's complex thought of the double, this is a motif, one of the most fundamental of all of Du Bois's thought and not just one among others, announced at its inception, as we are tracking it here, that will in its eventuality be given a ceaseless elaboration across his entire itinerary

(Du Bois 1897a[?], 1980b, 1985b, 1897c). Organized as the conjunctive thought that constitutes "The Present Outlook for the Dark Races of Mankind," which we will annotate extensively below, this motif undergoes a formative passage through the difficulty of proposing a rethinking of the aftermath of the failure of Reconstruction in the United States (Du Bois 1900a, 2015g, 1901b, 2015e). That rethinking yields the historiographical frame of the great small book that is *The Souls of Black Folk: Essays and Sketches* (Du Bois 1903l) and the reflection on the legacy of John Brown at the half-century mark of his death (Du Bois 1909, 1962, 1973d). While already announced in those earlier texts, the heading of the concept metaphor of the colonial "shadows" of the metropole of the nineteenth- and twentieth-century empires, extending this motif of the always irruptive double in variegated exfoliations, acquires a distinct legibility across the time of World War I and its immediate aftermath (Du Bois 1906a, 1975c, 1925). It is signal that the explicit provocation for its vocative announcement arose out of a radical order of crisis on a global scale. The 1915 essay "The African Roots of War" stands as a turning point, both a theoretical summary restatement and an original recalibration of a conception of the logic of modern historicity in the horizon of war on an unprecedented scale (Du Bois 1915a, 1982a). Produced on a rather spectacular level as the narrative of *Dark Princess* from 1928 (Du Bois 1974a, 1928), its theoretical promise broaches another fulfillment in the immediate aftermath of World War II in the pathbreaking essay *Color and Democracy: Colonies and Peace* (Du Bois 1975b, 1945; see also Chandler 2021). A certain other culmination of this thought—announced this time on the order of a subject of experience—will then be realized across the narrative of the *Black Flame* trilogy of 1957 to 1961 (Du Bois 1957, 1959, 1961), especially its last volume, *Worlds of Color* (Du Bois 1976c, 1961).

It formed the root and organized the principal branches of *Black Reconstruction: An Essay toward a History of the Part Which Black Folk Played in the Attempt to Reconstruct Democracy in America, 1860–1880*— which remains his magnum opus (Du Bois 1935, 1976d).

The "problem of the color line" in Du Bois's sense, then, is announced on that order of historicity that becomes at issue when the putative sovereign example exhibits the dysfunction of its supposed paternal status. Its ostensible capacity to stand (that is to say, to stand at all and not only as a claim of singular historial status) is recognized as maintained, if at all, only by way of a hierarchical organization of forms of privilege, exploitation, and dispensation. If the root of historicity should be understood as otherwise than the simple, as always ensemblic, then it can also be understood to announce a question of the status of relation in every sense. This is the irruptive ground of our problematic. On one register of the historial, at issue is the proclamation of the singular example of the passage beyond historical limit. On a different level, the question is the reimagination of historial possibility according to another or a new affirmation of relation. In this way, then, we can see that what is named by way of a critical deployment of such a concept metaphor—"the problem of the color line" or the dispositive effects of "the veil"—is a problematization of all previous presumption of the possibility of the sovereign example in the devolution of historicity. This is the form of problem that names the epoch of the so-called modern for Du Bois. For example, it is the very terms of the emergence of something called "America." And what of other such modern projects, those already announced and those that remain at stake for the future? (1) The "problem of the color line," then, is produced in *modern* history as a basic and fundamental aspect of new historical relations among groups of people. (2) In this historicity, the institution of Atlantic slavery and its relation to modern forms of imperialism, including its devolution in and as the practices of colonialism, with particular implication by way of its inscription into the unfolding forms of colonial usurpation of the legalities of those peoples already indigenous to various regions of the world (throughout the Americas, for example, but not only so), would stand as an incipient reference. (3) And an ensemble of symbolic operations (perhaps one could say, discourse in a general sense) is constitutively inscribed in the production and unfolding of these institutions and in their aftermath. This can entail practices in any social field, from the microscopic to the most general. (And such operations are certainly not only "linguistic.") And this order of the symbolic is not simply one level of problematization among others. As it pertains to the status of what in the Greek conceptuality inherited in Europe has been called truth, notably that which has been supposed as given or understood as the articulation of a judgment of correctness (cf. Heidegger 1998), its formal promulgation establishes the horizon of judgment with which any critical discourse in this domain must come to terms. It is the seam by which the problem of knowledge is announced as a part of the problematization in question—the global "problem of the color line."

This seam must be given a somewhat more explicit remark, for it is also the form or fold at which our own practice is announced to itself, even if only "darkly as through a veil," if we take reference to Du Bois's thought as he unfolds the metaphor in the opening paragraphs of the opening chapter of *The Souls of Black Folk: Essays and Sketches.*

Formal discourses beginning in the eighteenth century announced the fundamental bearing of this problematization in the formalization of a concept of "man," and later the human, in philosophy and science. It is here that one can see that the *concept* of race appears as the outcome of the way in which the manifest diversity of humans as a problematization of existence articulates with the imperatives of the faculty of reason as these are announced in critical thought (from David Hume to Immanuel Kant, and beyond, into German idealism and its contemporary legacies; from Benjamin Franklin to Thomas Jefferson, and beyond into the American nineteenth century) (see, for example, Kant 2007b, 2007c). Du Bois does not elaborate this account of the epistemic production, philosophical if you will, of what he understands as "the problem of the color line." Perhaps he was circumscribed by his own ambivalent inhabitation of critical thought (as I have indexed it) or by his focus on the general field of social subordination and exploitation (as this latter was so powerfully afoot in the time of his writing, at the turn to the twentieth century). Yet it can be done on the basis of premises in his work. I have begun to propose such a questioning, à partir de, by way of, or after Du Bois's order of attention both in this study as well as in additional elsewhere (Chandler, forthcoming).

The present elaboration offered here, in part II of this study, is simply a step in the solicitation of contemporary thought to sustain a larger critical engagement with Du Bois's legacy in this domain. Yet it has, I believe, a fundamental role and value. In a sense, it precedes the labor that should be accomplished by new theoretical work. Herein, I attempt a distinct form of elaboration, an attention to the letter of his text. Whereas earlier in this study, of necessity, I proceeded by a certain taut tracking of the discursive movement of several key passages in Du Bois's thought of the turn of the century by way of intertextual reference within enunciations signed by Du Bois, here the text at issue solicits an explicitly doubled tracking. In the reading of the essay "The Present Outlook for the Dark Races of Mankind," as the text simultaneously strains in two directions at once, the reading protocol must maintain itself on these counterposed and interwoven motific paths as well. Du Bois is at once attempting to announce a theoretical disposition, even as he does not call it by such a name at the time of his writing (nor does he do so later in any explicit manner), even as the disposition named in this study can be understood to remain definitive for the whole of his subsequent itinerary and to annotate and accentuate the representation of his historical present so as to render into relief a fundamental dimension, the futural implication of the forms of actual present and lived existence, in whatever sense we can possibly speak of the latter. One track of our consideration must proceed by way of the taut reference to the thetic and allusive interpretations proposed within the declarations of Du Bois's text proper, as we have so far practiced it in this study. The other track must annotate, according to the limits and possibilities given in existing forms of knowledge, the ensemble of contextual horizons (which remain in principle unclosed and illimitable, and hence knowledge of such must always remain unfinished and without fulsome realization in any present projection) placed at stake by such a theoretical disposition. This doubled tracking, while in principle always at issue in my remarks on other writings by Du Bois, will show most legibly in my discourse as I engage the essay "The Present Outlook for the Dark Races of Mankind" directly. In that reference, my practice can be understood as operating in two primary modes, iterative elaboration and direct annotation. In this sense, part II of the present study is primarily scholastic in its premise. It is an effort to allow a certain form of recollection of the character of an antecedent discourse, that given by Du Bois, to provide some terms or some ground according to which contemporary thought can critically reengage the challenge of Du Bois's discourse, general practice, and historical profile on this terrain—the thought of "the problem of the color line." The commitment here, then, is to a reinhabitation of the labor of thought by which Du Bois could first begin to name for himself a workable formulation of "the problem of the color line" as a problem for thought. We will track Du Bois's thinking by way of linking a specific scene of problematization, the African American, to a general one, "the world," as he put it at 1900. In this construal, the exemplary example—on all levels of individuation—is something other than a figure of the sovereign.

We can approach the whole proposition as a certain kind of epistemological question by engaging just a handful of texts from Du Bois's writings, three essays or passages of essay length, from the time of his first work as a thinker who had come to a certain understanding of his own declared sense of an intellectual itinerary—the time in question is from the middle months of 1897 to the last month of 1899, the latter being the moment of his first full epistemological statement of a thought of "the problem of the color line." Indeed, the most sustained consideration offered herein is of the text "The Present Outlook for the Dark Races of Mankind," presented in public on the 27th of December at the third annual meeting of the American Negro Academy in Washington, D.C. in 1899 (see the discussion below, and notes thereto, for bibliographic notations pertaining to this text) (Du Bois 1900a, 2015g, 125–26).

I. FORMULATION I: "THE CONSERVATION OF RACES," WASHINGTON, D.C., MARCH 1897

The first place that we can recognize the incipient formulation of "the problem of the color line" as a problem of thought in the work of Du Bois, that is to say, *as a certain object of critical theoretical reflection*, is in the fundamental essay "The Conservation of Races" from the early spring, March, of 1897.[1]

After acknowledging in an opening paragraph that his audience of African American leaders and intellectuals, all men in this instance, would tend to deprecate the idea of essential differences among humans that one might call race, Du Bois announces in the second paragraph of that essay the premise that he would take as fundamental to thinking about the question of the African American on this occasion:

> We must acknowledge that human beings are divided into races; that in this country the two most extreme types of the world's races have met, and the resulting problem as to the future relations of these types is not only of intense and living interest to us, but forms an epoch in the history of mankind. (CR 5, para. 2)

This is a historical problem, produced in the development of imperialism and colonialism, which together devolved by way of the inaugurating and constitutive organization of the institution of Atlantic systems of enslavement, all of which would in turn be constitutive in the history of the deployment of forms of capital, of capitalization, from the fifteenth through the nineteenth centuries. Yet, by the second half of the eighteenth century, the heading of supposed differences of race as an ontological proposition had been rendered coherent for forms and practices of knowledge, for a diverse ensemble of forms of thought and understanding, notably as forms of epistemology. And, by the time of Du Bois's writing, still within the wake of the American Civil War and the failures and reactions that followed, a sense of human difference as ostensibly given in some categorical manner (which might today be claimed as somehow ontological) had been rendered so broadly emphatic that it was almost presumptive for general forms of thought and practice. It is with this sense, thus, that Du Bois in "The Conservation of Races" describes the situation of his historical present, encompassing both its past and its future, as forming "an epoch in the history of mankind" (CR 5, para. 2).

In this address, on the one hand, Du Bois proposes that this historical situation or problem should be approached first of all as a problem of knowledge and understanding.

On the other hand, the orientation, the commitment that would guide an approach to this situation, will be to take a certain course of action, to make a decision, establish a policy, and organize an institution.

The matter of knowledge is, thus, a first consideration in that process.

Beginning with the premise that a certain authority has established this distinction, that is, a conception of something formulated under the heading of race as marking essential differences among humans, an authority that remains unnamed in the first three paragraphs but that will be presented in the fourth as the science of his time, a general evolutionism specified by Charles Darwin's theoretical accomplishment, Du Bois proposes "to survey the whole question of race in human philosophy" (CR 5, para. 3). In a sense, he proposes to formulate and develop, for the purposes of thinking through the problem of the Negro American situation, a whole question about the status of a difference that has been placed under the heading of race in human history, a certain kind of whole or theoretical totality. To do this, he proposes to take up the concept of race and to examine its place in a certain understanding of history, not so much history as an unfolding process of singular and irreversible events as historicity, as a showing forth of the supposed ontological or metaphysical organization of human existence. This will not be a factual account of the supposed actual events of the play of supposed race differences in history. Instead, it will be an attempt to explain the whole of this development as something comprehendible: that is, in the final sense, as devolving according to a kind of necessity. That is, Du Bois proposes to answer this question on the basis of philosophy and to ask of it a fundamental question about the basis of the differences among humans, at least as that difference is understood according to the proposed concept of race. The domain, or order of existence, that he will examine as the object of his inquiry, that which he will ask about or question, that which can reveal or show forth something essential pertaining to the distinction that may be construed according to the idea and concept of race, is history, historical processes, the movement of historicity as such, the historial in general, a domain that can be distinguished from other possible domains of inquiry, such as the physiological or internal processes of the human body or the devolution of theological truth. On the basis of such an inquiry, in this text Du Bois hopes "to recognize the hard limits of natural law," or, as he also says, to understand "the constitution of the world" as it pertains to this question of so-called racial differences and the question of the status of the Negro American (CR 5, para. 3).

This general problematic and question can then be summarized in one locution. In the third paragraph, Du Bois formulates it in the following way: "What is the real meaning of Race?" The term *real* in this sentence and its apparent insistence on the factual, the actual, the materially irreversible, should not mislead one to understand this as primarily a discourse about facts, the factum of human history. Rather, the entire emphasis should be placed on the idea of "meaning" as modifying such a presumption of "real." For Du Bois is concerned to understand the bearing of human differences, their implication, in historical processes. That undefinable, yet illimitable, gap will be the focus of Du Bois's attention. He then outlines his inquiry as proceeding in two temporal directions from the situation of his present: (a) "What has in the past been the law of race development?," that is, the "swift and slow" of history, as he will remark it in the closing paragraphs of the closing chapter of *The Souls of Black Folk: Essays and Sketches* (see the epigraph to part I); and (b) "What lessons has the past of race development to teach the rising Negro people?" (CR 5, para. 3). That is, what are the lessons from this past that might be of service in the future?

In this essay, "The Conservation of Races," Du Bois goes on to answer the overall or prncipal question, "What is the real meaning of Race?" He follows its derivative forms, about the past and then about the future, as the rhetorical and organizational headings of his address. As preliminary to those considerations, however, he questions the traditional concept of race as an essential and determining order of physical difference, a difference that had been understood as indicated by a physical character of the body in the sciences and the philosophy of the eighteenth and nineteenth centuries in Europe and the Americas. He then reformulates it as a primarily social and historical character of the internal relations among groups of people (CR 6–7, paras. 4–6).[2] Second, Du Bois then offers a speculative narrative of the past about the development and productivity of ideals in the constitution of groups that he alternately calls "races" and "nations." His account is one in which "intermingling" and intermixture stand as the essential infrastructural character of the entities produced in this history. And it is also one in which historicity, that is, a process of becoming and dissolution, as the mode of being of such differences or of such groups, is fundamental (CR 7–9, paras. 7–10).[3] Third, Du Bois formulates a theory of the future of such groups and on that basis proposes a course of action for the Negro American in the present. The course that he proposes would, he suggests, make it possible for the Negro to be at one with the movement of history, its "law(s)," or the "constitution of the world." That course of action, the theory, that he proposes is that they should foster their "racial" characteristics, "conserve" their racial differences, not oppositionally but differentially and affirmatively (CR 9–12, paras. 11–17). The American Negro Academy should, Du Bois proposes, represent the institutional realization of such a direction among African Americans in the United States (CR 12–15, paras. 18–32).

With this schematic statement of the stakes of "The Conservation of Races," a crucial and fundamental distinction within Du Bois's formulation of the problematic at hand can now be rendered. It is of fundamental epistemological importance for the contemporary interpretation of the work of Du Bois that his complicated negotiation with the concept of race as the nominalization within science or philosophy of the supposed ontological ground for a historical positivity that he would seek to affirm, for example, a group that might be called Negro American or African American, should not be simply subordinated or amalgamated to his epistemological nominalization of the term *color line* or better the phrase in his thought that issued as "the problem of the color line" that he proposed in order to bring into analytical relief a dimension of modern historicity that he wished to make the object of a fundamental critique.[4] In "The Conservation of Races," these two dimensions seemed to take shape in one discursive register. And in a sense this is so. However, in a more fundamental sense, it is the intersection of two different orders of the problem of the Negro as a problem of thought. We might call them, respectively, the question of possibility and the question of limit.

II. FORMULATION II: "A FINAL WORD" OF *THE PHILADELPHIA NEGRO: A SOCIAL STUDY*, ATLANTA, GEORGIA, MAY–JUNE 1899

In the late spring of 1899, in writing the short closing chapter, "A Final Word" of his justly famous sociological study *The Philadelphia Negro: A Social Study*, the preface of which he dates as June 1—just six days after the tragic, emotionally shattering death of his firstborn, a son, Burghardt—in fact, in the opening section of that epilogue, called "The Meaning of All This," Du Bois reflects on the global context of the Negro question as he had described it in his study of the conditions of Negro Americans in the Seventh Ward of Philadelphia of the late 1890s (Du Bois 1899a).[5] And he does so on the same order of generality, here in an epistemological articulation, that he had first formulated some fifteen months earlier, there an articulation with a supposed ontological problematization, we might say, in "The Conservation of Races."

The Negro problem in America, in the United States, as it is put in this discussion, is part of a very large question about the status of human relation in the modern epoch and its implication for the human practice of freedom.

So the Negro question is, *first*, only a particular form of an age-old question. It is a question that can in its broadest extension be understood as only a specific and distinctive formation in the context of common problems of society. Writing from the context of the "New World," Du Bois describes those perennial questions as "the old world problems of ignorance, poverty, crime, and the dislike of the stranger."

> They are after all the same difficulties over which the world has grown gray: the question as to how far human intelligence can be trusted and trained; as to whether we must always have the poor with us; as to whether it is possible for the masses of men to attain righteousness on earth. (PN 385)

In one sense, then, there is nothing new here, no new problematic in a comparative sense.

Second, however, an aspect or one kind of such a perennial question, a specific form of such a general social question, the age-old question of the relation to the other, a kind of problem that human groups have commonly faced throughout history, acquires a specific and fundamental character when it arises in relation to the Negro. That is to say that in this context a certain character within this question, a dimension that is not simply reducible to the immediate social level, acquired a certain relief. It acquired a texture that allows its philosophical appurtenance to come legibly into view. In the case of the Negro (certainly in Philadelphia but also beyond and including the whole of the African Diaspora and at its limit pertaining to the question of the status of all who would be called Negro or African globally), this question becomes an ontological one because it takes the specific, threshold or incipiting, form of a question of essence. The question asks about essence: (*ti est ti*), *what is, what is it?* Historically, the locution of its enunciation in discourses of the Negro is: "What, or who, is the Negro?" And this is a question that can only be answered as part of a broader frame of reference, namely, "What, or who, is the human?" And then, or therefore, the other side of such a question also acquires a certain legibility: What is the relative status of the human and the animal, or other animals; what is the status and character of such a distinction? Or, as Du Bois states it in this text, "After all who are Men?" (PN 385); so too, it is a question of the difference among such supposed kind as those called man or the human, in general:

> Is every featherless biped to be counted a man and brother? Are all races and types to be joint heirs of the new earth that men have striven to raise in thirty centuries and more? Shall we not swamp civilization in barbarism and drown genius in indulgence if we seek a mythical Humanity which shall shadow all men? (PN 385–86)

To this question, Du Bois first compares two answers, one from the past and another from his historical present. Du Bois himself will go on to propose a perspective from another horizon, that of the future, of the centuries yet to come.[6]

The answer of the past, of "the early centuries," was essentially peremptory. And here Du Bois seems to have in mind not only Europe but also, perhaps, the so-called ancient world of the Mediterranean and, perhaps, even beyond:

> [That] those of any nation who can be called men and endowed with rights are few: they are the privileged classes—the well-born and the accidents of low-birth called up by the King. The rest, the masses of the nation, the *pöbel*, the mob, are fit to follow, to obey, to dig and delve, but not to think or rule or play the gentleman. (PN 386)

Du Bois goes on to propose a suggestive translation or form of comparison, to which we shall return later:

> We who are born to another philosophy hardly realize how deep-seated and plausible this view of human capabilities and powers once was; how utterly incomprehensible this republic [the United States] would have been to Charlemagne or Charles V or Charles I. We rather hasten to forget that once the courtiers of English kings looked upon the ancestors of most Americans with far greater contempt than these Americans look upon Negroes—and perhaps,

indeed, had more cause. We forget that once French peasants were the "Niggers" of France, and that German princelings once discussed with doubt the brains and humanity of the *bauer.* (PN 386)

So, the present situation of the Negro, of the Negro American in the United States, of the Negro in Philadelphia, poses a question that stretches back into the history of modern Europe, to the very inception of modernity in general, to the question of a European modernity and its relation to the "New World" and to Africa.

The answer of the present, of Du Bois's time, which of course can be referred through the great revolutions of the eighteenth century, the American, the French, and the Haitian, to the movements of the sixteenth and seventeenth centuries for the recognition of rights, is for "a wider humanity, a wider respect for simple manhood unadorned by ancestors or privilege" (PN 386). Not that "all men are created free and equal, but that the differences in men are not so vast as we had assumed" (PN 386). But this "widening of the idea of common Humanity is of slow growth and to-day but dimly realized" (PN 386). There is, for Du Bois, a differential ranking of groups of humans. He outlines the declension as it pertains both to the question of a global humanity and to the question of the Negro:

> We grant full citizenship in the World-Commonwealth to the "Anglo-Saxon" (whatever that may mean), the Teuton and the Latin; then with just a shade of reluctance we extend it to the Celt and the Slav. We half deny it to the yellow races of Asia, admit the brown Indians to an ante-room only on the strength of an undeniable past; but with the Negroes of Africa we come to a full stop, and in its heart the civilized world with one accord denies that these come within the pale of nineteenth century Humanity. (PN 386–87)

This comparative global perspective is what surrounds and situates the question of the Negro in the United States. The persistent rebirth of this differentiation of who is understood as human, or, better, fully human (and a teleological structure is always implied in conceptions of such an entity), in the context of the idea of a global humanity is the broadest social and historical horizon for understanding the situation of the Negro in the United States as a problem. This hierarchy of value, articulated as a "feeling, widespread and deep-seated," has a unique and distinct bearing in the United States (PN 386).

Du Bois tries to name it according to two metaphors. Suggesting the image of an overlay or canopy, of a horizon, a vista receding to the limit of visibility, he describes it as, "in America, the vastest of the Negro problems" (PN 387). And just two paragraphs later, suggesting a kind of animated ether or ghostlike consciousness, a haunting perhaps, operating by way of a kind of immanent movement, producing itself by way of instituting differentiations in every domain of sociality, apart from which it is nothing, he describes it as "a spirit that enters in and complicates all Negro social problems."

Thus, in the United States, the Negro is seen as *not fully* human. But this should not be understood simply as a question of degree.[7] Du Bois understands it as oppositional, as categorical; that is, there is a "full stop" in the face of the question of the Negro.[8] The premise is that there is a telic conception of the human and that in the final analysis the Negro is not capable of becoming such or becoming commensurate with such.

It is exactly in the face of such an oppositional claim that Du Bois proposes a third answer to this question. Its temporality is resolutely an open one. It is a futural view, the view of "other centuries" yet to come, those that could be understood as "looking back on the culture of the nineteenth [century]." From this perspective, Du Bois describes this problem of the Negro, the Negro question, as one that should be addressed in the context of all humanity: "Only civilization and humanity can successfully solve" it. Thus, one might say, as does Du Bois, that it is a "battle for humanity and human culture" (PN 387–88).[9]

Such a futural perspective opens a rift within the ontological and categorical claims embedded within the prevailing judgment in discourses supposed as *of* the Negro in light of the question of what is human in general. This rift arises because any gesture to declare a categorical denial of the Negro could only sustain itself if it could hypostasize a telos or horizon that could withdraw completely into itself. That is to say, it would have to exist only in the temporal form of a present. Yet if it made such a claim, its own becoming would be rendered incoherent. Thus, Du Bois's present, a "hey day of the greatest of the world's civilizations," must account for its own possibility as rooted in an openness to a future whose bearing cannot be forgone or foreclosed. That openness might be the common root of both its own becoming and that of "the Negro American." A futural perspective, then, one coming from outside or on the margins of the present proscription of the Negro, poses the question of the justification of such a distinction, or, more radically, of the possibility of its ground, of its status with regard to universal historicity or the possibility of such. This is a question that, at the barest level, that of its being formulated and posed, points toward the agonistic organization of the question "What are Men?" in the context of the problem of the Negro as a problem for thought (PN 387–88).

III. ELABORATIONS: "THE PRESENT OUTLOOK FOR THE DARK RACES OF MANKIND," WASHINGTON, D.C., DECEMBER 1899

In December 1899, just six months after signing off on his preface to *The Philadelphia Negro*, Du Bois wrote a crucial text for understanding his thinking of the problematic at hand, the question of how to think the historicity of the Negro question in the United States in relation to modern historicity as a whole. That text is "The Present Outlook for the Dark Races of Mankind."[10] Perhaps composed over the weeks and days just before his departure and perhaps even completed on the train en route from Atlanta, Georgia, to Washington, D.C., as its style has the feel of the coming to voice of immediate speech, it was first presented to the public as the presidential address to the American Negro Academy (ANA) on the occasion of its third annual meeting, held on the 27th and 28th of December, 1899, at Lincoln Memorial Church in the capital city (figure 2.1). It was his second major address to that organization.

The 1899 address was subsequently put into print in the October 1900 issue of the *A.M.E. Church Review*, published at Philadelphia by the African Methodist Episcopal Church, with Hightower T. Kealing (a founding member of the ANA) as editor (Du Bois 1900a).[11]

As the reception of this text over the past century and a quarter is somewhat at odds with the interest of its thematic, I will indicate several aspects of its publication history. And, in addition, it has not often been reprinted in its entirety and hence remains not so easily accessible in complete and reliable form.[12]

Indeed, even the provenance, or occasion, of the first presentation of this text is of some interest in this context. In a monograph-length study of the ANA, completed almost two generations ago, citing records of the society's official proceedings, Alfred A. Moss Jr. indicates that in June 1900 "the executive committee voted to print this paper as Occasional Paper no. 7, knowing at the time that it was scheduled to appear in the July [1900] issue of the *AME Church Review*" (Moss 1981, 101). Moss concludes that "this decision was almost certainly the desire to lay claim to what it considered an ANA paper no matter the consequences." However, they did not follow through on this decision. Moss goes on to reference an unpublished letter from Du Bois to John Wesley Cromwell (from the papers of Cromwell, privately held at the time of Moss's research), then secretary for the ANA, indicating that the letter dates from sometime in "November 1900" (Moss 1981, 18n20, 101n17). As quoted by Moss, Du Bois wrote, "I am doubtful of the expediency of publishing my last year's address. Those colored people who may want it can find it in the *Review*. For others the matter is a little old and the Academy has already published one of my papers. You will of course follow your own and the committee's decision" (Moss 1981, 101). The ANA decided not to publish the Du Bois text and instead issued an essay by a different author as its next occasional paper.

Moss further indicates that to his understanding, "the July, 1900 issue of the *AME Church Review* is no longer extant making it impossible to see if the essay ['The Present Outlook for the Dark Races of Mankind'] appeared" (Moss 1981, 101n17). However, as noted above (at the opening of our discussion of this text), there is at least one extant copy of the *October* 1900 issue of the *Review*, the issue in which Du Bois's essay did in fact appear.

Later in his chapter on the ANA series of Occasional Papers, Moss notes that indeed the editor of the *A.M.E. Church Review*, Kealing, was also a member of the ANA. He quotes a March 1900 letter from Kealing to Cromwell where the former wrote that he sought the "co-operation" of the academy's other members "by contribution and otherwise, in making the [*A.M.E. Church*] *Review* the broadest and most scholarly publication ever issued by the race" and that he would be pleased if the ANA would use it to reach a "larger audience than any present medium at its command allows" (Moss 1981, 106–7). Indeed, at the third annual meeting, at which Du Bois's address was delivered, Kealing proposed a motion that the ANA enter a formal arrangement with the *A.M.E. Church Review*. At the insistence of Kelly Miller, another important and founding member of the ANA, the motion was amended to include other publications in addition to the African Methodist Episcopal Church's sponsored publication (Moss 1981, 107).

Certainly these records offer some sense of the ANA's internal efforts to organize itself in such a fashion as to produce and intervene in discourses concerning the Negro American. However, its pertinence in the context of the discussion of the essay at hand is that it also shows evidence of the sense among some members of the African American intelligentsia of the relation of their situation to a global horizon; that is to say, on the basis of these facts, it can be reasonably judged that the perspective of Du Bois's essay "The Present Outlook for the Dark Races of Mankind" was of presumptive currency and issue for the group to which it was most directly addressed during the year following its delivery.

I suggest that according to a certain order of attention, the epistemological (and it is an attunement that includes the context of the occasions of the essay's two original presentations, one oral and the other written), Du Bois's essay, while certainly "a little old" (already within the year following its original oral presentation, according to Du Bois himself) and we might say "a little occasional" (as opposed to the patience of the perennial that might attend and commend a scholarly effort), maintains within its enunciation a reference to a fundamental dimension of modern historicity, on the one hand, and records a formative development within Du Bois's thought as he attempts to come to terms with this difficult problematic, on the other. In its eventuality, Du Bois's efforts to come to terms with this reference will never cease. He punctiliously sustained an inhabitation of this question from one end of his itinerary to the other. Therefore, one should not look for a treatise in this domain of his work; rather, his entire itinerary was the elaboration of his engagement. Hence, our task should perhaps best be understood as an attention to the demands on thought that arise in the maintenance of the question at stake therein. It is in this epistemic sense that I propose to comment on the essay at hand—to ask, "What is the character of the thought that takes shape for us if we accept it (warts and all, the limits as well as the possibilities given therein) as our own responsibility?" It is also in this sense that it remains the contemporary of our own thought and is at stake for us in this globalized and supposedly postmodern world of the twenty-first century. A recognition of this contemporaneity, in parallel to both the historicity of Du Bois's lived itinerary and the historicity of his thought itself in its epistemic dimension, cannot be accessed by us all in one go, one blow, or one gesture. Its most telling sense may take shape only by way of a certain labor of elaboration.

A. CONCEPTUALIZATION

At an epistemic level and in a theoretical sense, it is a unique text in Du Bois's thought. And the principal conceptualization that Du Bois enunciates in it, even as it was an occasional and a laconic locution as a theoretical statement, remained fundamental to all of his subsequent thinking. It announces the lineaments of a thought of modernity as a whole according to a dimension of that historicity that he proposed to comprehend under the heading "the problem of the color line." Let us remark, for the sake of our own contemporaneity, that Du Bois began to announce this thought in the midst of the high stride of modern imperialism, which had sedimented itself most precisely and historically as an ongoing modern projection in the form of colonialism. It is a specific dimension of this historicity, which is yet not simply a relative one, and the problematic that takes shape within it, that Du Bois sought in this essay to render coherent for a theoretical inhabitation.

In one sense, "The Present Outlook for the Dark Races of Mankind" should be considered a sequel, a certain continuation of the meditation and the appeal that Du Bois had proposed in "The Conservation of Races." For in its broadest reference, the 1899 essay situates its concern at the same epochal level of the problematic that Du Bois had already formulated in the earlier one.

As I have already briefly noted above, there is an essential epistemological difference between these two essays. Yet the import of this difference is such that it should be remarked here, at the juncture of an explicit comparison between them. In the first essay, "The Conservation of Races," on the one hand, Du Bois's question concerned the relation of relation and possibility. He thus attempted a critical reformulation of the concept of race as a heading by which to announce a theory of historical possibility. In the second essay, "The Present Outlook for the Dark Races of Mankind," on the other, his question was about the relation of relation and limit. In the latter essay, he thus attempts to formulate a critical conception of a phenomenon that he calls "the problem of the color line" and to outline something of its theoretical implication. At the level of an analysis, that is, a certain kind of theoretical inquiry, the respective dimension of historicity to which these two essays are addressed should be rendered as distinct. To conflate the two aspects would be to submit the entire critical force of Du Bois's intervention, in both domains, to the terms of the very conditions that he is attempting to question and to the limits of the horizon that we, in our own turn and with him, would seek to move beyond.

In a rhetorical sense, Du Bois's discourse shifts vocative registers from the earlier text to the later one. While more philosophical and speculative in the earlier formulation, it is more historical and political in the later one. Reciprocally retrospective and prospective in both essays, producing interpretations of a past to propose a possible future that is yet to come, the principal horizon of the call to action is more explicitly or elaborately named as *a practice of the local or national within a worldwide or global situation* in the latter essay. And whereas the threshold naming of "the problem of the color line" is thematized more as the circumstantial and the conditional in the earlier essay, the realm of a certain ontological necessity that nonetheless has within it a domain of freedom, in that he sought therein to announce the terms of an originary possibility as historial according to which something called a Negro or Negro American could be announced as a figure in modern history, in the latter essay, the problem of the color line is of historicity itself, modern history, and thus the possibility of a certain complication and disruption of its determinations, the realm of a certain freedom that might be realized by action in accordance with a certain ethical imperative, one that Du Bois will present as a "duty," is more resolutely affirmed. Du Bois's address in the latter essay calls for an inhabitation of responsibility to a future that is beyond all boundaries.

With these general comparisons between these two essays in mind, perhaps I can now propose some more specific comparisons as a way to elucidate the original status of the later text in Du Bois's elaboration of the thought of the problem of the color line as an epistemological horizon, a vista for historiographical investigation, interpretation, and understanding.

Just as with "The Conservation of Races," where Du Bois proposed to analyze the situation of the African American in the United States with regard to the problem of relations across a putative color line from a point of view that stood above the everyday and surveyed the question from the viewpoint of "all human philosophy," in "The Present Outlook for the Dark Races of Mankind," Du Bois proposes that he and his audience "place themselves" at the level of a "larger point of view," one that he now characterizes as "the cold eye of the historian and social philosopher" (Outlook 95, para. 1). Just as he spoke of law and necessity in the earlier essay, here Du Bois speaks of "the secret of social progress [as] wide and thorough understanding of the social forces which move and modify your age" (Outlook 95, para. 1).

It can be said that both essays ask about the past in order to understand the present and in order to establish guidelines for action in the future. However, "The Conservation of Races" seems to pivot on articulating the Negro or African American relation to a past, "a vast historic race" called Negro, whose primary geographic scene of origination would be the "African" continent. "The Present Outlook for the Dark Races of Mankind" turns on the Negro or African American relation to a new horizon or situation, to a specific future, of a national and an international scene, of what might with caution be called "racial" intermingling, of which the American scene will be an exemplary example and of which the Negro or African American situation will thus also be exemplary (that is, within this American scene). Perhaps, this example, would be the exemplary of the exemplary, and will thus be exemplary on a global scale. As Du Bois can be understood to propose in the later essay, such will be the global situation of the twentieth century, a century that for him, on the eve of the year 1900, was yet to come.

Thus, Du Bois's formulation of the topic that he would address in the essay is a certain way of understanding, or thinking about, "the problem of the color line." If in "The Conservation of Races" Du Bois's focus was on conceptualizing the situation of the Negro American with regard to the specific scene of the United States, then in "The Present Outlook for the Dark Races of Mankind," he proposes to redeploy the question of the character of that situation by accenting another register of its organization.[13] If in the earlier text he questioned and reconceptualized the general and comparative ground of something like the Negro American as a group, in order to specify their situation and to outline a particular course of action in relation to it, then in the later essay Du Bois assumes his previous formulation of the specific historical "dilemma" of the African American as a fundamental reference and then operates that reference as a background theoretical fiction, or context, by which to elaborate a general thought of the problem of the color line, the concept of a global order of distinction.[14] Such an order, Du Bois proposes, can be analytically approached only by way of a comparative perspective that would include, at the limit, any and all social and historical contexts, in both a spatial, or horizontal, sense and a temporal, or vertical, sense. According to this register of attention, or analytical attunement, the "national or local" situation of the African American in the United States can be understood as "but the beginning of the problem" of the color line. From this perspective, the problem of the color line can be thrown into a new texture of relief and be seen to "belt the world" (Outlook 95, para. 2).

On the basis of this shift of perspective, in 1899 Du Bois could declare, not only that "the problem of the color line," understood on the basis of the problem of the relation of the Negro and the European in the United States, marked out a past and present "epoch in the history of mankind," as he had in the 1897 address, but if also understood or thought according to another possible context, that of a future or coming worldwide situation, "the social problem of the twentieth century is to be the relation of the civilized world to the dark races of mankind" (Outlook 95, 2). In this sense, the hypothesis of a global "problem of the color line," as Du Bois formulated it in the second paragraph of his 1899 address, is announced by him as a theoretical fiction or, better, a problem for thought, by which to investigate the historicity that enfolds the group that has come to be called African American. This problematic, within Du Bois's perspective, led in the most fundamental sense to a thought about the historicity of the entire epoch in which such a figure had (in its production and appearance) announced a problematization within existence, that is, had become a problem of existence and thought, on the modern worldwide horizon.

Whereas in the earlier essay, "The Conservation of Races," this problematic is announced primarily under the heading of a speculative proposition, a proposition that in this context serves to demarcate a given epistemological horizon, in terms of which an orientation or specification of the position of the Negro American in American and human history could be formulated (even though the ultimate horizon is not simply given), here, in the later essay, despite its appearance in the form of a declaration, this problematic is announced as a hypothesis, that is, as a proposition that would itself be the object of inquiry, a locution that is not so much the expression of an already established or given truth as it is a question that must first be properly understood and then utilized as a certain protocol for the practice of a critical attention.

The protocol in question would be the possibility of a certain account of historicity, that is to say, in brief, a certain possible narrative. What is involved here? The organization of this protocol would demand that at least two initial epistemological conditions be established. First, there must be the possibility of formulating a standpoint or position in terms of which, that is to say, *for* which, something could be gathered as the scene or object of which one might give an account. Second, beyond its variegation, heterogeneity, or dissemination, there must yet be some horizon of the common. However, beyond those general epistemic conditions, a certain theoretical organization of their relation must be rendered explicit as the very course of the analysis: at no point are the terms of this account, a putative theoretical subject position or a putative object, understood as simple, fixed and given. Rather, they acquire their historical pertinence by way of the relations that can be construed between them. As such, neither is attributable to an absolute finality. They might be better understood to define in reciprocal and mobile fashion the terms of a task of thinking as practice, as action, as an attempt to make something possible beyond a present. That is to say, such a narrative must be as resolutely submitted to imperatives of the future as future as it might be submitted to considerations of the past as past. In the critical sense, this is the relation of an investigation of historicity to the historial in general. This would be the understanding from which one could then speak of Du Bois's narrative as the practice of a certain kind of theoretical protocol, the practice of a kind of theoretical fiction, or a practice of formal problematization. In such a practice, a hypothesis might guide thought as a not necessarily impossible fiction and yet give rise to a kind of hyperbole that would be an attempt to render legible—as track or trace—the appearance of freedom or chance in or as history. Indeed, it might well be the opening to an elaboration not only of the past in a manner not yet seen or imagined but of a future that remains beyond and otherwise than the future as it might appear as forthcoming according to the present.

Now, on the basis of the formulations given so far, we might try to characterize the originality in terms of Du Bois's work as a whole of the general premises and implications of his practice in this text.

In the combined sense of its rhetorical form as a hypothetical declaration and of its semantic reference as a historical interpretation, a claim about the historicity of Du Bois's present at the time of his writing (the moment of the turn to the twentieth century) and its position within a broader historical horizon, a horizon that would pertain to all that is customarily called *modernity, the modern world*, or *the modern era*, this text can be understood as the first systematic enunciation by Du Bois of the concept-metaphor of "the problem of the color line" as a general theoretical formulation. It is the first text in which Du Bois is able to present a systematic statement of the concept metaphor of "the problem of the color line" as a way to think of modernity as the domain of a specific form of historicity. It is the first appearance, at the level of an achieved epistemic statement, of that formulation of Du Bois's that has become his most famous: "the problem of the twentieth century is the problem of the color line," the thought of which we are elaborating here.

This perspective is in contradistinction to the received understanding that the first such enunciation by Du Bois occurred at the first conference understood and commonly called by the descriptor "pan-African," that took place in London in July 1900. For example, the pioneering work from the late 1960s by Clarence Contee on Du Bois in relation to African nationalism mistakenly describes the manifesto of the conference that was written by Du Bois, "To the Nations of the World," as "the first occasion" of such this statement and then, to substantiate the thesis that he had put forward therein, he proposed that only over the subsequent years did this statement further issue from him (Contee 1969a; Du Bois 1900b). Although it may not be by way of direct influence from the work of Contee (a scholar whose texts I find of great ongoing value), it remains that in our moment this view can be found so widely dispersed throughout scholarship on Du Bois (and I include my own earlier efforts), even within the work of some of the most diligent scholars, as to make any further specific mention of such seem somewhat gratuitous. Indeed, so many scholars have mistakenly understood the later statement as the first occasion of his declaration of this phrase that I will forgo any other direct citation. So, it is six months after the occasion at hand, his December 1899 presidential address to the American Negro Academy, that Du Bois will append these same lines to the summary conference statement that he drafted in London in July 1900 (Du Bois 1900b, 1982k). Then it was some fifteen months later, in March 1901, that Du Bois's essay "The Freedmen's Bureau" was published, an account of the meaning of the Civil War and the failure of the Reconstruction project, which opens in its first paragraph with the famous sentence: "The problem of the 20th century is the problem of the color-line,—the relation of the darker to the lighter races of men in Asia and Africa, in America and the islands of the sea" (Du Bois 1901b, 2015e). Perhaps by way of its republication as the second chapter of *The Souls of Black Folk: Essays and Sketches* two years later and Du Bois's metonymic citation of it throughout that book, but especially in its "Forethought," the "Freedmen's Bureau" essay has become the most famous and recognized source of Du Bois's statement (Du Bois 1901b, 1903g, 1903a, 2015e). Yet both of these commonly quoted references are in every sense—including precisely the theoretical sense—*after* the formulations of the text at hand, "The Present Outlook for the Dark Races of Mankind."[15]

We might do well, then, to recall the opening words of the second paragraph of this address, for it is here that Du Bois first produces this formulation as a literal enunciation:

> It is but natural for us to consider that our race question is a purely national and local affair, confined to nine millions Americans and settled when their rights and opportunities are assured, and yet a glance over the world at the dawn of the new century will convince us that this is but the beginning of the

problem—that the color line belts the world and that the social problem of the twentieth century is to be the relation of the civilized world to the dark races of mankind. (Outlook 95, para. 2)

As an epistemological formulation, as a statement about the historicity of his time in a truly broad sense, it is a conceptualization that Du Bois would develop persistently—deepening and specifying its historical pertinence—throughout the remainder of his itinerary.

B. NARRATIVIZATION

Du Bois outlines the phenomenon that he calls "the problem of the color line" according to an order of generalization that he would situate as international or "the world," as in worldwide, as in the whole of *the* world. Whereas, not so long ago, we might have spoken primarily of our framing index as the international, or the transnational, we now—in our own time—tend to concatenate them with a "global" level of generality and to speak of the processes of globalization or *mondialisation*, by way of example, to account for our sense of a new threshold that has been broached in the historicity of our present in the long duration of the process of which Du Bois speaks. In his historical account, Du Bois describes modernity by way of tracking the history of systems of social ordination, especially as they articulate the supposed distinctions among groups of people. With regard to those temporalities that one might call modern, the forms of such articulation that are at the center of Du Bois's conceptualization and narrative are the configured processes of imperialism and colonialism. By way of this approach, he proposes what he calls "a larger perspective," one other than and beyond any that might take as its focal point of view America or the West as the basis for a thought of modernity as a whole.

Situated on that level, Du Bois proceeds to describe the problematic according to two modalities of historicity. One mode we may describe as a *spatial* topography, in which a form of *geo-graphy* or *mapping* yields the key concept metaphor of narrative order. He first examines the problem of the color line as a worldwide phenomenon *by way of a spatial or geographic* reference, beginning with Africa, "crossing the Red Sea" (hovering above the Indian Ocean) and moving through "Asia" in a complicated elliptical fashion (including "Arabia," perhaps Russia and Central Asia, India, China, and Japan), on across the Pacific Ocean to South America, and on to North America (focusing especially and at some length on the situation of African Americans in the United States), and finally traversing the Atlantic to (western) Europe. Yet the titular heading of a spatial metaphor should not obscure the fact that at each juncture in his geographic narrative, Du Bois formulates a historical perspective that is resolutely temporal, referring to the past in order to understand the present. The other mode we can describe as a *temporal* topography, in which a process of *temporization* offers the lineaments of the key concept metaphor for narrative organization. After the geographically organized account, Du Bois then turns to a discussion of the problem of the color line *by way of a series of temporal* references in which the reciprocity of duration and dissipation is fundamental. While he will focus specifically on the figure of "Europe" in this latter narrative, that is, on the temporal unfolding of a general problem of the status and historical bearing of differences among groups of humans in a nascent Europe over the course of the previous six hundred years, this temporality, through the particular relation of this domain to a modern emergent global historicity, is nonetheless inseparable from a sense of global spatiality that can be understood as specifically modern.

1. A FIRST NARRATIVE. In the *first narrative*, organized by geographic reference, Du Bois seeks to bring into relief something common across space. And yet, in doing so, he describes some differences in the ways in which this problem has been engaged. Those different ways have yielded the very texture of a global historicity, the historicity of Du Bois's present.

The orientation of this narrative, its directional marks, or origination and movement, is of propositional importance, even as it remains unthematized as an explicit theoretical or explanatory claim. The *standpoint* of the whole narrative is that of an African American intelligentsia situated in the United States. Perhaps it is more than symbolic that at the moment of Du Bois's presentation, the speaker and the addressees, the members of the American Negro Academy in their annual meeting, are located in Washington, in the District of Columbia, the national capital. However, the *beginning point* of the narrative is the continent of "Africa." Du Bois then moves eastward to "Asia" and includes Russia and Central "Asia" ambiguously as its northern border. From there, the narrative moves further eastward until it meets the "west" in South America and continues by proceeding northward to North America, specifically the United States, and then eastward again, to Europe. In this movement, the Negro or African American standpoint remains as the background pronominal figure, the putative epistemological subject, in the name of which this narrative incipits.[16] The interests of this subject position set afoot and guide this specific itinerary and the organization of the narrative reference to geography. Across the opening decades of the twentieth century, but perhaps specifically at the year of 1900, a certain narrative of modernity could begin with the idea of the ultimate singularity of a European epistemic subject (as, for example, in the influential one of Max Weber that was to come at the denouement of World War I).[17] Or such a narrative might take the devolution of the conditions of rights and the supposed arrival of new dispensations or capacities as indices of the modern (even as they can be found in the much earlier narratives of Karl Marx, for example).[18] And, to some extent, Du Bois will himself adduce such an account a bit further on in his story. Yet here, in this text, matters are not so simple—even if Du Bois in one measure of his thought can be understood to wish for such—for it remains that no such reference can come on the narrative scene as the heading of the story. To take the two examples given, of a certain historial singularity or of a certain singular universality, both are at once rendered relative by this "larger" perspective of *geographic* space and time. This is one of Du Bois's first narratives of the imperial and colonial organization of global modernity, and it cuts to the quick of a presumption still afoot in our own moment among the most contemporary of theoretical projections. For if modern historicity has the form of a singularity, in its origination and its devolution, it is less an accession to a replete totality (even as the name of a problem) or to universality than the distended concatenation of a radical and essentially agonistic heterogeneity operating at every level and in every sense. If modernity is marked by any dispensation to singularity, it is given in the radical heterogeneity of its origination and its devolution on all levels of historial generality. As such, it is this agonistic originary organization that remains the most fundamental possibility of the common of its horizons.

Let me now rhetorically follow the schema or outline of the whole of the geographic trajectory as the organization of my own reelaboration of Du Bois's thought in this stage of his essay.

A. AFRICAN-AMERICA. Writing from the standpoint of an African American intelligentsia, moving according to a mind's-eye projection, Du Bois opens his geographic narrative with a rhetorical gesture toward Africa that should be understood as a kind of stage setting for the discourse that will follow. He proposes to his audience: "If we start eastward to-night and land on the continent of Africa we land in the centre of the greater Negro problem—of the world problem of the black man" (Outlook 95, para. 2). Along with and yet beyond the African continent, the statement signals quite strongly that a reference to the East, an orientation toward such as the scene of a kind of originarity, perhaps in a multiply refracting sense, will be the first inclination of the perspective that he will proffer.

Yet, while one may quite legitimately elaborate this formulation under the heading of a rhetoric, for it certainly is performative as such, it may more generally be understood to carry a certain theoretical premise.

Why this turn to Africa? Why should the first narrative referent within a problematic supposed as global take its index as the continent of Africa?

In a word, it is because it maintains within its lineaments an incipient organization of the complex historicity according to which the Negro in the United States, but in truth the Negro in the Americas and the Caribbean in general, took shape within the horizon of a global problematic—the problem of the color line, a certain form of relation among peoples of different histories and locales. The decisive inaugural moment of such encounter in its modern form for the continent that bears the name Africa, whether considered from an internal or external perspective, regarded as a whole, was the institution of the Atlantic trade in Africans as slaves. This reference is in fact the analytical beginning point in the situation of his present era, that is, for Du Bois's global narrative of the problem of the color line. In this context, it is doubtless that this whole sense of beginning has for Du Bois everything to do with the oft set aside but absolutely fundamental role that the history of Atlantic slavery has played in inaugurating the historical epoch that has been called modernity, even as he will not belabor a specific nominalization. Thus, in Du Bois's perspective, the nineteenth century was but the continuation of the violent and destructive encounter of the peoples of this continent with Europe. For Du Bois, without that background, one cannot understand the situation in which Africa was undergoing a pervasive coerced colonization astride the height of the modern moment by way of those states of Europe committed to a new imperialism. The history of that inaugural subduction of African peoples into a European project of domination and exploitation is historical at the root—even if not the only one—of the global problem of the color line. Internally, so to speak, it brought African social organization into profound new relation to processes beyond any given locality (even though this was by no means the first time), often with massively destructive and dislocating effects. And, in terms of its external profile, at that juncture in time, writing just over a decade and a half after the fact,

Du Bois emphasizes the recently systematized general consolidation of colonialism on the continent by way of the Berlin conference of 1884–85 and its immediate aftermath. Even as he will note just a bit later in this essay (throughout the whole of its second paragraph) what he considers at the year 1899 a certain comparative benevolence of England as a colonial power, Du Bois underscores in the same gesture that this country's way in the colonial scene was still one of primary and fundamental injustice (and Belgium would thus be the foil for Du Bois, a kind of opposite of England). This horizon that Du Bois's gesture brings into view can be understood to name a key aspect of the premise that serves as the basis of Du Bois's practice of a generalized Africanism, a kind of pan-Africanism (*avant la lettre*, so do speak): that is to say, this whole historical problematic, not some primordial simplicity, is the basis of this commitment.

In the phrase "if we start eastward to-night and land on the continent of Africa we land in the centre of the greater Negro problem," then, is contained, in the background as it were, an entire and fundamental theoretical presumption with regard to modern historicity on a global scale.

From such a disposition, then, we can turn to recognize the implication of the apparently direct but somewhat subtle and punctilious observations that outline the thread of Du Bois's conception of the historical present of Africa or "the greater Negro problem" on the eve of the twentieth century. The matter of sovereignty and self-determination, of the possibilities for full historial realization, from the most mundane forms of territorial line or border to the distinctive capacity to originate a future, such is everywhere at issue, as we can recognize in this opening sweep of his purview:

> The nineteenth century of the Christian era has seen strange transformation in the continent where civilization was born twice nineteen centuries before the Christ-child. We must not overlook or forget the marvelous drama that is being played on that continent to-day, with the English at the North and on the cape, the Portuguese and Germans on the East and West coast, the French in Guinea and the Saharah, Belgium in the Congo, and everywhere the great seething masses of the Negro people. Two events of vast significance to the future of the Negro people have taken place in the year 1899—the recapture of Khartoum and the Boer war, or in other words the determined attempt to plant English civilization at two centres in the heart of Africa.[19] It is of interest to us because it means the wider extension among our own kith and kin of the influence of that European nation whose success in dealing with undeveloped races has been far greater than any others. Say what we will of England's rapacity and injustice,

(and much can be said) the plain fact remains that no other European nation—and America least of all—has governed its alien subjects with half the wisdom and justice that England has. While then the advance of England from the cape to Cairo is no unclouded good for our people, it is at least a vast improvement on Arab slave traders and Dutch brutality. Outside of America the greatest field of contrast between whites and Negroes to-day is in South Africa, and the situation there should be watched with great interest. We must not forget that the deep-lying cause of the present Boer war is the abolition of Negro slavery among the Cape Dutch by England. The great Trek or migration of the Transvaal Boers followed and in the [Orange] Free State no Negro has to-day a third of the rights which he enjoys in Georgia—he cannot hold land, cannot live in town, has practically no civil status, and is in all but name a slave. Among the English his treatment is by no means ideal and yet there he has the advantage of school, has the right of suffrage under some circumstances and has just courts before which he may plead his cause. We watch therefore this war with great interest and must regard the triumph of England as a step toward the solution of the greater Negro problem. In the Congo Free State we see the rapid development of trade and industry, the railroad has crept further in toward the heart of Africa and the slave trade has at least been checked.[20] Liberia stands hard pressed by France but she has begun to pay interest on the English debt and shows in some ways signs of industrial development along with her political decline.[21] Leaving our black brothers of Africa we travel northward to our brown cousins of Egypt; rescued from war and rapine slavery and centuries of misrule they are to-day enjoying stable government under England and rapid industrial advancement. (Outlook 95–96, para. 2)[22]

We may gather the narrative construal given here, in an initial sense, by way of its main strands. That is to ask: If this continental scene is the "center"—certainly in a historical and demographic sense—of the so-called Negro question in a global scenario, how might one give its summary character on the on the eve, so to speak, of the year 1900? Three interwoven thetic lines can be recognized here. At root is the unstated presumption that African peoples, of whatever kind, are essential to the future of the modern world conceived as a whole. Further, then, if one takes reference to a formulation that Du Bois will offer just a few years later, in the paragraphs that close *The Souls of Black Folk: Essays and Sketches*, "they are worth the saving." Thus, on a third line, at the juncture of the turn of the century, Du Bois offers a formulation that can be understood as liberal in its dispensation, in the sense that it presumes and indirectly petitions for the affirmative benevolence of those who would claim, or portend, to lead human civilization at the turn of that new century. Yet this moral proclivity will not lead Du Bois to withdraw from the critical arraignment of the practices in the modern era of such claimants to a principle of universal morality. In all truth, it can also be understood as a direct moral challenge to the historically existing organization of military and economic force on a global level. In "To the Nations of the World," the summary statement of the Pan-African Conference, as Du Bois penned it some seven months after the December address to the ANA, this motif forms the verso of its open proclamation (Du Bois 1982k). And then, in the 1901 essay "The Relation of the Negroes to the Whites in the South" (Du Bois 1901d), published almost exactly one year after the London declaration, in its two opening paragraphs (which are left out of its reprint as the ninth chapter of *The Souls of Black Folk: Essays and Sketches* just over eighteen months later, in March 1903), Du Bois formulates the judgment at length in the context of the history of the United States, and perhaps the hemisphere in which it is located in general:

> The world-old phenomenon of the contact of diverse races of men is to have new exemplification during the new century. Indeed, the characteristic of our age is the contact of European civilization with the world's undeveloped peoples. Whatever we may say of the results of such contact in the past, it certainly forms a chapter in human action not pleasant to look back upon. War, murder, slavery, extermination, and debauchery,—this has again and again been the result of carrying civilization and the blessed gospel to the isles of the sea and the heathen without the law. Nor does it altogether satisfy the conscience of the modern world to be told complacently that all this has been right and proper, the fated triumph of strength over weakness, of righteousness over evil, of superiors over inferiors. It would certainly be soothing if one could readily believe all this; and yet there are too many ugly facts for everything to be thus easily explained away. We feel and know that there are many delicate differences in race psychology, numberless changes that our crude social measurements are not yet able to follow minutely, which explain much of history and social development. At the same time, too, we know that these considerations have never adequately explained or excused the triumph of brute force and cunning over weakness and innocence.
>
> It is, then, the strife of all honorable men of the twentieth century to see that in the future competition of races the survival of the fittest shall mean the triumph of the good, the beautiful, and the true; that we may be able to

preserve for future civilization all that is really fine and noble and strong, and not continue to put a premium on greed and impudence and cruelty. To bring this hope to fruition, we are compelled daily to turn more and more to a conscientious study of the phenomena of race-contact,—frank and fair, and not falsified and colored by our wishes or our fears. And we have in the South as fine a field for such a study as the world affords,—a field, to be sure, which the average American scientist deems somewhat beneath his dignity, and which the average man who is not a scientist knows all about, but nevertheless a line of study which by reason of the enormous race complications with which God seems about to punish this nation must increasingly claim our sober attention, study, and thought, we must ask, what are the actual relations of whites and blacks in the South? and we must be answered, not by apology or faultfinding, but by a plain, unvarnished tale. (Du Bois 1901d, 121–22, paras. 1–3; 2015h, 189–90, paras. 1–3; see 1903j)

In the same breath, then, it can be said that throughout this variegated but closely strung discourse, across the last years of the nineteenth century and the opening years of the twentieth, Du Bois nonetheless maintains a resolute moral rectitude soliciting the initiative of Africans and African Americans to "strive" to remake themselves and hence make the world anew. It is in this sense that he proposed a profound mutuality—in this context, with reference to the Negro question in both its local and global frames—across "the *problem* of the color line" (emphasis mine), as he so often formulates the matter, soliciting those who would occupy both sides, respectively, in the address of a common modern historicity.

B. ASIA. Asia is for Du Bois, at the turn to the new century, at the year of 1900, "the mother continent." Later in his life, Du Bois will describe Africa as such.[23] For Du Bois, Russia is its northern limit, India its southern border, Turkey its western limit, and China, Korea, and Japan its eastern limit. It is perhaps with his proposal of a certain conception of this region as if a whole that Du Bois offers his most telling conception of the problem of the color line, simultaneously specific in the characterization that he gives it and yet exhibiting the lineaments of his general conception in a most legible manner.

It is not simply a matter of the supposed large and substantial differences according to physical character that are most important (or phenotype, in the language of the biological sciences of our day); rather, more fundamentally, it is the disposition of those who might have access to a certain form of domination, perhaps technological in some extended sense, that gives historical meaning to Du Bois's idea of a problem of the color line here. (And this will ultimately hold in general terms as well.) Apart from the obvious presumption of phenotypic difference that one might tend to assume in the relations of the peoples of Africa and Europe, within the contextual frame of what Du Bois calls Asia, both by historical distance and specific circumstance, even as they can be construed to exist, such differences cannot be simply and directly presumed as a sufficiently effective mark of prescription or proscription. Nor, in some cases, in the relations among the peoples of Asia, could they be presumed as directly pertinent at all; this might be especially questionable in supposed intra-contextual situations (of nation, state, or forms of empire, such as in India or China). The themes of power, violence, and exploitation in Du Bois's conception of the *problem* of the color line are thus rendered distinctly legible in his narrative of the history of this geographic region.

If the present of circa 1900 has arrived in this domain as a "congeries of race and color problems," in Du Bois's formulation, then, as he immediately continues to explain his perspective, a look at the past might offer an understanding of just how this has taken shape:

> The history of Asia is but the history of the moral and physical degeneration which follows the unbridled injustice of conquerors toward the conquered— of advanced toward the undeveloped races—of swaggering braggadacio toward dumb submission. (Outlook 97, para. 2)

And thus, for Du Bois, working with his hypothesis of a history of the global level production of "the problem of a global color line," the history of this region, the past, can be narrated along this specific track as the failure of civilizations by way of their promulgation of categorical distinction, of absolute proscription and its affirmative derivatives, among groups of humans through institution and general social practice, especially religious and legal structures in concatenation with specific forms of economic organization—in particular the control of land. Such "braggadocio" has led to the failure of civilizations, according to Du Bois. His respective characterizations of India (especially Mughal India), the Ottoman Empire, and dynastic China can help to clarify this interpretative orientation:

> The brown Turanians of India were overborne by their yellow conquerors and the resulting caste system to keep the despised down was the very cause of that wide-spread discontent and internal dissension which welcomed the armies and

government of England. So too when the case was reversed and the dark Turks swept over the white inhabitants of Asia Minor and southern Europe, it was the unjust determination to keep down the conquered, to recognize among Armenians no rights which a Turk was bound to respect. It was this that ultimately paralyzed the pristine vigor of the Ottoman and leaves them to-day beggars at the gates of Europe. And finally if we turn to China we have again an example of that marvelous internal decay that overcomes the nation that trifles with Truth and Right and Justice, and makes force and fraud and dishonesty and caste distinction the rule of its life and government. (Outlook 97–98, para. 2)[24]

For Du Bois, this history should be understood as a lesson to nations and civilizations that would attempt to place a fundamental proscription upon the possibilities of human ability and capacity, upon the possibilities opened in history as the human practice of freedom. At this step in his itinerary, while the implication of the judgment that he renders pertains to economic structures as such in their very historicity, it remains that the theoretical edge of Du Bois's critique foregrounds the historicity of morality as the terms of a passage to another form of relations among human groups, of general collectivities, of one kind or another. It is reasonable to suppose that in the background of his thought in this passage is a critical judgment of both America in particular and the modern nations of western Europe, and then, too, all states or national states practicing or seeking to practice modern forms of imperialism and colonialism. As I have done above, in part one of this study, and as I will reformulate the matter below, in the context of our present elaboration, Du Bois will eventually come to understand the practice in question—the imperial idea in its principle—as the very productive source of both "the problem of the color line" in general and its specific promulgation in the form of war, even "world war."

There were two contexts, in this region of the world at the moment of a turn to the new century, the year 1900, that would propose for Du Bois in his present the possibilities for a future of "the problem of the color line" that might be something different otherwise than it had been in the past, during the centuries that had just gone by.

(1) JAPAN. One might be construed as an example of external relation. It is the example of Japan. As was so often the case up to the time of World War II, in Du Bois's discourse, Japan is an exemplary example: "The one bright spot in Asia to-day is the island empire of Japan, and her recent admission to the ranks of modern civilized nations by the abolition of

foreign consular courts within her borders is the greatest concession to the color line which the nineteenth century has seen" (Outlook 98, para. 2).[25] If we recall Du Bois's characterization in his 1897 address, "The Conservation of Races," of the situation of Japan with regard to the internal development of its own ideals, that it must do so and on its own terms, then we can see, in this 1899 text at hand, an affirmation of an idea of sovereignty that is continuous with the earlier one, in terms of political ideals as well as actual political organization and exercise of authority.[26] At the end of the year 1899, for Du Bois, Japan's way would propose an exemplary path for the modern world, especially with regard to a global horizon in which a "problem of the color line" in his sense defined relations among groups of people. Du Bois does not recognize here the nascent, yet already virulent, articulation of Japan's own imperial projection and participation in the creation of what might be called an intra-Asian "problem of the color line," in his extended sense of the term. Indeed, he will affirm Japan's victory over Russia in the Russo-Japanese War of 1904–5, which he will anticipate in a sense a bit later on in the text at hand (as did others), preferring a limit to European and American imperialism in Asia even at the interpretive risk of ignoring another imperialism, that of an Asian power, in this case that of Japan, which the latter was already promulgating against the people of Korea and subsequently against other states and nations throughout the region. And this ambivalence remained well into the 1940s the frame of Du Bois's thought about Japan and its relation to other countries in the region, notably China (Chandler 2021).

(2) INDIA. Another example might be construed as one of internal relation. This is colonial India (under the Raj). While Du Bois had already described England in Africa as "that European nation whose success" in their relation to what he understood as "undeveloped races" (a formulation by which we may well understand Du Bois's mean the sense of *under*developed, as in whose accomplished future might be still yet to come), " has been far greater than any others," he had also declared that their "rapacity and injustice" made their contributions "no unclouded good" for Negroes on that continent or in the Americas. And such fundamental ambivalence is the background of his description of the colonization of India by England. And thus it can be said that Du Bois is ambivalent here even as he affirms England:

> [It is a] fairly honest attempt to make in some degree the welfare of the lowest
> classes of an alien race a distinct object of government. A system of education

with a well-equipped university at the head has long been established for the natives and in the last few years some natives have been admitted to administrative positions in government. The cordial sympathy shown toward Queen Victoria's black and brown subjects at the late jubilee has borne golden fruit. (Outlook 98, para. 2)[27]

Notwithstanding the extent to which we in our own time can recognize in the policies of the English in India described by Du Bois the project of a certain form of colonization that would attempt to promulgate what has been called an "empire of the mind" and that we would question its liberalism at the most profound levels, we can recognize Du Bois's inclination on the eve of the new century to affirm a disavowal of categorical proscription by the politically and economically dominant group over the subordinate one. It remains for us to emphasize that such a disavowal as Du Bois tries to imagine it here in a liberal guise was yet doubly confounded: for in fact the British in India sought precisely to sustain a formal categorical subordination on the order of a declared international horizon of legality, of the peoples of the Indian subcontinent, almost to the midterm mark of the new century; and then those whose liberation remains yet to come in the historicity of modern India, oft gathered under the heading of the subaltern groups in our own time, can be understood to appear, if at all, under this already twice-refracted form of subordination.[28]

However, on the eve of the twentieth century, Du Bois's main concern is the possibility that the past history of conflict and strife will be the general form of future relations across what he can be understood to think of as the articulations of the problem of the color line in a general sense.

C. SOUTH AMERICA. South America, according to Du Bois, is a land of the "intermingling" of the "races."[29] His account recalls to mind José Martí's description of the "other America" as a land of *mestizaje* in the same historical moment:[30]

South America [is a place] where the dark blood of the Indian and the Negro has mingled with that of the Spaniard and the whole has been deluged by a large German and Italian migration. The resulting social conditions are not clear to the student. The color line has been drawn here perhaps less than in any other continent and yet the condition of the dark masses is far from satisfactory. We must not forget these dark cousins of ours, for their uplifting, and the establishment of permanent government and for industrial conditions is the work of the new century. (Outlook 98, para. 3)

Thus, for Du Bois, South America is a place of promise, of hope, of the possibility of a new day. It already exemplifies what he will soon describe as the very path of the historicity of the future with regard to the situation of historical difference among humans. Quite simply, the question is, How will such new positions and relations be undertaken? For the African American intelligentsia, the question of the future of South America is of the essence. Yet what must be underscored here in the conceptual or epistemological sense, again, is exactly the extent to which, for Du Bois, the concept metaphor of "the problem of the color line" extends beyond any simple characterization of a physical attribute to entail in a fundamental sense matters of the political and economic proscription of whole groups and the promulgation of social hierarchy in such a manner that it would be fundamental in the production of the social order in general.

D. NORTH AMERICA. North America is the context on which Du Bois focuses with the greatest attention to detail. It is the specific scene in which the Negro American in the United States arises. While it is the standpoint from which the narrative is told, the permissive threshold from which it is enunciated, as it were, in the narrative of this address we arrive at this scene only by way of its comparative construal (in contradistinction to its direct narrative dominance in "The Conservation of Races"). At this juncture in the narrative, we can only think of this scene as a relative context, even if it is the object of a certain necessary theoretical privilege and commands a somewhat detailed examination.

This privilege, and thereby this detail, accrues because the operative question of this text, an address to a body of Negro American intellectual leaders, is, *What is to be done?* What should be their guiding policy in grappling with their historical situation? What should be their sense of matters, their understanding, with regard to different groups of humans on a worldwide scale of reference? How should such understanding affect or determine their actions and policies in relation to those groups? Like "The Conservation of Races," the 1899 address is an appeal for a certain course of action. This generic form, or rhetorical register, stands as the formal background of all of its claims and demarcations.

In the history of African American discourses, or Africanist discourses put forth by Negro, or African, Americans in the United States, the appeal, in the sense exemplified here by both "The Conservation of Races" and "The Present Outlook for the Dark Races of Mankind," can be understood as an epistemological mode or category. It operates in the domain of the treatise and of the oratory, or sermon, simultaneously (Porter 1971). As such, it is the very pathway of the articulation of a critical self-consciousness of an African American intelligentsia (Spillers 2003d). One recalls here the discourse of Absalom Jones and Richard Allen at Philadelphia in 1794, of David Walker's appeal of 1829 in Boston, or of Anna Julia Cooper at Xenia, Ohio, at the onset of the 1890s (A. Jones and Allen 1794; Walker 1829; Cooper 1892). Or, perhaps, then, one might recall Du Bois's own petitions of the mid-twentieth century, especially those addressed to the nascent United Nations (Du Bois 1980f, reel 85, frames 1491–1555). The truth claims of the appeal, if it maintains such, are by way of its construction and establishment of a mobile and differentially articulated point of view. Thus, the often defensive or anticipatory conditions of its incipit should not obscure the commitment to erudition that dominates its tone or vocative register. Rather than being a derivative, a reaction, or a *simple* partial view, it is best understood as exemplifying a "supraliteracy," or a "metaliteracy," or even a disposition and possibility that I would nominalize under the term *paraliteracy*.[31] It is not a limitation of an understanding of the world to a parochial disposition. Rather, it is the proposition of a double or redoubled understanding—a remark of both sides of a limit, so to speak—of various forms of limited and parochial understandings of the world that have been promulgated as universal, such that the layers of sedimentation in which such distinctions would ostensibly be secured can be rendered susceptible to a certain desedimentation. As such, it overturns existing claims of the relation of the universal and the particular in a given field of understanding and knowledge, especially in their direct political implication, and resituates such claims in a larger frame, perhaps a frame that will always remain illimitable. Such practice in principle will simultaneously specify the old claims according to their limits, which are brought into new relief in the context of this new epistemological construal, and yet also mark what is most at stake in them in such a way that it too is then given another elaboration, even if this latter is not simply, or entirely, a new one. This other elaboration amounts to a delimitation of its problematic.

And these contributions are possible not because of the perfection of the discourse but despite or beyond its imperfections. Du Bois will explicitly describe his own enunciation in this text as a "hasty and inadequate survey." Its implication arises solely from its transposition of view, not to a perfect, correct, or absolute one, but rather to one that in its articulation poses by way of its reflexive recognition of its partiality, as its integral possibility and internal demand, that is, by that which gives form to its own vocative register, the illimitability of what is at stake in the question that it accepts as its own. Partiality here is anything but parochial. It is an affirmation of the becoming of possibility itself, becoming and transformation, even as a certain distantiation, as the very terms of its own promulgation.

Let us also mark here that one such as Du Bois, in this case, for example, is led to this larger perspective because the African American problematic solicits one. His discourse is the practice of a form of receptivity to that solicitation. His practice, even as a form of reception, from its inception, is nonetheless a practical theoretical inhabitation of a situation of displacement from any putative primordial origin. This whole problematization, this development that is the practical theoretical situation specific to African Americans, and there is always specificity for any such situatioin, comes about only by way of social processes that are excessive to any locality, no matter how locality is defined. Thus, the very particularity of the African American situation is what sets in motion, or calls for, a form of supra-inhabitation of thought or demands that a certain metaperspective take shape right in the midst of experience, self-consciousness, or the particularities of existence. It solicits the development of a paraontological discourse.[32]

It is thus no rhetorical anomaly that in this section of his essay, Du Bois produces the most direct formal conceptualizations of historicity of any that he gives in the whole text. That is to say that in giving an account of the historicity of his contemporary era, including also the history of the African American in earlier decades and centuries, Du Bois is led to speak of the general rhythms of history, to pose a conceptualization or metaphorization of history in general, with regard to the human engagement with what he calls "social problems." He describes what we might call a dialectic of "sympathy" and "criticism," of generosity and reaction, in the way in which groups of humans tend to deal with social problems.

Let us take three brief indices at the textual level of his elaboration of this general concept metaphor.

(1) If the so-called or "half-named" Negro problem is but a local indication of a larger social problem, then, in terms of the present moment, December 1899, it can be said of African Americans: "There is no doubt of the significance of the present attitude of the public mind toward us; it is the critical rebound that follows every period of moral exhalation; the shadow of doubt that creeps silently after the age of faith; the cold reasoning that follows gloomy idealism" (Outlook 100, para. 12). And then

Du Bois goes on to situate this present in terms of his idea of a general dialectic of thought:

> Nor is this a thing to be unsparingly condemned. The human soul grasping—striving after dearly conceived ideals, needs ever the corrective and guiding power of sober afterthought. Human fancy must face plain facts. This is as true of nations as of men. We find great waves of sympathy seizing mankind at times and succeeded by cold criticism and doubt. Sometimes this latter reaction chokes and postpones reform or even kills it and lets the blind world flounder on. At other times it leads to more rational and practical measures than mere moral enthusiasm could possibly offer. It is not the critic as such that the idealist must oppose but only that attitude of human criticism and doubt which neglects and denies all ideals. (Outlook 100, para. 12)

What is the status of the ideal, or the movement of idealization, here? It is the name of possibility as it announces itself within thought and practice. It would be the name of a possible future as it can be approached, as if in the dark or under a blind, from within a given present. The ideal, or, better, ideals are a basic premise of his conception of historicity, of the movement of sociality that is historicity, that is its organization by way of a telic structure. The ideals are not a given or simply realized telos, but the form of its announcement as possibility. Perhaps we can say here that the novel form of this thought is its naming of ideals by way of a thought of the problems or problematics that arise in the course of existence. Ideals come by way of a problematization of existence. Perhaps, then, we can fold this formal dimension of Du Bois's thought of ideals back across the question of historicity. If so, then we can continue and say that criticism is the very path of the formulation and delimitation of ideals. The criticism of ideals is the very movement of possibility as idealization, as the movement of the construction of ideals. Criticism, here, in the passage at hand, is for Du Bois anything but a simple restriction; rather, it is an amplification of the resonance of possibility in the movement of human practice.

(2) If the time of Du Bois's own writing, the end of the nineteenth century, is a time of criticism, as distinguished from an era of sympathy, it can yet be said in a general sense that the history of the Negro or African American situation, as example, shows an affirmative movement within this contrapuntal rhythm:

> In this we can see progress—tremendous progress from the times when New England deacons invested their savings in slave trade ventures, passed the Dred

Scott decision and the [F]ugitive [S]lave [A]ct down to the lynchings and dis-
criminating laws of to-day.[33] To be sure the actual status to-day far from being
ideal is in many respects deplorable and far beyond those ideals of human
brotherhood which from time to time have animated the [nation],[34] and yet
we must be prepared in the progress of all reformatory movements for periods
of exhalation and depression, of rapid advance and retrogression, of hope and
fear. The Negro problem in America curiously illustrates this. Away back in
the [seventeenth] century Massachusetts arose in wrath and denounced the
slave trade, and the Pennsylvania Quakers asked: "Is slavery according to the
Golden Rule?"[35] [A]nd yet, 50 years later Massachusetts slave traders swarmed
on the coast of Africa and the Quakers held 10,000 slaves. Toward the end of
the eighteenth century the conscience of the nation was again aroused. Darien,
Ga., where the Delegal riot recently occurred[,] declared its abhorrence of the
unnatural practice of slavery.[36] [Thomas] Jefferson denounced the institution
as a crime against liberty, and the day of freedom seemed dawning, and yet
fifty years later a cargo of black bondsmen were landed near Darien, Georgia,
and the Vice President of the Confederacy declared Negro slavery the cornerstone of the new-born nation.[37] So again the dreams of [William Lloyd]
Garrison, [John] Brown, [Wendell] Phillips and [Charles] Sumner seemed
about to be realized after the war when the Negro was free, enfranchised and
protected in his civil rights, and yet a generation later finds the freedman in
economic serfdom, practically without a vote, denied in many cases common
law rights and subject to all sorts of petty discrimination. Notwithstanding all
this the progress of the nation toward a settlement of the Negro is patent—the
movement with all its retrogression is a spiral not a circle, and as long as there
is motion there is hope. (Outlook 99–100, para. 12)

With this summative conclusion to his capsule narrative in mind, Du Bois
goes on in this paragraph to make two thetic declarations about the history
of the problem of the color line in the North American situation, in what
has become the United States. One is that the movement is "a spiral and not
a circle." Du Bois wishes to declare that the return has not been a simple
repetition.[38] Another is that "error that ends in progress is still error," that
there is no simple recuperation of the past under the heading of sacrifice
or redemption. History has the character of actuality, of a first time and an
only time, of temporality as otherwise than the present. Thus, idealization
as the path of historicity occurs only in the movement of this irretrievable
displacement of the simple or pure origin or telos. The meaning of error, if
such could at all be announced, would be as the cost or liability of human

practice. Perhaps only in this way could the tension of sympathy and criticism be both a spiral and not a simple recuperation. All would remain at stake in practice. No origin or finality of history could be absolute.

(3) And yet—this is the imperative of the appeal as a form of knowledge—the historical future remains at stake in the present. The African American intelligentsia, for example, must take action to participate directly in the historical formation and reformation of ideals. Thus, there is a responsibility on the part of his auditors to make such history.

If so, the first form of such responsibility is to seek fundamental understanding, perhaps in the form of knowledge, of the historical present: "to study carefully and seek to understand the present social movement in America as far as it affects our interests" (Outlook 100, para. 12). The second form of such a response will be the formation of policy and the organization or reorganization of institutions to accord with such a form of understanding.

In the context of this address to the ANA in 1900, if such a fundamental understanding must always proceed by way of the act of reflection, of a questioning recursion, of a step back and revision of field or horizon in the direction of a beyond of the simply given or possible limit, then the sine qua non of the maintenance of such responsibility for Du Bois and his auditors is (as we have seen him declare from the outset) a principle of comparative reference within a global or worldwide historical horizon. He writes of the movement of idealization in actual history:

> [There is a] critical rebound that follows every period of moral exhalation; the shadow of doubt that creeps silently after the age of faith; the cold reasoning that follows gloomy idealism. Nor is this a thing to be unsparingly condemned. The human soul grasping—striving after dearly conceived ideals, needs ever the corrective and guiding power of sober afterthought. Human fancy must face plain facts. This is as true of nations as of men. We find great waves of sympathy seizing mankind at times and succeeded by cold criticism and doubt. Sometimes this latter reaction chokes and postpones reform or even kills it and lets the blind world flounder on. At other times it leads to more rational and practical measures than mere moral enthusiasm could possibly offer. It is not the critic as such that the idealist must oppose but only that attitude of human criticism and doubt which neglects and denies all ideals. (Outlook 100, para. 12)

And then, in turn, as an illustration of such historicity, to give the situation of the African American and the problem of the color line therein another, different, and perhaps larger amplification, a certain form of theoretical comparison, Du Bois turns to the resonance of this problem, of the complicated movement by which ideals acquire form, within the history of debates in the modern West (perhaps the United States and Europe) about poverty:

> This is curiously illustrated in the modern world's attitude toward poverty: first came stern unbending morality: the pauper, the tramp, it said[,] rascals and drones every one of them; punish them. Then came the century of sympathy[,] crying as it saw dumb toil and hopeless suffering and the paradox of progress and poverty:
>
> *Down all the stretch of Hell to its last gulf*
> *There is no shape more terrible than this—*
> *More tongued with censure of the world's blind greed,*
> *More filled with signs and portents for the soul,*
> *More fraught with menace to the universe.*[39]
>
> So the world sympathized until there came the era of calm criticism and doubt. Are all paupers pitiable? What makes men poor? Is the cause always the same? Is poverty or the fear of it an unmixed evil? Will not sympathy with the failures in the race of life increase the number of failures? Will not the strengthening of the weak weaken the strong and the enriching of the poor pauperize the rich?[40] To-day, in the world of social reform, we stand as it were between these two attitudes seeking some mode of reconciliation. The ideals of human betterment in our day could ill afford to lose the scientific attitude of statistics and sociology, and science without ideas would lose half its excuse for being. (Outlook 100–101, paras. 12–13)

If the opening temporal frame in this passage is the eighteenth century and the beginnings of industrialization, in both colony and metropole, then this sketch is principally of the modern West during the nineteenth century, the "century of sympathy."[41] Here, in the context of a discussion of poverty, ostensibly analyzed apart from any reference to physical character by way of a concept of race, the fundamental question returns that Du Bois raises elsewhere in his early itinerary, namely (as we noted above in our opening discussions in part II) in a text that predates "The Present Outlook for the Dark Races of Mankind" by six months, that is, "A Final Word" of his closing discussion of the Negro situation in Philadelphia. That question is, "Who, after all, are men?" Who counts as human, or fully human? Can there be some fundamental demarcation within or among those understood by this heading? We can say that this is the root predicative question of both the debate about poverty as Du Bois describes it and the question of the problem of the color line as a modern Western formation. Is the concept of man as a supposed universal being to be confounded or extended in the context of the problem of the poor? Or, might this perplexity articulate as our effort to understand their overlapping historicity, that of "the problem of the color line"?

Yet this entire account is in the service of developing an answer to one question: *What is to be done?* In this case, the question is addressed to the intellectual and political leadership of African Americans as it is represented on the occasion by the members of the ANA.

If, as Du Bois has claimed from the outset, such action should be based upon a deep and broad understanding of one's age, then he has sought thus far in his address to give a historical and comparative basis for such comprehension. But here, at this point in his text, he is specifically trying to name the concrete conditions and form of the problem of the color line for African Americans in the United States in 1900 so as to form the proper course of action. His general claim is that the question of action at present, on the eve of the turn to the twentieth century, is substantially different than such a question as it might have appeared at 1865, or even at 1885. And the accent, given along two tracks, will be on the futural form of the situation, or the aspect which opens toward the future in a distinct and powerful way.

With regard to African Americans specifically, if they think of themselves in the context of the time, the question of possibility takes shape not "as to slavery, not as to human equality, not as to universal suffrage, but rather as to individual efficiency, the proper utilization of the manifestly different endowments of men" (Outlook 102, para 15). While not susceptible to a full characterization in one breath, this claim can be shown to sustain no major contradiction of Du Bois's formulations of a sense of the collective in either "The Conservation of Races" or "Strivings of the Negro People" (the latter of which subsequently became the first chapter of *The Souls of Black Folk: Essays and Sketches*), both from 1897. In the former essay, the problematic of historical possibility appeared not as paradox, nor as anomaly, but rather under the guise of dilemma: the question of the respective commitment—what he will call "duty" in a nineteenth-century phrase—to a supposed subnational "national" collective (such as the Negro American), comprehended in a philosophical sense under the heading of the concept of race, or to a supposed supranational "national" collective (such as a certain "America"), thought under the heading of an unstated putative universal historicity. Here the same question, which again takes the shape of the historically particular relation of opportunity and obligation, brings into explicit relief another sense of the level of generality of the subject or historical carrier of such a problematic, that of the individual as person. He writes that the question of authority "is not so much of rights as of duties—not so much of desires as of abilities—not so much of leveling down the successful to the dead level of the masses, as of giving to individuals among the masses the opportunity to reach the highest" (Outlook 102, para. 15). In the relation of the texts of these two moments, 1897 and 1899, and then, too, their relation to the text of circa 1894, "The Afro-American," which we opened in part I of this study, we have essentially all of the theoretical terms that Du Bois will later use to formulate the idea of the "talented tenth" (see Du Bois 1903n, 2015m). In the rhetorical scene of the first moment, the accent is on the formation of a certain collective within a collective. In the scene of the second moment, the one under discussion here, Du Bois's discourse unfolds another layer of reference within the insurgent collectivity. The accent here is on the historical form of possibility: that is, how individual opportunity and the preparation for such, which must be affirmed, is also the seat of a larger responsibility. Certainly, it can be said that Du Bois is here seeking to affirm the idea or principle of illimitable opportunity in relation to ability (or capacity) as the heading of action. Yet he is also maintaining that such individualism must be oriented toward a collective horizon that will affirm such possibility as general. Near the end of "The Present Outlook for the Dark Races of Mankind," it will be indexed as "duty."

But beyond the situation of African Americans directly, Du Bois is attuned to what he believes will be another register of change in the situation of the problem of the color line in the United States. It is a change that will arise as a result of the "new imperial policy" of the United States. It can be understood as the rearticulation of the colonial in the midst of the putative postcolonial. It is that historical process by which the former colony established by way of the imperial imposition becomes itself in turn a practitioner of imperial colonization. Within the domain of historicity that Du Bois is rendering into relief, such a process can be understood as paradoxically fundamental within modern historicity. It is not its anachronistic vestige but the very way in which the historical present and future are produced. What is this historical process and moment? It is "the fact that the colored population of our land is, through the new imperial policy, about to be doubled by our ownership of Porto Rico, and Havana, our protectorate of Cuba, and conquest of the Philippines" (Outlook 102, para. 17).[42]

As what is referenced here is precisely that historical valence by which the on-the-ground configuration of the African American situation in the United States will become enfolded within a certain exfoliation of a new formation of "the problem of the color line" (or, alternatively put, undergo an implosion therein, as it were) as it devolved across the twentieth century and right into the twenty-first, across the North American continent, I will annotate this historical reference directly here on the surface of our discussion.

That is to say, the process in question simply renders into historical relief that this mode of the production of an ostensibly domestic organization of social field has been both originary and dominant in the making of all that has been called American in the modern moment. Within, upon, and in relation to forms of indigeneity—including the most ancient and enduring—the multiply imposed contradictory inscription and conscription of social groups of one kind or another becomes originary or reinaugurating; their arrival on the social horizon in question announces a new incipit. This turn-of-the-twentieth-century imperial relation, then, is one form of a general process of the process of arrival—in the Americas in general and in the United States in particular in the present reference given by Du Bois, but with implicative reference beyond this continental formation, as we shall notate below (a reference that has become historically dominant in our own contemporary moment)—from another shore and another heading of existence.

The relation of the Negro or African American as a group to these other groups should be, writes Du Bois, "an attitude of deepest sympathy and strongest alliance" (Outlook 102, para. 17). The former might be historicized by us as a nineteenth-century idea. The latter might be understood as a harbinger of the form of the question as it would take shape over the course of the twentieth century. The prospects of such alliance leads Du Bois to imagine the dawning of a "third millennium" when "the color line has faded as mists before the sun" (Outlook 103, para. 18).

E. EUROPE. Finally, then, it is after this tarrying with the North American form of this horizon that Du Bois narratively turns and crosses the North Atlantic and begins to propose a discussion of Europe at the end of the nineteenth century and in his historical present.

If we understand the question of the problem of the color line only according to a received idea of a distinction of civilized and uncivilized, or developed and undeveloped, then by definition this narrative would simply refer back to the traditional moorings in the accounts of modernity. However, as we have begun to see, perhaps such a premise should not be the basis of our analysis of this narrative. The question of the problem of the color line understood as a symbolic practice in material form on the global and historical scale that Du Bois has developed thus far in this essay has an essential premise that takes it beyond any simple dichotomy or simple categorical distinction. The operative premise of the narrative is not the presumption of simple or pure terms that are then brought into relation. Rather, the narrative focus is on historical practices that promulgate themselves as the production of social relations organized as if such a distinction were or could be their foundation. And, thus, the key aspect of this order of narrative attention is a certain social and historical production of hierarchy. The objects of attention are institutions and practices. They are forms of institution which orient themselves, in their practical operation, toward the telos or ideal of the production of categorical hierarchy. In this sense, Du Bois has been giving an account of the production of modern historicity, whether of Africa, Asia, the Americas, or now a certain Europe. What Du Bois's discourse can then be said to allow us to begin to notice are the simultaneously productive and yet destructive and constraining effects of such an orientation on what he calls the movement of human progress.

Thus, while the specific global character of the problem of the color line in Du Bois's present is not manifestly simply replicated within a context called "Europe," for him the root character of this global problematic can be recognized as showing forth there. We might thematize these aspects in a summary fashion as following two pathways. These are, respectively, the question of a supposed internal differentiation of groups within the context of a national fabric or tapestry and the relation of a given nation to its aspirations for a certain form of expansion and domination of an external group or such an ensemble.

Thus, for Du Bois, several contemporary problems in Europe seem to relate to the general "problem of the color line," even if none bear on it directly but only "touch it":

> There are three significant things in Europe of to-day which must attract us: the Jew and Socialist in France, the Expansion of Germany and Russia, and the race troubles of Austria. None of these bring us directly upon the question of color; and yet nearly all touch it indirectly. In France we have seen the exhibition of a

furious racial prejudice mingled with [deep-lying] economic causes, and not the whole public opinion of the world was able to secure an entirely satisfactory outcome.[43] The expansion of military Germany is a sinister thing, for with all her magnificent government and fine national traits, her dealings with undeveloped races hitherto have been conspicuous failures. Her contact with the blacks of [E]ast and [We]st Africa has been marked by a long series of disgraceful episodes, and we cannot view with complacency her recent bullying of Hayti and her high-handed seizure of Chinese territory.[44] The development of Russia is the vast unknown quantity of the European situation and has been during the 19th century. Her own great population of slaves stands midway racially between the white Germans and the yellow Tartar, and this makes the whole progress of the Bear a faint reflection of the color line.[45] With the advance of Russia in Asia, the completion of the great trans-Siberian railway, and the threatened seizure of Corea, comes the inevitable clash of the Slav with the yellow masses of Asia. Perhaps a Russia-Japanese war is in the near future.[46] At any rate a gigantic strife across the color line is impending during the next one hundred years. In Austria we see to-day the most curious and complicated race conflict between Germans, Hungarians, Czechs, Jews and Poles, the outcome of which is puzzling.[47] Finally in the lesser countries of Europe the race question as affecting the darker peoples is coming to the fore. In the question of the status of Turkey and the Balkan States, in the ventures of Italy in Africa and China, in the black membership of the Catholic church, indeed a survey of the civilized world at the end of the 19th century but confirms the proposition with which I started—the world problem of the 20th century is the Problem of the Color line—the question of the relation of the advanced races of men who happen to be white to the great majority of the undeveloped or half developed nations of mankind who happen to be yellow, brown or black. (Outlook 103–4, para. 19)[48]

In this passage, we can hear the full resonance of Du Bois's summary of the implication for an understanding of the historical figure of Europe of his guiding theoretical fiction in this essay. What Europe had proposed to displace from within its own domesticity to other domains and other climes has in fact returned anew to its shores, reinaugurating thus the originary heterogeneity of its supposed internal historicity, beyond any premise or presupposition of the homogeneity of the same.

Two further historicizing motifs of this account as it pertains to the question of a global horizon might be especially underscored. That is, one can note two specific effects of Du Bois's global perspective on how he characterizes Europe as a historical figure at the turn to the twentieth century: for it would guide and shape his understanding of this figure during the course of the century that was to come.

On the one hand, Du Bois understood Russia at 1900 as potentially part of a new world to come, to the extent that in his view it had not yet established its decisive modern historical character in a global sense. Yet Russia's imperial ambition with regard to Korea, as Du Bois characterized it, was a crucial step in its eventual indication that it would announce itself in the mold of the traditional imperialism of Europe in the modern period. And in that process it would define itself in relation to a global scenography beyond its domesticity that could legibly be read in terms of a question of a critical thought of what Du Bois means in this essay as "the problem of the color line." Du Bois was thus led to hypothesize that perhaps a Russo-Japanese war was in the near future. Four years later, it arrived. But we note that perhaps it matters little for us as to whether or not he was novel in this prediction. Far more important for us is a distinctive aspect of his interpretation, one rooted in the whole premise of his understanding of modernity as configured by way of a global problem of the color line. For Du Bois, a war such as the one that did occur in 1904–5 between Russia and Japan was an example of conflict at the conjunction of this global problem of the color line. Thus, he went on to write further, immediately, in this paragraph, "At any rate a gigantic strife across the color line is impending during the next one hundred years" (Outlook 104, para. 19). Here, Korea must also be understood to articulate precisely within (and now beyond, to make reference from our own moment) this twentieth-century form of the general problematic configured in this general discussion by Du Bois. Again, for Du Bois at this time, Japan appears as a potentially exemplary example in the unfolding global scene of this itinerary. Later, Du Bois in fact affirmed Japan's success in the war and declared it as a further concession across the putative color line, just as he had claimed such that about its abolition of "foreign consular courts" on its soil.[49]

On the other hand, at the year 1900, as we will shortly annotate further as he begins his temporal narrative of the problematic in question, Du Bois thought of Europe as the exemplar of "the civilized world of the present age."[50] However, the question that guided his account of a global problem of the color line, namely, the way in which a group of people—a so-called social class, a nation, a culture, or even a civilization (whatever may be understood as such)—addresses the matter of its relation to different human groups, provides Du Bois with profound historical criteria by which to understand the meaning and status of Europe in a context that we may understand as world historical. Thus, if by 1900 Du Bois was already critical of Europe's history in this domain, after World War I, in the early 1920s, Du Bois's doubts about the moral character of a certain essential dimension of what had taken shape across the modern period under the heading of a certain European civilization became fundamental. And, as noted elsewhere, in the months and years immediately following the end of World War II, he would come to critically remark the view of Europe that he had held in the year 1900 and decisively question the idea of Europe as a singular or even dominant source of ideals for the world of the future.[51] The irruption of two wars of worldwide scale and implication from within its domestic disposition and its promulgation of a near-total planetary colonization, which was in all truth for him the very mode of the implication of this domestic horizon for a planetary one, across the first half of the twentieth century can be understood to have confirmed at the most profound level his concerns at the turn of the century about the coming form of historical relations among groups of peoples within this whole scenography. As a theoretical lens, the problem of the color line, as a frame, proposed for Du Bois a simultaneously acute and flexible form of visibility, rendering both real and at stake (that is, a form of the not yet and the possible) the matter of new forms of difference as they acquire distinction within a heretofore unarticulated sense of horizon, a theoretical apperception in which this problematic names even itself as a problem of the form of knowledge.

In the context of a reference to a certain projection of Europe, then, it can be said that if the problem of the color line is global in the manner in which Du Bois has thus far construed it, then the question is not one of the supposed primordial status of one group in relation to another. And, most especially, it is not the question of the primordial status of any supposed singular group in relation to all others. Rather, the problem is one of historical practice. The present situation, when understood on the basis of a global background, can be described as relative in every sense. It has arisen historically and will devolve according to the same fundamental modalities of existence. The new imperialism and modern forms of colonialism then have been announced as historical forms—a certain sense of phase—of an unfolding devolution in which their pertinence cannot be understood as simple, ultimately given, or absolute in any sense.

2. A SECOND NARRATIVE. In the *second narrative*, Du Bois redeploys the operative question of this essay according to another mode of analyzing existence, a temporal one. It announces temporization as the movement of

the formation of ideals in or as historicity. It names the formation of ideals according to a movement of temporization as the very texture and organization of historicity.

"What in the light of historical experience is the meaning of such a world problem and how can it be solved?" (Outlook 104, para. 20).

If in the former narrative, organized spatially by way of geographic reference, Du Bois has emphasized a certain commonness among the different contexts, let us say a certain hypothesis or theoretical fiction as both an object of inquiry and a guide for thought, then in the second narrative, organized by temporal transitions, he wishes to emphasize that while social problems can be understood as persisting, that while there is a sameness to be tracked in both space and time, the more fundamental aspect of their historicity is that they arise in or as human existence. To the extent that human disposition is itself susceptible to temporization, indeed is only possible as such, transformation of ideals is the very path of the existence and becoming of social problems. Such transformation could be understood in a certain way as historicity in general, perhaps as the temporal organization of social problems, or perhaps as the movement of idealization. It is their historicity. Transformation, we might say, in all of its diverse forms, as they can be marked or tracked under the headings of temporality, is the mode of coming into being for social problems; it is their mode of existence.

Thus, for Du Bois, "in many respects the Negro question—the greater Negro question—the whole problem of the color line is peculiarly the child of the 19th and 20th centuries, and yet we may trace its elements, may trace the same social questions under different garbs back through centuries of European history" (Outlook 104, para. 20).

The only direct arena explored in this step-by-step temporal fashion will be the history of Europe. This is perhaps for one thetic reason and for two circumstantial ones. At an implicit level, "Europe" is a good example. For Du Bois places his declared intent at the head of this narrative as seeking "to see how other nations" dealt with such problems and "how other ages failed and prospered in their solution" (Outlook 104, para. 20). Perhaps his idea is that if the history of Europe is understood as the history of the current advancement of civilization, then an exploration of this history would acquaint one with the best that historiography has to offer at this point in the modern era. Yet it is also the case that circumstantially, through slavery and colonialism, the history of Europe pertains directly to the history of African Americans in the United States. And, through imperialism, the European example during the centuries that Du Bois will narrate was linked to a global problematic in a distinct fashion. That is to say that by way of the history of modern slavery and colonialism and an imperial project in general that extends a European reference to a global dimension, a global reference also extends itself into the very heart of the internal history of the European situation.

Du Bois takes his temporal orientation from the year 1900 and moves back in time across more than half a millennium, six hundred years, to the beginning of the modern period in European history. This earliest time is before the beginning of the slave trade. He shows the history of proscriptions internal to Europe, the previous history of differentiations and conflict in the relations among groups of people that might have been described at the end of the nineteenth century as the "same" when viewed in the context of a new colonial global scenography.

We can already remark that after narrating the progressive extension of respect for difference of patria or homeland, of religious tolerance, of the commonness of political rank and political right in European history, Du Bois can be understood to draw two morals or thematic conclusions from his story. These are narrative claims, one might say, about the formation of ideals and the evolution of moral values. The first conclusion is that many of the wisest thinkers and leaders of past eras, certainly in the European context, hesitated on the question of the general capacity of the masses. The second conclusion is that ideals only have existence in the form of a duration. As such form, they exist only as an order of change: the world has "grown" and changed its way of dealing with what was, as it were, has been understood as the basis of fundamental differences among groups. Perhaps such change, this history of actual openness to a future, would be the most important lesson to draw from this history of the extension of respect for the common among groups of humans.

Let us sketch the temporal narrative; Du Bois proceeds to give four markers:

A. "RIGHTS." At 1800 the problem was the "Political Rights of the Masses"— "the relation of the modern state to the great mass of its ignorant and poor laboring classes"—that is, the question of "Universal *suffrage*" (Outlook 105, para. 21, emphasis author):

> The matter did not seem so clear in 1800. There were men—and honest men too—who saw in the orgies of the French mob the destruction of all that was

decent in modern European civilization. There were men—and wise men, too—who believed that democratic government was simply impossible with human nature in its present condition. "Shall the tail wag the dog?" said they; shall a brutish mob sway the destines[52] of the intelligent and well-born of the nation? It was all very well for [Jean-Jacques] Rousseau to sing the Rights of Man, but this civic idealism must make way for calm criticism. What were the abilities of the mob any way? Must there not in the very nature of the case be a mass of ignorant inefficiency at the bottom of every nation—a strata of laborers whose business it was (as the German princeling said) to honor the king, pay their taxes, and hold their tongues? (Outlook 104–5, para. 21)

Then, to accent his reference, Du Bois provides a formulation, a conceptualization, that he highlights by making of it an entirely separate paragraph.

Over this the world struggled through the French Revolution, through the English chartist and reform movements, past the Frankfort Parliament and the upheavals of '48 down to the overthrow of the Federalists and the rise of Andrew Jackson, and to-day we have not to be sure a full realization of the dreams of the political philosophers of the 18th century, nor have we found the critic's distrust of the working classes justified. All civilized nations have found that the great mass of grown men can safely be given a voice in government and be represented in its deliberations, and that taxation without representation is tyranny. This is the revolution of one hundred years of thought and striving. (Outlook 104–5, para. 22)[53]

This is the question of universal suffrage, the root formal problem of democracy, of the status of the demos, here in its modern form. In this formal sense, such a new idea of "sovereignty," if such an old name retains its usefulness here, could now be understood as always heterogeneous to itself: as susceptible to its own becoming, as always multiple, as other than the one or the simple.

B. "RANK," OR SOCIAL STATUS. At 1700 one can grasp another horizon of "world problem" or "problem of the century." Suppose, Du Bois writes,

We had gone back past Napoleon [Bonaparte], past the French Revolution, past the day of [Jeanne Bécu, Comtesse] Du Barry and [Jeanne Antoinette Poisson, Marquise de] Pompadour—back to this bowed and stricken old man with his hooked nose and piercing eyes, his majestic figure and hands that grasped half the world—the 14th Louis, King of France. What was the problem of the year that dawned on 1700, almost the last year of the greatest monarch the world has known? It was the problem of the privileged class—the question as to whether or not the state existed for the sole privilege of the king and the king's friends; whether after all ordinary people not well born were really men in the broader meaning of that term. We who were born to sing with [Robert] Burns "The rank is but the guinea's stamp, / The Man's the gowd for a' that," have faint conception of the marvellous hold which the idea of rank, of high birth once held on earth.[54] How narrow and confined were the lives of all who were not their fathers' sons and how hard a battle the world fought before the low born had a right to go where he pleased, to work as he pleased, to be judged according to his deserts and to be held and treated as a man. (Outlook 106, para. 23)[55]

This idea of rank can be translated into a formal logic as the idea of categorical distinction, of categorical hierarchy, of categorical proscription and ascription. With reference to the European horizon, which is in fact Du Bois's orientation here, such forms of distinction would in only an apparent paradox index an originary heterogeneity within the formation of that horizon and persisting right through the birth of the supposed modern reorganization of forms of social ordination and configuration.[56]

3. RELIGION (OR THEOLOGY). At 1600 "the problem of the century" was the problem of religious and theological intolerance, a situation wherein "only those who went to your church were worthy of life and liberty and you roasted the others alive to the glory of God and the salvation of your soul" (Outlook 106, para. 24). The question was the stability of the border in a community of belief. Anyone understood as essentially of the outside could be purged or persecuted. In a certain formal language, this is an idea of the putative inside and the putative outside, another turn or form of the idea of category. It hardly need be remarked that such practical forms of distinction have rearticulated themselves within the new forms of the global as the very announcement of the twenty-first century.

4. PATRIA (NATALITY AND PATRIMONY). And at 1500 the problem of the century can be captured in the fact that the "Spaniards looked on Englishmen as Englishmen now look at Hottentots, and Frenchmen regarded Italians as Americans look upon Filipinos, when hatred and dislike of foreigners made war a holy pastime, and patriotism meant the murder of those who did not speak your language" (Outlook 106, para. 24).[57] This was a question of *patria*, or homeland. Anyone from outside but situated somehow

within some common frame of reference, a foreigner, could be treated with suspicion, dislike, or even hatred, with relative impunity. Here is a thought of the origin, of the pure as origin, of the origin as pure.

And such a thought is almost always a matter of the *Patron*—of a masculine gendered claim to a line of descent, of becoming in all senses (of supposed beginnings *and end*). Let us note, for future annotation, that within this text as given, this motif remains without explicit remark or elaboration by Du Bois. Thus, too, it must be remarked that within our own time, the universal extension of matters of suffrage by gender remains withheld in the most fundamental of senses, not only of sex and sexualization, but on the order of claims of being, namely, all that is understood as woman. And here I propose to signal the generality of the metaphor: *as "Black" woman*. We may take the liberty of responding to Harriet Tubman's rhetorical question to Frederick Douglass, with our own metaphorization: "Frederick, is God Dead?" No, and she is a *Black woman* (see Du Bois 1909, 121–22; 1962, 93).

Perhaps the bearing of this narrative for a fundamental thought about historicity is twofold. The historicity of ideals can be understood according to a certain temporality, that is, of temporization rather than the punctual present. Du Bois's account certainly proposes that ideals even as an announcement of a kind of fulfillment can only acquire pertinence in the form of a historicity in which temporization is the very form of being of ideals: that is to say that they are produced in history, by way of historical processes, both events that happen and actions that attempt to follow a certain course of practice or a policy. Yet perhaps more fundamentally still, such a realization should perhaps be understood only as the heading of another formation of problem, of world-historical problem, shall we say. This is to suggest that the mode or phenomenality of this temporization is that ideals appear under the blind heading of problems given to a social group, whatever is such, or by those in general who would ask about the historiality of the human, by its situation, in all of its specificity and illimitability. The historicity of ideals is the actuality of the engagement with such problems. Historicity is then such temporization as being an impossible possibility of ideals. Thus, Du Bois can characterize the meaning of his narrative from the standpoint of the year 1900 or of the year 2000, or perhaps even 2020. In this sense, we can recognize that Du Bois has been on the track of adducing a problem of the centuries, certainly those past but perhaps also of those yet to come.

At this point in this account of his present, Du Bois's discussion has arrived at a certain kind of theoretical joint or hinge. If so far in this address, Du Bois has proposed to think of his present by way of a reference to the past, after this double narrative, geographic and temporal, he turns to think of his present in relation to the question of the future. And this latter temporality is ultimately the horizon and guide of the text as a whole; it is oriented to the future and not to the past. It is oriented by the question of possibility, even as it seeks to give an account of limit. And even the narration of the past has been guided by this sense. Thus, the rhetorical movement of Du Bois's text at this juncture issues from a precise theoretical commitment. Du Bois's procedure in this essay is the same as that which he followed in "The Conservation of Races." His first gesture has been to formulate a "wide and thorough understanding" (CR 5, para. 3) of his situation, that of African Americans as a whole. Only then, and on that basis, could he formulate a judgment or a proposition, make a decision, and choose a definite course of action in contradistinction to another possible one. At this point in "The Present Outlook for the Dark Races of Mankind," we are at the moment of the final step in the construal of such an understanding. If we have some understanding of the past, how can we use that perspective to formulate a hypothesis about the future of the problem of the color line, if we think of this concept-metaphor in the sense that Du Bois has given it here? This turning from an account of the past *to an account of the future on the basis of an understanding of the past*, a past that has become narratable by way of the formulation of a certain epistemological fiction, which is also a proposed epistemic intervention and perhaps a certain kind of conceptual innovation, but which is not thereby false in any simple sense, is the theoretical hinge or joint across which the text moves at this point. The rhetorical construction of this hinge or joining is one of the major theoretical interventions of the text. Its successful molding will give direct rise to the articulation of a position that might situate and guide a course of action by African Americans in the future.

1. OF WAR. On the eve of 1900, Du Bois is hopeful, suggesting to his audience that "we can find much in our surroundings to encourage this hope," despite what he describes as obvious signs that would make such a view questionable, that is, the "armed court of Europe," and the "impending

clash in the East" (between Russia and Japan), and too, the "struggle in Africa" (Outlook 106–7, para. 25).

What is, or could be, the basis of such hope? What is the basis for Du Bois's optimism?

Perhaps we can track this at the level of a fundamental logic internal to the movement of Du Bois's narrative as a whole. He has already questioned the premise of categorical difference as a truth that could be sustained by history. While he does not offer what might be called an infraconceptual account of the untenability of categorical difference, that is, its internal conceptual aporias, he does describe its instability as an actual basis of human institution at the level of entire civilizations. As such, above all, he narrates a history of change in their promulgation (and change in the thetic character of a categorical claim is always a wearing and tearing away of the grounds of its very premise). Thus, in a sense, the internal logic of Du Bois's entire account leads him to imagine the dissolution of distinctions of *family or nation*, in an extended metaphorized sense of such ideas as the terms of human conflict. Further, if this text is an appeal addressed to an audience that must choose or establish a course of action with regard to their relation to other groups, and Du Bois has already proposed that such a decision ought to be based on an understanding of fundamental truth, and if the fundamental truth of history in the modern period is of the disruption and the wearing away of categorical distinction, then the internal logic of his narrative leads one to the idea that action committed to such categorical logic is doomed to fail—perhaps entailing tremendous cost in all senses, perhaps in a repetitive and ongoing fashion—in the broadest and deepest historical sense. Therein, perhaps, paradoxically, chance and possibility can arise.

2. OF WAR, AGAIN. It is perhaps on this basis that Du Bois could portend to anticipate the decadence of war in the twentieth century. "No age has shown such genuine dislike of war and such abhorrence of its brutalities as this, and the 20th century is destined to see national wars, not disappear to be sure, but to sink to the same ostracism in popular opinion as the street fight and the brawl among individuals" (Outlook 107, para. 25). Was he right? Obviously, the first and most decisive answer, if this thought is a simple idealism, is a fundamental and emphatic negative. However, the internal formation of a critical practice such as Du Bois is attempting here has its own complexity. We can specify it on two levels: the given as possible and as actual.

On the one hand, Du Bois was right in the sense that the old forms of war, especially those that had become definitive of the modern era as one in which the nation-state had arisen as the principal geo-global form of political entity, would be increasingly displaced by another order of conflict. In this sense alone, such war as Du Bois thought of it at the end of the nineteenth century did take on a different and somewhat diminished profile over the course of the twentieth century. In this specific sense, there has indeed been a marked change in the character of war. There is no need retrospectively to censure a hope that it could be affirmed as a fundamental practice of a new kind, even if it were to arise of necessity (as in the ongoing attempts at the institutionalization of a global order of the common among nations).

On the other hand, and this will hit the fundamental dimension, within Du Bois's discourse proper, it will be precisely the attention to that dimension of historicity that he is trying to recognize in an epistemological sense in "The Present Outlook for the Dark Races of Mankind" that will lead him over the decade and a half following its presentation to begin to step by step render into a decisive theoretical understanding the ongoing production of war through the promulgations of the problem of the color line as the very mode of the formation of a new twentieth-century global order. With the opening of World War I, this sense, already in profound conception in his discourse, became decisive (Du Bois 1973d, 1915a, 1982a, 1945, 1975b).

Thus, we can note rather directly that Du Bois was also wrong in his prediction. And this is fundamental. For the twentieth century saw instead the rise of new forms of categorical, or totalitarian, distinction and the promulgation of war on such a basis—with a concrete intensity and scale never before witnessed on the whole of the planet earth. Thus, the twentieth century became the century in which war was waged at a level that was utterly unprecedented in human history. And "the problem of the color line," this effort to promulgate a categorical distinction within the form of the human (in all senses—ontological, theological, sociological, political, and legal, for example) that we have seen Du Bois adducing in this essay, would become its fundament. Or, in an additional theoretical idiom, precisely the premise of such war was the placing at stake of a total, or categorical, proscription and its affirmative derivatives. That is to say, the totality of the ground, in every sense, of the entity, or group, proposing such a distinction was put at stake. And it was necessarily likewise for those groups that would challenge such a proscription—even if both, in some sense, took the form of humanity as a whole. The imperial premise—for that is what has been at issue, as Du Bois will theorize it—both shifted its axial reference and yet reaffirmed its most deep-seated presumption. In this sense, the problem of war shifted in its bearing onto another order of existence.

Perhaps, at the turn of the century, Du Bois was too much of a believer in the idea that the establishment of truth alone might make it directly possible for the world to be brought into accord with such understanding. Or at least the appeal, or petition, as a form, that discursive form the deployment of which Du Bois practices here, must operate on that epistemic and ethical basis: it solicits a sovereign truth or a putative sovereign subject that would produce such truth in history or as history, whether that sovereign be an ecclesiastical entity, a deity, God, or the demos organized as a people, that is, a family or nation, of some kind, perhaps humanity in general.

And he wished for the heterogeneous ensemble that he proposed to nominalize as the rising colored folks of the world to accord with this truth and announce this new epoch of historicity.

Thus, we might assume the other *futural* implication of the terms of Du Bois's own narrative and also say that he does not at this point, December 1900, recognize the extent to which what can be called a *civil* war in an extended sense, the war of different ideological positions that would each declare a putative sovereignty under one instituted heading, of nation *and* state, of nation *or* state, was already the hallmark of modernity. That is to say that perhaps it was not possible at 1900 for Du Bois to see precisely how a certain idea of sovereignty that itself had already become at issue over the course of the early moments of a global modernity would within a few decades become understandable in a fundamentally new way. And if we follow this thought of displaced sovereignty, the histories of the unfolding of such a problematic in the global colonial theater would be understood to have always played a crucial role in its modern devolution. Thus, the revolutions in the Americas, which yielded the United States and which yielded the state of Haiti, might be included here. And then, further, so could the Civil War in the United States, the so-called Boer war in southern Africa, the Cuban Revolution, or the war in Vietnam of the 1950s through the 1970s. And the twentieth-century wars of Europe, the Spanish Civil War of the 1930s, and the two world wars, in particular, if situated within the frame of Du Bois's narrative, could be understood precisely as projects of internal categorical proscription, of which the attack at Guernica declared its mark; of which, perhaps, we will come to recognize the Nanking Massacre as its decisive transformation; of which the project of Auschwitz in its entirety should stand as an example that confounds the limits of the example; or of which the "bombings" of Tokyo, Hiroshima, and Nagasaki would propose its hyperbolic translatability. While one retrospection might propose to understand certain examples of such war (war to protect from tyranny or to restrict tyranny) as an affirmation of freedom, and I would maintain such an affirmation here, it yet also remains that even those examples of the processes that configure this historicity cannot yet be removed from all possibility of being reinscribed under the heading of a maintenance of war, or the maintenance of a problem of the color line, in Du Bois's extended sense: that is, the maintenance of an attempt to promulgate categorical difference as the essence of the modern epoch. It remains, I suggest, that it is something like the order of historial attention that Du Bois adumbrates in this brief text, as one example, that offers us the traction to orient ourselves for such an account of the history of modernity. Such an account would be truly open to a recognition of both sides of the limit in the devolution of modern historicity on a planetwide scale, for it would be written under the impress of a thought of the dissemination of authority, rather than that of its maintenance or constitution.[58] This is the motif that Du Bois begins to render into thematic relief from the outset of World War I in Europe, and it will acquire a deepening, even if complex and at times contradictory, articulation in his thought across the remainder of his itinerary (Du Bois 1915a). I propose that it is such an order of attention that governs Du Bois's magisterial *Black Reconstruction: An Essay toward a History of the Part Which Black Folk Played in the Attempt to Reconstruct Democracy in America, 1860–1880*, from 1935 (Du Bois 1976d) and his searing redoubled retrospectives following World War II, *Color and Democracy: Colonies and Peace* (Du Bois 1975b), issued during the first half of the year 1945— and each the two texts just noted were cited in this respect above—as well as the epistemologically radical *The World and Africa: An Inquiry into the Part Which Africa Has Played in World History*, first published in 1947 (Du Bois 1976e). It is in *Color and Democracy* that this thought is given its most direct statement with reference to a historically present sense of the global multiplicity of peoples and situations (Chandler 2021).

3. OF THE NEW PROBLEM OF THE COLOR LINE. Du Bois also predicts the rise of new forms of internal differentiation within a national situation. This will be by way of novel transnational configurations.[59] It will occur by way of the "expansion and consolidation of nations." This would lead to novel forms of "intermixture."[60] That is, the kinds of social processes that

led to the formation of the United States and have been extended in its own imperial policy have become global or will become so soon. Du Bois believes at 1900 that such new forms of internal difference will become virtually universal. We can quote this passage in full as a way to stage its elaboration. It forms the entire second half of the one in which Du Bois announces his hypothesis about the future, about the century to come, about the twentieth century:

> At the same time the expansion and consolidation of nations to-day is leading to countless repetitions of that which we have in America to-day—the inclusion of nations within nations—of groups of undeveloped peoples brought into contact with advanced races under the same government, language and system of culture. The lower races will in nearly every case be dark races. German Negroes, Portuguese Negroes, Spanish Negroes, English East Indian, Russian Chinese, American Filipinos—such are the groups which following the example of the American Negroes will in the 20th century strive, not by war and rapine but by the mightier weapons of peace and culture to gain a place and name in the civilized world. (Outlook 107, para. 25)

The central claim of this passage is the parallel, or the corollary, of Du Bois's previous claim about the decadence of war in the century to come. Both are premised on the idea of a certain erosion of the supposed pre-eminent pertinence of a simple national border or boundary as the basis of either difference or identity among groups of humans.

If his idea of the decadence of war can be understood in our contemporary moment only in an ambivalent manner, at best, then what of his idea of new forms of relation, of difference and identity?

4. OF NEW ORDERS OF DIFFERENCE. Three direct thetic claims can be outlined here.

A. NEW OLD HIERARCHIES. First, according to Du Bois, there will be the articulation of new forms of hierarchy (yet occurring within the nexus and idioms of the old), of social ordination, specifically as the text gives it to us, an organization of relations of "lower" and "higher" *races*. As I remark elsewhere (Chandler, forthcoming), in my address of the essay "The Conservation of Races," in a formulation such as given here, by *a* race Du Bois means primarily a social and historical entity, rather than a group defined simply, first or only, by physical character, yet one that can be named as otherwise than simply under the heading of a nation or a state. The idea of ordination here is conceived less in terms of the coherence of theology or the premises of natality than it is gathered in thought and practice from a supposedly modern and critical (in the sense of the German and French inheritance of the Enlightenment and then the work of Immanuel Kant) *idea of the perfectibility of the human.* That there is such an idea or ideal, of the perfectibility of the human, is the first premise about ordination that should be underscored. It is also part of the inheritance that gives the sense of progress that is so ambivalently at the center of Du Bois's thought of historicity at this time. However, second, with regard to ordination, for Du Bois, any such process is historial; it is marked in its modes by temporization. All is not given at one go or in terms of any final or ultimate sense. Thus, in the most committed and radical sense of his thought, no historical group has an absolute privilege in its unfolding. Rather, by circumstance and event in the broadest and most durable sense of these terms, a given configuration of possibility unfolds in the relation of groups. Thus, for Du Bois, *in his present,* a given ensemble of diverse groups, perhaps nameable only in some differential sense under the heading of the metaphors "light" or "white," could be understood to have a certain status in the organization of historical possibility. And, thus, while the ordination of "lower," and by implication "higher," should certainly be understood to name a hierarchical relation, it does not denote in any genetic, primordial, ultimate, or final sense an idea of superiority or inferiority. It is rather a name for the situation of a given relation, that is, an instituted and circumstantial one, to historical possibility. In Du Bois's historical present at the turn of the twentieth century, the organization of such possibility was rooted in the violence and destruction of the practice of categorical proscription, what he has called "the problem of the color line" in the modern and global context, just as much as or more than (much more than) it was grounded in any chance, freedom, or ability announced within human practice. Thus, in the sense of logic or absolute necessity, it can be said that in Du Bois's terms, it is by chance that at the year, that the so-called "advanced races of men . . . happen to be white" or that "the great majority" of the so-called "undeveloped" or supposedly "half developed" nations of the world "happen to be yellow, brown or black." The semantics of such markers are derivative of instituted systems of hierarchy. Thus, the former are not the source of the latter's origination. For this reason, they are always relative, ambiguous, or incoherent as category, or as terms of a categorical mark or instantiated criterion, in the supposed instance of their bearing. Likewise it is no accident that the nominal headings that Du Bois gives for possible "lower races" can all be remarked as names for positions produced by way of the relations of imperial colonialism. For this history has played its definite part in the present institution of relations among groups of people, no matter the criteria by which one articulates such distinction. It is for this reason that he can speak of such groups to come as "German Negroes, Portuguese Negroes, Spanish Negroes, English East Indian, Russian Chinese, American Filipinos." And thus one can remark further just how prescient was Du Bois's prediction. In this sense, his claim has proved precisely accurate.[61] This interpretation of the "metropole" by way of the relation of metropole and colony will in all truth remain a fundament of Du Bois's thought throughout his entire itinerary.[62]

B. THE REMAKING OF WORLD—AS "CULTURE." Second, Du Bois proclaims that such groups, shorn of the sense of national necessity or prerogative, would seek to redefine the horizon of civilization by way of a certain reorganization of the terms of "culture." For Du Bois, the idea of culture here has the sense of a cultivation of the best, the development of the highest sense of the good or right. It has in this context a profound moral implication: it is the articulation of group ideals according to a protocol or modicum of "peace" in contradistinction to "war." If, on the one hand, Du Bois thought of Europe at 1900 as a source of ideals for the coming century and if there was a substantial basis for such affirmation on his part, on the other hand, at this turn to a new century, it was not alone in such status.[63] Indeed, in the context of the high-water mark of European colonial exploitation and oppression at the time of Du Bois's writing, his formulation calls for another kind of affirmation that would be pointedly at odds with the modern history of Europe or a putative Euro-America. Thus, not only would such new groups, "lower races," "strive" or seek "to gain a place and name in the civilized world," according to Du Bois they would in a fundamental sense make that world otherwise than what it had become thus far in the modern era (Outlook 107, para. 25).

C. THE "NEGRO" AMERICAN EXAMPLE, AGAIN. Third, for Du Bois, the American Negro is potentially a leader in this new world situation. And this is precisely the sense of their own place in historicity that Du Bois would have his audience, the assembled members of the American Negro Academy, most accept on the basis of the "wide and thorough understanding" whose possibility and orientation he has at least outlined, if not demonstrated, perhaps by way of circumstance, in the preceding sections of his address. As Du Bois had already proposed to this group in 1897, the Negro "race" as a whole, or a "vast historic race," as he formulated it in that earlier moment, had yet to deliver its full contribution to the promulgation of the ideals of human civilization. Yet the past and present situation of the Negro *American* meant that it was potentially a pioneer in the twentieth-century world to come, certainly a future world and perhaps a new world. In the one instance, the full Negro message was yet to come because it was relatively undeveloped as a historical subject or entity. Indeed, in "Strivings of the Negro People" from 1897, which became the opening chapter of *The Souls of Black Folk: Essays and Sketches*, Du Bois speaks of the Negro American situation as a condition of a "credulous race childhood."[64] In another instance, the Negro American owing to its situation at or as the site of a specific intermingling of ideals or as part of a scene of multiple ideals is potentially in the "vanguard" of the development of the forms of civilization in the century to come. This position meant that for Du Bois the Negro American *in the present of the time of his writing* had a historical burden: the question of "the success of many a people and largely the fate of the twentieth century" (Outlook 107, para. 26). Thus, in a resolutely masculinist and military fashion, not to say naïve, perhaps, Du Bois appeals to his audience, primarily male: "Let us acquit ourselves like men" (Outlook 107, para. 26). (Elsewhere, Du Bois will affirm the feminine, a persistent gesture for him, which thus marks a complex ambivalence within his thought. One notes here Josie in the fourth chapter of *The Souls of Black Folk: Essays and Sketches* of 1903, the first figure of forbearance and loss in his discourse, after his own autobiographical persona, and Jennie in the thirteenth chapter of that book [whom I also remarked at the end of part I], the sister of the titular character John, as also bearers of historical possibility. And, too, one notes that in that book, for example, in his discussion of American self-assertiveness and aggrandizement, Du Bois often affirmatively configures the Negro as a caretaker of supposed traditional feminine values of humility and self-sacrifice.) The possible meaning for the Negro American was that *in the future* their position would be "not simply to follow but to lead the civilization of the day—pressing onward with him who never followed but marched breast forward":

> Never dreamed tho' right were vanquished, wrong would triumph,
> Held we fall to rise, are baffled to fight better,
> Sleep to wake. (Outlook 107, para. 26)[65]

Thus, the Negro American, despite or beyond, and not simply because of, its passage through the exploitation of slavery and colonialism, articulates the historicity of modernity as new forms of relation, of difference and sameness, of hierarchy and position, of necessity and possibility. It is this complex horizon, of a certain relation of past and future, that Du Bois sought to adduce most specifically for his audience in this address. I have described these paragraphs of Du Bois's address as taking the theoretical position of a kind of joint or hinge. Such a figure should perhaps be understood as more than just a rhetorical form of passage. It would also be the thetic proposition announced here as a theory of the situation of the historical present of the Negro or African American. This means not simply that the organization of the situation of the Negro American in the present forms the terms of this passage of the past to the future. It also means that the organization of the Negro American's present situation bespeaks the possibility of the future in such a way that the relation of the past to any possible present, including the one on the eve of the year 1900, is not given fully or all at once. This relation remains at stake in the future. Historicity understood as a relation to origin would be nameable only in and through such movement, through this reciprocity of end and origin. This would be the form of a specifically Negro American historicity in the modern age. Yet, and more profoundly, while such futural form is indeed the privileged heading under which to situate the organization of Negro American historicity, at another level it would be in the most fundamental sense exemplary of the modernity that remained to come for Du Bois, perhaps, in the form of the twentieth century and, perhaps, beyond.

D. DECISION

Yet Du Bois will try here to step to the side, at least, of this blind that is the unfolding of historicity and to propose the possibility of intervening in the making of history, of organizing one's relation to futural possibility on the basis of a heading, a plan, a decision, a direct and responsible form of action.

How does Du Bois formulate such a project? What is its heading? By what course of action should the Negro or African American at 1900 proceed according to the terms of Du Bois's address?

His answer is that they should proceed by way of a commitment to a form of relation among groups that would be otherwise than the past: otherwise than by way of "war" or otherwise than the model, or ideal, of war. It would be by way of a commitment to "peace and culture" as the defining terms of their horizon, of a critical affirmation of the past and of a critical affirmation of the future. This would be "the one true path to victory: the moral mastery over the minds of men—true desert, unquestioned ability, thorough work and purity of purpose—those things alone will ensure victory to any group of men if the 20th century fulfills its promise" (Outlook 108, para. 20).

An affirmation with regard to the past can be thought as an affirmation of difference in every sense, as to both emergence and maintenance. Du Bois would give up no past or future source of the good, the true, or the beautiful. The question of just what such terms could mean would always remain at stake.

An affirmation with regard to the future could be understood as an affirmation of relation, let us say otherwise than first of all as identity. On the one hand, Du Bois seems to speak of a certain cultivation of the self in the name of a larger possibility. In one sense, this would be relation as the articulation of *duty*, or even of *sacrifice*, that is, of duty to the group beyond the self as atomic. The motif of Du Bois's idea of the "talented tenth," which will be rendered explicit in his work in the half dozen years following the composition of our text at hand, is woven from and on the fabric of this cloth. Its historical enunciation in Negro American discourses would mark it as irrupting during the course of the institution of slavery in the United States but also acquiring a deep legibility during the last decades of the nineteenth century as a more sharply variegated pattern of historical opportunity emerged among African Americans. Du Bois thematizes this difference under the heading of the duty of those with opportunity to those without.[66] In another sense, this would be relation as the name of *responsibility*. One can imagine this thought as addressed to the future, certainly to the twentieth century but perhaps even beyond. This would be a kind of respect for the other, certainly with regard to those groups that are contiguous in some national scene but also those dispersed across a global scenography that can be thought of or understood as already in relation. In the language of the discourse afoot in this address, at the limit, such a scene would include all of humanity. Du Bois will speak of this demand or call in terms of a moral imperative for a certain Europe (and the word *certain* here is meant to specify that for Du Bois Europe was a heterogeneous figure) and a certain Euro-America. There is a responsibility "for the white races of mankind to see to it that the culture they have developed is not debauched by the Philistine, the Fool, and the Lyncher—by the wholesale murder falsely called expansion, and by retail torture falsely called race pride" (Outlook 108, para. 20). Just as in "The Conservation of Races," where Du Bois affirmed the great and universal ideals of the American horizon as one that might be understood as a republic, here he will affirm a fundamental contribution of a certain Europe to the development of modern civilization: but here it is placed under the heading of responsibility to a larger horizon than the idea or figure of Europe. In the same way, Du Bois will elaborate a critical thought of responsibility for the Negro, especially the Negro American as a group, to reform, that is to say, to overcome its present limits, first by way of an acknowledged self-criticism, to accede to the best of its possibilities, that is, to its historically given opportunity.[67] It is a responsibility that Du Bois addresses directly to his immediate audience "to build up our strength, efficiency and culture" and thus become "an advance guard of that renaissance of the black races of men."[68] Thus, the Negro American here must accept responsibility as the name of a relation to another and larger horizon than that of the idea or figure of the Negro American or even the Negro in general.

This affirmation of difference and relation would distantiate the historical pertinence of "the problem of the color line." It would attempt to operate a kind of displacement of the limits imposed upon the future by way of a supposedly given origin of the present. Thus, even if Du Bois's most famous words here issue as a prediction, "the problem of the twentieth century *is to be* the relation of the civilized world to the dark races of mankind" (my emphasis), as he puts it in the opening of the second paragraph of our essay, "The Present Outlook for the Dark Races of Mankind," his most resolute concern in this text is to imagine the forms of engagement that would render to such relation the character of possibility rather than the character of a limit for humankind.

IV. ANNOTATION

If the problematic named in Du Bois's discourse must in all appearance begin with a constative reference to the specific historical situation of the Negro in America—in the part that has become the United States, according to a necessity that cannot and should not be simply avoided, it is nonetheless the case that if such an example is not to produce an uncritical prejudgment of its own general possibility and the radical dimension of such, it demands from thought a certain complicated performative operation in the formulation of its object. Thus, if Du Bois, as we have outlined, sought to situate this specificity in its most general historical horizons by an act of theoretical projection, announcing the orientation of his intuition almost as if by way of a constative reference, that is, stating the hypothesis of the existence of a global "problem of the color line," *in the first turn* of this discourse, this is simply a certain fiction that makes possible a narrative. This narrative, both geographic and temporal, in the instance, is a performative gesture. It adduces an object for inquiry, a dimension of historicity, by a progressive act of naming the eventualities of the past according to a specific order of attention. This whole operation can thus be understood as a theoretical practice of *renarrativization*. What has been ostensibly given as the terms of historiographical understanding is remarked in this reelaboration. This yields a specific order of thematization, which amounts to a hyperthematization, of a dimension of historicity, which may well have remained sedimented or suppressed according to the previously given orders of thought and understanding and which would have thus been obscure or unsusceptible to a critical reflection. It can thus be understood, in *the second turn* of this discourse, that the object in question is not a simply given thing—a punctual point, perhaps—but an objectivity adduced by way of a certain theoretical attention. Therein this attention can remark and thus render into phenomenal relief a historical organization of relation according to which the order of thing can be named. And the theoretical discourse is itself part of that relation. That is to say, the object in question is a certain order of *problem*, of the problematization of existence, of the announcement of existence as an organization of problem: the *problem* of the so-called color line. Such a problem is always and already in its announcement—whatever its ensemblic and general modes beyond such—a problem for thought as thought. Thus, Du Bois's discourse is not oriented toward a thing as a finality—that is the hypostasization of an absolute. Rather, his practice as thought is solicited by the difficulty of naming for itself an always temporal organization of relation that would predetermine and even foreclose its announcement of historical possibility. Thus, he is led to formulate the thought of a historical relation among putative groups of humans in which the status of such groups is announced as an always previous question. Thus, while such an objectivity is produced *for* consciousness, in and as consciousness, or *for* a subject, in and as subject position, it does not arrive on the scene after consciousness or subjectivation. Rather, it takes its place, if at all, as the historical lineaments according to which consciousness and subjectivity are formed and can be announced. Its announcement for thought as a problem for thought, then, can likewise occur only by way of the ineluctable complication of the constative by the performative in the naming of its object. All along the seams of its announcement, it is through and through a matter of the instituted mark that is at issue. It is according to this epistemic necessity that Du Bois's theoretical projection and generalization should be understood. What it names is the heading of a problem for thought whose status cannot be given all in one go. Thought can only address it by way of a practice of hypothetical elaboration that is always still a form of re-marking (another inscription, a re-inscription) of the given—a kind of re-narrativization. To the extent that it brings into epistemological relief that which had remained obscured or unthematized, it can be called a form of *hyperbolic* renarrativization.

In the instance at hand, we can propose that Du Bois accomplishes such. Across the three essays that I have considered in our present elaboration, dating from March 1897 to December 1899, that is, "The Conservation of Races," "A Final Word" in *The Philadelphia Negro*, and "The Present Outlook for the Dark Races of Mankind," we see the first realization as an achieved theoretical statement of a nascent critical concept of "the problem of the color line" in the work of Du Bois. Also, and in the same epistemological breath, so to speak, we see the first attempt by him at a theoretical production by way of the concept that he has formulated. In an analytical sense, these two gestures are interwoven on different registers of the same enunciation—they can be understood as its theoretical (or performative) and descriptive (or constative) levels—neither of which can be rigorously extricated from the other.

As a theoretical production, it yields a distinct order of narrative.

It is not the narrative of an event. Nor is it the account of the formation of a subject. Rather, it remarks the suspended organization of problem, of a problematization of historical existence, the eventuality of which in its very announcement for thought is always at stake and, in that sense, never quite yet fully realized or accomplished and yet always already effective in its partiality.

It can be said on an apparently more mundane level, then, that across these three essays Du Bois can be understood as disentangling a conception of "the problem of the color line" as a general social and historical *phenomenon* from the situation of the Negro American in the United States as a specific social and historical *condition*, even as such phenomenality and conditionality as modes of problem are *everywhere* given in the other and are in truth distinguishable only by the practice of a theoretical reflection.

Further, whereas in 1897 these two dimensions of historicity—the specific and the general—appear almost confounded, with the situation of the Negro American serving as the analytic envelope within which the problem of the color line could be named and situated, in 1899 the problematization that is announced as the so-called matter of "the problem of the color line" in a global dimension is theoretically recognized as a general name for the organization of the so-called problem of the Negro, or the Negro question, or the "race question" in America (which Du Bois describes in the ninth paragraph of the opening chapter of *The Souls of Black Folk: Essays and Sketches*, the original essay version of which was published just past the mid-point of 1897, as "half-named" [Du Bois 1903d, 1897c]). This traversal thus makes possible for Du Bois the delineation of a certain dimension of the historicity of his present at the turn of the twentieth century. Du Bois is able to recognize and name in a critical discourse the spatial and temporal organization of the historicity of his present as a certain form of problem. This, we might say then, is the passage of a theoretical labor and accomplishment.

Thus, a narrativization of the historicity of the *problem* named by Du Bois under the concept-metaphor of the color line, which would amount to a renarrativization, would generalize it to all that can be called modern, as distinct from the supposed ancient.

In this sense, Du Bois's thought might be usefully juxtaposed, if such might facilitate its apprehension in contemporary discourse, with that renarrativization of modernity involving the heading of "race"—even if still apparently subordinated to a supposedly more general problem of sovereignty—as such is given in the writings of Michel Foucault in the later part of his itinerary. For Du Bois, while his most famous phrase is undoubtedly that "the problem of the twentieth century is the problem of the color line," the key thought (as we have proposed in our own elaboration here, and as almost everywhere elaborated by Du Bois himself, as beyond the apparition of its implicit presentist presentation in this phrase) is that the problematic in question pertains to the whole of anything that we might call modernity, the modern era, or the modern epoch and not just to the twentieth century, perhaps also including centuries to come. Thus, it can be said that while Foucault in his later work narrated a historical movement from practices of hierarchization tendentiously toward a kind of practice of governance that would promote or affirm a kind of self-legislated commitment to norm, normalization, practices of normativity and the level of subjectivation, if we assume such terminology for the moment, then we may surmise that Du Bois had already formulated a thought of the hierarchical elaboration of the supposed normal, of presumptions thereof, across the essays leading up to the turn to the twentieth century. This ensemblic formulation notably includes those texts that we have considered here in part II of our study (Du Bois1894a, 2015a, 1897b, 2015c, 1901b, 2015e, 1899a; Foucault 1980, 2003).

We can now thematically summarize this theoretical work as proceeding along two tracks. Du Bois most certainly noted the reelaboration of a form of categorical distinction within Europe and America (which cannot be radically elaborated by way of a theory or in an analysis as separate from the very idea of race, indeed most especially as this latter is produced as a concept in thought). Indeed, in Du Bois's thought it makes possible a focus on the status of the various "national" working classes.[69] He also formulated the problem of the elaboration of a new hierarchy according to which Europe and so-called European Americans, if there is such, stood over against and above an ensemble of dispersed and "colored" human groups throughout the world (the majority of whom were constituted as classes of laborers, often subordinated and exploited according to violent hierarchies maintained within those "colored" groups).[70] The formulations of a general problem of historicity on a planet-wide scale of implication as we have recognized them according to our elaborations in part II of this study bears out the reciprocal formulations by Du Bois according to which, as we remarked in part I of this study, he sought to name the sense of matters African American in terms of its apparent specific horizons of problematization.

Beyond the texts that I have remarked above, so far, we can recognize the fundamental character of this whole problematic and problematization for his thought. In his 1909 study of John Brown, as a signal example, Du Bois wrote:

> We are in fact to-day repeating in our intercourse between races all the former evils of class distinction within the nation: personal hatred and abuse, mutual injustice, unequal taxation and rigid caste. Individual nations outgrew these fatal things by breaking down the horizontal barriers between classes. We are bringing them back by seeking to erect vertical barriers between races" (Du Bois 1909, 381–83, chap. 13, para. 38; 1962, 286–87, chap. 13, para. 38; 1973d, 286–87, chap. 13, para. 38)

The historical situation concerns the devolution of imperial relations as exploitation. The situation of a supposed ontological claim, as we might name it, involves the devolution of imperial relation as the conceptualization of categorical or absolute hierarchy among persons. Here too, in the context of this study, in Du Bois's thought, the problem in question would be a fundamental dimension of modernity. It names precisely the problem of the common nexus—in a spatial sense, the question of world and worlds; in a temporal sense, the question of the epoch—or reopens in another way the matter of epochality, perhaps, in general. Or, so we can now, in light of our study, understand Du Bois to so propose such an understanding.

Despite the sustained elaboration given herein, it remains that I have adumbrated my recollection of Du Bois's thought of "the problem of the color line," for it could be extended in the immediate scene of discussion of his signal essay "The Present Outlook for the Dark Races of Mankind" to include in detail and in depth his most famous text, *The Souls of Black Folk: Essays and Sketches*, whose "Forethought" offers this appeal or apology: "This meaning is not without interest to you Gentle Reader for the problem of the twentieth century is the problem of the color line." But, as I suggested in our opening "A Notation" above, in truth this thought runs throughout the whole of that text, forming the sinew that threads its binding and holds it together in an epistemological sense. And, beyond this singular reference, our study suggests that it can be shown that one might gather up and tie together, as in a thematic ensemble, the sheaves of all of the major critical work of Du Bois's practice by way of this specific aspect of his general problematic, from the 1890s through to the 1960s.

Du Bois's treatment of two figures from the nineteenth century in his great 1935 study *Black Reconstruction*, can be adduced here, in brief, both to suggest a bit further the availability for a future critical scholarship of this continuity within his itinerary and practice and to further name the character of the bearing of his thought of "the problem of the color line" for contemporary critical discourses. These figures are, respectively, John Brown and Andrew Johnson. In this context, we see not only the critical side of Du Bois's thought of modernity but also his sense of possibility. On the one hand, in *Black Reconstruction* Du Bois titled his long chapter on Johnson, the American president who presided over the reaction to the project of Reconstruction, "The Transubstantiation of a Poor White" (Du Bois 1976d, 237–324, chap. 8). It narrates Johnson's attempt to situate his presidency as the benefactor of a rising middle class by way of, indeed on the basis of the rejection of any possible identification with a radical sense of democracy, to the extent that the latter would have meant a disavowal of those emergent privileges of "whiteness" that Du Bois called "the wages of whiteness," which, in relation to Johnson's presidency, would have compromised the support that he received from those (both laborers and the owners of capital) in the South who were the beneficiaries of those privileges. This thematic had already been announced in Du Bois's thought at the advent of World War I in Europe (Du Bois 1976d, 700; 1910; 1915a; 1917). And it prefigures all that has come to be placed under the heading of the study of "whiteness" in our own time, as, for example, in a turnkey work for contemporary discourses in the United States since the 1960s that takes its very title from Du Bois's 1935 statement of concept (Roediger 1991). On the other hand, already in his 1909 biographical study of John Brown, the so-called White abolitionist who sought to foster a violent overthrow of slavery and was, after capture, thus tried and convicted of treason and then executed by hanging (and this thought is recalled later on in the threading of references to the example of Brown throughout the 1935 study), Du Bois adduced a figure who accepted the solicitation by a group considered radically other in a historical sense, in this case the Negro American as enslaved, and thus took a completely different orientation than Johnson toward the possibility of a democracy that might still be historically forthcoming in his time and in his engagement of "the problem of the color line" (Du Bois 1909, 1962). For Du Bois, Brown moved to undo every dimension of those privileges, by any means necessary (Chandler 2014c, 112–28, 230–33). Perhaps we can think this gesture, not just in relation to the mundane orders of privilege, but also in the sense that Jacques Derrida proposed and briefly elaborated with regard to Nelson Mandela in the context of the struggle against apartheid in South Africa as at once the problem of a radical question of the historicity at stake in the production of idealization, most precisely as traditions thereof, and the affirmation of *a certain democracy to come whose memory is at stake in the present* (Mandela 1979, 1986; Derrida, 2007, 1987, 2005, 1978, 87–107). This would be an immanent formulation of the thought of what has been for too long understood only under the heading of a rather staid conception of the transcendental. The opening of the question of law to an illimitable horizon, or to a beyond of horizon, to the question of justice in Derrida's terms of the last decade of the twentieth century, would already have been described in Du Bois's narrative of the first decade of the same century by way of the latter's conceptualization of the problematic that constituted the itinerary and the life course of one John Brown. This latter figure then stands as a *hyperbolic* character in the past-present who might still portend a future that remains yet to come for *us*—whomever or whatever is such. Du Bois's practice exemplifies a certain kind of historiography that can be described as the critical production of hyperbole, what we might call a hyperbolic historicization of the present by a futural thought of the past. One might even call it a kind of prophetic historiography, for it attends to that within the present that is yet to come as a guide to a radicalization of any thought of the past.

Such may well be the still irruptive possibility for thought here—astride a century that is still searching for its way, the so-called twenty-first century, and perhaps for those to come—of the discourse of one W. E. B. Du Bois on "The Present Outlook for the Dark Races of Mankind" on that restless eve, the 27th of December 1899, of the advent of a still long twentieth century.

Another Coda, the Explicit—Revisited

An annotation, doubled, may serve as a coda to our recital of this work, as we have found it in writings by W. E. B. Du Bois.

One notation is political, which may be framed, for example, in terms of reference beyond the supposed nation-state. The African American is the example by which Du Bois places at stake the question of the project of America as itself a world-historical supposed exemplary example. It is in fact from the base of this abiding critical example as a crucible that all of Du Bois's reflections on historicity unfolded. It would put one on the wrong track to declare this privilege to be a simple chauvinism, for this was the historically produced form of Du Bois's problematic. Even his supposed vanguard disposition—whether of the "talented tenth" or of the Negro in America—is rooted less in an arrogance or a judgment of a supposedly proper (or preternaturally given) hierarchy than in a sense of *historically given duty*, an imperative beyond choice, for those who might arise in and by way of the conjunction of chance and necessity as realized possibility. The question of the future of this group entailed a rethinking of the sources of their emergence. In the first moment of that incipit of thought that it can only precomprehend, even if critically, this was posed in concrete terms. In this case, it required an engagement with the history of modern Atlantic systems of enslavement and then, by way of the history of that process, their reciprocal relation to a project called "America," as well as to both a historical "diaspora" throughout the Americas and Europe, indeed across the earth, and the situation of the continent of Africa. On this point it is instructive to take reference to the sense of "diaspora" in *The Negro* from 1915, especially its closing chapters. For there one finds the configured sense of the "black horizon" long before and otherwise than our contemporary discourses of a "Black Atlantic" or a certain "Africana" (Du Bois 1915b). Yet, just as certain, within this same torsion, a question of the relation of this configured group to proclaimed or declared Europe was also posed throughout for him, although it has of course certain specifics in its internal organization of questions and the rhythms of its devolution, not only by way of the broad historicity of the institutions of modern enslavement, stretching from one opening of our epoch to another, but also by the way in which the problematic of the so-called Negro question has placed all that has now been claimed as Europe across that historicity under the force of a kind of suspension, the necessity of what ought to be considered most at stake from within the historical projection often assumed under that name for a future that would remain beyond the limits so far given. The stakes of the futural forms of idealization remain just as much as the materially realized imperatives given from the complexity of a certain form of shared past.

Herein can be located a key example for Du Bois—as such, it may eventually be shown as not just one among others, in thought—that articulates with all of the scenes of modern historicity that are at stake in these few lines of remark (at once of the Americas—and the Caribbean thereof—of Europe, of Africa), and that is the historial profile of Hayti, or Haiti. Along this track one finds that Du Bois has named the historically singular situation—not the spiritual profile—of the Haitian example in modern historicity. This began with his doctoral study on the suppression of the Atlantic slave trade, which he completed just a century after, more or less, the incipit of the revolution there—the island domain then known as Saint-Domingue (or San Domingo)—and runs right through to his last published texts. Among the latter is one concerning the bearing of the Haitian Revolution for an understanding of the French Revolution (Du Bois 1961a). This historial example might be allowed to rearticulate all of the stress points within this study.

The other annotation is epistemological. For to think the historical situation of this group, that supposed as Negro, poses the question of the capacity and limits of philosophy and science, philosophy as science— notably the science of the human—to bespeak the truth of the futural historicity of any supposed human group. In this latter instance, and in a sense ultimately, it posed the speculative question of the status-as-a-kind of the

Negro as a *historial* being. Does such a form of human being actually exist in a traditional metaphysical sense, understood here as a theological reference or a philosophical premise? And if so, on what terms? Thinking with Du Bois, we can note that according to the history of modern thought in Europe and the Americas, the question of the Negro first (a priority that is not so much a chronological eventuality but rather the sense of a problem for thought and understanding) took the shape of a question about that group's place within the terms of what should properly be called *the philosophical concept*, and hence the *historial concept*, of race.

For it can be said here, in a word, that the concept of race itself took shape as the scientific side of a question about the metaphysical ground of the entity called "man" or, later, "the human." It is in this precise sense that I think of it as philosophical. And, further, while the concept may be used to name an object of a science (biology, sociology, history) and so forth or as the heading for a play of power (as law, politics, or economics, for example), it remains through and through a fundamentally philosophical problematic. Indeed, it is a concept that would propose to name a supposed ontological status with regard to human being. An elaboration of this question in this specific idiomatic form of thought—the philosophical—is now fully at issue for contemporary thought. The concept under impress here, the concept of race, is one that would propose to name an ontological status with regard to human beings. Thus, such a delimitation might aid in the clarification of what is at stake under the headings that I have come to propose in this study as decisive. For the sense of limit and possibility at stake here addresses in its course the whole of knowledge and thought in all of its forms.

Yet the understanding of the problem of the concept of race is not a restriction to the philosophical; rather, it is a delimitation of the problem of the philosophical. For while the question bears fully on all that might be understood as philosophy, from ontology to ethics, from epistemology to aesthetics, for example, its bearing and implication exceed any strict thought of what is or so far has been understood as philosophy in traditions that have been hegemonic in the modern era. The political sense of an African American problematic that we have noted in this study by way of the example of Du Bois's practice would indicate such excess or exorbitance. It may be thus that we can now underline and affirm Du Bois's own path of attention and recognition of problematization as general—implicating the general social field—"the problem of the color line."

It may be that the metaphorization in Du Bois's nominal practice is precisely what subtends his attention for our own ongoing reflection and renders supple his apparently staid and somewhat opaque discourse, making it available for our contemporary critical reelaboration of his thought—in the form of our own translative and transformative questions, both to his discourse and to ourselves, in turn, by way of such address to this aspect of his legacies.

Amid our tracking of Du Bois's own formulations of discourse, I can now rearticulate our ongoing and titular consideration of the African American problematic—the practice of W. E. B. Du Bois and the problem of the Negro as a problem for thought—this time on the plane of a world-historical frame of reference, that is to say, as a historiographical example that we might place in today's parlance as bespeaking an order that pertains to the whole of the planet earth.

The crucial sense for contemporary thought to reckon with is that, for Du Bois, the Negro American example takes its place as the incipit for him as a thinker, as fate or instituted chance, overdetermined in both its freedom and its necessity. The example given to him, that which solicited him most immediately, ineluctably, and without ceasing, posed a question about possibility—supposed as ontological and historical, *ontohistorial* in the traditional senses of ontology—that yet remained exorbitant for traditional formulations of philosophical question in the modern epoch. Herein I have begun to remark our own, my own, engagement of that problematization under the heading of a *para*ontology—a critical practice that attends to that within discourse, or forms of existence in general, practices that would operate *as if* there were indeed such a matter as present being, available for knowledge that would produce an ontology (a disposition from which the thought of a paraontology takes profound, fundamental, unfungible reserve). On such a path of thought, a certain practice of reengagement (that is to say, our own efforts) of the problematization that announced itself as the supposed question of the Negro or the African American example—by way of Du Bois's elaboration of its configuration as the movement of an always complex organization of heading—I have been led to suggest that his example may yet be able to help us to open, or, better, reopen, most precisely some resources for a new thought of the contemporary, for both its past and its future. Yet, if so, all this simply makes it possible for us to now commit to discursive passage toward the thought of another horizon of historicity with and by way of the discourse of Du Bois—a horizon that in a radical sense has no proper name, and so we will leave it remarked only in relief and retrospect here.

What has now been put to issue is the status of the historiographical reference as example, as example of possibility, not so much as a supposed simple and direct thought of the whole in general, whatever is such. The dimension of problem cannot be named by way of the analogy of a simple linearity or discrete contiguity. If we have presented our discourse as if an unfolding of sheaves, the matter of their binding still remains loose and undrawn, if not undrawable. For the effort of my practice here has been a matter of *paleonymy*, that is, the study of old names, old words. The spacing of such work is perhaps, thereby, an ineluctable form of annotation and elaboration, unceasing, for which if there is closure such is without end. In its eventuality, it might yield the problem of a difficult thought of horizon as otherwise than the given or that which could *be*—even in the staid sense of the term—as thought or concept. The sense of space and spacing will always have been *in its very immanence* beyond or otherwise than the simple form of a here and now. This matter of *the way in which*, the question of possibility in its actuality, should remain our guide. Orchestration of thought and practice in this dimension of practice must always be of at least double reference—of here and there, of then and now—for the matter is always *of* relation.

Thus, at this close in my own discourse, a kind of fold, another fold, if you will, I propose an affirmation of this thought-metaphor of spacing—the movement that forms space or time (as duration). Our question is at once always of the given and yet also always other than simply given.

We may thus place all that we have proposed for thought in this study, nonetheless, under a distinct heading: *atopia*. It is by way of an attention according to that heading that I have sought to enable another (different and otherwise, and somewhat new, even if it also retains the same, as it were) rearticulation of Du Bois's concern with the figurations of historicity—even that supposed as his own.

I have sought to propose that thereby we may discover that the matter in question will have always been—in the sense that he inscribed it in *The Souls of Black Folk: Essays and Sketches*, from the turn to the twentieth century—"beyond this narrow Now."

THE EXPLICIT

This study has taken W. E. B. Du Bois as an example—as example of both the problem of the Negro for thought and the problem of the practitioner of thought who would study matters of the Negro.

My central effort has been to enable delimitations of the manner in which we might approach Du Bois as such an example. On the one hand,

I have sought to contribute to a better understanding of the terms on which he was solicited in the engagement of the question of the Negro as a problematic for understanding. On the other hand, I have proposed a certain thoughtful critical reception of his initial formulations of this problematic.

The lead and ultimate concern of my study has been to attend to the question within Du Bois's practice of the *historial* status of the group placed under such a heading: as "Afro-American," within the horizon of a putative "America," astride the fin de siècle of the nineteenth century, yet, too, as "a people," in a putative sense, within the horizon of the world-historical efflorescence of the "peoples" of the modern world, that is, modern historicity on a planetwide scale of reference, just past the dawn of the new century, the twentieth, during his itinerary of a lifetime.

Too, however, I have thus followed how, in his efforts to understand the historicity in which and by which such a group could emerge, Du Bois was led to formulate a conceptualization of the horizon of a distinctive collective problematization that became constitutive in general across the modern epoch.

The dimension thus brought into a certain theoretical and interpretive relief would attend not only to that group understood as the Negro or African American or matters attendant thereto, but to all such groups configured in the production and emergence of the general historial domain that we might name as modernity, or as the modern epoch.

One aspect of Du Bois's formulation of this general dimension of historicity, not often understood on these terms, is his early generalization of matters African American as a world-historical example of the articulations, of modern historicity, notably as possibility, which has been given some considered remark in part I of this study, clustered according to two texts—"The Afro-American," from circa 1894, and "The Development of a People," of 1904—from the two decades that frame the turn to the twentieth century. If understood with regard to Du Bois's practice in general, these texts may be understood to both affirm and rearticulate for us the broad sense of historial affirmation with regard to all that might be called African or Negro American that was gathered by Du Bois between 1897 and 1903 under the heading of the text *The Souls of Black Folk: Essays and Sketches*, which was produced out of the same moment and locutions of his early itinerary as those two texts considered in this study as exemplary.

Another aspect of his formulation of the historial as modern historicity— not yet fully recognized in thought according to the general implication proposed for it within Du Bois's own discourse—is the formulation for which his thought has often been taken as infamous, that is, his conceptualization of "the problem of the color line" on a global scale of reference. In the second part of this study, I have been concerned not only to restitute somewhat our scholarly emplacement of the emergence of this idea within Du Bois's problematization and practice but to suggest, by way of a certain practice of elaboration, the way in which his thought may be understood to implicate any conception of modern historicity in general. For Du Bois, "the problem of the color line" emerged and remained as a problem of the centuries, configuring the whole of all that has come to be thought as the modern epoch in general, taking the middle of the fifteenth century as a nodal reference, to the past. For Du Bois, matters that have been announced in historicity as African American or Negro, both since its emergence and by way of its maintenance, implicate the production of the whole of the planet. At once, Europe, and so too Asia, and the "islands of the sea," along with Africa, the Caribbean, and the Americas, are gathered and articulated in and through the common vortex of the histories that have produced and still maintain, for the futures of the present, "the problem of the color line." In sum, this study has sought, too, to elaborate this aspect of Du Bois's general understanding of his problematic at the outset of his itinerary.

In terms of Du Bois's own initial development and early practice in thought, notably as scholarship, I have thought to approach his itinerary as something otherwise than simply a derivative expression, in an apparently seamless continuity with its contexts, of whatever kind.

Indeed, I have adjudged to approach his practice as also the operation of a kind of freedom, at once as both principle and surreptitious play. Thus herein I have proposed that we might take the itinerary of doubled possible apparitional forms for analysis of his passage—autobiographical, historiographical—as at stake for us, as a heading for the radical possibility of the practical theoretical organization of project, in the contemporary moment.

On this mark I have worked from certain premises and considerations.

The essential premise is that Du Bois's practice is in some radical sense itself a form of example, for me, in my own practice.

Perhaps it is so, too, for us, for a "we" that may be still to come.

Perhaps it will remain, likewise, in the future—precisely—as the form of a question.

If so, at such a conjuncture, a potential practical theoretical concatenation, a paradox may appear. It may be that it is the apparently "dead" order of the letter of the text, that which is in all its appearance opaque, that can remain a legible carrier of a certain *atopic* movement of freedom or chance, showing at the level of thought.

In my own reckoning, opacity as a kind of passive force of solicitation can be taken as a name for the emergent possibility given within the text—in its writing. It is thus by way of the movement of freedom or chance showing forth in discourse as a practice of thought, within writing.

It is thus that I have proposed herein an example of the possible reelaboration of Du Bois's thought as a task for a critical labor in our time.

Thus my work in this study has taken the form of the proposition of my effort toward a responsibility for conceptual, rhetorical, and theoretical labor in and across the topography—in the general sense—of his discourse. I have sought to attend to that in Du Bois's discourse that might render the paradoxical legibility of a projection that yet might remain *atopic* in the implication of its revelations and in its ultimate commitment. Its time of appearance will have always been a bit other than punctual, for it is always, in a sense, yet to come. Its spatial referents cannot, finally, be given.

It follows finally, then, that the approach that I have offered with all of its limits and complications should be understood otherwise than simply as a statement. It is rather a certain formulation, or reformulation, of a question, another introduction to the problem of the thought of Du Bois for our time. I have proposed, in sum, that one might most powerfully engage the limits of Du Bois's thought by way of a kind of acceptance of the given in his discourse, so that in turn a rather hyperbolic practice within our own engagement may be allowed to emerge, perhaps with uncanny force: that is, to read him on the order of the letter of his text, of his writing, yet as given by the manner of his own locution, that is, on the bias—taking Du Bois himself in the first instance at this letter of his own declarations.

As I have already suggested on several occasions, the practice in question is a theoretical accession, the practice of a *paleonymy*. The work is paleonymic in disposition, to turn a phrase. To *reresonate* (as Cecil Taylor once wrote of such practice) with the coda already given here, it is a study of the old words, as it were, in such a way that it allows that within such a word to find anew the passage of its form toward another, if not altogether novel, ensemble of possible references and projections. It attends to the internal historicity of the enunciation, of the mark—the inscription, the site, sight, a position (always in the plural, for position is also always relation, thus beyond any simple topos), and the inhabitation of the sonorous or legible "voice"—of that which is writing, in the most general sense of that concept metaphor.

In such a practice, the apparently given letter in both its perdurance and its dissipation may be shown to remain open to its futural form. In this sense, as the opacity of the text, the given as that which will not give way, if you will, can yet be understood to mark "both sides" of the limit. It is the practice of thought at the limit of possible world.

It is thus under the heading of a response to the solicitation to such a practice—a material thought of the illimitable—that we might find and maintain in our own discourse the generosity of the writings of a certain W. E. B. Du Bois on the question of the example.

This commitment has guided my practice in this study.

NOTES

....

A NOTATION

1 In the margin of the sheet issue of these stamps, this hierarchy is replicated, with Du Bois described first as a "Civil Rights advocate" and a "founder of the NAACP" and only then, after the fact so to speak, as a "noted writer, historian, scholar, educator, and sociologist."

2 The scale of the curatorial work carried out by the late Dr. Herbert Aptheker over the course of some forty years, but especially after 1961, can be glimpsed from his annotated bibliography of Du Bois's writings (Aptheker 1973a), in which one should especially note his brief introduction, as well as the volume collecting his introductions to Du Bois's major books (Aptheker 1989a), which still seems to me to provide the best introduction to the sense of Du Bois's writing as an intellectual practice whose very form is a political work. Likewise, I have also annotated the work of Dr. Aptheker above in the Note on Citations for this study.

3 Hortense Spillers, more than two and a half decades ago, in a superb and incisive intervention that remains yet to be truly thought and fully engaged, "*The Crisis of the Negro Intellectual*: A Post-Date" (an essay of 1994), an essay which took the passing of the quarter-century mark after the publication of Harold Cruse's classic statement (see Cruse 1967) as its own occasion, called for an assumption of general theoretical work as the task of the African American intellectual. The recollection now stands as the closing chapter of Spillers's pivotal collection of essays *Black, White, and in Color: Essays in American Literature and Culture* (Spillers 2003b, 2003a). If this is so, then perhaps it is not too much today to call for a renewed engagement with earlier projects and texts in the African Americanist domain or field that took their form prior to full-scale institutionalization of such practices in the 1960s and 1970s. The idea here, then, is that such legacies must be reengaged as or at the level of the philosophical in the general sense.

4 It should be remarked that the status of forms of proscription that we conceptualize today in relation to supposed difference of sex and usually construe in relation to a concept of gender as a titular heading should be understood to show forth another unique relation to this epistemic horizon. What is common to both is that in the domain of philosophy as science, they each announce a radical form of ontological problematic, even if ontology does not itself remain radical for thought. And yet it should almost go without saying that neither uniqueness precludes its articulation in the same existential circumstance or on the same epistemic plane as the other. Their differential uniqueness has to do with the historical form of their emergence as a problematization

of existence in the order of thought; it does not have to do with any supposed onto-logical status nor with supposed absolute epistemic priority. Yet if one were to insist on posing such a question, we indeed should recognize the priority of formulation as question in general what has been so poorly named under the idea of difference of sex (and all of the concomitant articulations that cluster according to its *historial* problematization) for a *philosophical* organization of the general question of historical difference.

5 It was in part through my ongoing dialogue with Professor Koji Takenaka, both dur-ing our yearlong seminar at Tohoku University on Du Bois's idea of the color line and modernity and then, in particular, by way of the provocation of his questions that followed my presentation at the international conference, "W. E. B. Du Bois and the Question of Another World," held at Tohoku University (Sendai, Japan), June 15–17, 2006, that I have come to realize just how crucial it is to clarify this distinction in Du Bois's thought. I thank him for his exemplary collegiality and form of interlocution. It should almost go without saying that Du Bois did not naively inhabit the term *race*; nor did he uncritically maintain it as a nomination for that aspect of existence that he sought to adduce under the heading of ideals and to affirm as an immanent movement beyond the given.

6 Du Bois wrote in "The Present Outlook for the Dark Races of Mankind," on the eve of the year 1900, that "if the third millennium of Jesus Christ dawns as we devoutly believe it will upon a brown and yellow world out of whose advancing civilization the color line has faded as mists before the sun," then "its consummation" as a realization of opportunity would depend on the actions of his auditors, that is, the assembled members of the American Negro Academy (Du Bois 1900a, 2015g). The quotation is from paragraph 11.

7 This line of my own research on Du Bois was given renewed stimulation in the spring of 1999 by way of the kind invitation (via personal correspondence) of the late Theo-dore Cross, then publisher of *Black Issues in Higher Education*, to consider comment-ing on Du Bois's most famous phrase "the problem of the twentieth century is the problem of the color line," on the occasion of the turn to the twenty-first century. It served as a provocation for a still ongoing reflection. While I had certainly formulated the question of the twentieth century as but a "phase" of a larger and global problem-atic as early as 1991, it seemed to me that a sound-bite restatement of this thought was not so useful or appropriate (Chandler 1996, 265–66n2). And such was all that I thought that I could manage at the time. I was chagrined to realize that the deep scholastic work on this fundamental motif had not yet been properly attempted by anyone, including me. Only now, a few years on, in the wake of my efforts at a certain necessary scholastic labor, do I feel that I can begin to contribute to an answer to Mr. Cross's solicitation. In part II of this study, I pursue such an account.

8 And, of course, others have proposed the thought, based on Du Bois's own autobio-graphical statements, that such a global perspective was born from his experience in Europe as a student from 1892 to 1894. However, even this formulation is too simple. For Du Bois's apprehension of his experience in Europe was grounded in his ongoing

and complicated critical engagement with the situation of the African American in the United States. I briefly explore one aspect of this question in the opening stages of part I. The Pan-African Conference of 1900 was organized by Henry Sylvester Williams, a Trinidadian-born London-based barrister and founding member and leader of the "African Association of London," which should perhaps be considered as inspired in part by the American Negro Academy in the United States. Indeed, Williams was in correspondence with African American leaders in the United States in formulating his association. As I note in part II of this study, Alexander Crummell met with Williams during the elder clergyman's visit to London in the summer and autumn of 1897 (Moss 1981, 53–54). See also Clarence Contee's early work on the history of the 1900 Pan-African Conference in London (Contee 1969a, 1969b, 1973).

9   Some of the writing of Paul Gilroy provides generalizable examples of both points. See in particular his discussion of the famous line as it appears in the second chapter of *The Souls of Black Folk: Essays and Sketches*, the chapter on the Freedmen's Bureau, in his widely read text from the early 1990s (Gilroy 1993, 127).

10 In both senses Du Bois can be understood retrospectively as the trailblazer. However, in our time, it is especially apposite to remark the latter. His work, in its persistence and scope, along with what I understand as a deep grasp of the philosophical sense, or more properly the persisting metaphysical order, of the problem of historicity that is often without recognition in the later literature, remains a high benchmark. The key texts include his major historical studies, from the doctoral dissertation from 1896, to his global account of the Negro from 1915, to his massive study of the meaning of Reconstruction in the United States from 1935, to his prescient and profound critique in 1945 of the gathering horizon according to which a post–World War II global order was being instituted as well as his biographical and fictional narratives, for example, *John Brown* (1909), *Dark Princess* (1928), and *The Black Flame: A Trilogy* (1957–61) (Du Bois 1896, 1973h, 1909, 1973d, 1915b, 1975e, 1928, 1974a, 1935, 1976d, 1945, 1975b, 1947, 1976e, 1957, 1976b, 1959, 1976a , 1961, 1976c). In this sense, Du Bois's work can still be understood not only as a resource, whether affirmed or neglected, but as an interrogation in an epistemological sense of the work of recent scholars who have also proposed the decisive status of the processes of Atlantic slavery in a global history of modernity (Hall 1980; Rodney 1982; Robinson 2000b [1983]; Blackburn 1988, 1997a; Holt 1992). Such point holds a fortiori for those scholars who address this question of slavery at the level of historicity itself in a somewhat indirect manner (Hardt and Negri 2000). And his definitive work preceded, and in part informed, the two classic interventions from the 1930s and 1940s concerning the role of slavery in the making of both the horizon for democratic revolutions of the nineteenth and twentieth centuries and in the making of capitalism generally as a historical form: C. L. R. James's *The Black Jacobins*, first published in 1938, and Eric Williams's *Capitalism and Slavery*, first issued in 1944 (see James 1938; Williams 1944). This precedence remains pertinent despite or beyond the disputation of the well-known open secret of James's claim that the Williams thesis was derived from his guidance of the author (James

1972). The reinauguration of this problematic that has ensued across the past three decades, stemming in part from debates in the revisionist historiography of slavery in the U.S. context, especially a renewed concern with the differential forms of the immediate aftermath of the legal abolition of slavery throughout the Americas and the Caribbean, on the one hand, and the interwoven debates on the feasibility of slavery as an economic institution in tandem with a discussion of the role of accumulation in the rise of slavery as it is related to capital formation in the modern era and thus, in part, to the modern world economic system, on the other, and then, too, its relation to a whole set of debates within the context of scholarship in economic history in Britain, can now be understood in summation, at least in an initial sense (Solow and Engerman 1987; Darity 1988; Holt 1990; Solow 1991; Blackburn 1997b; Klein 1999).

11 The idea of *example* here is anything but the thought of a pure idea. It should go without saying then that *exemplarity*, then, may issue from multiple sites and situations, each with their revelatory and limiting capacities for thought, none of which are absolutely given. It is the responsibility of critical discourse to accept the task of thinking such a dynamic concept of limit as possibility.

12 The term *l'énonciation* references Michel Foucault's discussion in the second chapter, "The Enunciative Function," of part 3, "The Statement and the Archive," of *The Archaeology of Knowledge*, which I cite here only in the English translation (Foucault 1972, 77–131, esp. 88–105; but see also Foucault 1969, 116–38). Although I wish to emphasize here that I seek to call attention to the general sense of the political character, nonneutral, of the "enunciative function," in some contrast to Foucault's disposition in his text (which I cited here), I have also elsewhere annotated the distinction that I intend. For to "enunciate" at all is to already do so on the bias; it is a political action, remarking distributions and arrangements of force, and thus forms and relations of empowerment; practices that adduce an example are always the practice of power. Elsewhere it is the poetic practice of Phillis Wheatley—both then, in the eighteenth century, and now, in the twenty-first—that I have cited as a theoretical example (Chandler 2014c, 190n9).

PART I. "BEYOND THIS NARROW NOW"

1 This opening paragraph also stands at the head of *Toward an African Future—Of the Limit of World* (Chandler 2021). For that essay is of the same locution and premise as the writing offered in this study; it is another kind of elaboration of what is offered here.

2 It was my hearing of Cecil Taylor and Elvin Jones in a duo performance of Taylor's compositions with drums, piano, voice, and dance at the Blue Note in New York City on August 29 and 30, 1999, that set in motion the thought offered in part I of this study. Later, Fred Moten, by example, helped to bring new language here: if my reading is apposite, we can place in parallax relation with what has been said so far his formulation of what is at stake: "the differentially repeating plane that intersects and animates the comparativist sphere" (Moten 2008, 1746).

3   In using the word *historial* here, most especially as I propose to operate it across the second half of part I of this study, rather than the word *historical*, I propose the former term as mnemonic in my practice. The theoretical concern is to propose the interest of a step toward something just beyond a simple or naive historicism in the strict sense when one seeks to address a thought of possibility, of some order beyond the given. I propose it to prompt a rethinking—in the context of discourse about something like "the African American"—of the problematic named under the heading or concept of history as something otherwise than the events of time (whatever is such) or a chronology, however we might adduce meaning for such. Instead, perhaps the matter here concerns the movement in which the very possibility of the event—including the subjectum—is opened precisely in and as a problem. In this sense, I seek to affirm that the very possibility or impossibility of existence is always at stake in any thought of history, and above all in that which is yet to come. That is to say, history or historicity always arises by way of a constitutive passage within the movement by which existence is announced as a form of problem. The sense of possibility and limit for subjectiva-tion on all levels of generality then is a constitutive, always dynamic, incomplete ar-ticulation of what I have here remarked under the heading of the historial, irresolvable in any final sense to its supposed terms of reference. I propose the thought as radical, guided by principle, even as it must yet remain pragmatic.

4   I examine this text in "The Figure of the X: An Elaboration of the Autobiographical Example in the Thought of W. E. B. Du Bois"; part I of this study may be understood as a companion to that text (Chandler 2014c, 68–111, 213–30).

5   It is apparently not the earliest *written* account. In an essay that remained unpub-lished during his lifetime, discussed later in this study, "The Afro-American," pre-pared most likely within months of his return to the United States from Europe in June 1894, perhaps sometime during the autumn of that year during his first semester of teaching at Wilberforce University in Ohio, or the term following, Du Bois opens and closes his text with an autobiographical reference to his travels in a "third class continental railway carriage" in Europe. And as we will notice later on in the present chapter in our discussion of this essay, the sense of "Europe" that we are tracing here in the 1897 text has a fictional component—as it should, perhaps—interlaced within its interstices. The earlier essay, from 1894–95, shows the first nascent formulations in Du Bois's thought of the concept-metaphors of "the veil" and "double-consciousness," and a certain thought of "the Negro problem" as a global one that bespeaks "the prob-lem of the color line" that Du Bois will later develop, even as none appear as such by name. It also proposes, no doubt following T. Thomas Fortune on the matter what was at the very least still at that time an unusual nominalization for the so-called Negro in the United States of America: the "Afro-American" (Du Bois 1894a[?], 1980a, 2015a; Fortune 2008 [1890]) We will consider Du Bois's essay later on in part 1.

6   As a nodal index of this perspective as a leitmotif of Du Bois's thought of the turn to the twentieth century, it is apposite to take note of his essay "Die Negerfrage in den Vereinigten Staaten" (The Negro Question in the United States)—the opening section of which concerns the conditions of African Americans during the decades

from the end of the civil war to the turn to the twentieth century, which was yet titled by him, with wry irony, as "The Bondsman"—which he gathered in mid-1905 from some of his diverse previously published writings for translation and publication by Max Weber under one essay heading. The turn-of-the-century formulations of Du Bois that adduce this interpretive analogy are annotated, including his unremarked citation to the eighteenth-century writer Arthur Young, in the recent translation of this essay from the German (Du Bois 2015f, 287–91, 331–33; 1906b).

7 I thank the late Cheryl Wall for generously and quietly suggesting this useful phrase to me in October 2003, on the occasion of the delivery of a portion of this essay at a conference celebrating the centenary of *The Souls of Black Folk: Essays and Sketches* at Northwestern University. I also thank Dwight McBride and Robert Gooding-Williams, organizers, for making that occasion possible.

8 The complete extant text that was published only in 1985 by Herbert Aptheker in a collection of some previously unpublished writings by Du Bois, in its expressiveness and singularity, demands to be read in extenso. We cannot do so here. Hence, I wish to simply fold into our discussion an essential reference as leavening and leave aside for now further exploration of its specific internal properties and implications (Du Bois 1985c). Du Bois quotes most, but not all, of this text in the manuscript that was posthumously published as his *Autobiography* (Du Bois 1968, 170–71).

9 This word is published as "now" in the 1985 version of the text but as "not" in Du Bois's posthumous autobiography, first published in 1968 (Du Bois 1968, 171; 1985c, 28). The original manuscript of the text in question, among the Du Bois Papers, confirms for us that the word that Du Bois originally inscribed on the page numbered 7 therein is "not" (see the microfilm edition of Du Bois's papers: Du Bois 1980f, reel 87, frames 468–79). In the quotation I have corrected the 1985 publication (the only one of the two that is a complete version of the extant text).

10 And *we* might add, from the standpoint of *our* present, "or its opposite: a dictatorial disposition in adjudicating the truth of the world and the course of action which should follow therefrom." Du Bois's own bravado and "youthful bumptiousness" at this time might have placed this latter risk in the shadows. And it was a risk that would show forth at each stage of his career as he maintained an occasionally reserved but consistently forthright admiration for strong leadership, including the leadership of ideas (Du Bois 1975c). As the rebirth of a project of absolute sovereignty in the twentieth century would become one of the most fundamental problematics of our time, this constitutive risk and torsion in Du Bois's thought and practice, recognized here in an early moment, showed forth across the entirety of his career. Many of his most difficult and problematic historical-political judgments, from the standpoint of our own dispositions, cluster along this axis: his support for Woodrow Wilson and the call for African American support of U.S. participation in the First World War, his affirmation of Japan as a potential bulwark against Western imperialism becoming globally total, and his stalwart and unmitigated affirmation of the "modernization projects" of Joseph Stalin and Mao Tse-tung in Russia and China, respectively. This whole question must be thought otherwise than a simple and blanket negative judgment

and closure upon this dimension of Du Bois's thought. For one will find that he also affirms from the same disposition those many projects of democratic initiative that we would today be so wont to champion. We share this vortex with Du Bois; we are not simply free of it.

11 The posthumous *Autobiography* on which Du Bois was working in his last days recollects this earlier "recollection" and retrieval from 1893 that we are tracking here. He writes of his sense upon watching the pomp and circumstance of patriotism surrounding the German kaiser at the Brandenburg Gate and on Unter den Linden: "I *began* to feel that dichotomy which all my life has characterized my thought: how far can love for my oppressed race accord with love for the oppressing country? And when these loyalties diverge, where shall my soul find refuge?" (Du Bois 1968, 169). Among the Du Bois Papers is a text of three pages titled "A Plot for a Story/Faded [Shattered] Ideals." The word "shattered," given here in brackets, is crossed through. At the end of the text is the inscription of a date and place: "7 Dec. '92 Berlin" (Du Bois 1980g). The story sketched therein is about the fracturing and breaking of dreams and horizons—of youthful love and hope, of marriage (irrespective of a putative color line), of crusading hope. All end in failure. What survives is a commitment to the uplift of her race by a young woman who is gifted. The text was published by Aptheker in 1985 (Du Bois 1985e).

12 In his first extended autobiographical reflection, and one of the first on this moment, Du Bois at age fifty in "The Shadow of Years" (included in *Darkwater*) describes his life according to four stages: "an age of miracles," which includes his time in Europe as a student; "the days of disillusion," which includes his return to America and the death of his son; "the discipline of work and play," which includes his forced departure from the academy (and which overlapped the previous stage); and "a second age of miracles," which includes the time of his writing, 1918. Du Bois writes poignantly of the whole course of his life up to that time:

Then, after two long years, I dropped suddenly back into "nigger"-hating America! My Days of Disillusion were not disappointing enough to discourage me. I was still upheld by that fund of infinite faith, although dimly about me I saw the shadow of disaster. I began to realize how much of what I had called Will and Ability was sheer Luck! *Suppose* my good mother had preferred a steady income from my child labor rather than bank on the precarious dividend of my higher training? *Suppose* that pompous old village judge, whose dignity we often ruffled and whose apples we stole, had had his way and sent me while a child to a "reform" school to learn a "trade"? *Suppose* Principal Hosmer had been born with no faith in "darkies," and instead of giving me Greek and Latin had taught me carpentry and the making of tin pans? *Suppose* I had missed a Harvard scholarship? *Suppose* the Slater Board had then, as now, distinct ideas as to where the education of Negroes should stop? Suppose *and* suppose! As I sat down calmly on flat earth and looked at my life a certain great fear seized me. Was I the masterful captain or the pawn of laughing sprites? Who was I to fight a world of color prejudice? I raise my hat to myself when I remember that, even with these thoughts, I did not hesitate or waver; but just went doggedly to work, and therein lay whatever salvation I have achieved. (Du Bois 1975c, 16–17)

13　The essay was published for the first time in 2010 and then a second time with annotation in 2015 (Du Bois 2010, 2015a); all references to "The Afro-American" herein are to the 2015 publication, with specific citations given as AA followed by the paragraph number (e.g., AA para. 19). See also Du Bois (1894a[?], 1980a).

14　Kenneth Barkin retrieved these texts from the unpublished archive of Du Bois's papers and completed in resolute form the demanding yeoman's work of transcribing and editing them for their first ever publication in the late 1990s. He proposed 1893, during the time that Du Bois was in Berlin, as the year for the composition of one of the two texts (see Barkin 1998). However, on the basis of internal references within these two texts, respectively and together—in particular, their internal self-referential statements—I propose that the composition of the extant form of each text, respectively, was most likely realized sometime from mid-to-late 1894 through the first half of 1896, with much of the latter part of the period during Du Bois's time at Wilberforce University (Du Bois 1894c[?], 1980h[?], 1980h, 1998a, 1998b). I date the composition of the extant form of both of these texts to the period following the time of Du Bois as a student in Berlin—that is from the middle of 1894. If either or both texts were in part drafted before the middle of 1894, on the basis of internal historical references in the texts, respectively, it seems likely that Du Bois emended each text at some later point, but before mid-1896. This is a matter that I will annotate more directly in further work, namely, as part of my ongoing study of Du Bois and Max Weber at the turn of the twentieth century (Chandler 2006a, 2007).

15　In this sense, it should be placed right in the center—temporally and thematically—of that tradition named so well in the work of Farah Griffin and Cheryl Fish that has renewed this problematic (Griffin 1995; Griffin and Fish 1998).

16　The eventuality by which this thought takes shape within Du Bois's discourse and its radical general implication, including the place of this essay within its devolution, is the proper concern of a more fulsome annotation. Here I wish only to situate this thought as a stage of the discourse of the essay "The Afro-American" in a discrete sense. Elsewhere I have indeed argued for its generalizable implication (Chandler 2014c, 129–70, 233–46). This thought draws in part from the work of Hortense Spillers in a general sense; thus, I note her incisive interlocution on the question (Spillers 2006).

17　The autobiographical register becomes explicit again only at the end of the five paragraphs of this opening section of the essay, when Du Bois makes reference to "even the boy born, as I was, in Puritan New England" (AA para. 9).

18　This last phrase is purloined from the work of Kevin Thomas Miles, who, it might be proposed, outlined such a sense, aligning it with a pre-Socratic sense of world given in archaic discourse and the tragedies of ancient Greece, in a remarkable discourse under the title "The Other World after Paradise: The Musical Aesthetic in *The Souls of Black Folk*" (Miles 2006).

19　Here one may index the complex emergence of the narrative and example of Zora, the dark-skinned heroine of Du Bois's first novel—begun in the immediate wake of the completion of *The Souls of Black Folk: Essays and Sketches* but published only in 1911— for she will emerge within the story line as not only the lost and willfully exploited or set aside but as the emergent, unifying exemplar for a radical democratic ideal that had been set aside in the aftermath of Reconstruction by not only the American South but the American nation as a whole (Du Bois 1911, 1974b).

20 Du Bois will go on in the remainder of this paragraph to render the operation of this structure of distinction as a kind of social "wall":

I had thereafter no desire to tear down that veil, to creep through; I held all beyond it in common contempt, and lived above it in a region of blue sky and great wandering shadows. That sky was bluest when I could beat my mates at examination-time, or beat them at a foot-race, or even beat their stringy heads. Alas, with the years all this fine contempt began to fade; for the world I longed for, and all its dazzling opportunities, were theirs, not mine. But they should not keep these prizes, I said; some, all, I would wrest from them. Just how I would do it I could never decide: by reading law, by healing the sick, by telling the wonderful tales that swam in my head,—some way. With other black boys the strife was not so fiercely sunny: their youth shrunk into tasteless sycophancy, or into silent hatred of the pale world about them and mocking distrust of everything white; or wasted itself in a bitter cry, Why did God make me an outcast and a stranger in mine own house? The "shades of the prison-house" closed round about us all: *walls* strait and stubborn to the whitest, but relentlessly narrow, tall, and unscalable to sons of night who must plod darkly on in resignation, or beat unavailing palms against the stone, or steadily, half hopelessly watch the streak of blue above. (Du Bois 1897c, 194; 2015k, 68, para. 2)

The metaphor of a blocked path, as in a closed gate or door, appears in "The Afro-American" at paragraph 9 (Du Bois 2015a, 37, para. 9). And such a metaphor, now specified as a "door" or "doors," reappears in the fourth paragraph of the opening chapter of *The Souls of Black Folk: Essays and Sketches* (Du Bois 1903d, 4, chap. 1, para. 4). However, it is not present in the text of the first version of this chapter, the 1897 essay "Strivings of the Negro People" (Du Bois 1897c, 2015k).

Late in his itinerary, just after his seventieth year, in *Dusk of Dawn*, Du Bois will adduce the image of a "plate glass" to remark this distinction:

It is difficult to let others see the full psychological meaning of caste segregation. It is as though one, looking out from a dark cave in a side of an impending mountain, sees the world passing and speaks to it; speaks courteously and persuasively, showing them how these entombed souls are hindered in their natural movements, expression, and development; and how their loosening from prison would be a matter not simply of courtesy, sympathy, and help to them, but aid to all the world. One talks on evenly and logically in this way, but notices that the passing throng does not even turn its head, or if it does, glances curiously and walks on. It gradually penetrates the minds of the prisoners that the people passing do not hear; that some thick sheet of invisible but horribly tangible plate glass is between them and the world. They get excited; they talk louder; they gesticulate. Some of the passing world stop in curiosity; these gesticulations seem so pointless; they laugh and pass on. They still either do not hear at all, or hear but dimly, and even what they hear, they do not understand. Then the people within may become hysterical. They scream and hurl themselves against the barriers, hardly realizing in their bewilderment that they are screaming in a vacuum unheard and that their antics may actually seem funny to those outside looking in. They may even, here and there, break through in blood and disfigurement, and find themselves faced by a horrified, implacable, and quite overwhelming mob of people frightened for their own very existence. (Du Bois 1975d, 130–32; see also 1940, 130–32)

While I will only note it here, there is no reason to turn aside from considering Du Bois's formulation, while distinct on its own terms, as yet also a critical citation of Plato's thought in his "allegory of the cave" in *The Republic* (Plato 1971). Yet, whereas Plato may be understood to insist that the enlightened may teach those enchained to turn and face the light, that is, to do so without being blinded by it, and thus to move to a higher order of understanding and truth, Du Bois may be understood in his practice of an allegoresis in *Dusk of Dawn* to presume that those entombed in "a dark cave in the side of an impending mountain," as he put it, to have already turned (just how so, we must leave aside for now) toward the light (of ostensibly new senses of ideal, perhaps of justice and democracy and opportunity, etc.), but the supposed enlightened either are not so wise or simply will not assume a sense of duty or any responsibility (two distinct senses of obligation) to uplift those who have been or become entombed.

21 This text, which now exists as a hand script of three pages among the Du Bois Papers, was first published by Aptheker in 1985 (Du Bois 1985b). However, I have consulted and followed the original manuscript here (Du Bois 1897a[?], 1980b). Whereas Du Bois has a long dash followed by the suffix *-ville*, as in "——ville," Aptheker has interpolated the prefix "Farm" inside brackets in place of the dash, making it "[Farm] ville." As well, I am uncertain of both my own attempt and Aptheker's in deciphering several words in Du Bois's script, especially in the last paragraph of the sketch. Such uncertainty is indicated throughout by placing the relevant word in brackets.

22 The word in brackets in this sentence, "where," is not in the original manuscript. It has been added here by me, following Aptheker's interpolation of the same in the published version.

23 It will acquire its fulsome elaboration in the narrative production of his biographical study *John Brown* of 1909 (Du Bois 1973d). And this is then maintained across the era of the First World War in the signal essays "The Souls of White Folk" (1910) and "Of the Culture of White Folk" (1917), which were conjoined and re-presented as the theoretical frame of *Darkwater*, published in the immediate aftermath of the war in 1920 (Du Bois 1975c, 1910, 1917). It is then this general view that subtends two remarkably underread conjoined chapters—"The White World" and "The Colored World Within"—of *Dusk of Dawn* from 1940 (Du Bois 1940, 134–72, 173–220; 1975d; Chandler 2014c, 206–8n52). And, beyond the American horizon, it orients the critical account of Europe given in the two great essays that Du Bois issued in the immediate aftermath of World War II: *Color and Democracy: Colonies and Peace* in 1945 and *The World and Africa: An Inquiry into the Part Which Africa Has Played in World History* in 1947 (Du Bois 1975b, 1976d, 1945, 1947).

24 On the original typescript, the word "chance" is crossed out, and the word "spade" is written next to it in hand script.

25 As noted above, I address some dimensions of this question in some considerations on the relation of the work of Du Bois and that of Max Weber (Chandler 2006b; 2007, 260n14).

26 The typescript has the word "poase" here. However, this word, if it is such, is perhaps a typographical error, for there is a famous saying that is attributed to Benjamin Franklin: "He that would live in peace and at ease, / Must not speak all he knows, nor judge all he sees" (see, for example, Franklin 1960). It is plausible that Du Bois is inverting the meaning of such a phrase by suggesting that the African American has a form of legal equality with other American citizens after the American Civil War and hence is at peace, but his condition is not a state of "ease." If so, the inscription "poase" should read as the word "peace." As the words "poase" and "ease" are both in quotation marks, this transposition seems plausible.

27 The key statement is as follows: "The fourth division of this investigation is sociological interpretation; it should include the arrangement and interpretation of historical and statistical matter in the light of the experience of other nations and other ages; it should aim to study those finer manifestations of social life which history can but mention and which statistics can not count, such as the expression of Negro life as found in their hundred newspapers, their considerable literature, their music and folklore and their germ of aesthetic life—in fine, in all the movements and customs among them that manifest the existence of a distinct social mind" (Du Bois 1898c, 20, para. 42; 2015l, 92, para. 42).

28 All words in brackets are my own interpolations into Du Bois's text for the sake of clarity.

29 This claim about the "invariable" is of the same order of postulation that we shall see Du Bois invoke some three years later in his address to the opening session of the American Negro Academy under the heading "The Conservation of Races" (Du Bois 1897a[?], 2015c). He speaks of it there as the "constitution" of the world. And, as will be obvious to those familiar with other aspects of Du Bois's discourse, the passage at hand now appears as the first thematic statement of the problem and theoretical project that should set afoot a leadership group among African Americans that he will later call "the talented tenth," in a statement whose preparation and publication occur in the immediate aftermath of his productive assemblage of *The Souls of Black Folk: Essays and Sketches* (Du Bois 1903n, 2015m). The question of leadership in relation to democracy remained the domain of the deepest complications in his thought. While acknowledging no presumptive limit on the possible sources of leadership, that is to say, for him no group, however defined, maintained a preternaturally given capacity, for such historical role or status, he nonetheless sought a resolute basis for recognizing both the incipient sense of duty (or responsibility) and the accomplishments of the acts of leadership.

30 Already on the scene when Du Bois began to announce himself, Cooper and Wells-Barnett would each, respectively, come to articulate forcefully on their own terms with Du Bois's itinerary (Cooper 1892; Wells-Barnett 1892, 1895; Giddings 2008). While the list of others that Du Bois had noticed could be long, we can notate, for example,

that Du Bois was most certainly attuned to the thought of T. Thomas Fortune, a journalist and publisher, who had founded the National Afro-American League in 1887, in whose newspapers (the *New York Globe* and its successor, the *New York Freeman*) Du Bois's first published writings appeared, and from whom he had most likely purloined his titular nominalization (Fortune 1884, 1890; Bracey 1970; Du Bois 1986b, 1–22). He can be understood to have indirectly mentioned Richard Robert Wright (as noted above). And he was already an admirer of William S. Scarborough (Scarborough 2006, 2005), whom he was unfortunately designated to replace at Wilberforce. Later, Du Bois would admit that while he had read the poems of Paul Laurence Dunbar he discovered that he was "Negro" only when the latter visited Wilberforce, sometime proximate to the composition of "The Afro-American" (see Dunbar 1893). As noted earlier, it was at Wilberforce that Du Bois first met Crummell. Du Bois would reprise this whole problematic, on a more secure footing, in the chapter of *The Souls of Black Folk: Essays and Sketches* focused on Booker T. Washington, but this latter time Du Bois perspective was telescoped to recognize a political frame. The quite substantial revision of the previously published essay on leadership, notably titled "The Evolution of Negro Leadership," into the chapter titled "Of Mr. Booker T. Washington and Others" sharpened the edge of Du Bois's criticism of the position from which, by 1903, he wished to distinguish his own (Du Bois 1901a, 1903c). And, as subsequent history has its bearing for us, it must again be recalled in light of the essay at hand, "The Afro-American," that Du Bois wrote to Washington immediately after the latter's famous "Atlanta Exposition" speech that it was a "word fitly spoken" (Du Bois 1973a, 39). This accords with Du Bois's thematization of the economic within "The Afro-American." It is a status that Du Bois would never disavow, even as he would come more and more to insist on the problem of ideals in general as against a simple and resolute prior insistence on the necessity of material reproduction on the part of Washington and his followers. This is quite apart from his later relation to an ensemble of perspectives adducing a whole other kind or sense of problematic, announced as a critique of the devolution of the modern organization of economic relations as a projection of exploitative capital accumulation.

31 And this register of moral rectitude is a powerful motif in all of the discourse of Du Bois. While I have remarked it earlier, it must be recalled again here, for it leads to perhaps the single distinctively troubling dimension of this early essay: his hypothesization of the dangers of "majority worship and deification of mob-rule" (AA para. 19) and his proposition that the general franchise should be restricted for a time, declaring that "in its blind worship of democracy, that [America] is today ruled more from its gutters than from its homes" (AA para. 24). This premise of the authority to judge who has the capacity or status to *best* determine the ideals of a group remained the locus of an abiding conundrum in Du Bois's thought. Paradoxically, he would insist that the source of genius could not be precomprehended, and yet he would resolutely insist on the right of already constituted forms of such ingenuity to render decisions of leadership on the matter. This hesitation remains notwithstanding that Du Bois is asserting his own claim to authority (or that of others like him) as

one of a resolute *duty* to the collective or that he is writing amid the vigilantism (an epidemic of the lynching of African Americans) that was afoot in the American South during the 1890s (cf. Brundage 1993).

32 The reference is to Antão (or Antonio) Gonçalves, the key "trader" whose narrative of the 1441 and 1442 expeditions down the west coast of the African continent, prepared in 1455, was pivotal in sparking renewed exploratory expeditions throughout much of Europe. Du Bois may be understood to annotate that it was in fact the ensuing trade in humans that constituted the "river of Gold" (Galvão 1731, 23; 1601, 27; Vincent 1807, 217; Lach 1965a, 50–58). From the 1731 Portuguese language edition of Galvão's text, published at Lisbon, a translation may be instructive here as to the manner of its presentation over the first two centuries that followed the world historical moment, of the first Africans brought to Lisbon: "Treatise of discoveries ancient, and modern, from their first origins to the year 1550, with the particular names of those who made them: In what season, and in what latitude, and the uncommon routes by which pepper and spices came from India to our parts; a work certainly very remarkable and copious" (Galvão 1731). Most especially, the reference to India and thereby in fact to the Indian Ocean trading system and Asia in a general sense, can be directly brought to a threshold recognition. The translation is my own.

33 Without understanding the matter as one of opposition, the terms of Du Bois's theoretical perspective may be understood to annotate diverse projections of contemporary critical thought that proceed according to different premises on conceptions of modern historicity (Wallerstein 1974; Blackburn 1997a, 1997b; Thornton 1998; Arrighi 1994, 2002; Hardt and Negri 2000). Of scholarship in historiography from the latter decades of the twentieth century, the principle guiding the work of Walter Rodney may have been the most attuned to the order of attention formulated by Du Bois at the opening of that century (Rodney 1970). Of this latter, as already indicated, likewise may be said for the understanding of the Genoese-rooted, Portugal-based initiative within the promulgation of the inception of modern systems of enslavement throughout the Atlantic basin as proposed by Cedric Robinson (2000a [1983]). One may note here the thetic position of Charles Verlinden, eventually definitive in much of the post–World War II era of twentieth-century traditional scholarship (Verlinden 1970).

34 The work of Leslie A. Adelson on the demand and terms of the imagination of futurity in the context of matters German and European in the still ongoing aftermath of the Second World War of the twentieth century, as she adduces it in the work of Alexander Kluge, is of apposite reference for what may be understood to concern Du Bois at the turn to the twentieth century in the aftermath of the American Civil War, in the wake of a disaster of a "cosmic" character, no matter the scale of the metaphor, notably what she unfolds around matters of connection or relation (Adelson 2017).

35 This order is an aspect of the essay that could obscure its theoretical claim for some thinkers and practitioners of the twenty-first century who may not remain so attuned to the commitment to a project of reform or transfiguration of the human, both individual and collective, that organized so much the general project of a science of the human, or specifically the German defined projection of *Geisteswissenschaft*, of

the nineteenth century. Du Bois will remark his sense of a commitment to change the world through science in 1956, that is, even within the last decade of his long life (Du Bois 1956).

36 Robert Gooding-Williams and David W. Blight included a version of "The Development of a People" as an appendix to their first-ever, thus pioneering, annotated edition of *The Souls of Black Folk: Essays and Sketches*, issued in 1997. In their notations, they called attention to the import of this essay, a reference that I still regard as decisive in the contemporary reception of this essay (Du Bois 1997).

37 The import of this thematic is recognizable, for example, in the fact that John Locke authored in 1704, late in his life, a text on the history of navigation in which the place of these technologies in his thought as in relation to the developments made possible by the scientific Renaissance in Europe are susceptible to direct and fulsome annotation (J. Locke 1732; Du Bois 2015d, 261n2) Likewise, although Marcus Rediker's study rightly privileges by his consistent annotation throughout his work the massive, mortally violent, nearly existential, destructive operations of the so-called slave ship for all Africans entailed in its deployment, his history has also given us a new and telling access to that technology's emplacement within the history of modern technologies of Europe pertaining to ships, oceans, and "seafaring" (Rediker 2007). This is a thematic that Du Bois's perspective in this essay's narrative may be taken to affirm, if not so directly adduce. Indeed, we may not be wont to understand Rediker's work in general in this domain to take up its position in light of or in the wake of the thought of Du Bois on modern history, notably the 1935 book *Black Reconstruction* (Du Bois, 1935, esp. 3, 727, 1976d, esp. 3, 727).

38 Herbert Spencer's work was given a handsome multivolume, cumulative, and authoritative reproduction in the United States astride the years just before and after the turn to the twentieth century. In "Sociology Hesitant" (most likely written between late 1904 and the mid-year of 1905) Du Bois specifically names and criticizes Spencer's promulgation of this analogy (Du Bois 1905[?], 2015i, 272–73 para. 4). See also my related annotation to the essay "The Present Outlook for the Dark Races of Mankind," which Du Bois had written some four years earlier—for that text, too, he had already hesitated over the biological analogy that he was led to remark in "Sociology Hesitant" (Du Bois 2015g, esp. 131–33n19).

39 Hortense Spillers's meditations on this problematic remain signal for our moment, most particularly as one thinks the reference Negro or African American (but in all truth, the human in general) (Spillers 2006).

40 Elsewhere, I have offered general considerations on this problematic in the context of a discussion of the project of thought or study of the "Negro" in Du Bois's early writings (Chandler 2014c, 40–55). And, further, as I have suggested earlier in this study, a critical elaboration of the antinomies and contradictions of philosophy and science since the European Enlightenment with regard to matters of the conception of difference among humans can and ought to be produced. In ongoing work, a companion study to the present work, I propose the opening possibilities of such an effort, an elaboration of this difficulty, with reference to a philosophical formulation of

problem (Chandler, forthcoming). I have published an excerpt from that latter work (Chandler 2014b).

41 The discourse of Immanuel Kant astride the 1780s is indexed here, for his discourse registers in thought the events and the archive of the revolutionary English events of the seventeenth century and the Scottish thought of this early modern era, encoding the emerging "American" revolution, and attendant to both matters of the British Isles and the continent, on the one hand, and the records of the imperial journeys of the moment, as it were, of the various nations that are now often thought of as western Europe, on the other (Kant 2007b, 2001, 2007a). So, too, we must note Thomas Jefferson, precisely on this point (Jefferson 1984; Chandler 2014c, 20–30)

42 One may note here the watershed exhibition by the Monticello Foundation Exhibition, launched in 2018, titled "The Life of Sally Hemings" with a strong online curatorial presentation; accessed October 21, 2019, https://www.monticello.org /sallyhemings/?ref=briefaccount. In addition to the references on that website to recent scholarship in general on this whole problematic, as I indicate elsewhere in this study, one must especially take note of the historiographical work of Annette Gordon-Reed (Gordon-Reed 1997, 2008, 2018).

43 As I noted earlier, I seek to unfold this thought elsewhere on another plane of discourse and textual attention, and example, with regard to Du Bois's practice, somewhat on its own terms (Chandler 2013).

44 *The Quest of the Silver Fleece* was a fictional account of the understanding that Du Bois had cultivated in a historiographical sociological study that he completed in Lowndes County, Alabama, in the summer of 1906. As Du Bois tells us, the study was carried out with funding from the U.S. Bureau of Labor, which had commissioned, funded, and published several previous local town-based or county-level studies by Du Bois, for at least some half dozen years. Following his delivery of the final report, after some delay upon his inquiry, Du Bois was informed that due to cost, it would not be published; then upon his further request, for the return of the report, he received a reply stating that it had been lost. As I confirmed through my own search over several days in 1991, among the records of the bureau at the U.S. National Archives, it apparently remains that there is no extant documentary confirmation of the existence of this report, or any part of the ensemble thereof. To my own knowledge, there has been no confirmation otherwise some nearly three decades later. (Located at approximately sixty miles from the Tuskegee Institute, the research locale was a site that would be given an additional historical mark abreast the 1960s. A political configuration was organized there in 1965 under the name "Lowndes County Freedom Organization." It took as its emblem a "black panther," in contrast with the "white rooster" of a statewide white-identified dominant political party.) Du Bois considered his 1906 research there, working with some three dozen assistants or more, one of his best works of scholarship. Although I note these historical indices, which I have done previously in reference to Germany and Du Bois in relation to Max Weber, I leave aside substantive remark here, for they must be addressed elsewhere on their own fulsome and general terms (Chandler 2006b; see also Du Bois 1940, 1975d).

1   It was first published as W. E. B. Du Bois, "The Conservation of Races," American
    Negro Academy Occasional Papers, No. 2 (Washington D.C.: American Negro Acad-
    emy, 1897) (Du Bois 1897b, 2015c, and see 1986a). This text is also available as a scho-
    lastically reliable reprint in *W. E. B. Du Bois Writings*, ed. Nathan Huggins (New York:
    Random House/The Library of America Edition, 1986), 815–26. Also, see the "Note
    on Citations" given at the head of this study. According to Alfred Moss, there were
    eighteen founding members present on the occasion of the inaugural meeting of the
    American Negro Academy at A. P. Miller's Lincoln Memorial Congregational Church:
    including eight of the nine Washington-based members—John Wesley Cromwell,
    Alexander Crummell, Francis J. Grimké, Walter B. Hayson, John A. Johnson, John L.
    Love, Albert P. Miller, Kelly Miller—and ten from other locales: Matthew Anderson,
    Charles C. Cook, Levi J. Coppin, W. E. B. Du Bois, William H. Ferris, George N.
    Grisham, W. T. S. Jackson, Lewis B. Moore, William S. Scarborough, and Richard R.
    Wright. However, the Academy specifically did not include women, and it seems that
    it could not in situ resolve a query on the point, that is to say, even as the matter was
    directly posed at its opening meeting (Moss 1981, 31, 35–57, esp. 38, 40–41).

2   I will not address in detail here the matter of a reading of the pivotal fourth paragraph
    of this essay, in which Du Bois carries out this distantiation of a biological concept of
    race, principally the thematization of the way "intermingling" of physical traits or signs
    of such difference render the thought of a physical ground of such a conception logi-
    cally incoherent. I only recall the problematic here, as I address this question in a sepa-
    rate study of Du Bois's overall conception of the historicity of the African American,
    with a central engagement of the philosophical concept of race that this work necessar-
    ily entailed, a study that I consider a companion of the present volume. Likewise, I have
    already presented an excerpt from that larger study (Chandler 2014b, forthcoming).

3   Although this speculative frame from "The Conservation of Races" is not reducible
    to a simple biologism, Du Bois will turn away from this gesture, it seems, and toward
    a more concrete historical analysis and will begin to develop—almost immediately,
    that is, from the midpoint of 1897—a more and more specific narrative of the actual
    historical processes of imperialism, colonialism, and slavery as the configuration of a
    "problem" (his word, my emphasis) of the color line in or as modern history. While
    the speculative gesture will remain therein, it will take place as a theoretical labor in
    the service of narrating an ostensibly actual historicity. A few key examples can be
    remarked seven years on, during 1904, a pivotal year in Du Bois's itinerary, following
    upon the accomplishment of the thought proposed in *The Souls of Black Folk: Essays
    and Sketches* during the previous year (Du Bois 1904, 1982c 1982h, 1982b, 1982g).

4   It was in part through my ongoing dialogue with Professor Koji Takenaka both during
    our yearlong seminar at Tohoku University on Du Bois's idea of the color line and mo-
    dernity and then, in particular, by way of the provocation of his questions that followed
    my presentation at the international conference W. E. B. Du Bois and the Question
    of Another World, held at Tohoku on June 15–17, 2006, that I came to realize just

how crucial it is to clarify this distinction in Du Bois's thought. I thank him for his exemplary collegiality and form of interlocution. It should almost go without saying that Du Bois did not naively inhabit the term *race*, nor did he uncritically maintain it as a nomination for that aspect of existence that he sought to adduce under the heading of ideals and to affirm as an immanent movement beyond the given.

5 *The Philadelphia Negro: A Social Study* text is cited hereinafter as PN followed by the page number. While I reference here the first edition of the text, issued in 1899, I also take scholarly note of the edition of the book published by Herbert Aptheker in 1973 in the series of the Complete Published Works of W. E. B. Du Bois for it notably includes Du Bois's own preface to that study (Du Bois 1899c, 1899d, 1973g). That preface is not included in all reprint editions of this text. Also, the bibliographic citation as given in the reference list indicates the full original title of this text, including that the text in its original publication includes a text by Isabel Eaton on the domestic work of African American women in Philadelphia at the time of publication (Du Bois and Eaton 1899, 1973). Also, see the "Note on Citations" given at the head of this study.

6 As the primary character of our attention in this chapter is scholastic, I shall not at this specific rhetorical moment attempt to unfold in a critical manner this complex question of "man" or "the human" as it organizes itself here. However, I hope to broach an engagement elsewhere.

7 Certainly, in some empirical or historical sense, a greater or lesser degree of any practice is possible with regard to racial distinction. And here Du Bois wishes to specify a hierarchy that would name such differentiation by degree. Such specification can be understood as the sine qua non of the practice of racial distinction. However, at least as Du Bois is formulating it here, such practices are not constitutive; they are constituted. Rather, it is the presumption or explicit presupposition of the possibility of a categorical distinction that authorizes and gives kinetic force to the minutiae of distinction that devolves as racial distinction in practice. Any distinction that would purport to be racial always maintains within its claim the postulation of a categorical difference, no matter how sedimented or withdrawn in its announcement. There must be the imagined possibility of saying, "I am not you; I am not the same as you," or "We (or they) are not the same as them (or you)," in this order of distinction.

8 I would suggest that we can recognize an ontological claim (not a truth) as embedded in the categorical character of this disposition (not by Du Bois, but within the discourses ostensibly about the Negro), but the concern should be understood as not so much about the Negro, the African, or "blackness" as it is about a certain figure of what is often thought of as the European, the supposed European American, or as "whiteness." Or, better, it entails anyone who might try to claim on the basis of such a distinction, "I am not you; I am not the same as you." Or one could say "we." This can be followed in a layer of the discourse of Thomas Jefferson (Chandler 2014c, 20–30).

9 In the context of this recollection, I will not analyze this reference at this specific textual juncture. Yet due to its epistemological importance for understanding all of Du Bois's work and the continuity of his thought of the problem of the color line across his itinerary, it is necessary to cite the fact that Du Bois will use this very formulation and

conceptualization as the frame for one of his two most important texts (which is perhaps his magnum opus in the truest sense, that is, of the full maturity of his practice, a text published in 1935 when Du Bois was in his late sixties): *Black Reconstruction in America: An Essay toward a History of the Part Which Black Folk Played in the Attempt to Reconstruct Democracy in America, 1860–1880* (Du Bois 1935, 1976d).

10 I acknowledge and thank Jacqueline Y. Brown, archive librarian of the Rembert E. Stokes Library of Wilberforce University, for locating a copy of the original publication in the university's archives and making a copy of it available to me in March 2006. This concluded a search of several years on my part to locate an original copy of the October 1899 issue of the *A.M.E. Church Review* and thus a copy of the original published text of Du Bois's essay.

11 The essay "The Present Outlook for the Dark Races of Mankind" is hereinafter cited in part II as "Outlook," followed by the original page number and then paragraph number (e.g., Outlook 95, para. 1). As indicated in the "Note on Citations" given at the head of this study, and as with the essay "The Conservation of Races" discussed above, while the essay under discussion here is always cited according to its original publication (Du Bois 1900a), with regard to specific quotation and citation by paragraph, as I do extensively here, as a scholastic reference, the reader can also note the version of this text included in the collection of early essays by Du Bois, specifically edited and annotated, with numbered paragraphs, in order to support the study that I offer herein (Du Bois 2015g).

12 Prior to the 2015 annotated edition (Du Bois 2015g), apparently, the essay was reprinted in its entirety twice since its original publication: in a volume of the Complete Published Works of W. E. B. Du Bois, edited by Herbert Aptheker (Du Bois 1982f), and in a reprint collection of documents of the African Methodist Episcopal Church dating from the era of the Civil War up to World War II (Du Bois 2000a). In the latter reprint, the title is incorrectly given as "The Present Outlook for the Dark *Ages* of Mankind" (my emphasis). Editorial decisions have deeply marked the publication history of this essay over the past half century. According to my best ascertainment, all other reprints of this essay have in fact been excerpts from the whole, usually constituted by editorial excisions that render the thetic claims of the text more obscure rather than less, thus at times making those postulations uncertain with regard to their potential use for basic scholarly understanding and theoretical interpretation. This fact holds a fortiori for those anthologies that remain in print today and contain some but not all of the text of this essay as originally published by Du Bois (Du Bois 1996). Many contemporary anthologies of Du Bois's writing, the majority, contain almost no reference at all to this text, we may specifically note an example of those issued since the early 1990s (Du Bois 1995).

13 We should emphasize here in this rhetorical locution that Du Bois was indeed focused on addressing the specifics of the African American situation in the "The Conservation of Races," even as he felt compelled to address it by way of a consideration of both a general ontological question about the ground of a social group called *Negro* or *African*, namely, in terms of an ontological distinction among humans called *race*,

and a general moral and ethical question about the relation of that same group to a larger political and historical entity. And, further, at key junctures in that text, Du Bois makes reference to a panoply of groups of people throughout the world as the contextual horizon for his discussion of the Negro American, especially "the Slav" and "the Japanese." I have commented on the Japanese example in this essay elsewhere (Chandler, forthcoming, 2021). Thus, there is a fundamental general and comparative level of attention in his characterization of the Negro situation in the United States in this earliest of his formulations of "the problem of the color line."

14 Du Bois's auditors for the 1899 address might well be presumed to have known the 1897 address, especially since (a) it had been the subject of substantial discussion at the organization's founding meeting; (b) partly through the affirmation of its central ideas, especially by Alexander Crummell, the godfather of the organization so to speak, Du Bois eventually became the second president of the ANA, following Crummell; and (c) the essay had been published by the ANA as a stand-alone pamphlet shortly after its presentation as the second of its Occasional Papers.

15 One should specifically note that the often alternatively cited supposed first source for this most famous phrase of Du Bois, the manifesto for the first Pan-African meeting in London in July 1900 (Du Bois 1900b), is also *after*—in the theoretical sense that I am proposing can be elaborated, even more than its dating—the text under direct discussion here.

16 Consider here Edward Said's brilliant essay "Permission to Narrate" (Said 1984).

17 See especially the prefatory text that Weber prepared in 1920 for his essays on the sociology of religion (Weber 2002). Placed as if it were the original preface of Weber's *The Protestant Ethic and the Spirit of Capitalism* in Talcott Parsons's English translation of the book version of the study, it doubtless articulated the root premise, or implicit presumption, of a perspective in discourses about modernity that was widely distributed in Europe and a certain America during the time of Du Bois's writing his earliest essays through to the time of World War I and, perhaps, beyond (Weber 1930). I have remarked this problematic in a discussion of Du Bois and Weber in relation (Chandler 2006b; 2007, esp. 252–55).

18 Pertinent here, generally, is the analysis of the inception of capitalism as a system in his *Grundrisse* (Marx 1973). With Du Bois's example in thought no doubt on the horizon of his discourse, even if ambivalently, just over a generation ago, in a now classic intervention, which I also note elsewhere (Chandler 2014c, 172–73), Cedric Robinson proposed a reconceptualization of certain key terms of this problematic: "Capitalism was less a catastrophic revolution (negation) of feudal social orders than the extension of these social relations into the larger tapestry of the modern world's political and economic relations" (2000c [1983], 10).

19 Several parallel annotations, following the broad yet specific sweep of Du Bois's narrative in these two sentences, can be offered here: (a) The "recapture of Khartoum" references the Battle of Omdurman (September 2, 1898), a nodal turning point in the ongoing colonial conflict in the Sudan across the nineteenth century between the Sudanese peoples, the Egyptians, and the British (Zilfū 1980; Daly 1986; Spiers 1998).

It marked the military reassertion of British colonial authority and political governance within the Sudan, which would last until 1956, when formal independence was granted to the new Republic of Sudan. (b) The "Boer war" refers to the last and decisive stage of an ongoing conflict in southern Africa across the last quarter of the nineteenth century between the English and the Dutch settlers (Nasson 2010). It is from this historicity that the twentieth-century promulgation of a principle of "apartheid" subsequently took shape across the whole of the region of southern Africa, in particular in the state established under that name. (c) As the first global empire and the longest-lived of modern European colonial empires, the Portuguese had arrived in Africa in the fifteenth century and would remain there even through the last quarter of the twentieth century. While the Portuguese took initiative at different times in many parts of the continent, we can note with reference to the time of Du Bois's writing that in Africa's eventuality in their colonial projections formed respectively, in the west of the continent, Portuguese Guinea, now Guinea-Bissau (1474–1974), and a colony mainly coterminous with what is now Angola (1575–1975) and, in the east of the continent, a colony in what now constitutes Mozambique (1498–1975) (Lobban and Mendy 1997; Bender 1978; Newitt 1995). (d) The Germans, however, came to the colonial project in Africa only at the end of the nineteenth century, following the 1884–85 Berlin Conference that led to the "partition" of the continent among the major states of Europe. (e) While France undertook imperial ventures in Africa from 1624, it was only after the Franco-Prussian War of 1870–71, during the Third Republic, that France acquired most of its colonial claims in Africa that existed at the turn of the twentieth century (including much of what is today the states of Tunisia, Algeria, Mauritania, Senegal, Guinea, Mali, Côte d'Ivoire, Benin, Niger, Chad, the Central African Republic, and the Republic of the Congo). Across this latter period, they pursued a policy of "assimilation" or "association" that had a distinctive profile, even as scholarship has annotated the de facto historical contradiction of this principle (Fanon 1975, 1976; Betts 2005; Saada 2012).

20   The État Indépendant du Congo (Congo Free State), which remains infamous for the atrocities it carried out against indigenous Africans, was a government set up and privately controlled by King Leopold II of Belgium from the time of the Berlin Conference in 1885 (in which the European powers agreed to a kind of partition of Africa) to 1908 (Ndaywel è Nziem 2009). The character and scale of those atrocities began to emerge into full view in England and the United States in late 1900 as E. D. Morel published a series of anonymous articles on the colony, followed by an inquiry commissioned by the British House of Commons in 1903, which resulted in the infamous Casement Report of 1904, by Roger Casement (see Hochschild 1999).

21   Throughout the 1890s, amid ongoing internal instability within its political leadership, the independent state of Liberia (which had been founded decades earlier by freed New World–born African-descended former slaves and "free Blacks," primarily from the United States) was under heavy pressure to concede claims made by France on its southern and western boundaries. This culminated in October 1898 with a French decree enlarging French Guinea to include France's territorial claims, boundaries

that remained unchanged through midcentury (Brownlie 1979, 305; Johnston and Stapf 1906, 277–311).

22 Du Bois is indexing here, but passing quickly over, the advent of British colonial occupation of Egypt from 1882, in an acute political and economic manner, a control that lasted nominally until 1922 but in practice into the 1950s. The British displaced more than a century of big power rivalry in Egypt, notably entailing French efforts and the existing corrupt and economically unstable lingering vestige of the dynasty founded in 1805 by Muhammad 'Ali, an Ottoman tributary government (Daly 1998, esp. 139–284; Mansfield 1971). The resumption of British control in the Sudan in 1898, was part and parcel of this move by the British into North Africa. And Du Bois's formulation here parallels his notations above.

23 For example, in *The Negro* of 1915, a pioneering narrative of the position of Africa and its diaspora in the context of global historicity (Du Bois 1915b, 1975e). One could also pose the thought that perhaps Africa and Asia can be understood under a common frame of reference, according to another temporality and level of historicity.

24 A questioning of the whole dispensation to empire might be adduced here, along three parallel lines: (a) In the first instance, it is the history of the Mughal Empire (from the fourteenth to the nineteenth centuries) on the Indian subcontinent that Du Bois is most likely indexing here (Richards 1992). Across the second half of the nineteenth century, the widely influential F. Max Müller, a German-born Oxford-based linguist and orientalist, proposed "Turanian" as one of the three main divisions of language along with the Aryan and the Semitic (Müller 1855, 86–138). By the time of World War I, it was no longer considered a viable theorization. Even so, Du Bois's reference might be understood to cut against the bias of a formulation such as Müller's, one that privileges what he thought of as Aryan in India. (b) One of the major empires of modern times, spanning three continents at its height in the sixteenth and seventeenth centuries, the Ottoman Empire was in the last stages of its terminal decline, after some six centuries, at the time of Du Bois's writing (Inalcik 1994; Barkey and Von Hagen 1997). It is of this historicity that he proposes an interpretation. (c) In terms of China, Du Bois is especially making reference to the Qing dynasty (1644–1912) and its resistance to transformation toward a more egalitarian society (Fairbank 1978; Fairbank and Liu 1980; Struve 2004). As Du Bois was speaking, the Boxer Rebellion was in full development and would erupt over the coming months and begin the radical modern transformation of China that would unfold across the twentieth century (Xiang 2003).

25 Du Bois was writing in the moment of the late Meiji era, a historical juncture during which Japan had embarked on a massive, urgent, and oligarchic program of modernization over the two preceding generations (Jansen 1995). Specifically, he is referencing the conclusion of a process much underway throughout the 1890s, although vigorously opposed by the foreign powers in question, by which Japan succeeded in abolishing the concessions dating from the 1850s (and modeled on such courts in China) that had allowed extraterritorial jurisdiction to be held in Japan by the United States and many European states, notably the United Kingdom (F. C. Jones 1931;

Hoare 1970; Norman 1975; LaFeber 1998a). This included foreign consular courts. The diminishing of extraterritoriality in Japan occurred in the aftermath of Japan's victory in the Sino-Japanese War (1894–95). Japan would then subsequently impose its own extraterritorial claims in China and Korea, as well as other countries (Lee and Quigley 2008, 13–14; Duus 1995). This process ran parallel with and was thus in a sense part of the promulgation of a new constitution (the Meiji constitution) and national legal code in Japan. The transformation of such extraterritoriality also coincided with Japan's victory in the first Sino-Japanese War (1894–95) and thus marked its emergence as a major world power, indeed as a new imperial power.

26 As I also propose elsewhere, for Du Bois this should not perhaps be understood as an affirmation of sovereignty as an absolute. Further, it remains that as the rebirth of a project of absolute sovereignty (in Japan and Germany in particular) during the course of the twentieth century would become one of the most fundamental problematics of our time, a constitutive risk and torsion in Du Bois's thought and practice can be recognized here: in seeking a decisive break with past and present forms of imperialism and injustice, the very form of such decisiveness replicates the premise and implication of the system it would challenge and overthrow. Yet this is not an affirmation of sovereignty as an absolute. This is a whole matter that is complex enough that it demands to be addressed on it own. Some of my initiatives, so far, with this question may be indexed in my notations: on Du Bois, Max Weber, and Germany; on Du Bois's thought concerning Japan, China, and "Asia," in a general sense; and then, too, his concerns about a planet-wide sense of historicity, this latter understood from the immediate aftermath of World War II (Chandler 2007, 242–55; 2012; 2021). Too, below, in text and notation, I briefly annotate further Du Bois's engagement with the *historial* figure of Japan (see note 53).

27 Du Bois is referencing two dimensions of British colonial practice, abroad and at home (which later scholarship has come to thematize as fundamentally interwoven): (a) It is most likely that on colonial education Du Bois has in mind Fort William College, established at Calcutta in 1800, as well as, perhaps, other institutions similar in concept or function that followed in its wake in other parts of the Indian subcontinent throughout the nineteenth century (Das 1978; Kopf 1969). Our understanding of the contradictions of the British promulgations for the "welfare" of the peoples of India in general and of their concept of education in particular in relation to forms of knowledge long established in the subcontinent, often of ancient tradition and practice, has benefited from considerable critical scholarship across the past two generations (Cohn 1996b, esp. 45–53; Guha 1997b, esp. 165–83; Viswanathan 1989; Dirks 2001). (b) With regard to the home front of the metropole, Du Bois references here the diamond jubilee of Queen Victoria of Great Britain, held on June 20–21, 1897, to mark the sixtieth year of her reign (eventually the longest of any British monarch). Representation of the empire at the festivities was a key aspect, with many Indian princes and the heads of eleven imperial dominions in attendance, while, as well, two regiments of Indian cavalry were on hand. Along with some fifty monarchs or heads of state in attendance, it is estimated that upward of three million persons witnessed the event live on the streets of London (King 2007).

28 The work of Ranajit Guha and Bernard S. Cohn should be cited as reopening these questions in the historiography of colonial India in our time, along with others whose work was announced in the horizon of the problematic named by these two figures (Cohn 1987, 1996a; Guha 1999, 1997a; Guha and Spivak 1988; see also Guha 1997c). Also see Thomas C. Holt (1982) on the paradoxes of an "empire over the mind" as a projection of British colonialism. With regard to Du Bois's references at 1899, the discourses of the twentieth century from the South Asian subcontinent toward a certain independence remained yet to come (Guha 1999, 333–37; Spivak 1988).

29 And one can suppose that Du Bois includes the Caribbean under this heading, just as in other contexts he will include it in a discussion of the diaspora of Africa along with the United States. See, for example, his account in *The Negro* of 1915 (Du Bois 1915b, 1975e) and *Black Folk Then and Now* of 1939 (Du Bois 1939, 1975a).

30 See Jose Martí's "Nuestra America," first published in *La Revista Ilustrada de Nueva York* on January 10, 1891 (Martí 1891, 1977). Du Bois would sustain this thematic in his work, notably in *The Negro* of 1915. He can be understood thus to have anticipated certain key aspects of scholarship in this area as it developed during the past century, especially across the past two or three generations of scholars (Whitten and Torres 1998; Hyatt and Nettleford 1995; Yelvington 2005).

31 Taking theoretical reference to Shakespeare's play *The Tempest* in an essay of the mid-1980s, "Caliban's Triple Play," Houston Baker writes briefly of Caliban's "supra-literacy" in relation to Prospero (Baker 1986; Shakespeare 2013). And Srinivas Aravamudan, writing just over a decade later, on several poignant occasions speaks of a certain "meta-literacy" practiced by what he calls "tropicopolitans," for example, Olaudah Equiano, during the eighteenth century (Aravamudan 1999). In an earlier formulation, with both the ideas of Du Bois as a fundamental reference and Baker's brief nominalization in mind, I proposed that a more universal inhabitation of thought and culture could arise from a so-called partial position by way of its double position as simultaneously both within and outside of the mainstream, as a panel member for a "conversation on the contemporary scene of education" (WBEZ 91.5 FM, National Public Radio affiliate, interview by Mara Tapp for *The Mara Tapp Show*, Chicago, Illinois, during March 1991). For me, these nominalizations can be understood to address a fundamental question for theoretical reflection in our time. If one calls such inhabitation *paraliteracy*, then, it is the name of a problem for theory in the practice of critical thought. It names not only a so-called minority or majority but also the radical falseness of such a distinction and thus points to the need for thinking the whole but in such a way as to displace the topographical premise of a punctual resting point that would be understood as the neutral.

32 The thought of a practical theoretical engagement as articulated in this paragraph follows from the formulation of an African American problematic under the heading of the Negro as a problem for thought that I have formulated elsewhere (see Chandler 2014, 11–20, 185n1). We may here annotate that such engagement is a receptive inhabitation or resting-with in thought, an affirmation, of a certain kind of exorbitance, that is at stake for contemporary thought. The situation solicits an affirmation, the

rhetorical or poetic recognition of the catachresis that will always show forth in any practice in thought that would be contemporary for us. Any such practice will always have been an elaboration. Yet, it moves always beyond and otherwise than a sense of exorbitance would remark its incipit as if by way only of principle and decision. For the generative character of any such thought will always have been at least doubled or enfolded, redoubled, in both its emergence and possibility. It opens another sense of exorbitance. For what it sets in motion moves always beyond and otherwise than what may be given. It becomes illimitable. (See Chandler 2014, 29.)

33 In September 1850, as part of a compromise between southern slaveholders and northern free-soil advocates, the U.S. Congress amended the 1793 Fugitive Slave Act, declaring henceforth that any runaway slave, even if in a state in which slavery was illegal according to the state law, must be returned to their legal owner. The Dred Scott decision, put forth by the U.S. Supreme Court in 1857, declared that no person of African descent or their descendants were protected by the U.S. Constitution, that they were not and could never be U.S. citizens (Fehrenbacher 1978). In the aftermath of the Civil War, as measures to maintain a supply of labor at the lowest possible cost, southern states began to pass a series of laws, usually known as the Black Codes, to restrict and control the movement and independence of newly freed former slaves (Litwack 1979).

34 In the original published text of 1900, the word printed here in this sentence is "nature" (Du Bois 1900a).

35 In the original published text of 1900, this sentence has "sixth." It may be that Du Bois meant either to refer to the seventeenth century or to reference the sixteen hundreds. Du Bois's 1896 doctoral dissertation, *The Suppression of the African Slave-Trade to the United States of America, 1638–1870*, is one of the earliest efforts and an exhaustive account of the development of antislavery legal discourse in the United States and documents the actions in both Massachusetts and Pennsylvania (Du Bois 1896, 28–31, 37–39, 199, 201; Whitmore 1890, 52, 54). According to Du Bois's discussion therein, I suppose the possibility of such intended references. For the earliest antislavery statement in the colony of Massachusetts dates from the 1641 code "The Body of Liberties," which pertained to all inhabitants of the colony, Article 91 of which limited slavery to "lawful captives taken in just wars" or those who "willingly sell themselves" or are sold in such manner by others. Further, as noted by Du Bois, in 1646 the Massachusetts General Court ruled that certain Africans brought to the colony by a Captain Smith had been unlawfully abducted into slavery and should be returned to their homeland at the colony's expense, in the course of which the court took the first opportunity to issue a statement against the practice of "manstealing." Also, similar statements among the Quakers, specifically the leading preacher George Fox (who wrote against slavery in 1657, but ambiguously so) and a group of four Quakers who were part of the Germantown Meeting in Pennsylvania (who wrote a statement of protest in 1688), date from the second half of that century. In the Germantown Meeting document that Du Bois annotates in this paragraph (12) of his essay (see Du Bois 2015g for my own further annotations), the four Quakers use "the Golden Rule" to argue against the practice of slavery (Hendericks et al. 1980; Frost 1993; Nash and Soderlund 1991).

36 In August 1899, Henry Delegale, an affluent and influential African American in the town of Darien in McIntosh County on the coast of Georgia where the Altamaha River arrives at the coastal wetlands, was accused of rape and arrested. When the local sheriff proposed to transfer him to Savannah for holding and trial, members of the African American community surrounded the jail and prevented officials from moving him, on the premise that he would likely be lynched in transit. The state's chief executive ordered in the militia. Upon the promise that the militia would protect Delegale during the transfer, African Americans relinquished the standoff. Subsequently, however, two white men who were temporary deputies went to the Delegale family home to arrest his sons for participating in the blockade. The sons agreed to surrender, but when a gun was brandished by a deputy, a shotgun erupted from the Delegale house, killing one deputy and wounding the other. Eventually, although Henry Delegale was acquitted of the spurious charge against him and charges were dropped against forty of the suspected "rioters," some twenty-three of his supporters received heavy fines and were sentenced to prison terms of a year of hard labor for their participation in the insurrectionary defense. As well, while one son and a daughter were acquitted of murder charges, two of his sons (John and Edward Delegale) were each given life sentences for the result of the armed confrontation at the Delegale home (Brundage 1993, 132–37; 1990). At this time Du Bois was living in Atlanta, Georgia, where he was a professor of sociology and history at Atlanta University. There he had begun to carry out his program to pursue a comprehensive study of the social and historical life of African Americans in the United States, in both rural and urban contexts. Among the early publications of this work are considerations of landholding, farming, housing, education, etc., some of which include field notes taken by his students in the summer of the year following the crisis noted above, in which there are strewn references to the low-country coastal region of Georgia, McIntosh County and the town of Darien in particular (Du Bois 1980e, 115–16, 189–91; 1980d, 259–65, 290–95; 1899b). In a text issued in 1901, describing Darien in a reference to a "a typical 'black belt' county," Du Bois's work records that African Americans therein outnumbered white Americans nearly four to one in the town in the 1890 census (Du Bois 1980e, 189). It is Du Bois himself, in his 1896 study on the suppression of the slave trade in the United States, who notated the town of Darien's 1775 declaration against the trade in the midst of the debates about the institution of slavery during the American Revolution (Du Bois 1896, 51–52). Finally, it was in April 1899 that Sam Holt was murdered by lynching in front of two thousand whites, following a sensationalized two-week manhunt in central Georgia on the basis of a rumor carried allegation that he had killed his employer and raped the latter's wife. It marked the inception of a kind of tidal wave of lynching throughout that state; at least nineteen occurred between May and November of that year (Brundage 1990, 235–36). A few years later, in *The Souls of Black Folk: Essays and Sketches*, at the very beginning of the pivotal chapter "Of the Black Belt" (itself comprising the first half of an essay published in 1901), Du Bois wrote, "And a little past Atlanta, to the southwest, is the land of the Cherokees, and there, not far from where Sam Hose was crucified, you may stand on the spot which is to-day the centre

of the Negro problem,—the centre of those nine million men who are America's dark heritage from slavery and the slave trade" (Du Bois 1903e, 111 [chapter 7, para. 1]; see also Du Bois 1901c). Du Bois may be taken to in fact refer, more exactly, to the fate of Sam Holt (rather than Sam Hose). Forty years later, in an autobiographical reference, in his book *Dusk of Dawn*, Du Bois wrote that those events cut like a "red ray" across his fulsome plans for research as the sine qua non of his effort to address "the so-called Negro question," and thus he began to "turn away" from such study as the ultimate form of his life's work (Du Bois 1975d, 67; 1940, 67).

37 Herein Du Bois is referring to the infamous Cornerstone Speech given in Savannah, Georgia, on March 21, 1861, by Alexander Hamilton Stephens as vice president of the "new-born nation" of the "Confederate States of America," which had been proclaimed in February of that year by seven states proposing to secede from the United States of America (Cleveland 1866, 721–23). Three weeks later, the military hostilities that would mark the onset of the American Civil War would erupt.

38 And perhaps Ralph Ellison's narrator half a century later can be understood to signify on this thought (if not this text or Du Bois's discourse itself) when he sardonically muses in the prologue of the novel (which, in the fiction of the study is issued from underground, from the dark wisdom of the denouement of his journey, from the sub-subbasement of history, so to speak), "But that (by contradiction, I mean) is how the world moves: Not like an arrow, but a boomerang. (Beware of those who speak of the *spiral* of history: they are preparing a boomerang. Keep a steel helmet handy.) I know; I have been boomeranged across my head so much that I now can see the darkness of lightness. And I love light" (Ellison 1989, 6; emphasis in the original).

39 These lines are from Edwin Markham's famous poem "The Man with the Hoe." The poem was written in late 1898 after Markham saw Jean-François Millet's painting *L'homme à la houe* (dating from 1860–62 and now in the permanent collection of the Getty Museum in Los Angeles, California). Originally read in San Francisco at a gathering on the eve of the New Year in 1898, the poem was published as a chapbook the next month, widely reprinted in newspapers throughout the United States during the following year, and presented as the title poem in a book collection of Markham's poetry (Markham 1899, 1–4). It is commonly understood to have been translated into more than thirty languages.

40 In *The Principles of Biology*, first published serially from 1864 to 1867 and later integrated into his "system of synthetic philosophy," Herbert Spencer translated the idea of "natural selection" (based on a process of "descent with modification") from Charles Darwin's then recently published *The Origin of Species by Means of Natural Selection, or The Preservation of Favored Races in the Struggle for Life* (1859) into his own formulation of a concept of race as the theoretical mark of the outcome of the relation of a biosocial entity to its environment. In Spencer's formulation "natural selection is capable of *producing* fitness between organisms and their circumstances"; as such, the process would serve as "an ever acting cause of divergence among organic forms" (Spencer 1898, 2:443–46; emphasis in the original; see also Darwin 1897). In an essay titled "Sociology Hesitant" that he wrote, perhaps in late 1904 or early 1905,

several years after "The Present Outlook," but which remained unpublished during his lifetime, Du Bois would take exception to Spencer's proposal in his *Principles of Sociology* that the biological entity could be understood as the analogue ("we consistently regard a society as an entity") by which the object of a sociology might then be construed (Du Bois 2015i, 272–73, para 5; Spencer 1899, vol. 1, pt. II, chap. 1, sec. 212, 436). One should note that the availability of Spencer's discourse in the United States (not to remark Europe or elsewhere) was at its height at the turn of the century, with his whole "system of synthetic philosophy" being brought out in an authorized edition during the years 1898–1905, along with his autobiography, just before his death in 1903. With regard to a larger frame, Du Bois was writing at a historical juncture in which the presumption of the possibility of a science of eugenics that might intervene on the terms of "natural selection" in order to augment this ostensible process within the socius had been set afoot within the United States and would, subsequently come to play a major role in social policy, including the promulgation of war, and the project to eliminate or subjugate various social, cultural, and religious groups across the twentieth century, most especially in the project of genocide by Adolf Hitler's regime toward all Jews, the Roma, and all those understood as "homosexual" (as well as several other groups) in Europe, and Germany in particular, during the 1930s and 1940s. Perhaps, then, we can herein recognize the theoretical pertinence and an additional resonance, but one definitely sounded within its formulations by Du Bois and concerning its very formation within the field of knowledge, of the question for thought that we are following generally within the text at hand under the heading of "the problem of the color line." I thank Professor Karen Fields for calling this passage in Du Bois's text into relief for me and directing me to Edwin Black's work on the history of eugenics, this latter of which I index herein (Black 2003).

41 In the sixth paragraph of the chapter on Alexander Crummell in *The Souls of Black Folk: Essays and Sketches*, an essay written expressly for the book (which thus was most likely drafted within two years or so of "The Present Outlook for the Dark Races of Mankind"), Du Bois gives the indication of a historicizing perspective in relation to this term *sympathy* (Du Bois 1903b, 218, chap. 12, para. 6). That paragraph stands as the epigraph of coda I in part I of this study.

42 These references notate the historical juncture at which the United States began to promulgate an empire beyond its continental borders. This followed by way of and in the wake of the Spanish-American War of 1898 (Foner 1972). As a result of the military outcome of the war, Spain relinquished imperial and colonial control of Cuba, Puerto Rico, the Philippines, and Guam. While the latter three were variously ceded to the United States by Spain, Cuba was occupied from January 1899 for some four years as a protectorate, an occupation that concluded on the basis of the infamous terms of the Platt Amendment of 1903. Even as some African Americans served as soldiers in the war of 1898, general dispositions toward that war among both soldiers and the public in general from African American communities were highly ambivalent (Gatewood 1975, 1971). And, in addition to articulating its presence within the Caribbean and South America on a new level in a historical sense (including especially the

promulgation in 1904 of the Roosevelt Corollary to the Monroe Doctrine, claiming Caribbean and South American states as subject to direct intervention by the United States to protect its interests therein, and its actions in Haiti and the Dominican Republic that would shortly follow), the outcome of the war established the United States as a major political and military power in the Pacific. It is thus that some ten months before the time of Du Bois's writing, resistance to inscription into the domain of U.S. imperial power had erupted within the Philippines as the first stages of the Philippine-American War, a war that would last in its declared form through 1902 and more indirectly up to the eve of World War I (Agoncillo 1956; Ileto 1979; Rafael 2010). Within this same historical moment but specifically in the course of the Spanish-American War—as a mid-Pacific fueling station and naval base became of strategic value for the U.S. military—the U.S. government would annex the islands of Hawaii and claim them as a territory of the United States, an action that was illegal according to existing international law (N. K. Silva 2004, 143–63).

43 In the original text of 1900, the word "deep-lying" is printed as "deeplying." The Dreyfus affair, in which Alfred Dreyfus, a young French army captain of an assimilated Alsatian Jewish family, was falsely convicted of espionage and sent to prison in exile (solitary confinement in French Guiana) for five years, is most likely Du Bois's reference here. In 1899 Dreyfus was at first retried and reconvicted but then granted a presidential pardon. He received full exoneration in 1906 and fought in World War I, rising to the rank of lieutenant-colonel. Precisely current at the time of Du Bois's address, more than a century after its formal denouement, the affair continues to resonate both within France and on an international level (M. Burns 1999; S. Wilson 1982).

44 During the last two decades of the nineteenth century, Germany acquired territories in Africa: forming in the west from 1884 Deutsch-Südwestafrika (German South West Africa, what is now Namibia; which entailed attempted genocide, perhaps the first of the twentieth century, against the Herero and Namaqua peoples of this region during the first decade of the new century), German Kamerun (now Cameroon), and Togoland (including what is today the state of Togo and most of what is now the Volta Region in Ghana) and forming in the east from 1885 the Schutzgebiet Deutsch-Ostafrika (Protectorate of German East Africa, which included what is now Burundi, Rwanda, and the mainland part of Tanzania). Over this same period of time, Germany gained territories in the Pacific (including, among others, colonies in part of New Guinea and among the Samoan Islands, the latter both now part of independent states) through purchase and treaties. (Germany's Samoa acquisition, for example, by way of a tripartite agreement with the United States and Great Britain, who each also took a share of the islands, was finalized in Washington, D.C., just weeks before Du Bois's ANA address.) In addition, in 1898 a ninety-nine-year lease for territory in northeastern China at Kiautschou (which is romanized today as Jiaozhou Bay) was acquired (the administrative center of which was at Tsingtao [sometimes written today as Qingdao]). These colonies and concessions in their diversity were yet collectively and comparatively promulgations of the German constitutional imperial monarchy (Steinmetz 2007). They were brought to an end during and just after the

end of World War I (Chickering 1996, esp. 430–53; Wehler 1985). While the specific terms of Du Bois's reference to Germany's relation to Haiti remain ambiguous, across the two decades previous to the time of Du Bois's speech, the German imperial government had repeatedly intervened in Haiti to support German business interests on the island, including the diplomatic and military demand of indemnity as compensation for supposed losses or risks (Dupuy 1989, cf. 115–42; Plummer 1988; Logan 1941). It is also possible, however, that Du Bois had in mind an event of 1896, in which the German government sent a warship to Port-au-Prince Bay to support such a claim by a "biracial" Germano-Haitian of dual citizenship, Émile Lüders; the whole episode became known as *l'affaire Lüders* (Woodson 2010; Ménos 1898; Gaillard 1984). I thank Drexel G. Woodson for his superb general bibliographic guidance on the German-Haitian matters noted here but especially for his referral to the 1896 event and its resonance through the turn of the century. One should also note that the Dominican Republic—which shares the island of Hispaniola with Haiti—faced similar pressure by several European states, including Germany, during the late 1890s, which culminated in part in the virtual placement of the country in economic receivership to banks from North America and the promulgation in 1904 of the Roosevelt Corollary to the Monroe Doctrine by the U.S. government (also noted above; see note 46), claiming a right of intervention to protect its interests in the region and hemisphere, a principle according to which it would later occupy both Haiti and the Dominican Republic, as well as intervene subsequently in other states throughout the hemisphere (Healy 1988; LaFeber 1998b). I thank Nicholas De Genova for calling to my mind the historical proximity and relevance of the Roosevelt Corollary to the circumstances in Haiti that are the object of Du Bois's direct reference.

45 The whole history of populist movements in the context of imperial Russia, but especially the developments that followed in the wake of the 1848 revolutions across Europe, might be considered Du Bois's key index here (Venturi 2001; Lieven 2006). It must be noted that Du Bois was writing just before the 1904–5 revolutions and more or less a generation ahead of the Bolshevik Revolution of 1917. Across those cataclysmic events, the "unknown" to which Du Bois refers in this sentence may be understood to have begun to show itself. Yet, paradoxically, it may be that the historical unfolding of the collapse of the Soviet Union at the end of the twentieth century and its aftermath, at once straddling the century mark and still ongoing one hundred and twenty years after Du Bois's writing can be understood to articulate the long-unfolding global-level complex historical processes, and their ambivalent outcomes, to which he refers at the time of his writing (Suny 1993).

46 Four years after Du Bois's address, in February 1904, war would erupt between Japan and Russia (ending only twenty months later) in pursuit of competing imperial and colonial claims on Korea, a competition made possible by Japan's defeat of China in the first Sino-Japanese War a decade earlier (Warner and Warner 1974; Nish 1985; Wells and Wilson 1999). While Du Bois was not alone in predicting the Russo-Japanese conflict, it remains that the bases on which he adjudged such a historical movement—as offered in this passage of his ANA address—may be distinctive: the

sense of a struggle over categorical claims to status, played out on an international level in the form of competing sovereign states. In this schema of interpretation, in the year following the event, in a text that is a summary restatement of the thetic position of this 1900 address to the ANA, Du Bois would affirm Japan's success in the war in relation to Russia, declaring that it "marked an epoch" (Du Bois 1906a; Kearney 1998, 18–38). In both texts, Du Bois leaves Japan's own imperial and expansionist initiatives unremarked (Chandler 2012; Duus 1995).

47 Writing two generations after the 1867 compromise and the establishment of the dual monarchy of Austria-Hungary, a heterogeneous regime in which nonetheless German and Magyar groups dominated in both politics and economics at the expense of other linguistic and ethnic groups, Du Bois is notating the potential (at the time of his writing) but indefinite impact of this suppression and resistance to it (Jászi 1929; Kann 1950; Cornwall 2002; see also Kann 1974). As is so well known, fourteen years later, the assassination of the Austrian heir apparent to the throne, Archduke Franz Ferdinand of Austria, by operatives set in motion by a militant political organization from such a suppressed group sparked the events that in their own eventuality would lead to World War I.

48 With regard to "Turkey and the Balkan States," the large-scale question that concerned leaders in France and England, and then, too, the United States, at the time of Du Bois's writing was their future status—whether as independent states or as states subject to the authority of a major power such as Germany or Russia—beyond the disintegration of the Ottoman Empire and the coterminous difficulties facing the Hapsburg monarchy. In this same time frame, in its first imperial venture in Africa, Italy invaded and annexed the Eritrean port of Massawa in 1885 and claimed the country as its colony in 1891 (Negash 1987). In this same period, it colonized part of the Somali people and territory in another part of the Horn of Africa and attempted a first, but failed, invasion of Ethiopia (Hess 1966). Half a dozen years later, in 1895–96, the Italians in seeking to force protectorate status on Ethiopia were decisively defeated, in what is now known as the First Italo-Ethiopian War, culminating in the famous Battle of Adwa (Ahmad 1998; Del Boca 1997). However, the Italians continued to hold Eritrea and part of the Somali area of the Horn of Africa up to World War II; while failing to persuade France to partition the Ottoman province of Tunisia, they would pressure Turkey on the Ottoman colony of Libya across the first decade of the century, invading it just before World War I, leading to eventual colonization until World War II. All of this presaged Italy's full-scale imperial venture in North and East Africa during the first half of the twentieth century (Del Boca 1992; Rochat 1974). And then, in China in the last years of the 1890s, Italy began to press the Qing dynasty for extraterritorial rights, as had most European powers since the 1860s, gaining a concession in 1901 at Tientsin (now romanized as Tianjin) on the northeast coast of China (Xiang 2003, 79–103).

49 As I have noted at an earlier stage of our consideration of "The Present Outlook for the Dark Races of Mankind," the figure of Japan as noted here marks the locus of a persisting paradox of Du Bois's thought with regard to global imperialism: How does one judge sovereign judgment in an epoch when the status of sovereignty has been

placed in question? While Japan, an instance announced on the level of the global or humankind as a whole in general, is the example at hand, the question holds for any act of historical judgment that would issue as peremptory action that would seek to intervene in history—whether to foreclose or to open a possibility. It would stand at the so-called domestic level of whatever kind, just as much as at the level of the crossing of a titular boundary of some kind. I notate some dimensions of this paradox in Du Bois's thought throughout this study. As indicated above, elsewhere in this second part of this study, I have noted this problematic in a comparative discussion of Du Bois's relation to Weber, and likewise I have begun to annotate the figure of Japan in his thought (Chandler 2006b, 2007, 2012, 2021). However, I reserve for another occasion a more fulsome address of this question in Du Bois's thought on its own specific terms.

50 And note here Du Bois's essay "The Spirit of Modern Europe," unpublished during his lifetime but notated by Herbert Aptheker upon its first publication in 1985 as "presented to an all Black audience in Louisville, Kentucky," in the autumn of 1900 (Du Bois 1985f, 2015j). However, the original manuscript of this text is apparently lost at the present time. For it cannot be located among the extant papers of Du Bois in the W. E. B. Du Bois Papers in the Special Collections department at the W. E. B. Du Bois Library at the University of Massachusetts Amherst (this is according to my correspondence with Danielle Kovacs, curator of the collection, in October 2006), nor does it appear to be included in the microfilm edition of the Du Bois Papers (Du Bois 1980f). In correspondence with the author, as of early 2015, the University of Massachusetts Press confirmed that it was unable at that time to locate any manuscript or typescript version of the text.

51 See *Darkwater: Voices from within the Veil*, especially the preface, published in 1920 (Du Bois 1920, 1975c), and *The World and Africa: An Inquiry into the Part Which Africa Has Played in World History*, first published in 1947 (Du Bois 1947, 1976e), especially the opening three chapters of the latter book. These texts were gathered (from existing texts prepared during the time of war) or written and published just after each of the two European-led "world wars," respectively (see Du Bois 1975d).

52 In the original text published in 1900, the word printed here, in this sentence, is "destines" (Outlook 105, para 21).

53 In paragraph 21, the immediately preceding one, in this address, Du Bois has already begun to index the French Revolution, perhaps the signal transformative moment of modern European political historicity, which of course had worldwide implication (K. M. Baker 1987). The campaign for the "People's Charter," a democratic movement that thrived in the decade after 1838, may be considered Britain's formative civil rights movement and was probably the most important mass movement in British history (Chase 2007). The Frankfurter Nationalversammlung (Frankfurt National Assembly), the first freely elected parliament for all of Germany, sat from May 1848 to May 1849 (producing the so-called Paulskirche Constitution, which proclaimed a German empire while proposing a constitutional democracy headed by a hereditary kaiser [or emperor] and principles of parliamentary democracy) (Valentin 1930; Mommsen 1998). It was part of the famous Revolutions of 1848 that took place across much of the European continent and the just noted Chartist movement in the British

Isles during those years (P. H. Wilson 2006; Sperber 2005). Andrew Jackson came to the U.S. presidency proclaiming the rise of the common man, which in its principal claim proposed to effect the extension of the franchise to include all white male adult citizens, rather than only landowners in that group, while still affirming the removal of Native Americans from their homelands and a general national level acquiescence on the part of those supposed as "white" in the face of the institution of slavery (Wilentz 2005; Remini 1984; Hofstadter 1948).

54 These lines are from the famous song-poem by Robert Burns, "A Man's a Man for A' That"—first published anonymously in the *Glasgow Magazine* in August 1795. As printed in the *A.M.E. Church Review* in October 1900, the strophe mistakenly reads as follows: "The rank is but the guineas *stand*, the man's the gawd for a' that." As printed in that original publication of Du Bois's essay, as well as virtually all reprints of his essay (if the paragraph is included at all), the lines of the Burns poem are in essence unintelligible. Along with punctuation, I note in particular the mistaken printing of the word "stand" for "stamp." The mistakes in this quotation as printed are perhaps as likely to have been due to the printer's errors as to Du Bois's memory or manner of quotation. The full stanza reads (R. Burns 2001, 516):

> Is there for honest Poverty
> That hings his head, an' a' that;
> The coward slave—we pass him by,
> We dare be poor for a' that!
> For a' that, an' a' that.
> Our toils obscure an' a' that,
> The rank is but the guinea's stamp,
> The Man's the gowd for a' that.

Here must be noted that the guinea, the first English machine-struck gold coin minted in the Kingdom of England and later the United Kingdom between 1663 and 1813, was stamped on its obverse side with the bust of royalty. "Gowd" is old Scottish for gold. The name *guinea*, while not official, was the common name used for the coin and was a reference to the Atlantic coast of West Africa on the Gulf of Guinea on the northern reach of the Bight of Benin, which in the English discourses of the seventeenth and eighteenth centuries was known as the Guinea Coast (from a sixteenth-century Portuguese term to nominalize the peoples of the coastal regions of the continent south of the Senegal River), from which most of the gold used in its minting was derived—this during the time frame that marked the high tide of Atlantic systems of enslavement that inscribed, in substantial part, persons originating from that region of the west coast of the continent (as well, of course, from the coastal regions southern to it, down through the Congo Basin, to include what is now the coastal regions of the country of Angola). The guinea was originally understood as equal to an English pound sterling (twenty shillings), although its valuation fluctuated to as high as thirty shillings and was subsequently fixed at twenty-one shillings by royal decree in 1717. Burns's poem was also a favorite of William Lloyd Garrison, printed and referenced in his weekly *The Liberator*, and thus was of ongoing currency in abolitionist discourses in the United States dating at least from the 1830s and could thereby perhaps be considered of known reference to the auditors of Du Bois's 1899 ANA presidential address (see Du Bois 2015g, 136n31).

55 More than two generations ago, Hortense Spillers called attention to the symbolic lineaments of such a problematic in the formation of both an African American and an American historial profile as a figuration of the modern—of the disavowed offspring as progeny and progenitor—indexing its persisting legacies (if not simply as rank) in the afterlives of the history of slavery in the United States (Spillers 2003c).

56 With regard to the early modern moment, it is a theme that would indeed come to be recognized and placed as fundamental in the work of Cedric Robinson, some four generations later, perhaps in part by way of the implication of Du Bois's resonance within the younger scholars own distinctive order of theoretical attention rich elaboration (Robinson 2000c [1983]).

57 The term "Hottentot(s)" is a name derived by European travelers and settlers in southern Africa to describe some groups of the societies indigenous to the region. In its eventuality a derogatory term, the name was in high currency at the time of Du Bois's writing. Following Linda Evi Merians, I place "Hottentot(s)" in quotes because I mean for the term to stand for the constructions invented and developed by Europeans, especially the British and the Dutch, and thus to distinguish the imagined people from the actual societies in question, the Khoisan of southern Africa, in both their heterogeneity and commonality (Merians 2001, 14; Fauvelle-Aymar 2002; Bank 1998; Schapera 1930; Barnard 1992).

58 Such a thought would be otherwise than the apparently resolute commitment or orientation to the speculative as *first* a question of the whole or the totality that seems still to govern the itinerary of new projects in the thinking of immanence such as that proposed by Michael Hardt and Antonio Negri in their signal and remarkable interventions, *Empire* (2000) and *Multitude* (2004), as well as *Commonwealth* (2009) (especially the first volume; each volume of which I cite here only under its respective main title in order to annotate the declarative aspect of the titles, even as metaphors). It may well be that lucidity in this domain carries within it its own lability. At the nexus of our modern colonial horizons, tendentiously afoot on the order of temporarily that we might annotate in units constituted at a base level of reference as centuries, it is perhaps no surprise that all cannot be thought in one go in this domain and in our time. Such, might be understood to register as given, for example, in the apparent necessity that what must be named might only be remarked by at least two headings, the first two, rather than one, of the respective titles that I have annotated here, these by two exemplary thinkers, whose itinerary I would yet profoundly affirm (Chandler 2014c, esp. 11–20, 56–67).

59 I note here a provocative collection, emerging in a theoretical sense prior to the current efflorescence on the theme, in which the subjects of such historicities that take shape within such configurations, usually simply objects of knowledge, are also subjects of knowledge—writing "from" as well as "about" such a situation (Lavie and Swedenburg 1996).

60 This motif is part of a very broad and powerful general idea in Du Bois's thought. Thus, here I am transposing a term, *intermixture*, that Du Bois will operate later, in his 1940

text *Dusk of Dawn* (Du Bois 1975d). It is at the center of my elaboration of Du Bois's idea of an autobiography of a concept (Chandler 2014c, 68–111, 213–30). In "The Conservation of Races," for example, this motif is placed under the heading of an idea of the ineluctable "intermingling" of racial character, which I have remarked in a study that I understand as theoretically adjacent to this one (Chandler, forthcoming; see 2014b).

61 Apart from the worldwide purview of this question (for one thinks of Korean Japanese, for example), does not Du Bois foresee at one turn of the century the problematic that scholarship and critical thought in Europe and about Europe of the first two decades of the twenty-first century, including in particular philosophical reflection, such as the touchstone work of Étienne Balibar (Balibar 2004; 2016)? Thus we can note Turkish Germans or Senegalese Italians, not to mention Algerian French, Surinamese Dutch, and so forth (Adelson 2005; Carter 1997). This was already a dominant theme at the 2006 World Economic Forum in Davos, Switzerland. However, in the ongoing movement of the first mass migrations of this century, it is no longer the 2006 query of "What, or who, is Europe?" The question has become, in a tendentious manner, "What is home if it no longer belongs only to us?" However, I intend the citation here not so much as a confirmation of Du Bois as perhaps a solicitation for an ongoing contemporary discussion (Chandler 2021).

62 For example, see "Worlds of Color" from 1925 (Du Bois 1925), which was later reprinted as "The Negro Mind Reaches Out" in the famous Harlem Renaissance anthology *The New Negro: An Interpretation* (A. L. Locke 1925). See also the 1928 novel *Dark Princess* (Du Bois 1928, 1974a); *Color and Democracy* from 1945 (Du Bois 1945, 1975b); and *Worlds of Color* (the third novel in the *Black Flame* trilogy) from 1961 (Du Bois 1961b, 1976c).

63 This is a theoretical place, following upon notations in an adjacent and contiguous study (Chandler 2021) to remark the importance and character of Du Bois's thought about the historial profile of Europe. First, at the end of this essay, "The Present Outlook for the Dark Races of Mankind," Du Bois will formulate a responsibility for "the white races," and specifically the peoples of "Europe" (as he conceived them at 1900) to sustain the "best" of their traditions, as opposed to their "worst." Further, one must note Du Bois's poignant essay "The Spirit of Modern Europe" (Du Bois 1985f, 2015j). However, as the problematic is quite substantial and important, I hope to consider it elsewhere (in the second half of part I and in several annotations on Du Bois's understanding modern Africa), in terms of its own register. And it must be placed in the context of his later writing on Europe, especially after each of the two world wars, as noted above with reference to both *Darkwater* from 1920 (Du Bois 1920, 1975c) and *The World and Africa* from 1947 (Du Bois 1947, 1976e; and see Chandler 2021).

64 I should emphasize here that before one hesitates too much before these words, from the standpoint of our contemporary debates, one should recall that Du Bois in 1900 does not want the history of slavery to remain the principal heading by which to articulate the status of Negro peoples in world history. The rethinking of the history of Africa was yet to come, and indeed Du Bois may be understood to formulate a prescient approach to such an undertaking. And, further, as we are remarking in this

study, Du Bois's most fulsome narrative of the historical contribution of the African American to the making of the American project and a certain idea of modernity was also yet to come, and indeed, here as well, Du Bois was already in the midst of formulating radical premises thereto. While remarked and subjected to comment everywhere, as it were, from another register of thought the epistemic contributions of Du Bois on both these levels which showed forth at the midpoint and later stages of his itinerary still remain to be fully comprehended in thought along these lines. See by way of a few examples *The Negro* of 1915 and *Black Folk Then and Now* of 1939, as well as, *The World and Africa* from 1947, on the former (Du Bois 1915, 1975e, 1939, 1947, 1976e), and then see *The Gift of Black Folk* of 1923 and *Black Reconstruction* of 1935, on the latter (Du Bois 1923, 1935, 1976d).

65 These lines—inexactly quoted in the printed text as "Never dreamed tho' right were vanquished, wrong would triumph, / Held we fall to rise, are baffled to fight better, / Sleep to wake," are from the third stanza of the famous "Epilogue" of Robert Browning's long poem *Asolando*, originally published on December 12, 1889, almost exactly one decade before the first presentation of the essay that we are reading as Du Bois's presidential lecture for the ANA. I thank Rebecka Rutledge Fisher and Nicole Waligora-Davis for assistance in adducing this reference. The full stanza reads:

> One who never turned his back but marched breast forward,
> Never doubted clouds would break,
> Never dreamed, though right were worsted, wrong would triumph,
> Held we fall to rise, are baffled to fight better,
> Sleep to wake. (Browning 1890, 157)

66 This theme runs throughout the book *The Souls of Black Folk: Essays and Sketches* in a manner specific to Du Bois's thought. Three chapters can be understood to signal it in an ensembial way: "Of the Meaning of Progress," through the figure of Josie; "Of Alexander Crummell"; and "Of the Coming of John," in the latter two signaled through their title figures (Du Bois 1903h, 1903f, 1903b, 1903l).

67 In order to address the present limits for realizing such opportunity in its fullest sense, just as he had done near the end of "The Conservation of Races," at the end of "The Present Outlook for the Dark Races of Mankind," and in a manner that he will often repeat, Du Bois proposes a ringing (self-)criticism of the Negro American. On the one hand, he claims that at the year 1900 the Negro in the United States was "developing alarming criminal tendencies." Thus, Du Bois "hails" the establishment of a reformatory for boys in the state of Virginia during the previous year. It should be noted that although here, in the moment of critical address to a Negro leadership, Du Bois does not qualify this censure and participates in a quite critical moral discourse that was essentially a denigration of the Negro American, especially the poor (even, as we saw above he could be quite critical of those who would simply denigrate the poor). Elsewhere, in *The Philadelphia Negro: A Social Study*, which he had completed just six months earlier, for example, he questioned the flat-footed opprobrium of such discourse (Du Bois 1899a, 1899d). On the other hand, Du Bois declares that "as a race: the Negro was not

doing thoroughly excellent work." Here he speaks of "a desire for notoriety rather than a search for excellence" that "continually spoils the efforts and cheapens the deeds of so many of us." His elaboration might well be quoted in full here as a matter of historical record: "A man will throw away ten years of his life writing careless essays and catchy addresses when this time put on a serious thorough book might have given the world something of permanent value instead of a heap of trash. A woman will play musical fireworks and catchy nothings all her life when half her day persistently and doggedly put into study and practice might have made her a musician instead of a hand organ. Young men and women continually graduate from our schools, and then satisfy their souls not with a masterpiece, a thoroughly excellent bit of work, but with a cut in the newspaper and a column of lies. Excellence, thoroughness, though it be in sweat and poverty, in obscurity, or even in ridicule, this must characterize the work of Negroes whether they plough or preach" (Outlook 109, para. 23).

Du Bois goes on to affirm the work of the preeminent African American literary figures of that time, especially Paul Laurence Dunbar and Charles Chesnutt. In our own moment we can note that the problematic remains, even as it has shifted, even beyond including the matter of scholarship, to involve the practice of a theoretical production within the movement of social science and humanistic research. Spillers's formulation of this question in her 1994 essay "The *Crisis of the Negro Intellectual*: A Post-Date," now the closing text of her collection *Black, White, and in Color*, may be signal for our time; see especially her remarks on the object of the attention of the "black creative intellectual" and the order of their practice (Spillers 2003b, 450–51, 456–58; and see Cruse 1967).

As an answer to this situation—that is, the way to overcome limits present within the Negro group at his time—Du Bois calls for a sense of *duty* and a "spirit of personal sacrifice." This idea is not one of "sentiment." Instead, it is premised on a precise form of historical "calculation" (Outlook 109, para. 24). However, Du Bois admits that he cannot give any a priori justification of such a call or the response to it that it posits. He cannot give a principle or other form of account of the source of such an obligation. (And this question remains at issue in the contemporary discussion; see, for example, its passage in Spiller's essay cited above.) In two texts, a biographical essay, "Of Alexander Crummell," and a short story, "Of the Coming of John," both of which were probably prepared in the autumn and winter of 1902–3 and were included in *The Souls of Black Folk: Essays and Sketches* as accounts of matters from "within the veil" as Du Bois phrases the matter within the forethought of that book (Du Bois 1903f, 1903b, and see 1903l: vii–viii), Du Bois presents figures that would be exemplary of the sense or "spirit" that he has in mind here. Those figures are the historical persona of Alexander Crummell, who remained committed throughout his life to the Negro "race" and to an idea of a collective Negro American community, and the fictional character of John Jones, a recent college graduate who sacrificed his own happiness to return home and work for the uplift of "his people." Yet such commitment must itself in turn be displaced toward the good of an even larger horizon of freedom and responsibility, humankind in general. And that horizon is the frame that in turn enables the delineation of the thematic center and guide of Du Bois's essay at hand. The essay "The Talented Tenth," widely mistaken as a form elitism, published within the three months that followed the publication of the book *The Souls of Black Folk: Essays and Sketches* in April of 1903 is the theoretical construal of this line of a kind of auto-critique within Du Bois's thought at the turn of the twentieth century (Du Bois 1903n, 2015m).

68 It is on this notation that, recalling his almost military reference to Browning earlier in the essay, Du Bois concludes his discourse with a reference to Ralph Waldo Emerson's well-known quatrain "Sacrifice," from the latter's *May-Day, and Other Pieces* (1867, 189). The quatrain as originally published reads:

> Though love repine, and reason chafe,
> There came a voice without reply,—
> "'Tis man's perdition to be safe,
> When for the truth he ought to die."

Du Bois often shortens *though* to *tho'* when he quotes poetry, but with this quotation from Emerson, whether by the writer, editor, or printer, it is *also* notable that the punctuation has been changed in Du Bois's quotation of these lines as printed at the conclusion of his essay: "Tho' love repine and reason chafe, / There came a voice without reply, / 'Tis man's perdition to be safe / When, for the truth he ought to die" (Outlook 110, para. 35). The closing two lines are placed in quotes in Emerson's original text.

69 As noted above, Du Bois writes in the closing chapter of *The Philadelphia Negro: A Social Study* from 1899, discussing the global context of the so-called Negro problem in the United States: "We forget that once French peasants were the 'Niggers' of France, and that German princelings once discussed with doubt the brains and humanity of the *bauer*" (PN 386). Though we must recall precisely within this global horizon of reference that this text is "a social study" of the local that includes an account of African American women as contemporary domestic workers (Du Bois and Eaton 1899c, 1973g).

70 This is most powerfully done in his magnum opus, the full subtitle of which must be recalled here: *Black Reconstruction: An Essay toward a History of the Part Which Black Folk Played in the Attempt to Reconstruct Democracy in America, 1860–1880* (Du Bois 1935, 1976d). However, on the one side, it is already conceptualized in texts from 1897 to 1901, but then especially in the later text, *John Brown*, published in 1909 (Du Bois 1909, 1962, 1973d), and in the two essays of the 1910s that form a kind of double coda of that text, the 1910 "The Souls of White Folk" (Du Bois 1982i) and the 1915 "The African Roots of War" (Du Bois 1982a); but too, we can not simple leave aside here the 1917 essay "Of the Culture of White Folk." (Du Bois 1917). Then, among other later references, it notably stands as the lead or guiding theme of *Color and Democracy: Colonies and Peace*, issued in January of 1945 amid the immediate aftermath of World War II (Du Bois 1945; Chandler 2021).

REFERENCES

....

Adelson, L. 2005. *The Turkish Turn in Contemporary German Literature: Toward a New Critical Grammar of Migration*. New York: Palgrave Macmillan.

Adelson, L. 2017. *Cosmic Miniatures and the Future Sense: Alexander Kluge's 21st-Century Literary Experiments in German Culture and Narrative Form*. Berlin: de Gruyter.

Agoncillo, T. A. 1956. *The Revolt of the Masses: The Story of Bonifacio and the Katipunan*. Quezon City: University of the Philippines.

Ahmad, A. H., ed. 1998. *Adwa Victory Centenary Conference, 26 February–2 March 1996*. Addis Ababa: Institute of Ethiopian Studies, Addis Ababa University.

Aptheker, H. 1973. *Annotated Bibliography of the Published Writings of W. E. B. Du Bois*. Millwood, NY: Kraus-Thomson Organization.

Aptheker, H. 1989a. *The Literary Legacy of W. E. B. Du Bois*. White Plains, NY: Kraus International.

Aptheker, H. 1989b. "The Suppression of the African Slave Trade." In *The Literary Legacy of W. E. B. Du Bois*, ed. Herbert Aptheker, 1–13. White Plains, NY: Kraus International.

Aravamudan, S. 1999. *Tropicopolitans: Colonialism and Agency, 1688–1804*. Durham, NC: Duke University Press.

Arrighi, G. 1994. *The Long Twentieth Century: Money, Power, and the Origin of Our Times*. London: Verso.

Arrighi, G. 2002. "Lineages of Empire." *Philosophia Africana* 5 (2): 13–23.

Baker, H. 1986. "Caliban's Triple Play." In *"Race," Writing, and Difference*, ed. H. L. Gates, 381–95. Chicago: University of Chicago Press.

Baker, K. M., gen. ed. 1987. *The French Revolution and the Creation of Modern Political Culture*. 4 vols. Oxford, UK: Pergamon.

Balibar, E. 2004. *We, the People of Europe? Reflections on Transnational Citizenship*. Princeton, NJ: Princeton University Press.

Balibar, E. 2016. *Citizen Subject: Foundations for Philosophical Anthropology*. New York: Fordham University Press

Bank, A., ed. 1998. *The Proceedings of the Khoisan Identities and Cultural Heritage Conference Organised by the Institute for Historical Research, University of the Western Cape: Held at the South African Museum, Cape Town: 12–16 July 1997*. [Bellville, South Africa]: Institute for Historical Research, University of the Western Cape.

Barkey, K., and M. Von Hagen, eds. 1997. *After Empire: Multiethnic Societies and Nation-Building: The Soviet Union and the Russian, Ottoman, and Habsburg Empires*. Ed. K. Barkey. Boulder, CO: Westview.

Barkin, K. D. 1998. "W. E. B. Du Bois and the Kaiserreich," *Central European History* 31 (3): 155–70.

Barkin, K. D. 2000. "'Berlin Days,' 1892–1894: W. E. B. Du Bois and German Political Economy." *boundary 2: An International Journal of Literature and Culture* 27 (3): 79–101.

Barkin, K. D. 2005. "W. E. B. Du Bois' Love Affair with Imperial Germany." *German Studies Review* 28 (2): 285–302.

Barnard, A. 1992. *Hunters and Herders of Southern Africa: A Comparative Ethnography of the Khoisan Peoples.* Cambridge: Cambridge University Press.

Beck, H. H. 1998. "Censoring Your Ally: W. E. B. Du Bois in the German Democratic Republic." In *Crosscurrents: African Americans, Africa, and Germany in the Modern World,* ed. D. McBride, L. Hopkins, and C. Blackshire-Belay, 197–232. Columbia, SC: Camden House.

Bender, G. J. 1978. *Angola under the Portuguese: The Myth and the Reality.* Berkeley: University of California Press.

Betts, R. F. 2005. *Assimilation and Association in French Colonial Theory, 1890–1914.* Lincoln: University of Nebraska Press.

Black, E. 2003. *War against the Weak: Eugenics and America's Campaign to Create a Master Race.* New York: Four Walls Eight Windows.

Blackburn, R. 1988. *The Overthrow of Colonial Slavery, 1776–1848.* London: Verso.

Blackburn, R. 1997a. *The Making of New World Slavery: From the Baroque to the Modern, 1492–1800.* London: Verso.

Blackburn, R. 1997b. "New World Slavery, Primitive Accumulation and British Industrialization." In *The Making of New World Slavery: From the Baroque to the Modern, 1492–1800,* 509–80. London: Verso.

Boas, F. 1911. *The Mind of Primitive Man: A Course of Lectures Delivered before the Lowell Institute, Boston, Mass., and the National University of Mexico, 1910–1911.* New York: Macmillan.

Boas, F. 1989. *The Shaping of American Anthropology, 1883–1911: A Franz Boas Reader.* Ed. G. W. Stocking. Chicago: University of Chicago Press.

Bracey, J. H., Jr. 1970. Foreword to T. T. Fortune, *Black and White: Land, Labor, and Politics in the South,* v–x. Chicago: Johnson.

Browning, R. 1890. Epilogue to *The Poetical Works of Robert Browning,* vol. 17, *Asolando,* ed. E. Berdoe, 106–10. London: Smith, Elder.

Brownlie, I., ed. 1979. *African Boundaries: A Legal and Diplomatic Encyclopaedia.* London: Hurst; Berkeley: University of California Press for the Royal Institute of International Affairs.

Brundage, W. F. 1990. "The Darien 'Insurrection' of 1899: Black Protest during the Nadir of Race Relations." *Georgia Historical Quarterly* 74:234–53.

Brundage, W. F. 1993. *Lynching in the New South: Georgia and Virginia, 1880–1930.* Urbana: University of Illinois Press.

Burns, M., ed. 1999. *France and the Dreyfus Affair: A Documentary History.* Boston: Bedford/St. Martin's.

Burns, R. 2001. *The Canongate Burns*. Ed. A. Noble and P. S. Hogg. Introduction by A. Noble. Edinburgh: Canongate.

Carter, D. M. 1997. *States of Grace: Senegalese in Italy and the New European Immigration*. Minneapolis: University of Minnesota Press.

Chandler, N. D. 1996. "The Figure of the X: An Elaboration of the Du Boisian Autobiographical Example." In *Displacement, Diaspora, and Geographies of Identity*, ed. S. Lavie and T. Swedenburg, 235–72. Durham, NC: Duke University Press.

Chandler, N. D. 2006a. "The Figure of W. E. B. Du Bois as a Problem for Thought." CR: *The New Centennial Review* 6 (3): 29–55.

Chandler, N. D. 2006b. "The Possible Form of an Interlocution: W. E. B. Du Bois and Max Weber in Correspondence, 1904–1905, Part I: The Letters and the Essay." CR: *The New Centennial Review* 6 (3): 193–239.

Chandler, N. D. 2007. "The Possible Form of an Interlocution: W. E. B. Du Bois and Max Weber in Correspondence, 1904–1905, Part II: The Terms of Discussion." CR: *The New Centennial Review* 7 (1): 213–72.

Chandler, N. D. 2012. "A Persistent Parallax: On W. E. B. Du Bois's Writings on Japan and China, 1936–1937." CR: *The New Centennial Review* 12 (1): 291–316.

Chandler, N. D. 2014a. "Anacrusis." In *X: The Problem of the Negro as a Problem for Thought*, 1–10. New York: Fordham University Press.

Chandler, N. D. 2014b. "On Paragraph Four of 'The Conservation of Races.'" CR: *The New Centennial Review* 14 (3): 255–88.

Chandler, N. D. 2014c. *X: The Problem of the Negro as a Problem for Thought*. New York: Fordham University Press.

Chandler, N. D. 2021. *Toward an African Future—Of the Limit of World*. New York: State University of New York Press.

Chandler, N. D. Forthcoming. *Annotations: On the Early Thought of W. E. B. Du Bois*. Durham, NC: Duke University Press.

Chase, M. 2007. *Chartism: A New History*. Manchester: Manchester University Press.

Chickering, R., ed. 1996. *Imperial Germany: A Historiographical Companion*. Westport, CT: Greenwood.

Clarke, A. 2015. "W. E. B. Du Bois's Fugitive Writing, or Sociology at the Turn of the Twentieth Century." CR: *The New Centennial Review* 15 (2): 171–209.

Cleveland, H. 1866. *Alexander H. Stephens in Public and Private: With Letters and Speeches Before, During, and Since the War*. Philadelphia: National Publishing Co.

Cohn, B. S. 1987. *An Anthropologist among the Historians and Other Essays*. Delhi: Oxford University Press.

Cohn, B. S. 1996a. *Colonialism and Its Forms of Knowledge: The British in India*. Princeton, NJ: Princeton University Press.

Cohn, B. S. 1996b. "The Command of Language and the Language of Command." In *Colonialism and Its Forms of Knowledge: The British in India*, 16–56. Princeton Studies in Culture/Power/History. Princeton, NJ: Princeton University Press.

Contee, C. G. 1969a. "The Emergence of W. E. B. Du Bois as an African Nationalist." *Journal of Negro History* 54 (1): 48–63.

Contee, C. G. 1969b. "W. E. B. Du Bois and African Nationalism, 1914–1945." PhD diss., American University.

Contee, C. G. 1973. *Henry Sylvester Williams and Origins of Organizational Pan-Africanism, 1897–1902*. Washington, DC: Department of History, Howard University.

Cooper, A. J. 1892. *A Voice from the South*. Xenia, OH: Aldine.

Cornwall, M., ed. 2002. *The Last Years of Austria-Hungary: A Multi-national Experiment in Early Twentieth-Century Europe*. Exeter: University of Exeter Press.

Cruse, H. 1967. *The Crisis of the Negro Intellectual*. New York: Morrow.

Daly, M. W. 1986. *Empire on the Nile: The Anglo-Egyptian Sudan, 1898–1934*. Cambridge: Cambridge University Press.

Daly, M. W., ed. 1998. *The Cambridge History of Egypt*. Vol. 2, *Modern Egypt, from 1517 to the End of the Twentieth Century*. Cambridge: Cambridge University Press.

Darity, W. 1988. "The Williams Thesis before Williams." *Slavery and Abolition* 9:29–41.

Darwin, C. 1897. *The Origin of Species by Means of Natural Selection, or The Preservation of Favored Races in the Struggle for Life*. New York: Appleton.

Das, S. K. 1978. *Sahibs and Munshis: An Account of the College of Fort William*. New Delhi: Orion.

Del Boca, A. 1992. *Gli Italiani in Africa orientale*. Vols. 33, 41, 43, 44. Milan: Mondadori.

Del Boca, A., ed. 1997. *Adua: Le ragioni di una sconfitta*. Rome: Laterza.

Derrida, J. 1978. Introduction to "The Origin of Geometry." In Edmund Husserl, *The Origin of Geometry: An Introduction*, ed. David B. Allison, trans. J. P. Leavey, 25–153. Stony Brook, NY: Nicholas Hays Ltd.

Derrida, J. 1987. *For Nelson Mandela*. Ed. J. Derrida and M. Tlili. New York: Seaver.

Derrida, J. 1994. *Specters of Marx: The State of the Debt, the Work of Mourning, and the New International*. Trans. P. Kamuf. Introduction by B. Magnus and S. Cullenberg. New York: Routledge.

Derrida, J. 2005. "Part II: The 'World' of the Enlightenment to Come (Exception, Calculation, and Sovereignty)." In *Rogues: Two Essays on Reason*, trans. P.-A. Brault and M. Naas, 118–59. Meridian. Stanford, CA: Stanford University Press.

Derrida, J. 2007. "The Laws of Reflection: Nelson Mandela, in Admiration." Trans. M. A. Caws and I. Lorenz. In *Psyche: Inventions of the Other. Vol. 2*, ed. P. Kamuf and E. G. Rottenberg, 63–86. Stanford, CA: Stanford University Press.

Dirks, N. B. 2001. "The Imperial Archive: Colonial Knowledge and Colonial Rule." In *Castes of Mind: Colonialism and the Making of Modern India*, 106–23. Princeton, NJ: Princeton University Press.

Du Bois, W. E. B. 1893. "1868–1893. Berlin, Germany, Oranienstrasse No. 130a. Program for the Celebration of My Twenty-Fifth Birthday." Series 3, subseries C, W. E. B. Du Bois Papers (MS 312), Special Collections and University Archives, University of Massachusetts Amherst Libraries.

Du Bois, W. E. B. 1894a[?]. "The Afro-American." Series 3, subseries C, W. E. B. Du Bois Papers (MS 312), Special Collections and University Archives, University of Massachusetts Amherst Libraries.

Du Bois, W. E. B. 1894b. "A Spring Wandering." Series 3, subseries C , W. E. B. Du Bois Papers (MS 312), Special Collections and University Archives, University of Massachusetts Amherst Libraries.

Du Bois, W. E. B. 1894c[?]. "The Socialism of German Socialists." Series 3, subseries C, W. E. B. Du Bois Papers (MS 312), Special Collections and University Archives, University of Massachusetts Amherst Libraries.

Du Bois, W. E. B. 1896. *The Suppression of the African Slave-Trade to the United States of America, 1638–1870.* Harvard Historical Studies. New York: Longmans, Green.

Du Bois, W. E. B. 1897a[?]. "Beyond the Veil in a Virginia Town." Series 3, subseries C, W. E. B. Du Bois Papers (MS 312), Special Collections and University Archives, University of Massachusetts Amherst Libraries.

Du Bois, W. E. B. 1897b. "The Conservation of Races." American Negro Academy Occasional Papers, No. 2. Washington, DC: American Negro Academy.

Du Bois, W. E. B. 1897c. "Strivings of the Negro People." *Atlantic Monthly* 80 (August): 194–98.

Du Bois, W. E. B. 1897d. "W. E. B. Du Bois Presents Plans for the Proposed Study of the Negro Question," Philadelphia, May 5, 1897. Department of Labor Records, National Archives and Records Administration, Washington, DC.

Du Bois, W. E. B. 1897e. "W. E. B. Du Bois Presents Plans for the Proposed Study of the Negro Question," Philadelphia, June 14, 1897. Department of Labor Records, National Archives and Records Administration, Washington, DC.

Du Bois, W. E. B. 1898a. "The Negroes of Farmville, Virginia: A Social Study." *Bulletin of the Department of Labor* 3 (14): 1–38.

Du Bois, W. E. B. 1898b. "The Study of the Negro Problems." A paper submitted to the American Academy of Political and Social Science, together with a report of the discussion of this subject at the Forty-fourth Scientific Session of the Academy. Publications of the American Academy of Political and Social Science, No. 219. Issued fortnightly. February 12, 1898. Philadelphia: American Academy of Political and Social Science.

Du Bois, W. E. B. 1898c. "The Study of the Negro Problems." *Annals of the American Academy of Political and Social Science* 11 (1): 1–23.

Du Bois, W. E. B. 1899a. "A Final Word." In W. E. B. Du Bois and I. Eaton, *The Philadelphia Negro: A Social Study, by W. E. B. Du Bois; Together with a Special Report on Domestic Service by Isabel Eaton,* 385–97. Publications of the University of Pennsylvania. Series in Political Economy and Public Law, No. 14. Philadelphia: Published for the University.

Du Bois, W. E. B. 1899b. "The Negro in the Black Belt: Some Social Sketches." *U.S. Department of Labor Bulletin* 4 (22): 401–17.

Du Bois, W. E. B. 1899c. *The Philadelphia Negro: A Social Study.* In W. E. B. Du Bois and I. Eaton, *The Philadelphia Negro: A Social Study, by W. E. B. Du Bois; Together with a Special Report on Domestic Service by Isabel Eaton,* 1–423. Publications of the University of Pennsylvania. Series in Political Economy and Public Law, No. 14. Philadelphia: Published for the University.

Du Bois, W. E. B. 1899d. "Preface." In W. E. B. Du Bois and I. Eaton, *The Philadelphia Negro: A Social Study, by W. E. B. Du Bois; Together with a Special Report on Domestic Service by Isabel Eaton*, iii–v. Publications of the University of Pennsylvania. Series in Political Economy and Public Law, No. 14. Philadelphia: Published for the University.

Du Bois, W. E. B. 1900a. "The Present Outlook for the Dark Races of Mankind." *A.M.E. Church Review* 17 (2): 95–110.

Du Bois, W. E. B. 1900b. "To the Nations of the World." Series 3, subseries C, W. E. B. Du Bois Papers (MS 312), Special Collections and University Archives, University of Massachusetts Amherst Libraries.

Du Bois, W. E. B. 1901a. "The Evolution of Negro Leadership." *The Dial* 31 (July): 53–55.

Du Bois, W. E. B. 1901b. "The Freedmen's Bureau." *Atlantic Monthly* 87 (March): 354–65.

Du Bois, W. E. B. 1901c. "The Negro as He Really Is." *World's Work* 2 (2): 848–66.

Du Bois, W. E. B. 1901d. "The Relation of the Negroes to the Whites in the South." *Annals of the American Academy of Political and Social Science* 18 (1): 121–40.

Du Bois, W. E. B. 1903a. "Forethought." In *The Souls of Black Folk: Essays and Sketches*, vii–viii. Chicago: McClurg.

Du Bois, W. E. B. 1903b. "Of Alexander Crummell." In *The Souls of Black Folk: Essays and Sketches*, 215–27. Chicago: McClurg.

Du Bois, W. E. B. 1903c. "Of Mr. Booker T. Washington and Others." In *The Souls of Black Folk: Essays and Sketches*, 41–59. Chicago: McClurg.

Du Bois, W. E. B. 1903d. "Of Our Spiritual Strivings." In *The Souls of Black Folk: Essays and Sketches*, 1–12. Chicago: McClurg.

Du Bois, W. E. B. 1903e. "Of the Black Belt." In *The Souls of Black Folk: Essays and Sketches*, 110–34. Chicago: McClurg.

Du Bois, W. E. B. 1903f. "Of the Coming of John." In *The Souls of Black Folk: Essays and Sketches*, 228–49. Chicago: McClurg.

Du Bois, W. E. B. 1903g. "Of the Dawn of Freedom." In *The Souls of Black Folk: Essays and Sketches*, 13–40. Chicago: McClurg.

Du Bois, W. E. B. 1903h. "Of the Meaning of Progress." In *The Souls of Black Folk: Essays and Sketches*, 60–74. Chicago: McClurg.

Du Bois, W. E. B. 1903i. "Of the Passing of the First Born." In *The Souls of Black Folk: Essays and Sketches*, 207–14. Chicago: McClurg.

Du Bois, W. E. B. 1903j. "Of the Sons of Master and Man." In *The Souls of Black Folk: Essays and Sketches*, 163–88. Chicago: McClurg.

Du Bois, W. E. B. 1903k. "The Sorrow Songs." In *The Souls of Black Folk: Essays and Sketches*, 250–64. Chicago: McClurg.

Du Bois, W. E. B. 1903l. *The Souls of Black Folk: Essays and Sketches*. 1st ed. Chicago: McClurg.

Du Bois, W. E. B. 1903m. *The Souls of Black Folk: Essays and Sketches*. 2nd ed. Chicago: McClurg. Electronic edition available at Documenting the American South, http://docsouth.unc.edu/church/duboissouls/dubois.html.

Du Bois, W. E. B. 1903n. "The Talented Tenth." In *The Negro Problem: A Series of Articles by Representative American Negroes of Today; Contributions by Booker T. Washington,*

W. E. Burghardt Du Bois, Paul Laurence Dunbar, Charles W. Chesnutt, and Others,
by B. T. Washington, W. E. Burghardt Du Bois, Charles W. Chesnutt, Wilford H.
Smith, H. T. Kealing, Paul Laurence Dunbar, T. Thomas Fortune, 33–75. New York:
James Pott and Co.

Du Bois, W. E. B. 1904. "The Development of a People." *International Journal of Ethics*
14 (3): 292–311.

Du Bois, W. E. B. 1905[?]. "Sociology Hesitant." Series 3, subseries C, W. E. B. Du Bois
Papers (MS 312), Special Collections and University Archives, University of Massachusetts Amherst Libraries.

Du Bois, W. E. B. 1906a. "The Color Line Belts the World." *Collier's Weekly*, October 20,
1906, 20.

Du Bois, W. E. B. 1906b. "Die Negerfrage in den Vereinigten Staaten." *Archiv für Sozial-
wissenschaft und Sozialpolitik* 22 (January): 31–79.

Du Bois, W. E. B. 1909. *John Brown.* American Crisis Biographies. Philadelphia: Jacobs.

Du Bois, W. E. B. 1910. "The Souls of White Folk." *Independent*, August 18, 1910,
339–42.

Du Bois, W. E. B. 1911. *The Quest of the Silver Fleece: A Novel.* Chicago: McClurg.

Du Bois, W. E. B. 1915a. "The African Roots of War." *Atlantic Monthly* 115 (May):
707–14.

Du Bois, W. E. B. 1915b. *The Negro.* Home University Library of Modern Knowledge, 91.
New York: Holt.

Du Bois, W. E. B. 1917. "Of the Culture of White Folk." *Journal of Race Development* 7
(April): 434–47.

Du Bois, W. E. B. 1920. *Darkwater: Voices from within the Veil.* New York: Harcourt,
Brace and Howe.

Du Bois, W. E. B. 1923. *The Gift of Black Folk: The Negroes in the Making of America.*
Boston: Stratford and Co.

Du Bois, W. E. B. 1925. "Worlds of Color." *Foreign Affairs* 20:423–44.

Du Bois, W. E. B. 1928. *Dark Princess: A Romance.* New York: Harcourt, Brace and Co.

Du Bois, W. E. B. 1935. *Black Reconstruction: An Essay toward a History of the Part Which
Black Folk Played in the Attempt to Reconstruct Democracy in America, 1860–1880.*
New York: Harcourt, Brace and Co.

Du Bois, W. E. B. 1939. *Black Folk Then and Now: An Essay in the History and Sociology
of the Negro Race.* New York: Henry Holt and Co.

Du Bois, W. E. B. 1940. *Dusk of Dawn: An Essay toward an Autobiography of a Race
Concept.* New York: Harcourt, Brace and Co.

Du Bois, W. E. B. 1945. *Color and Democracy: Colonies and Peace.* New York: Harcourt,
Brace.

Du Bois, W. E. B. 1947. *The World and Africa: An Inquiry into the Part Which Africa Has
Played in World History.* New York: Viking.

Du Bois, W. E. B. 1956. Letter to Herbert Aptheker, January 10, 1956. Series 3, subseries
C, W. E. B. Du Bois Papers (MS 312), Special Collections and University Archives,
University of Massachusetts Amherst Libraries.

Du Bois, W. E. B. 1957. *The Black Flame: A Trilogy.* Vol. 1, *The Ordeal of Mansart.* New York: Mainstream.

Du Bois, W. E. B. 1959. *The Black Flame: A Trilogy.* Vol. 2, *Mansart Builds a School.* New York: Mainstream.

Du Bois, W. E. B. 1961a. "Africa and the French Revolution." *Freedomways: A Quarterly Review of the Negro Freedom Movement* 1 (2): 136–51.

Du Bois, W. E. B. 1961b. *The Black Flame: A Trilogy.* Vol. 3, *Worlds of Color.* New York: Mainstream.

Du Bois, W. E. B. 1962. *John Brown.* Centennial ed. New York: International.

Du Bois, W. E. B. 1964. "Du Bois on Douglass: 1895." *Journal of Negro History* 49 (4): 264–68.

Du Bois, W. E. B. 1968. *The Autobiography of W. E. B. Du Bois: A Soliloquy on Viewing My Life from the Last Decade of Its First Century.* Ed. H. Aptheker. New York: International.

Du Bois, W. E. B. 1973a. *The Correspondence of W. E. B. Du Bois.* Vol. 1, *Selections, 1877–1934.* Comp. and ed. H. Aptheker. Amherst: University of Massachusetts Press.

Du Bois, W. E. B. 1973b. *The Correspondence of W. E. B. Du Bois.* Vol. 2, *Selections, 1934–1944.* Comp. and ed. H. Aptheker. Amherst: University of Massachusetts Press.

Du Bois, W. E. B. 1973c. *The Correspondence of W. E. B. Du Bois.* Vol. 3, *Selections, 1945–1963.* Comp. and ed. H. Aptheker. Amherst: University of Massachusetts Press.

Du Bois, W. E. B. 1973d. *John Brown.* Ed. H. Aptheker. Complete Published Works of W. E. B. Du Bois. Millwood, NY: Kraus-Thomson Organization.

Du Bois, W. E. B. 1973e. Letter to Daniel C. Gilman. In *The Correspondence of W. E. B. Du Bois*, vol. 1, *Selections, 1877–1934*, comp. and ed. H. Aptheker, 38–39. Amherst: University of Massachusetts Press.

Du Bois, W. E. B. 1973f. Letter to Rutherford B. Hayes. In *The Correspondence of W. E. B. Du Bois*, vol. 1, *Selections, 1877–1934*, comp. and ed. H. Aptheker, 16–17. Amherst: University of Massachusetts Press.

Du Bois, W. E. B. 1973g. *The Philadelphia Negro: A Social Study.* In W. E. B. Du Bois and I. Eaton, *The Philadelphia Negro: A Social Study*, 1–423. Ed. H. Aptheker. Complete Published Works of W. E. B. Du Bois. Millwood, NY: Kraus-Thomson Organization.

Du Bois, W. E. B. 1973h. *The Suppression of the African Slave-Trade to the United States of America, 1638–1870.* Ed. H. Aptheker. Complete Published Works of W. E. B. Du Bois. Millwood, NY: Kraus-Thomson Organization.

Du Bois, W. E. B. 1974a. *Dark Princess: A Romance.* Ed. H. Aptheker. Complete Published Works of W. E. B. Du Bois. Millwood, NY: Kraus-Thomson Organization.

Du Bois, W. E. B. 1974b. *The Quest of the Silver Fleece: A Novel.* Ed. H. Aptheker. Complete Published Works of W. E. B. Du Bois. Millwood, NY: Kraus-Thomson Organization.

Du Bois, W. E. B. 1975a. *Black Folk Then and Now: An Essay in the History and Sociology of the Negro Race.* Ed. H. Aptheker. Complete Published Works of W. E. B. Du Bois. Millwood, NY: Kraus-Thomson Organization.

Du Bois, W. E. B. 1975b. *Color and Democracy: Colonies and Peace.* Ed. H. Aptheker. Complete Published Works of W. E. B. Du Bois. Millwood, NY: Kraus-Thomson Organization.

Du Bois, W. E. B. 1975c. *Darkwater: Voices from within the Veil.* Ed. H. Aptheker. Complete Published Works of W. E. B. Du Bois. Millwood, NY: Kraus-Thomson Organization.

Du Bois, W. E. B. 1975d. *Dusk of Dawn: An Essay toward an Autobiography of a Race Concept.* Ed. H. Aptheker. Complete Published Works of W. E. B. Du Bois. Millwood, NY: Kraus-Thomson Organization.

Du Bois, W. E. B. 1975e. *The Negro.* Ed. H. Aptheker. Complete Published Works of W. E. B. Du Bois. Millwood, NY: Kraus-Thomson Organization.

Du Bois, W. E. B. 1976a. *The Black Flame: A Trilogy.* Vol. 2, *Mansart Builds a School.* Ed. H. Aptheker. Complete Published Works of W. E. B. Du Bois. Millwood, NY: Kraus-Thomson Organization.

Du Bois, W. E. B. 1976b. *The Black Flame: A Trilogy.* Vol. 1, *The Ordeal of Mansart.* Ed. H. Aptheker. Complete Published Works of W. E. B. Du Bois. Millwood, NY: Kraus-Thomson Organization.

Du Bois, W. E. B. 1976c. *The Black Flame: A Trilogy.* Vol. 3, *Worlds of Color.* Ed. H. Aptheker. Complete Published Works of W. E. B. Du Bois. Millwood, NY: Kraus-Thomson Organization.

Du Bois, W. E. B. 1976d. *Black Reconstruction: An Essay toward a History of the Part Which Black Folk Played in the Attempt to Reconstruct Democracy in America, 1860–1880.* Ed. H. Aptheker. Complete Published Works of W. E. B. Du Bois. Millwood, NY: Kraus-Thomson Organization.

Du Bois, W. E. B. 1976e. *The World and Africa: An Inquiry into the Part Which Africa Has Played in World History.* Ed. H. Aptheker. Complete Published Works of W. E. B. Du Bois. Millwood, NY: Kraus-Thomson Organization.

Du Bois, W. E. B. 1980a. "The Afro-American." In *The Papers of W. E. B. Du Bois, 1803 (1877–1963) 1979*, comp. and ed. H. Aptheker, reel 82, frames 1232–42. Sanford, NC: Microfilming Corporation of America.

Du Bois, W. E. B. 1980b. "Beyond the Veil in a Virginia Town." In *The Papers of W. E. B. Du Bois, 1803 (1877–1963) 1979*, comp. and ed. H. Aptheker, reel 82, frame 1258. Sanford, NC: Microfilming Corporation of America.

Du Bois, W. E. B. 1980c. "The Negroes of Farmville, Virginia: A Social Study." In *Contributions by W. E. B. Du Bois in Government Publications and Proceedings*, ed. H. Aptheker, 5–44. Complete Published Works of W. E. B. Du Bois. Millwood, NY: Kraus-Thomson Organization.

Du Bois, W. E. B. 1980d. "The Negro Farmer." In *Contributions by W. E. B. Du Bois in Government Publications and Proceedings*, ed. H. Aptheker, 231–95. Complete Published Works of W. E. B. Du Bois. Millwood, NY: Kraus-Thomson Organization.

Du Bois, W. E. B. 1980e. "The Negro Landholder of Georgia." In *Contributions by W. E. B. Du Bois in Government Publications and Proceedings*, ed. H. Aptheker,

95–228. Complete Published Works of W. E. B. Du Bois. Millwood, NY: Kraus-Thomson Organization.

Du Bois, W. E. B. 1980f. *The Papers of W. E. B. Du Bois, 1803 (1877–1963) 1979*. Comp. and ed. H. Aptheker and Robert C. McDonnell. Sanford, NC: Microfilming Corporation of America.

Du Bois, W. E. B. 1980g. "A Plot for a Story/Faded [Shattered] Ideals." In *The Papers of W. E. B. Du Bois, 1803 (1877–1963) 1965*, comp. and ed. H. Aptheker. Sanford, NC: Microfilming Corporation of America.

Du Bois, W. E. B. 1980h. "The Socialism of German Socialists." In *The Papers of W. E. B. Du Bois, 1803 (1877–1963) 1965*, comp. and ed. H. Aptheker, reel 87, frames 413–29. Sanford, NC: Microfilming Corporation of America.

Du Bois, W. E. B. 1980i. "Sociology Hesitant." In *The Papers of W. E. B. Du Bois, 1803 (1877–1963) 1965*, comp. and ed. H. Aptheker, reel 82, frames 1307–12. Sanford, NC: Microfilming Corporation of America.

Du Bois, W. E. B. 1980j. "Testimony before the United States Industrial Commission." In *Contributions by W. E. B. Du Bois in Government Publications and Proceedings*, ed. H. Aptheker, 65–94. Complete Published Works of W. E. B. Du Bois. Millwood, NY: Kraus-Thomson Organization.

Du Bois, W. E. B. 1982a. "The African Roots of War." In *Writings by W. E. B. Du Bois in Periodicals Edited by Others*, vol. 2, *1910–1934*, comp. and ed. H. Aptheker, 96–104. Complete Published Works of W. E. B. Du Bois. Millwood, NY: Kraus-Thomson Organization.

Du Bois, W. E. B. 1982b. "The Beginning of Emancipation." In *Writings by W. E. B. Du Bois in Periodicals Edited by Others*, vol. 1, *1891–1909*, comp. and ed. H. Aptheker, 242–45. Complete Published Works of W. E. B. Du Bois. Millwood, NY: Kraus-Thomson Organization.

Du Bois, W. E. B. 1982c. "The Beginning of Slavery." In *Writings by W. E. B. Du Bois in Periodicals Edited by Others*, vol. 1, *1891–1909*, comp. and ed. H. Aptheker, 235–37. Complete Published Works of W. E. B. Du Bois. Millwood, NY: Kraus-Thomson Organization.

Du Bois, W. E. B. 1982d. "The Development of a People." In *Writings by W. E. B. Du Bois in Periodicals Edited by Others*, vol. 1, 1891–1909, comp. and ed. H. Aptheker, 203–15. Complete Published Works of W. E. B. Du Bois. Millwood, NY: Kraus-Thomson Organization.

Du Bois, W. E. B. 1982e. "Douglass as Statesman." In *Writings by W. E. B. Du Bois in Periodicals Edited by Others*, vol. 1, *1891–1909*, comp. and ed. H. Aptheker, 28–30. Complete Published Works of W. E. B. Du Bois. Millwood, NY: Kraus-Thomson Organization.

Du Bois, W. E. B. 1982f. "The Present Outlook for the Dark Races of Mankind." In *Writings by W. E. B. Du Bois in Periodicals Edited by Others*, vol. 1, *1891–1909*, comp. and ed. H. Aptheker, 73–82. Complete Published Works of W. E. B. Du Bois. Millwood, NY: Kraus-Thomson Organization.

Du Bois, W. E. B. 1982g. "Serfdom." In *Writings by W. E. B. Du Bois in Periodicals Edited by Others*, vol. 1, *1891–1909*, comp. and ed. H. Aptheker, 246–49. Complete Published Works of W. E. B. Du Bois. Millwood, NY: Kraus-Thomson Organization.

Du Bois, W. E. B. 1982h. "Slavery in Greece and Rome." In *Writings by W. E. B. Du Bois in Periodicals Edited by Others*, vol. 1, *1891–1909*, comp. and ed. H. Aptheker, 238–41. Complete Published Works of W. E. B. Du Bois. Millwood, NY: Kraus-Thomson Organization.

Du Bois, W. E. B. 1982i. "The Souls of White Folk." In *Writings by W. E. B. Du Bois in Periodicals Edited by Others*, vol. 2, *1910–1934*, comp. and ed. H. Aptheker, 25–29. Complete Published Works of W. E. B. Du Bois. Millwood, NY: Kraus-Thomson Organization.

Du Bois, W. E. B. 1982j. "The Talented Tenth Memorial Address." In *Writings by W. E. B. Du Bois in Periodicals Edited by Others*, vol. 4, *1945–1961*, comp. and ed. H. Aptheker, 78–88. Complete Published Works of W. E. B. Du Bois. Millwood, NY: Kraus-Thomson Organization.

Du Bois, W. E. B. 1982k. "To the Nations of the World." In *Writings by W. E. B. Du Bois in Non-periodical Literature Edited by Others*, comp. and ed. H. Aptheker, 11–12. Complete Published Works of W. E. B. Du Bois. Millwood, NY: Kraus-Thomson Organization.

Du Bois, W. E. B. 1985a. "The Art and Art Galleries of Modern Europe (1896?)." In *Against Racism: Unpublished Essays, Papers, Addresses, 1887–1961*, ed. H. Aptheker, 33–43. Amherst: University of Massachusetts Press.

Du Bois, W. E. B. 1985b. "Beyond the Veil in a Virginia Town." In *Against Racism: Unpublished Essays, Papers, Addresses, 1887–1961*, ed. H. Aptheker, 49–50. Amherst: University of Massachusetts Press.

Du Bois, W. E. B. 1985c. "Celebrating His Twenty-Fifth Birthday." In *Against Racism Unpublished Essays, Papers, Addresses, 1887–1961*, ed. H. Aptheker, 26–29. Amherst: University of Massachusetts Press.

Du Bois, W. E. B. 1985d. "Harvard (1887–92)." In *Against Racism: Unpublished Essays, Papers, Addresses, 1887–1961*, ed. H. Aptheker, 4–25. Amherst: University of Massachusetts Press.

Du Bois, W. E. B. 1985e. "A Plot for a Story." In *Against Racism: Unpublished Essays, Papers, Addresses, 1887–1961*, ed. H. Aptheker. Amherst: University of Massachusetts Press.

Du Bois, W. E. B. 1985f. "The Spirit of Modern Europe." In *Against Racism: Unpublished Essays, Papers, Addresses, 1887–1961*, ed. H. Aptheker, 50–64. Amherst: University of Massachusetts Press.

Du Bois, W. E. B. 1986a. "The Conservation of Races." In *Pamphlets and Leaflets*, comp. and ed. H. Aptheker, 1–8. Complete Published Works of W. E. B. Du Bois. White Plains, NY: Kraus-Thomson Organization.

Du Bois, W. E. B. 1986b. *Newspaper Columns*. Vol. 1, *1883–1944*. Comp. and ed. H. Aptheker. Complete Published Works of W. E. B. Du Bois. White Plains, NY: Kraus-Thomson Organization.

Du Bois, W. E. B. 1995. *W. E. B. Du Bois: A Reader*. Ed. D. L. Lewis. New York: Holt.

Du Bois, W. E. B. 1996. *The Oxford W. E. B. Du Bois Reader*. Ed. E. J. Sundquist. New York: Oxford University Press.

Du Bois, W. E. B. 1997. "The Development of a People." In *The Souls of Black Folk*, ed. D. W. Blight and R. Gooding-Williams, 238–54. Bedford Series in History and Culture. Boston: Bedford Books.

Du Bois, W. E. B. 1998a. "The Present Condition of German Politics (1893)." *Central European History* 31 (3): 170–87.

Du Bois, W. E. B. 1998b. "The Socialism of German Socialists." *Central European History* 31 (3): 189–96.

Du Bois, W. E. B. 2000a. "The Present Outlook for the Dark Ages of Mankind." In *Social Protest Thought in the African Methodist Episcopal Church, 1862–1939*, ed. S. W. Angell and A. B. Pinn, 23–33. Knoxville: University of Tennessee Press.

Du Bois, W. E. B. 2000b. "Sociology Hesitant." *boundary 2: An International Journal of Literature and Culture* 27 (3): 37–44.

Du Bois, W. E. B. 2006. "Die Negerfrage in den Vereinigten Staaten (The Negro Question in the United States)." Trans. J. Fracchia. *CR: The New Centennial Review* 6 (3): 241–90.

Du Bois, W. E. B. 2010. "The Afro-American." *Journal of Transnational American Studies* 2 (1). https://escholarship.org/uc/item/2pm9g4q2.

Du Bois, W. E. B. 2015a. "The Afro-American." In *The Problem of the Color Line at the Turn of the Twentieth Century: The Essential Early Essays*, comp. and ed. N. D. Chandler, 33–50. New York: Fordham University Press.

Du Bois, W. E. B. 2015b. "Appendix: Résumé of the Discussion of the Negro Problems." In *The Problem of the Color Line at the Turn of the Twentieth Century: The Essential Early Essays*, comp. and ed. N. D. Chandler, 99–110. New York: Fordham University Press.

Du Bois, W. E. B. 2015c. "The Conservation of Races." In *The Problem of the Color Line at the Turn of the Twentieth Century: The Essential Early Essays*, comp. and ed. N. D. Chandler, 51–66. New York: Fordham University Press.

Du Bois, W. E. B. 2015d. "The Development of a People." In *The Problem of the Color Line at the Turn of the Twentieth Century: The Essential Early Essays*, comp. and ed. N. D. Chandler, 243–70. New York: Fordham University Press.

Du Bois, W. E. B. 2015e. "The Freedmen's Bureau." In *The Problem of the Color Line at the Turn of the Twentieth Century: The Essential Early Essays*, comp. and ed. N. D. Chandler, 167–88. New York: Fordham University Press.

Du Bois, W. E. B. 2015f. "Die Negerfrage in den Vereinigten Staaten (The Negro Question in the United States)." Trans. J. Fracchia. In *The Problem of the Color Line at the Turn of the Twentieth Century: The Essential Early Essays*, comp. and ed. N. D. Chandler, 285–338. New York: Fordham University Press.

Du Bois, W. E. B. 2015g. "The Present Outlook for the Dark Races of Mankind." In *The Problem of the Color Line at the Turn of the Twentieth Century: The Essential Early Essays*, comp. and ed. N. D. Chandler, 111–38. New York: Fordham University Press.

Du Bois, W. E. B. 2015h. *The Problem of the Color Line at the Turn of the Twentieth Century: The Essential Early Essays*. Comp. and ed. N. D. Chandler. New York: Fordham University Press.

Du Bois, W. E. B. 2015i. "Sociology Hesitant." In *The Problem of the Color Line at the Turn of the Twentieth Century: The Essential Early Essays*, comp. and ed. N. D. Chandler, 271–84. New York: Fordham University Press.

Du Bois, W. E. B. 2015j. "The Spirit of Modern Europe." In *The Problem of the Color Line at the Turn of the Twentieth Century: The Essential Early Essays*, comp. and ed. N. D. Chandler, 139–66. New York: Fordham University Press.

Du Bois, W. E. B. 2015k. "Strivings of the Negro People." In *The Problem of the Color Line at the Turn of the Twentieth Century: The Essential Early Essays*, comp. and ed. N. D. Chandler, 67–76. New York: Fordham University Press.

Du Bois, W. E. B. 2015l. "The Study of the Negro Problems." In *The Problem of the Color Line at the Turn of the Twentieth Century: The Essential Early Essays*, comp. and ed. N. D. Chandler, 77–98. New York: Fordham University Press.

Du Bois, W. E. B. 2015m. "The Talented Tenth." In *The Problem of the Color Line at the Turn of the Twentieth Century: The Essential Early Essays*, comp. and ed. N. D. Chandler, 209–42. New York: Fordham University Press.

Du Bois, W. E. B. and I. Eaton. 1899. *The Philadelphia Negro: A Social Study, by W. E. B. Du Bois; Together with a Special Report on Domestic Service by Isabel Eaton*. Publications of the University of Pennsylvania. Series in Political Economy and Public Law, No. 14. Philadelphia: Published for the University.

Du Bois, W. E. B. and I. Eaton. 1973. *The Philadelphia Negro: A Social Study*. Ed. H. Aptheker. Complete Published Works of W. E. B. Du Bois. Millwood, NY: Kraus-Thomson Organization.

Dunbar, P. L. 1893. *Oak and Ivy*. Dayton, OH: Press of United Brethren Publishing House.

Dupuy, A. 1989. *Haiti in the World: Economy Class, Race, and Underdevelopment since 1700*. Boulder, CO: Westview.

Duus, P. 1995. *The Abacus and the Sword: The Japanese Penetration of Korea, 1895–1910*. Twentieth-Century Japan. Berkeley: University of California Press.

Ellison, R. 1989. *Invisible Man*. New York: Vintage.

Emerson, R. W. 1867. *May-Day, and Other Pieces*. Boston: Ticknor and Fields.

Fairbank, J. F., ed. 1978. *The Cambridge History of China*. Vol. 10, *Late Ch'ing, 1800–1911, Pt. 1*. Gen. Ed. D. C. Twitchett and J. K. Fairbank. Cambridge: Cambridge University Press.

Fairbank, J. F., and K.-C. Liu, eds. 1980. *The Cambridge History of China*. Vol. 11, *Late Ch'ing, 1800–1911, Pt. 2*. Gen. ed. D. C. Twitchett and J. K. Fairbank. Cambridge: Cambridge University Press.

Fanon, F. 1975. *Peau noire, masques blancs*. Paris: Seuil.

Fanon, F. 1976. *Les damnés de la terre*. Paris: Maspero.

Fauvelle-Aymar, F.-X. 2002. *L'invention du Hottentot: Histoire du regard occidental sur les Khoisan, Xve–Xixe siècle*. Paris: Publications de la Sorbonne.

Fehrenbacher, D. E. 1978. *The Dred Scott Case: Its Significance in American Law and Politics*. New York: Oxford University Press.

Foner, P. S. 1972. *The Spanish-Cuban-American War and the Birth of American Imperialism, 1895–1902*. New York: Monthly Review Press.

Fortune, T. T. 1884. *Black and White: Land, Labor, and Politics in the South*. New York: Fords, Howard, and Hulbert.

Fortune, T. T. "The Afro-American (1890)." In *T. Thomas Fortune, the Afro-American Agitator: A Collection of His Writings, 1880–1928*, ed. Shawn Leigh Alexander, 215–20. Gainesville: University Press of Florida.

Foucault, M. 1966. *Les mots et les choses: Une archéologie des sciences humaines*. Paris: Gallimard.

Foucault, M. 1969. *L'archéologie du savoir*. Paris: Gallimard.

Foucault, M. 1972. *The Archaeology of Knowledge and the Discourse on Language*. Trans. A. M. S. Smith. New York: Pantheon.

Foucault, M. 1973. *The Order of Things: An Archaeology of the Human Sciences*. New York: Vintage.

Foucault, M. 1980. "Right of Death and Power over Life." In *The History of Sexuality*, vol. 1, *An Introduction*, trans. R. Hurley, 135–59. New York: Vintage.

Foucault, M. 2003. *Society Must Be Defended: Lectures at the Collège de France, 1975–76*. Ed. M. Bertani. Trans. D. Macey. New York: Picador.

Franklin, B. 1960. "An Almanack for the Year of Christ 1736." In *The Papers of Benjamin Franklin*, vol. 2, *January 1, 1735 through December 31, 1744*, ed. L. W. Labaree, W. J. Bell Jr., H. C. Boatfield, and H. H. Fineman, 136–45. New Haven, CT: Yale University Press.

Frost, J. W. 1993. "George Fox's Ambiguous Anti-slavery Legacy." In *New Light on George Fox (1624–1691)*, ed. M. A. Mullett, 69–88. York, UK: Sessions.

Gaillard, R. 1984. *La république exterminatrice*. Vol. 2, *L'etat vassal (1896–1902)*. Port-au-Prince, Haiti: Gaillard.

Galvão, A. 1601. *The Discoueries of the World from Their First Originall vnto the Yeere of Our Lord 1555. Briefly Written in the Portugall Tongue by Antonie Galuano, Gouernour of Ternate, the Chiefe Island of the Malucos: Corrected, Quoted, and Now Published in English by Richard Hakluyt, Sometimes Student of Christ Church in Oxford*. Trans. and ed. R. Hakluyt. London: Bishop.

Galvão, A. 1731. *Tratado dos descobrimentos antigos, e modernos, feitos até a era de 1550 com os nomes particulares das pessoas que os fizeraõ: E em que tempos, e as suas alturas, e dos desuairados caminhos por onde a pimenta, e especiaria veyo da India as nossas partes; obra certo muy notavel, e copiosa*. Lisbon: Ferreiriana.

Gatewood, W. B., ed. and comp. 1971. *"Smoked Yankees" and the Struggle for Empire: Letters from Negro Soldiers, 1898–1902*. Urbana: University of Illinois Press.

Gatewood, W. B. 1975. *Black Americans and the White Man's Burden, 1898–1903*. Urbana: University of Illinois Press.

Giddings, P. 2008. *Ida: A Sword among Lions; Ida B. Wells and the Campaign against Lynching*. New York: Amistad.

Gilroy, P. 1993. "'Cheer the Weary Traveller': W. E. B. Du Bois, Germany and the Politics of (Dis)Placement." In *The Black Atlantic: Modernity and Double Consciousness*, 111–45. Cambridge, MA: Harvard University Press.

Gooding-Williams, R. 2009. *In the Shadow of Du Bois: Afro-Modern Political Thought in America*. Cambridge, MA: Harvard University Press.

Gordon-Reed, A. 1997. *Thomas Jefferson and Sally Hemings: An American Controversy*. Charlottesville: University Press of Virginia.

Gordon-Reed, A. 2008. *The Hemingses of Monticello: An American Family*. New York: Norton.

Gordon-Reed, A. 2018. "Sally Hemings Takes Center Stage." *New York Times*. Accessed October 31, 2019. https://www.nytimes.com/2018/06/15/opinion/sally-hemings -monticello-thomas-jefferson.html?searchResultPosition=1.

Griffin, F. J. 1995. *"Who Set You Flowin'?": The African-American Migration Narrative*. Race and American Culture. New York: Oxford University Press.

Griffin, F. J., and C. J. Fish, eds. 1998. *A Stranger in the Village: Two Centuries of African-American Travel Writing*. Boston: Beacon.

Guha, R. 1997a. *Dominance without Hegemony: History and Power in Colonial India*. Cambridge, MA: Harvard University Press.

Guha, R. 1997b. "An Indian Historiography of India: Hegemonic Implications of a Nineteenth-Century Agenda." In *Dominance without Hegemony: History and Power in Colonial India*, 115–212. Cambridge, MA: Harvard University Press.

Guha, R. 1997c. *A Subaltern Studies Reader, 1986–1995*. Minneapolis: University of Minnesota Press.

Guha, R. 1999. *Elementary Aspects of Peasant Insurgency in Colonial India*. Durham, NC: Duke University Press.

Guha, R., and G. C. Spivak, eds. 1988. *Selected Subaltern Studies*. New York: Oxford University Press.

Hall, S. 1980. "Race, Articulation, and Societies Structured in Dominance." In *Sociological Theories: Race and Colonialism*, ed. UNESCO, 305–45. Paris: UNESCO.

Hardt, M., and A. Negri. 2000. *Empire*. Cambridge, MA: Harvard University Press.

Hardt, M., and A. Negri. 2004. *Multitude: War and Democracy in the Age of Empire*. New York: Penguin.

Hardt, M., and A. Negri. 2009. *Commonwealth*. Cambridge, MA: Harvard University Press.

Healy, D. 1988. *Drive to Hegemony: The United States in the Caribbean, 1898–1917*. Madison: University of Wisconsin Press.

Heidegger, M. 1998. "On the Essence of Truth (1930)," trans. John Sallis. In *Pathmarks*, ed. William McNeill, 136–54. Cambridge: Cambridge University Press.

Hendericks, G., D. u. d. Graeff, F. D. Pastorius, and A. u. d. Graef. 1980. "Germantown Protest." In *The Quaker Origins of Antislavery*, ed. J. William, 69. Norwood, PA: Norwood.

Hening, W. W., ed. 1810. *The Statutes at Large: Being a Collection of All the Laws of Virginia*. Richmond, VA: Pleasants.

Hess, R. L. 1966. *Italian Colonialism in Somalia*. Chicago: University of Chicago Press.

Hoare, J. 1970. "The Japanese Treaty Ports, 1868–1899: A Study of the Foreign Settlements." PhD diss., University of London.

Hochschild, A. 1999. *King Leopold's Ghost: A Story of Greed, Terror, and Heroism in Colonial Africa.* London: Macmillan.

Hofstadter, R. 1948. *The American Political Tradition and the Men Who Made It.* New York: Knopf.

Holt, T. C. 1982. "'An Empire over the Mind': Emancipation, Race, and Ideology in the British West Indies and the American South." In *Region, Race, and Reconstruction: Essays in Honor of C. Vann Woodward,* ed. J. M. Kousser and J. M. McPherson, 283–313. New York: Oxford University Press.

Holt, T. C. 1990. "Explaining Abolition." *Journal of Social History* 24 (2): 371–78.

Holt, T. C. 1992. *The Problem of Freedom: Race, Labor, and Politics in Jamaica and Britain, 1832–1938.* Baltimore: Johns Hopkins University Press.

Holt, T. C. 2010. "Many Thousands Born: The Roots of African America." In *Children of Fire: A History of African Americans,* 53–88. New York: Hill and Wang.

Hyatt, V. L., and R. M. Nettleford, eds. 1995. *Race, Discourse, and the Origins of the Americas: A New World View.* Washington, DC: Smithsonian Institution Press.

Ileto, R. C. 1979. *Pasyon and Revolution: Popular Movements in the Philippines, 1840–1910.* Quezon City, Philippines: Ateneo de Manila University Press.

Inalcik, H., ed. 1994. *An Economic and Social History of the Ottoman Empire, 1300–1914.* Assisted by D. Quataert. Cambridge: Cambridge University Press.

James, C. L. R. 1938. *The Black Jacobins: Toussaint L'Ouverture and the San Domingo Revolution.* New York: Dial.

James, C. L. R. 1972. "Interview." In *Kas-Kas: Interviews with Three Caribbean Writers in Texas; George Lamming, C. L. R. James [and] Wilson Harris,* ed. I. Munro and R. Sander, 22–41. Austin: African and Afro-American Research Institute, University of Texas at Austin.

James, C. L. R. 1989. *The Black Jacobins: Toussaint L'Ouverture and the San Domingo Revolution.* New York: Vintage.

Jansen, M. B., ed. 1995. *The Emergence of Meiji Japan.* New York: Cambridge University Press.

Jászi, O. 1929. *The Dissolution of the Habsburg Monarchy.* Chicago: University of Chicago Press.

Jefferson, T. 1984 [1785]. *Notes on the State of Virginia.* In *Writings,* ed. M. D. Peterson, 123–325. Library of America, Vol. 17. New York: Viking.

Jefferson, T. 1999. "The Declaration of Independence [as Amended and Adopted in Congress], July 4, 1776." In *Thomas Jefferson, Political Writings,* ed. J. O. Appleby and T. Ball, 102–5. Cambridge Texts in the History of Political Thought. New York: Cambridge University Press.

Johnston, H. H., and O. Stapf. 1906. *Liberia.* London: Hutchinson.

Jones, A., and R. Allen. 1794. *A Narrative of the Proceedings of the Black People, during the Late Awful Calamity in Philadelphia, in the Year 1793 and a Refutation of Some Censures, Thrown upon Them in Some Late Publications.* Philadelphia: Woodward.

Jones, F. C. 1931. *Extraterritoriality in Japan and the Diplomatic Relations Resulting in Its Abolition, 1853–1899*. New Haven, CT: Yale University Press.

Kann, R. A. 1950. *The Multinational Empire: Nationalism and National Reform in the Habsburg Monarchy, 1848–1918*. New York: Columbia University Press.

Kann, R. A. 1974. *A History of the Habsburg Empire, 1526–1918*. Berkeley: University of California Press.

Kant, I. 2001. "On the Use of Teleological Principles in Philosophy (1788)." Trans. J. M. Mikkelsen. In *Race*, ed. R. Bernasconi, 37–56. Malden, MA: Blackwell.

Kant, I. 2007a. "Anthropology from a Pragmatic Point of View (1798)." Trans. R. B. Louden. In *Anthropology, History, and Education*, ed. G. Zöller and R. B. Louden, 227–429. New York: Cambridge University Press.

Kant, I. 2007b. "Determination of the Concept of a Human Race (1785)." Trans. H. Wilson and G. Zöller. In *Anthropology, History, and Education*, ed. and trans. R. B. Louden and G. Zöller, 145–59. New York: Cambridge University Press.

Kant, I. 2007c. "On the Use of Teleological Principles in Philosophy (1788)." Trans. G. Zöller. In *Anthropology, History, and Education*, ed. and trans. R. B. Louden and G. Zöller, 195–218. New York: Cambridge University Press.

Kearney, R. 1998. *African American Views of the Japanese: Solidarity or Sedition?* Albany: State University of New York Press.

King, G. 2007. *Twilight of Splendor: The Court of Queen Victoria during Her Diamond Jubilee Year*. Hoboken, NJ: Wiley.

Klein, H. S. 1999. *The Atlantic Slave Trade*. New York: Cambridge University Press.

Kopf, D. 1969. *British Orientalism and the Bengal Renaissance: The Dynamics of Indian Modernization, 1773–1835*. Berkeley: University of California Press.

Lach, D. F. 1965a. *Asia in the Making of Europe. Volume 1. The Century of Discovery. Book One*. Chicago: University of Chicago Press.

Lach, D. F. 1965b. *Asia in the Making of Europe. Volume 1. The Century of Discovery. Book Two*. Chicago: University of Chicago Press.

Lach, D. F. 1965–93. *Asia in the Making of Europe*. 4 Vols. Chicago: University of Chicago Press.

LaFeber, W. 1998a. *The Clash: U.S.-Japanese Relations throughout History*. New York: Norton.

LaFeber, W. 1998b. *The New Empire: An Interpretation of American Expansion, 1860–1898*. Ithaca, NY: Cornell University Press.

Lavie, S., and T. Swedenburg, eds. 1996. *Displacement, Diaspora, and Geographies of Identity*. Ed. S. Lavie. Durham, NC: Duke University Press.

Lee, L. T., and J. B. Quigley. 2008. "Historical Evolution." In *Consular Law and Practice*, 3–25. New York: Oxford University Press.

Lewis, D. L. 1993. *W. E. B. Du Bois: Biography of a Race, 1868–1919*. New York: Holt.

Lieven, D. C. B., ed. 2006. *The Cambridge History of Russia*. Vol. 2, *Imperial Russia, 1689–1917*. Cambridge: Cambridge University Press.

Litwack, L. F. 1979. *Been in the Storm So Long: The Aftermath of Slavery*. New York: Knopf.

Lobban, R., and P. M. K. Mendy. 1997. *Historical Dictionary of the Republic of Guinea-Bissau*. Lanham, MD: Scarecrow.

Locke, A. L., ed. 1925. *The New Negro: An Interpretation*. New York: Albert and Charles Boni.

Locke, J. 1732. "An Introductory Discourse Containing the Whole History of Navigation from Its Original to This Time." In *A Collection of Voyages and Travels: Some Now First Printed from Original Manuscripts, Others Now First Published in English. To Which Is Prefixed, an Introductory Discourse (Supposed to Be Written by the Celebrated Mr. Locke) Intitled, the Whole History of Navigation from Its Original to This Time*, comp. and ed. A. Churchill and J. Churchill, 1: ix–xciv. London: Churchill.

Logan, R. W. 1941. *The Diplomatic Relations of the United States with Haiti, 1776–1891*. Chapel Hill: University of North Carolina Press.

Mandela, N. 1979. *I Am Prepared to Die*. London: International Defence and Aid Fund for Southern Africa.

Mandela, N. 1986. *The Struggle Is My Life: His Speeches and Writings Brought Together with Historical Documents and Accounts of Mandela in Prison by Fellow-Prisoners*. London: International Defence and Aid Fund for Southern Africa.

Mansfield, P. 1971. *The British in Egypt*. New York: Holt, Rinehart and Winston.

Markham, E. 1899. *The Man with the Hoe and Other Poems*. New York: Doubleday and McClure.

Martí, J. 1891. "Nuestra América." *La Revista Ilustrada de Nueva York*, January 10, 1891.

Martí, J. 1977. *Our America: Writings on Latin America and the Struggle for Cuban Independence*. Ed. and trans. P. S. Foner. New York: Monthly Review Press.

Marx, K. 1973. *Grundrisse: Foundations of the Critique of Political Economy*. Trans. and foreword by M. Nicolaus. New York: Random House, Vintage.

Ménos, S. 1898. *L'affaire Luders*. Port-au-Prince, Haiti: Verrollot.

Merians, L. E. 2001. *Envisioning the Worst: Representations of "Hottentots" in Early-Modern England*. Newark: University of Delaware Press.

Miles, K. T. 2006. "The Other World after Paradise: The Musical Aesthetic of *The Souls of Black Folk*." Paper presented at An International Conference: W. E. B. Du Bois and the Question of Another World, Graduate School of Education, Tohoku University, Sendai, Japan, June 15–17, 2006.

Mommsen, W. J. 1998. *1848, die ungewollte Revolution: Die revolutionären Bewegungen in Europa, 1830–1849*. Frankfurt am Main: Fischer.

Moss, A. A., Jr. 1981. *The American Negro Academy: Voice of the Talented Tenth*. Baton Rouge: Louisiana State University Press.

Moten, F. 2008. "Black Op." *PMLA* 123 (5): 1743–47.

Mudimbe, V. Y. 1988. *The Invention of Africa: Gnosis, Philosophy, and the Order of Knowledge*. Bloomington: Indiana University Press.

Müller, F. M. 1855. *The Languages of the Seat of War in the East: With a Survey of the Three Families of Language, Semitic, Arian, and Turanian*. London: Williams and Norgate.

Nash, G. B., and J. R. Soderlund. 1991. *Freedom by Degrees: Emancipation in Pennsylvania and Its Aftermath*. New York: Oxford University Press.

Nasson, B. 2010. *The War for South Africa*. Cape Town: Tafelberg.

Ndaywel é Nziem, I. 2009. *Nouvelle histoire du Congo: Des origines à la république démocratique*. Preface by E. M'bokolo. Foreword by G. Gryseels. Brussels: Le Cri.

Negash, T. 1987. *Italian Colonialism in Eritrea, 1882–1941: Policies, Praxis, and Impact*. Acta Universitatis Upsaliensis. Uppsala: Uppsala University.

Newitt, M. D. 1995. *A History of Mozambique*. Bloomington: Indiana University Press.

Nish, I. H. 1985. *The Origins of the Russo-Japanese War*. London: Longman.

Norman, E. H. 1975. *Origins of the Modern Japanese State: Selected Writings of E. H. Norman*. Ed. J. W. Dower. New York: Pantheon.

Pagden, A. 1987. *The Fall of Natural Man: The American Indian and the Origins of Comparative Anthropology*. Cambridge: Cambridge University Press.

Partington, P. G. 1977. *W. E. B. Du Bois: A Bibliography of His Published Writings*. Whittier, CA: Penn-Lithographics.

Plato. 1971. *The Republic*. Trans. P. Shorey. In *Plato in Twelve Volumes*, trans. H. N. Fowler, W. R. M. Lamb, P. Shorey, and R. G. Bury, vols. 5 and 6. Cambridge, MA: Harvard University Press.

Plummer, B. G. 1988. *Haiti and the Great Powers, 1902–1915*. Baton Rouge: Louisiana State University Press.

Porter, D. B., comp. and ed. 1971. *Early Negro Writing, 1760–1837*. Boston: Beacon.

Rafael, V. L. 2010. "Welcoming What Comes: Sovereignty and Revolution in the Colonial Philippines." *Comparative Studies in Society and History* 52 (1): 157–79.

Rediker, M. 2007. *The Slave Ship: A Human History*. New York: Viking.

Remini, R. V. 1984. *Andrew Jackson and the Course of American Democracy, 1833–1845*. New York: Harper and Row.

Richards, J. F. 1992. *The Mughal Empire*. Cambridge: Cambridge University Press.

Robinson, C. J. 2000a (1983). "The Atlantic Slave Trade and African Labor." In *Black Marxism: The Making of the Black Radical Tradition*, 101–20. Chapel Hill: University of North Carolina Press.

Robinson, C. J. 2000b (1983). *Black Marxism: The Making of the Black Radical Tradition*. Foreword by R. D. G. Kelley. Chapel Hill: University of North Carolina Press.

Robinson, C. J. 2000c (1983). "Racial Capitalism: The Nonobjective Character of Capitalist Development." In *Black Marxism: The Making of the Black Radical Tradition*, 9–28. Chapel Hill: University of North Carolina Press.

Rochat, G. 1974. *Il colonialismo italiano*. Turin: Loescher.

Rodney, W. 1970. *A History of the Upper Guinea Coast, 1545–1800*. Oxford, UK: Clarendon.

Rodney, W. 1982. *How Europe Underdeveloped Africa*. Washington, DC: Howard University Press.

Roediger, D. R. 1991. *The Wages of Whiteness: Race and the Making of the American Working Class*. London: Verso.

Rothberg, M. 2001. "W. E. B. Du Bois in Warsaw: Holocaust Memory and the Color Line, 1949–1952." *Yale Journal of Criticism* 14 (1): 169–89.

Saada, E. 2012. *Empire's Children: Race, Filiation, and Citizenship in the French Colonies*. Chicago: University of Chicago Press.

Sahlins, M. 2012. *What Kinship Is—and Is Not*. Chicago: University of Chicago Press.

Said, E. 1984. "Permission to Narrate." *London Review of Books*, February 16–29, 13–17.

Saller, R. P. 1994. "Pietas and Patria Potestas: Obligation and Power in the Roman Household." In *Patriarchy, Property and Death in the Roman Family*, 102–32. Cambridge: Cambridge University Press.

Scarborough, W. S. 2005. *The Autobiography of William Sanders Scarborough: An American Journey from Slavery to Scholarship*. Ed. M. V. Ronnick. Detroit: Wayne State University Press.

Scarborough, W. S. 2006. *The Works of William Sanders Scarborough: Black Classicist and Race Leader*. Ed. M. V. Ronnick. Oxford: Oxford University Press.

Schäfer, A. R. 2001. "W. E. B. Du Bois, German Social Thought, and the Racial Divide in American Progressivism, 1892–1909." *Journal of American History* 88 (3): 925–49.

Schapera, I. 1930. *The Khoisan Peoples of South Africa: Bushmen and Hottentots*. London: Routledge.

Schneider, D. M. 1972. "What Is Kinship All About?" In *Kinship Studies in the Morgan Centennial Year*, ed. P. Reining, 32–63. Washington, DC: American Anthropological Society.

Schneider, D. M. 1984. *A Critique of the Study of Kinship*. Ann Arbor: University of Michigan Press.

Shakespeare, W. 2006. *Hamlet*. Ed. A. Thompson and N. Taylor. London: Bloomsbury Arden Shakespeare.

Shakespeare, W. 2013. *The Tempest*. Ed. V. M. Vaughan and A. T. Vaughan. London: Bloomsbury Arden Shakespeare.

Silva, D. F. D. 2007. *Toward a Global Idea of Race*. Minneapolis: University of Minnesota Press.

Silva, N. K. 2004. *Aloha Betrayed: Native Hawaiian Resistance to American Colonialism*. Durham, NC: Duke University Press.

Sollors, W. 1999. "W. E. B. Du Bois in Nazi Germany, 1936." *Amerikastudien/American Studies* 44 (2): 207–22.

Solow, B. L., ed. 1991. *Slavery and the Rise of the Atlantic System*. Cambridge: Cambridge University Press; Cambridge, MA: W. E. B. DuBois Institute for Afro-American Research, Harvard University.

Solow, B. L., and S. L. Engerman, eds. 1987. *British Capitalism and Caribbean Slavery: The Legacy of Eric Williams*. Cambridge: Cambridge University Press.

Spencer, H. 1898. *The Principles of Biology*. Rev. and enlarged ed. 2 vols. New York: Appleton.

Spencer, H. 1899. *The Principles of Sociology*. 3rd ed. 3 vols. New York: Appleton.

Sperber, J. 2005. *The European Revolutions, 1848–1851*. Cambridge: Cambridge University Press.

Spiers, E. M., ed. 1998. *Sudan: The Reconquest Reappraised*. London: Cass.

Spillers, H. J. 2003a. *Black, White, and in Color: Essays on American Literature and Culture*. Chicago: University of Chicago Press.

Spillers, H. J. 2003b. "*The Crisis of the Negro Intellectual*: A Post-Date." In *Black, White, and in Color: Essays on American Literature and Culture*, 428–70. Chicago: University of Chicago Press.

Spillers, H. J. 2003c. "Mama's Baby, Papa's Maybe: An American Grammar Book." In *Black, White, and in Color: Essays on American Literature and Culture*, 203–29. Chicago: University of Chicago Press.

Spillers, H. J. 2003d. "Moving on Down the Line: Variations on the African-American Sermon." In *Black, White, and in Color: Essays on American Literature and Culture*, 251–76. Chicago: University of Chicago Press.

Spillers, H. J. 2006. "The Idea of Black Culture." *CR: The New Centennial Review* 6 (3): 7–28.

Spivak, G. C. 1988. "Subaltern Studies: Deconstructing Historiography." In *Selected Subaltern Studies*, ed. R. Guha and G. C. Spivak, 3–32. New York: Oxford University Press.

Steinmetz, G. 2007. *The Devil's Handwriting: Precoloniality and the German Colonial State in Qingdao, Samoa, and Southwest Africa*. Chicago: University of Chicago Press.

Stocking, G. W. 1982. *Race, Culture, and Evolution: Essays in the History of Anthropology*. Chicago: University of Chicago Press.

Struve, L. A., ed. 2004. *The Qing Formation in World-Historical Time*. Cambridge, MA: Harvard University Asia Center.

Suny, R. G. 1993. *The Revenge of the Past: Nationalism, Revolution, and the Collapse of the Soviet Union*. Foreword by N. M. Naimark. Stanford, CA: Stanford University Press.

Thornton, J. K. 1998. *Africa and Africans in the Making of the Atlantic World, 1400–1800*. Cambridge: Cambridge University Press.

Valentin, V. 1930. *Geschichte der deutschen Revolution von 1848–49*. 2 vols. Berlin: Ullstein.

Venturi, F. 2001. *Roots of Revolution: A History of the Populist and Socialist Movements in 19th Century Russia*. Trans. F. Haskell. Introduction by I. Berlin. London: Phoenix.

Verlinden, C. 1970. *The Beginnings of Modern Colonization*. Ithaca, NY: Cornell University Press.

Vincent, W. 1807. "Section 26. Discoveries of the Portuguese." In *The Commerce and Navigation of the Ancients in the Indian Ocean*, 2: 214–34. London: Cadell and Davies.

Viswanathan, G. 1989. *Masks of Conquest: Literary Study and British Rule in India*. New York: Columbia University Press.

Waligora-Davis, N. 2006. "W. E. B. Du Bois and the Fourth Dimension." *CR: The New Centennial Review* 6 (3): 57–90.

Walker, D. 1829. *Walker's Appeal, in Four Articles: Together with a Preamble, to the Colored Citizens of the World, but in Particular, and Very Expressly to Those of the United States of America. Written in Boston, in the State of Massachusetts, Sept. 28th, 1829*. Boston: Walker.

Wallerstein, I. 1974. *The Modern-World System: Capitalist Agriculture and the Origins of the European World-Economy in the Sixteenth Century.* New York: Academic Press.

Warner, D. A., and P. Warner. 1974. *The Tide at Sunrise: A History of the Russo-Japanese War, 1904–1905.* New York: Charterhouse.

Weber, M. 1930. *The Protestant Ethic and the Spirit of Capitalism.* Trans. T. Parsons, Foreword by R. H. Tawney. New York: Scribner's.

Weber, M. 2002. "Appendix: Prefatory Remarks to Collected Essays in the Sociology of Religion." In *The Protestant Ethic and the "Spirit" of Capitalism and Other Writings,* ed. and trans. P. R. Baehr and G. C. Wells, 356–72. New York: Penguin.

Wehler, H. U. 1985. *The German Empire, 1871–1918.* Trans. K. Traynor. Dover, NH: Berg.

Wells, D., and S. Wilson, eds. 1999. *The Russo-Japanese War in Cultural Perspective, 1904–05.* New York: St. Martin's.

Wells-Barnett, I. B. 1892. *Southern Horrors: Lynch Law in All Its Phases.* New York: New York Age Print.

Wells-Barnett, I. B. 1895. *A Red Record: Tabulated Statistics and Alleged Causes of Lynchings in the United States, 1892–1893–1894.* Chicago: Donohue and Henneberry.

Whitmore, W. H., comp. and ed. 1890. *A Bibliographical Sketch of the Laws of the Massachusetts Colony from 1630 to 1686: In Which Are Included the Body of Liberties of 1641, and the Records of the Court of Assistants, 1641–1644; Arranged to Accompany the Reprints of the Laws of 1660 and of 1672.* Boston: Rockwell and Churchill.

Whitten, N. E., and A. Torres, comps. and eds. 1998. *Blackness in Latin America and the Caribbean: Social Dynamics and Cultural Transformations.* Bloomington: Indiana University Press.

Whittier, J. G. 1869. "Howard at Atlanta." *Atlantic Monthly* 23 (March): 367–69.

Wilentz, S. 2005. *The Rise of American Democracy: Jefferson to Lincoln.* New York: Norton.

Williams, E. E. 1994. *Capitalism and Slavery.* Chapel Hill: University of North Carolina Press.

Wilson, P. H., ed. 2006. *1848: The Year of Revolutions.* Aldershot, UK: Ashgate.

Wilson, S. 1982. *Ideology and Experience: Antisemitism in France at the Time of the Dreyfus Affair.* Rutherford, NJ: Fairleigh Dickinson University Press.

Woodson, D. G. 2010. Memorandum on Haiti and Germany. Personal written electronic communication. March 29, 2010.

Wynter, S. 2003. "Unsettling the Coloniality of Being/Power/Truth/Freedom: Towards the Human, after Man, Its Overrepresentation—an Argument." *CR: The New Centennial Review* 3 (3): 257–337.

Xiang, L. 2003. *The Origins of the Boxer War: A Multinational Study.* London: Routledge Curzon.

Yelvington, K. A., ed. 2005. *Afro-Atlantic Dialogues: Anthropology in the Diaspora.* Santa Fe, NM: School of American Research Press.

Zilfū, I. H. 1980. *Karari: The Sudanese Account of the Battle of Omdurman.* Trans. P. Clark. London: Warne.

INDEX

....

among the human, 204; as proscription, 208.
See also race, concept of; "the problem of the
color line"
categorical distinction: idea of, 200 categorical
insistence, 122
categorical limits, 146 Caucasian race, 82
cave, allegory of the (Plato), 239n20
"century of sympathy," 189
chance, 9, 141, 203, 228
change, 203
charity: spasmodic charity, 81
Chartist movement, 261n53
Chesnutt, Charles, 266n67
child, figure of the, 33
childhood, 35
China, 101, 171, 178, 179, 180, 194, 236n10, 251n24,
251n25, 259n46, 260n48; Kiautschou (Jiaozhou)
Bay, 258n44; Tientsin (Tianjin), 260n48
Christianity, 119, 175
civil rights, Du Bois described as advocate of, 231n1
civil war, 205
Civil War, American, 69, 131, 154, 241n26, 243n34,
256n37
claim to the common, 121 class, 73–74
closed gate, metaphor of, 239n20. *See also* veil
coerced labor, xvii, 93, 119, 120
Cohn, Bernard S., 253n28
collective, 53, 101, 191; collective problematization,
226; collective sense, 112; collectivity, 97
colonial: colonialism, 165, 171, 246n3; colonists, 121;
colonization, 174; colonized people, 99; exploitation and oppression, America as world-historical
example of, 209; rearticulation of, in the midst of
the putative postcolonial, 191; slavery, 22; Virginia,
125
color, 60, 65; color prejudice, a world of, 237n12
Color and Democracy (Du Bois), 14, 150, 206, 240n23,
267n70
"colored population of our land," 191
color line, 73; as a term of reference and thought, 157
"color line belts the world," 171
commercial imperative, 94
commitment: committed practice, 140; to historial
genesis, 138; to peace and culture, 212
common: common good, 112; commonness, 121;
refusal of the common, 122 commoner, 121
commonwealth, 121
Commonwealth (Hardt and Negri), 263n67
community of belief, 200
comparative sense, 158
Complete Published Works of W. E. B. Du Bois, 3,
248n12

complex movement of affirmation, 34
concatenation, 78
conceptualization, 91
condition, 215
Confederate States of America, 256n37
Congo Free State (État Indépendant du Congo), 176,
250n20
Congress of Arts and Sciences (St. Louis, Missouri), 114
"The Conservation of Races" (Du Bois), 16, 32, 105,
106, 107, 108, 113, 154, 156, 158, 165, 166, 167, 168,
181, 183, 190, 202, 207, 215, 241n29, 246n3, 248n11,
248n13, 264n60, 265n67; as American Negro
Academy Occasional Papers, 246n1
Constitution, U.S., 254n33
"constitution of the world," 92, 105, 113, 156
constitutive: difficulty in Du Bois's thought, 118;
genesis, 139; opacity, 141
consular courts, 181
Contee, Clarence, 169–70
contempt, 36
contextualization, 18; contextualist orientation, 4
contrapuntal rhythm, of thought, 186
Cook, Charles C., 246n1. *See also* American Negro
Academy (ANA)
Cooper, Anna Julia, 184, 241n30
cooperative, 133
Coppin, Levi J., 246n1. *See also* American Negro
Academy (ANA)
Cornerstone Speech (Stephens), 256n37
correspondence, of W. E. B. Du Bois, 4
"cost of liberty is less than the price of repression": in
John Brown (Du Bois), 74
"*The Crisis of the Negro Intellectual*" (Spillers), 231n3,
266n67
criteria of life and the objects of living, 26
critical: critique, 9; discourse, 140; labor, theoretical
labor, 141; perspective, 104; practice, 26; self-
reflection, 105; thought, 152
criticism, 186; and sympathy, 185, 188
Cromwell, John Wesley, 163, 246n1. *See also* American Negro Academy (ANA)
Cross, Theodore, 232n7
Crummell, Alexander, 54, 85, 131, 233n8, 242n30,
246n1, 249n14, 257n41, 266n67. *See also* American
Negro Academy (ANA)
Cruse, Harold, 231n3
Cuba, 257n42
Cuban Revolution, 205
culture, 92, 123, 131, 209; concept of, 136

Darien, Georgia, 187, 255n36
"darker" peoples, 99

Enrique (Taino indigenous leader), 117

enslaved status: of the African woman as heritable, 120

enslavement, 93, 119; Atlantic systems of, 221, 262nn54; modern epoch of, xvii, 93, 115, 246n3; the modern slave trade, as a "child of the Renaissance," 145; reciprocity of freedom and, 95; systems of, 110

episteme, 116

epistemic: ensemble, 26; sense, 120

epistemological, 12, 14, 77, 140; annotation, 115; formulation, 171; horizon, 166; intervention, 148; subject, 172

epoch, 154

Eppes, Susannah, 125

Equiano, Olaudah, 253n31

era of calm criticism and doubt, 189 Eritrea, 260n48

error, 187

essence, 64; the question of, 159

État Indépendant du Congo (Congo Free State), 250n20

ethical, 102; ethical imperative, 166; ethics and morals, 8

Ethiopia, 260n48

Europe, 25, 31, 38, 39, 40, 42, 43, 46, 56, 57, 61, 74, 80, 99, 100, 102, 109, 110, 111, 174, 192–93, 194, 196, 222, 227, 235n15; early modern, 159; history of, in relation to U.S. African Americans, 197; Du Bois's relation to, 40–43, 56

European, 98, 119, 243n34; child, 67, 68; civilization, 73, 196; colonialism, 122; Enlightenment, 244n40; Europeans, 82; history, 197, 198; horizon, 200

evolution, 112

evolutionism, 155

example, 21, 23, 43, 44, 51, 52, 61, 90, 110, 134, 136, 139, 141, 142, 221, 224, 225, 229; Du Bois as, 24; exemplarity, 22; exemplary example, 140, 221; exemplary on a global scale, 167; historial, 140; orders of, 29, 135

exchange, 36

exemplary path, 181

existential, 102, 135; existence as problem, 50; existential horror, of middle passage, 103; existential journey, 136

exorbitance, 46, 253n32

"expansion and consolidation of nations," 206–7. See also "the problem of the color line" exploitation, 10, 217; systems of, 138

Exposition Universelle, Paris (1900), 13

external association, 41, 45, 47

fabric, 116

factum, 111

faith, 136

family, 123. See also kinship

family, of Du Bois: Burghardt Du Bois (son), 33, 131, 158; Yolande Du Bois (daughter), 33

Farmville, Virginia, 75, 76, 95, 147

father's declaration, in "Of the Passing of the First Born" (Du Bois), 34

feminine, 210

Ferris, William H., 246n1. See also American Negro Academy (ANA)

Fields, Karen, 257n40

1500 (year), "problem of the century" in, 200

"The Figure of the X" (Chandler), 235n4

"A Final Word": in The Philadelphia Negro (Du Bois), 158, 215

first narrative: spatial narrative, 197 first-person, 89; plural, 86

Fish, Cheryl, 238n15

Fisk University (Nashville, Tennessee), 41, 43, 62

fissure, 67, 68, 73, 76; fissured social horizon, 78

fold, 53; folding, 52

folk, 91

followership, 134

foreign "human," 118

"Forethought": in The Souls of Black Folk (Du Bois), 131, 218

formal problematization, 169

Fortune, T. Thomas, 235n5, 242n30

Fort William College (India), 252n47

Foucault, Michel, 38, 116, 216; l'énonciation, in The Archaeology of Knowledge, 234n12 Fox, George, 254n35

fractual, 136

France, 39, 193; as colonial power, 250n19; French Revolution, 39, 199, 160, 261n53

Frankfurter Nationalversammlung (Frankfurt National Assembly), 261n53

Franklin, Benjamin, 241n26

free competition, so-called, 80

Freedmen's Bureau, 71; "The Freedmen's Bureau" (Du Bois), 14, 16, 170

freedom, 9, 135, 141, 145, 146, 166, 227, 228; and enslavement, reciprocity of, 95; and instituted limit, tension between, 145–46; of movement, 72

French (language), 60, 62

Fugitive Slave Act, 187, 254n33

futural, 104, 108, 109, 161, 205; form, 141; thought of the past, 220

future, xix, 23, 50, 93, 96, 103, 128, 129, 166, 169, 210, 211; account of, on the basis of an understanding of the past, 202; theory of the, the Du Bois's, 157

futurity, 93, 243n34; affirmation of, 134; futural implication, 153; futural perspective, 161; the future that is at stake in the present, 135; yet to come, 31, 141

Garrison, William Lloyd, 187, 262n54

Geisteswissenschaft, 92, 243n35

gender, 122, 201; concept of, 231n4

genealogy, 38, 63, 127; genealogical, 66; and kinship, 123

generation, the passive in, 103

generations, 128, 133, 134; generational cohort, 129; in "Of the Coming of John" (Du Bois), 131; past, 129; yet to come, 129

genocide, 257n40; attempted, 258n44

geographic, 173; reference, 171

Georgia (U.S. state), 35, 71, 134, 176, 255n36

German, 66, 243; inheritance of the Enlightenment, 208; language, 62

Germantown (Pennsylvania) Meeting, 254n35

Germany, 39, 40, 41, 53, 56, 193, 194, 252n26, 260n48; as colonial power, 250n19, 258n44; Du Bois in, 39–41

gesture: as a social practice, 37; as a style of practice in thought, 20

Ghana, 94

gifted children, 133

"gigantic strife across the color line," 195

Gilroy, Paul, 233n9

"glance," as a line of force, 36

global, 10, 11, 13, 14, 15, 103, 149, 227; as horizon, 194; imperialism, 260; order of distinction, 167; perspective, 147, 160, 232n8; practice of the local or national within the global, 165; "problem of the color line," 195

globalization, 17, 171

Glorious Revolution, 117

gold ("gowd"), 262n54

Gonçalves, Antão (Antonio), 243n32

Gooding-Williams, Robert, 236n7, 244n36

Gordon-Reed, Annette, 245n42

"gorgeous visiting-cards": in *The Souls of Black Folk* (Du Bois), 36

Greek: Greek conceptuality, 151; Greek thought as conceptuality, 49

greeting card: in *The Souls of Black Folk* (Du Bois), 76

Griffin, Farah, 238n15

Grimké, Francis J., 246n1. *See also* American Negro Academy (ANA)

Grisham, George N., 246n1. *See also* American Negro Academy (ANA)

Grundrisse (Marx), 249n18

Guernica, attack on, 205

Guha, Ranajit, 253n28

"guinea's stamp": in "A Man's a Man for A' That" (Burns), 262n54

habitation, 109

Haiti, 205, 222, 259n44; Haitian Revolution, 160

harbinger of a new world, 138

"hard limits of natural law": in "The Conservation of Races" (Du Bois), 105, 156

Hardt, Michael, and Antonio Negri, 263n58

Hart, Albert Bushnell, 54

Harvard University (Massachusetts), 40, 41, 43, 54; Du Bois's scholarship to study at, 237n12

Hawaii: U.S. annexation of, 258n42

Hayson, Walter B., 246n1. *See also* American Negro Academy (ANA)

Hayti. *See* Haiti

Hemings, Elizabeth, 124, 125. *See also* Hemings, Sally

Hemings, Sally, 126, 127, 128, 129, 134; children of, 124–25; "The Life of Sally Hemings" (exhibition), 245n42; and Thomas Jefferson, 124–25

heredity, 123. *See also* kinship

Herero, 258n44

heritable, 120

heterogeneous, 32, 45, 91

hierarchy, 119, 208, 247n7; hierarchical organization, 150

hinge, 211

Hiroshima, Japan, 206

historial, 28, 50, 92, 101, 102, 108, 109, 113, 121, 126, 128, 151, 156, 226, 235n3; being, 117;

historiality of the human, 201; historicity and the, 169; and istoria, 96; limit, 42; Negro as a historial being, 223; originary historial genesis, 137; possibility, xviii; as problematization, 232n4; relation, 128; sense, 104; status of the African American, 107

historial example, 50

historical, 208; burden, 210; domain, 120; eventuality, 118; historically given duty, 221; and political, 165; possibility, 52; practice, 193, 196

historicity, xix, 8, 12, 18, 19, 24, 45, 48, 49, 50, 51, 71, 74, 90, 105, 107, 109, 113, 130, 133, 139, 156, 169, 186, 197, 201, 202, 226; African American, 136; Du Bois on error in history, 187; field of, 37; forms of, 27; and the historial, 169; historical process as a spiral, 187; historical processes, 155; history of differentiations, 198; of ideals, 201; modern, 136, 164; modern historicity of enslavement, 174; of morality, 180; originary historial articulation from and among African Americans, 137; of the present, 38; question of, 49; subject of history, 137

historiographical, 27, 29, 48, 52, 53, 90, 100, 106, 128, 135, 136, 140; autohistoriographical

desedimentation, 142; historiographic, 109; historiography, 125, 133; practice, 136

Hitler, Adolf, 257n40

Holt, Sam, 255n36

Holt, Thomas C., 253n28

homeland, 200

hope, 136, 203. *See also* futurity

hopelessness, 134

horizon, 64, 110, 121, 160; of the common, 168

Horn of Africa, 260n48

Hosmer, Frank (principal of Du Bois's high school), 237n12

Hottentots, 200; use of quotation marks with term, 263n57

Howard, Oliver Otis, 70, 71

"Howard at Atlanta" (Whittier), 69, 70

human, 121, 146; action, 114; concept of the, 115, 116, 223; development, 25; disposition, 197; humans, 149; idea of, as a certain legal fiction, 120; idea of, across modern era, 124; progress, 106; social organization, 114; understanding and action, 113; who counts as human, or fully human?, 189

humanities, and human sciences, 78

hyperbolic practice, 141, 228; hyperbolic character, 219; hyperbolic historicization, 220; hyperbolic renarrativization, 215; hyperthematization, 214

hypothesis, 168

ideals, 9, 96, 107, 122, 134, 188, 201; destruction of, 130; idealization, 131, 187; idealization, movement of, 188; of living, 95; production of, 130; the shared as a practice of idealization, 122

illegitimate, in kinship, 126

illimitable, 97, 116, 140, 142, 185, 229, 254n32; illimitable concatenation of association, 135; illimitable form of association, 139

immanence, 15

imperial: the European example, 198; and historicity, 174; imperial and colonial, 173; imperialism, 171, 246; imperialism and colonialism, 154, 171, 180; imperialism of Europe, 195; modern imperialism, 165; policy, 191; policy, U.S., 207; as premise, 204

imperial idea, 180

impossible: impossible possibility, 50, 136; impossible possible new world, 133. *See also* possibility

indenture, 119

indetermination, 112

India, 60, 63, 111, 171, 178, 179, 181, 243n32, 252n27; colonization of, by England, 181; Mughal Empire, 179, 251n24

indigenous peoples, 119

infrastructure, 76

inhabitation, 8

instability, 203

instance, 20. *See also* elaboration

intellectual, 7, 48, 56; intellectual audience, 98; intellectual formation of Du Bois, 28; intelligentsia, 59

intelligentsia, 84; African American, 58

"intercourse between races," 73

interlocution, 64

interlocutor, 65

intermarriage, 126

interminable, 136

intermingling, 246n2; in Du Bois's thought, 108; "racial," 167

intermixture, 126, 206, 263n60

internal differentiation, 206

internal dissociation, 37, 45, 46, 47

interpretive, 106

ipse, 125. ipseity, xx, 90, 139; self as *ipse*, 135

istoria, 28, 96, 97. *See also* historial

Italian (language), 62

Italy, 39, 260n48; Senegalese Italians, 264n61

Jackson, Andrew, 199, 262n53

Jackson, W. T. S., 246n1. *See also* American Negro Academy (ANA)

James, C. L. R.: *The Black Jacobins*, 233n10

Jamestown, 119, 120, 126, 128

Japan, 101, 111, 171, 178, 180, 181, 203, 236n10, 251n25, 259n46, 260n49; historial figure of, 252n26; Japanese, 74, 249n13; Tohoku University, W. E. B. Du Bois and the Question of Another World (conference), 232n5, 246n4

Jefferson, Martha Wayles Skelton, 124–25; and Sally Hemings, 126, 127

Jefferson, Thomas, 116, 121, 152, 187, 245n41, 247n8; Rousseau-Jefferson half-truth, 81; and Sally Hemings, 124–25, 127, 128

Jennie Jones (character in chapter 13 of *The Souls of Black Folk*), 132, 133, 134, 210

Jews, 41, 193, 194

John Brown (Du Bois), 73, 150, 233n10, 240n23, 267n70

John Jones (character in chapter 13 of *The Souls of Black Folk*), 210

Johnson, Andrew, 218–19

Johnson, John A., 246n1. *See also* American Negro Academy (ANA)

joint, 211

Jones, Absalom, 184

Jones, Elvin, 234n2

Josie (character in chapter 4 of *The Souls of Black Folk*), 35, 72, 131, 134

justice, 219

monarchy, 260n47

mondialisation, 17, 171

monogram, Josie (character) as, 131

monstrous, 61; comprehendible monstrosity, 65

Monticello, 124, 125, 128

Moore, Lewis B., 246n1. *See also* American Negro
Academy (ANA)

morals: moral forms, of African Americans (Du
Bois), 87; moral imperative, 212; moral rectitude,
242n31

Morel, E. D., 250n20

Moss, Alfred A., Jr., 162–63, 246n1. *See also* American
Negro Academy (ANA)

Moten, Fred, 234n2

Mozambique, 250n19

Mughal Empire (India), 251n24

Müller, F. Max, 251n24

Multitude (Hardt and Negri), 263n58

NAACP (National Association for the Advancement
of Colored People), 231n1

Nagasaki, Japan, 206

Namaqua, 258n44

Namibia, 258n44

Nanking Massacre, 205

narrative, 93; of modernity, 173; narration, 91; narrator, 64; order, 171; narrativization, of the historicity of the "problem of the color line," 216

natal, 66; natality, 64, 139, 200

nation, 123; "nations" as alternative term for "races,"
by Du Bois, 156

National Afro-American League, 242n30

national-local, 109

native: as natality, 63

natural law, 106

Negri, Antonio, and Michael Hardt, 263n58

Negro, 65, 110; Negro American, 79; Negroes, 74, 134;
Negroes of Africa, 160; "'Negro' meant a greater,
broader sense of humanity and world-fellowship,"
40; "Negro problem," 68, 86–87, 158, 185; Negro
question, 80, 87; New Negro vanguard, 41

The Negro (Du Bois), 32, 95, 222, 251n23, 253n30

New England, 68, 70, 238n17

New Guinea, 258n44

new social forms: of difference, 196; of hierarchy, 207;
of internal difference, 207; new hierarchy, 217; new
historicity, 95; new problem of the color line, 206

New South, 72, 87, 131

New World, 108, 109 Nietzsche, Friedrich, 38

nominalization, 61

nonsynchronous simultaneity, 48 normal, the supposed, 217

North America, 183

Northwestern University (Illinois), 236n7

"Not dead, not dead, but escaped; not bond, but
free": in *The Souls of Black Folk* (Du Bois), 34

"Nuestra América" (Martí), 253n30

object: for analysis, 112; of critical theoretical reflection, 154; objectification, 66; subject of thought
rendered as an, 135

"O black boy of Atlanta!": in "Howard at Atlanta"
(Whittier), 70

Occasional Papers of the ANA, 162, 163

"Of Alexander Crummell": in *The Souls of Black Folk*
(Du Bois), 134, 265n66, 266n67

"Of Mr. Booker T. Washington and Others": in *The
Souls of Black Folk* (Du Bois), 242n30

"Of the Black Belt": in *The Souls of Black Folk*
(Du Bois), 255n36

"Of the Coming of John": in *The Souls of Black Folk*
(Du Bois), 35, 131, 265n66, 266n67

"Of the Culture of White Folk" (Du Bois), 240n23,
267n70

"Of the Meaning of Progress": in *The Souls of Black
Folk* (Du Bois), 35, 131, 265n66

"Of the Wings of Atalanta": in *The Souls of Black
Folk* (Du Bois), 69

"once French peasants were the 'Niggers' of France,"
160

ontological: distinction, 248n13; ontohistorial, 224;
problematic, 231n4; question, 248n13; supposed
ontological claim, 217

opacity, 141, 228

openness, 161

opportunity, 36; and obligation, 191

opposition, 10

oppression, 138

optimism, 203

oratory, 184

organization, of society, 112

origami, a contemporary sense of, 53

originary, 51; originary historial articulation from and
among African Americans, 137; originary historical
configuration, 109

origin as pure: idea of, 201

The Origin of Species (Darwin), 256n40

oscillating gesture and movement, 53

the other, 125; as not yet fully human, 119

other America, 63; Jose Martí's description of,
182

other-worlds, 134

Ottoman Empire, 179, 251n24, 260n48; as described
by Du Bois, 180

Scarborough, William Sanders, 71, 242n30, 246n1. *See also* American Negro Academy (ANA)

Schmoller, Gustav, 40

Schutzgebiet Deutsch-Ostafrika (Protectorate of German East Africa), 258n44

scientific study of the situation of the Negro in the United States, 55

second narrative: temporal narrative, 196–97

second sight: in *The Souls of Black Folk* (Du Bois), 33

"see the world thus darkly through the Veil": in *The Souls of Black Folk* (Du Bois), 33. See also "double-consciousness"

self-consciousness, 33

self-reflex: self-reflexive, 67, 104; self-reflexivity, 59, 76

seme, 20. *See also* elaboration

Senegalese Italians, 264n61

Senegambia region, 110

sense: of being, 50; making of, 109; of the partial, 19; of self, 55; of the whole of Du Bois's itinerary, 17; of world, 137

sensus communis, 118, 121

sermon, 184

servitude, 95

1700 (year), "problem of the century" in, 199–200

Seventh Ward, of Philadelphia, 158

sexualization, 122

"shades of the prison-house closed round about us all": in *The Souls of Black Folk* (Du Bois), 36, 239n20

"The Shadow of Years" (Du Bois), 237n12

shadows, 150

Shakespeare, William, 25, 39; *Hamlet*, 35; *The Tempest*, 253n31

share cropping, 72

sheaf, 53

signal: as example or examples, 52, 140

singularity, of a European epistemic subject, 173

Sino-Japanese War, first (1894–95), 252n25, 259n46

situation, 140

1600 (year), "problem of the century" in, 200

slave trade, African, 100

Slavs, 249n13

slumming, 122

Smith, Adam: and Ricardo, David, economic theories of, 80–81

social: class, 68; condition, 73; fissure, 79; hierarchy, 183; and historical problem, 31; mind, 84, 241n27; paradox, 65; process, 100; reform, 189; status, 199; wall, Du Bois's metaphor of, 239n20

socialism, 57

"The Socialism of German Socialists" (Du Bois), 57

sociology, 110, 113, 114; sociological, 138; sociological interpretation, in "The Study of the Negro

Problems" (Du Bois), 241n27; sociological knowledge, 25

"Sociology Hesitant" (Du Bois), 98, 244n38, 256n40

solicitation of a world that has not yet been, 138

Somalia, 260n48

song: in penultimate paragraph of *The Souls of Black Folk* (Du Bois), 103

Song Dynasty: see also technologies, as in two world historical technologies from China, 101 sorrow, 134

"The Sorrow Songs" (Du Bois), 25

soul: also psyche, 130

souls of Black folk: inheritance of, 127

The Souls of Black Folk (Du Bois), 10, 16, 30, 31, 32, 33, 35, 39, 42, 46, 54, 58, 72, 78, 89, 92, 97, 98, 103, 106, 107, 108, 109, 113, 116, 130, 131, 132, 133, 134, 136, 138, 149, 150, 152, 156, 170, 176, 177, 190, 210, 225, 226, 233n9, 236n7, 238n19, 239n20, 241n29, 242n30, 244n36, 246n3, 255n36, 257n41, 265n66, 266n67

"The Souls of White Folk" (Du Bois), 240n23, 267n70

South Africa, 176, 219; Boer war, 175–76, 250n19

South America, 183

sovereignty, 181, 236n10, 252n26; sovereign, 135, 153, 205; sovereign, as the exception, 119; sovereign example, 151

Soviet Union, 259n45

spacing, 49, 225

Spain, 117; Spanish-American War, 257n42

Spanish (language), 60, 62

spatial, 167; first narrative, as, 197; referents, 228; topography, 171

Spencer, Herbert, 114, 244n38; *The Principles of Biology*, 256n40; *The Principles of Sociology*, 257n40

Spillers, Hortense J., 35, 124, 184, 231n3, 238n16, 244n39, 263n55; *Black, White, and in Color*, 266n67

spirit: in penultimate paragraph of *The Souls of Black Folk* (Du Bois), 103

"The Spirit of Modern Europe" (Du Bois), 32, 261n50, 264n63

spirituals, 129; tradition of, 93

Spivak, Gayatri Chakravorty: theoretical fiction, formulation from, 168 Stalin, Joseph, 236n10

stamp: W. E. B. Du Bois postage stamp, 1–2

state, 123

statement: in "The Development of a People" (Du Bois), 91

step, 20. *See also* elaboration

Stephens, Alexander Hamilton, 256n37

St. Louis, Missouri, 114

strategy: in Du Bois's practice, 118

stratified social order, 68

striving: key word in early writings of Du Bois, 129; "striving to make my life all that life may be," 43

"Strivings of the Negro People" (Du Bois), 58, 190, 210, 239n20

"The Study of the Negro Problems" (Du Bois), 88, 241n27; Du Bois's lecture to the AAPSS (1897), 55

Sturm und Drang, 39, 85

subject, 66, 83, 135; of the locution, 137; position, 138, 173

subjectivity, 84; subjection, 119; subjectity, 48, 67; subjectivation, of a putatively "Black" social subject, 78; subjectivation, of a putatively "white" social subject, 78

subsistence, 93

Sudan, 249n19, 251n22; Republic of, 250n19

Sumner, Charles, 187 superimposed worlds, 67

The Suppression of the African Slave-Trade to the United States of America, 1638–1870 (Du Bois), 105, 254n35

supraliteracy, 184

Surinamese Dutch, 264n61

surprise, statements of repeated in "The Afro-American," (Du Bois), 62

surreptitious play, 227

"survey the whole question of race in human philosophy": in "The Conservation of Races" (Du Bois), 155

sweat: as in African American labor, 103

sycophancy, 36

symbolization, 137; symbolic inheritance, 129; symbolic operations, 151

sympathy, 134, 257n41; and criticism, dialectic of, 185; and criticism, tension of, 188

systems of exploitation, 138

Taino, 117

Takenaka, Koji, 232n5

talented tenth, 57, 71, 134

"The Talented Tenth" (Du Bois), 98, 130, 267n67

Tang Dynasty, 101

task, 141; of thinking, 168

Taylor, Cecil, 228, 234n2

techniques, 140

technologies, world historical, 101

telic structure, 186

telos, 49

The Tempest (Shakespeare), 253n31

temporal, 167, 198, 214; narrative, 195, 198; narrative, second narrative, 196–97; temporality, 88; temporization, 196–97, 201, 208

textile, 116

theology, 200; theological, 114

theoretical: discourse, 135; disposition, 152; fiction, 168, 169, 194; hinge, 202, 203; implication, 165; labor, 140, 141, 216, 228, 246n3; perspicacity, 133; premise, 96; protocol, 169; sense, 87

thinking as practice, 168–69

third millennium: "when the color line has faded as mists before the sun," 192

third-person point of view, 69 "this narrow Now," 135

thought, 59; at the limit of possible world, 142; movement of, 20; as theoretical practice, 149 "time out of joint," 35

"to be both a Negro and an American": in *The Souls of Black Folk* (Du Bois), 32

Tohoku University (Japan): W. E. B. Du Bois and the Question of Another World (conference), 232n5, 246n4

"to make a way out of no way," 136

"to place themselves at stake," 23

topos, 27; topographical metaphor, 112

"To the Nations of the World" (Du Bois), summary statement of Pan-African Conference (1900), 170, 177

trace, 70

trade, 102

tradition, 93, 96, 128

transformation, 197

transnational configuration, 206

"The Transubstantiation of a Poor White": in *Black Reconstruction* (Du Bois), 218

travel, 61

trope, as metaphor or catachresis, 29

truth, 151

Tubman, Harriet, 201

Turkey, 178, 194, 260n48. *See also* Ottoman Empire

Turkish Germans, 264n61

two different registers, 124

"two warring ideals in one dark body": in *The Souls of Black Folk* (Du Bois), 32

understanding, of sameness or difference, 121

"unfaltering commerce with the stars": in *Dusk of Dawn* (Du Bois), 31

unhappy, 132

unhopeful hope, 129, 140

unimaginable, 129

United Nations, 184

United States of America, 57, 60, 64, 90, 172, 191; as imperial power, 258n42

"unity beneath all life clutched me": in *Darkwater* (Du Bois), 40

universal, 135; historicity, 161; opportunity, 9; suffrage, 198, 199

University of Massachusetts Amherst: W. E. B. Du
  Bois Library, 53, 261n50
"unresting water": in *The Souls of Black Folk*
  (Du Bois), 132
"unter den Juden?": in *The Autobiography of W. E. B.
  Du Bois*, 41
uplift, 92, 266n67; uplifting the whole, 85
U.S. Bureau of Labor, 245n44
U.S. National Archives, 245n44
U.S. Supreme Court, 254n33
utopic, 27

values, 127
"a vast veil": in *The Souls of Black Folk* (Du Bois), 76
veil, 10, 58, 74, 78, 86, 89, 149, 235n5, 239n20; within
  the Veil, 131; as verb, 75
the Veil, 34, 77
violence, 37
Virginia (colony), 121, 127, 134; "Jamestown," 126;
  legislative action in, seventeenth century, 120; as
  world historical example, 119
Virginia (state): Farmville, 77
vocation, 55
voice, 228; vocative in thought, 20; vocative position,
  86; voicing, 131

Wagner, Adolph, 40
Waligora-Davis, Nicole, 265n65
Walker, David, 184
Wall, Cheryl, 236n7
war, 203, 204, 209; maintenance of, 206
warp and weft (warp and woof): in *The Souls of Black
  Folk* (Du Bois), 103, 116, 139
Washington, Booker T., 85, 242n30; Atlanta Exposi-
  tion speech, 55
Washington, DC, 154, 162
Wayles, John, 124.
Wayles, Martha. *See* Jefferson, Martha Wayles
  Skelton
*W. E. B. Du Bois and the Question of Another
  World* (conference), 232n5, 246n4
Weber, Max, 98, 173, 236n6, 238n14, 241n25, 245n44,
  252n26, 261n49; *The Protestant Ethic and the Spirit
  of Capitalism*, 249n17
Wells-Barnett, Ida B., 85, 241n30
West Africa, 110–11
"What is the real meaning of Race?" (Du Bois), 156
What is to be done?, 183, 190
What, or who, is Europe?, 264n61
What, or who, is the human?, 159

What, or who, is the Negro?, 159
Wheatley, Phillis, 117, 129, 234n12
white American child, 67, 68
white man's country, claim of, 82
whiteness, 247n8
"The White World": in *Dusk of Dawn* (Du Bois),
  240n23
Whittier, John Greenleaf, 69, 70
"Who, after all, are men?": in *The Philadelphia Negro*
  (Du Bois), 189
whole problem of the Negro as world, 43
"Why did God make me an outcast and a stranger
  in mine own house?": in *The Souls of Black Folk*
  (Du Bois), 36
Wilberforce University (Ohio), 54, 71, 238n14,
  242n30; Rembert E. Stokes Library of, 248n10
Williams, Eric: *Capitalism and Slavery*, 233n10
Williams, Henry Sylvester, 233 n8
without any accession or passageway to home, 135
Wilson, Woodrow, 236n10
Woodson, Drexel, 259n44
"word fitly spoken": Du Bois to Booker T. Washington, 242n30
Wordsworth, William: as indirectly quoted by
  Du Bois in *The Souls of Black Folk*, 36
work, 237
working classes, 199, 217
world, 68, 107; sense of, 98
The World and Africa (Du Bois), 14, 95, 206, 240n23,
  261n51, 264n63, 265n64
"world . . . as changing growth": in *Dusk of Dawn*
  (Du Bois), 31
World Economic Forum (Switzerland, 2006), 264n61
world-historical, 121
"world problem of the 20th century is the Problem of
  the Color line" (Du Bois), 194
"worlds I longed for": in *The Souls of Black* Folk
  (Du Bois), 36
Worlds of Color (Du Bois), 150
World War I, 196, 204, 206, 236n10, 251n24, 258n43,
  259n44, 260n47
World War II, 14, 180, 206, 252n26, 260n48, 267n70
Wright, Richard Robert, 70, 242, 246n1. *See also*
  American Negro Academy (ANA)

Young, Arthur, 236n6

Zeitgeist, 22
Zora (character in *The Quest of the Silver Fleece*),
  132–33, 134, 238n19

CPSIA information can be obtained
at www.ICGtesting.com
Printed in the USA
LVHW080331220122
709067LV00013B/489

9 781478 014805